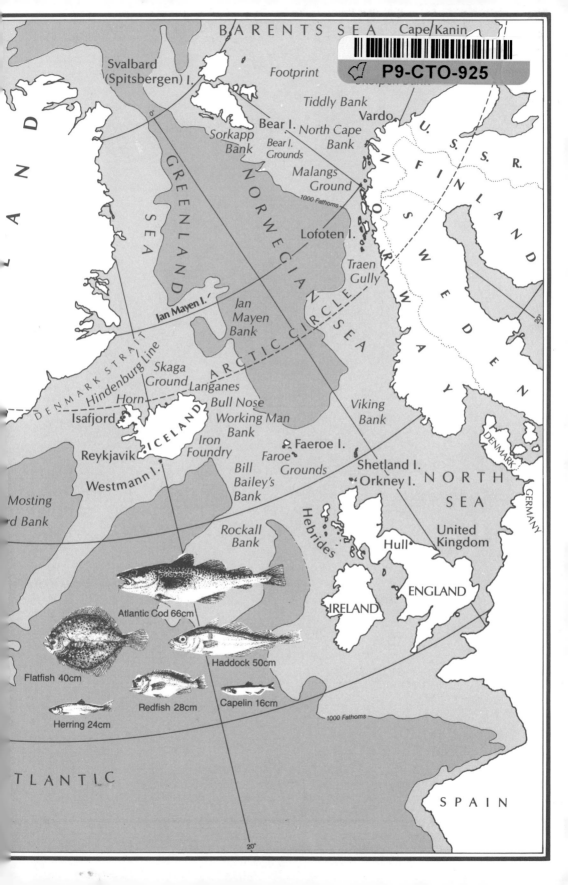

BARENTS SEA    Cape Kanin

Svalbard
(Spitsbergen) I.

Footprint

Tiddly Bank

Bear I.  North Cape    Vardo
Sorkapp    Bear I.    Bank
Bank       Grounds

Malangs
Ground

GREENLAND    NORWEGIAN    1000 Fathoms

SEA

Lofoten I.

Traen
Gully

Jan Mayen I.

Jan
Mayen
Bank

ARCTIC CIRCLE

DENMARK STRAIT
Hindenburg Line    Skaga
Ground    Langanes    Viking
Horn                  Bank

Isafjord    Bull Nose
Working Man
Bank

ICELAND

Reykjavik    Iron        Faeroe I.
Foundry    Faroe    Shetland I.
Westmann I.    Bill     Grounds    Orkney I.    NORTH
Bailey's
Bank                              SEA

Mosting
rd Bank    Rockall    Hebrides
Bank                  Hull    United
                              Kingdom

Atlantic Cod 66cm    IRELAND    ENGLAND

Flatfish 40cm

Haddock 50cm

Redfish 28cm    Capelin 16cm

Herring 24cm    1000 Fathoms

TLANTIC

SPAIN

U. S. S. R.

FINLAND

SWEDEN

NORWAY

DENMARK

GERMANY

20°

20°

# Distant Water

*Also by William W. Warner*

BEAUTIFUL SWIMMERS
*Watermen, Crabs, and the Chesapeake Bay*

# Distant Water

## The Fate of the North Atlantic Fisherman

## by WILLIAM W. WARNER

*An Atlantic Monthly Press Book*
LITTLE, BROWN AND COMPANY · BOSTON · TORONTO

Property of Library
Cape Fear Technical Institute
Wilmington, N

FIRST EDITION

Portions of this book have appeared in *The Atlantic, The Reader's Digest, Allgemeine Fischwirtschaftzeitung,* and *Das Beste aus Reader's Digest.*

LIBRARY OF CONGRESS CATALOGING IN PUBLICATION DATA

Warner, William W.
     Distant water.

     "An Atlantic Monthly Press book."
     1. Fisheries — North Atlantic Ocean.   2. Trawls and
trawling — North Atlantic Ocean.   3. Fishermen — North
Atlantic Ocean.   I. Title.
SH213.2.W37   1983          639'.22          82-24908
ISBN 0-316-92328-1

ATLANTIC–LITTLE, BROWN BOOKS
ARE PUBLISHED BY
LITTLE, BROWN AND COMPANY
IN ASSOCIATION WITH
THE ATLANTIC MONTHLY PRESS

MV
*Published simultaneously in Canada
by Little, Brown & Company (Canada) Limited*

PRINTED IN THE UNITED STATES OF AMERICA

*To Kathleen, for her great patience*

They that go down to the sea in ships,
that do business in great waters;
These see the works of the Lord,
and his wonders in the deep.

Book of Psalms, 107:23–24

"The floating Ritz, we called her."
The *Fairtry I* during sea trials, 1954.
(Credit: Christian Salvesen Ltd.)

# *Foreword*

IN the mid-1950s a new kind of fishing vessel began to cross the Atlantic. It was very large, it fished from the stern, and it quickly processed and deep-froze nearly all the fish it caught. Its operations were continuous, all around the clock and in all but the worst weather.

"They're fishing out there with ocean liners!" is the way astounded Canadian and American fishermen who first saw these vessels invariably described their arrival. The description is accurate, with only a trace of pardonable exaggeration. Seen from afar, the new ships did look very much like passenger liners. And they were big — bigger in length and much bigger in tonnage than any and all fishing vessels that preceded them.

Factory-equipped freezer stern trawlers, these ships were called — factory trawlers, for short. Although they combined various technologies new to fishing and were of a totally unorthodox design, factory trawlers at first went about their work in relative isolation, little noted outside the fishing industries in the countries of their origin. In time this changed, as the big ships moved out of the North Atlantic and extended their operations to all the world oceans, catching more and more fish. Often factory trawlers were not the most numerous ships in the fishing fleets of the nations who built them. In some cases these distant water fleets, as they came to be called, had many more older vessels of conventional design. But what the factory trawlers lacked in numbers they more than made up for in catching power. So awesome was this power in the early years of their prime (and so good was the fishing) that it is perhaps best described by hypothetical analogy to dry land. First, assume a vast continental forest, free for the cutting or only ineffectively guarded. Then try to imagine a mobile and completely self-contained timber-cutting machine that could smash through the roughest trails of the forest, cut down the trees, mill them, and deliver consumer-ready lumber in half the time of normal logging and milling operations. This was exactly what factory trawlers did — this was exactly their effect on fish — in the forests of the deep. It could not long go unnoticed.

I first saw a modern factory trawler in the harbor of St. John's, Newfoundland, in the spring of 1976, precisely as described in the text. So great was her size and so unusual her appearance that I felt an immediate urge to climb aboard and look her over more thoroughly. The ship, as it happened, was Russian, and I was not permitted to do so. But the memory of her stayed, as it would with anyone interested in ships and the sea. It stayed and festered, moreover, like a nagging virus that flared up into something more than a simple desire to examine a new kind of ship. In the course of writing *Beautiful Swimmers: Watermen, Crabs and the Chesapeake Bay,* I had gone out in what were in many cases the smallest of all commercial fishing vessels and had learned much of value by sharing the life of Chesapeake fishermen. The factory trawlers represented by the Russian ship at St. John's were at the other end of the scale, the ultimate fishing machines. The gap was a large one — electronic instead of artisanal fishing, the storm track of the North Atlantic in place of the Chesapeake, and, above all, fishermen who measured their trips in months and years rather than hours and days. Perhaps the gap's very span, the differences between its extremes, was the attraction. Whatever it was, I wanted to jump it all at once. I can offer no more rational explanation.

Thus, origins. At the very same time, in the spring of 1976, distant water fleets and the factory trawlers that were always their strength suddenly made world news. They had in fact become a principal issue in the long-standing United Nations debate about whether nations might exercise control over high-seas resources beyond three or twelve miles. The conflict ended, as far as fishing rights were concerned, after seven years of fruitless debate in the marathon third U.N. Law of the Sea Conference. During all the time the debate droned on, the factory trawlers continued to do their work much too well. Some coastal nations found their fish stocks were being reduced almost to the vanishing point. One of them eventually lost patience. In April of 1976 the United States enacted legislation that extended its fishing sovereignty out to two hundred miles. As a result of this unilateral action, U.N. delegations saw much of their long effort to construct a global fishery sharing system (as they were also trying to do with continental-shelf oil and seabed minerals) suddenly come to nothing. Canada followed suit within less than two months, and the "great sea grab," as critics still call it, was on. Almost without exception, many nations that had patiently waited on the fence rushed to establish exclusive two-hundred-mile economic zones for either fishing or seabed resources. Or, most commonly, both.

These were heady times, of course, for anyone interested in the world of fishing. "Cod wars" and other international fishery disputes, the rapid revision of law of the sea, the contrasting attitudes of the U.N. toward the big prize of offshore oil versus the minor irritant of fishing — all these things, it seemed to me, had to be studied and included in any work on modern fishing. To my editor's dismay (and now mine, as I gaze at discarded chapters), I did in fact study and write about them for too long a time. But the first trips with distant water fishing fleets virtually forced a change of plan. What I was witnessing, it was immediately apparent, was a unique way of maritime life. Equally apparent was the possibility that this way of life might soon disappear. It seemed clear that the two-hundred-mile fishing zones and the low catch quotas that their new owners immediately established within them would soon undermine the economic viability of distant water fleets and their costly factory trawlers. Though the law of the sea and global marine resources were already the subject of much scholarly research, no one was giving like attention to what was taking place at sea, to the high-technology fishing vessels seen from on board. (Or so I was led to believe from the startled reactions of fishing company and foreign government officials when I first asked permission to visit aboard their ships.) To make a foredeck chronicle, to document the age of the factory trawler at sea, before it passed away, seemed the most urgent and necessary task.

Such is the aim of this book, no more. Its principal arena is the North Atlantic, though the North Pacific has also felt the weight of factory trawlers (and is now a more productive fishing area). The principal characters are fishermen of five nations — the United States, Great Britain, West Germany, Spain, and the Soviet Union, each of which has played a distinctive role in distant water fishing — rather than, say, the fishermen of Norway, Iceland, and Denmark, whose rich home waters (or Greenland and the Faroe Islands, in the case of Denmark) made unnecessary the development of large distant water fleets. Or of Japan, whose principal fishing effort has always been in the Pacific.

The fish in this book are not salmon, tuna, and swordfish, which together constitute less than five percent of the world marine catch. They are rather what the factory trawlers most caught, the fish loosely grouped as the cod and the herring families. These fish make up about forty percent of the total marine catch.

In the chapters on Soviet fishing, nothing is said of spying, a subject of great concern to many. There are various reasons. First, I observed none on the Soviet trawler I visited. It is my personal belief that Soviet oceanographic and fishery research vessels, not the trawlers, perform the more sophisticated intelligence-gathering. Second, there is not much of particular interest about ship-to-ship "spying," which is a routine practice everywhere. (British trawlers in the Barents and White seas, for example, have long been a firsthand source of intelligence on new Soviet ships; Soviet trawlers, of course, do the same vis-à-vis British shipping.) For want of strict inspection, Soviet trawlers *did* make off with millions of dollars' worth of fish caught over and above the quotas set by international agreements. The same, in fact, is true, but less so, of nearly all other distant water fleets.

The fishermen in some chapters swear more than others. No national slights are thereby intended. All fishermen have their choice epithets. Some save them for moments of exasperation; others use them all the time. This does not mean, for example, that the Spanish fishermen who continuously employ religious oaths or the British fishermen who use all possible variants of a well-known four-letter verb are therefore either sacrilegious or foul minded. Their oaths and swearwords are mere interstices — points of emphasis, like raising one's voice — devoid of literal meaning. The reader should so understand them, and take no offense.

If in all chapters, here and there, the reader finds a note of melancholy over the decline of a kind of fishing that was seriously threatening world fish supplies, I readily confess to it. It is directed to the fishermen, not their ships or their fishing technologies. Most distant water fishermen began their careers when the world at large led them to believe they were waging a vital struggle against hunger, when, for more specific example, a former official of the Woods Hole Oceanographic Institute and a curator of the American Museum of Natural History confidently entitled their coauthored work "The Inexhaustible Sea." The fishermen who went out to carry forward the struggle were company employees, not decision makers. Their dream was to save money — to have just a few more good trips, they would always say — and then retire to less demanding pursuits. But, suddenly, their vital task was redefined as ruthless overexploitation, and the choice was no longer theirs. Many, at this writing, are out of work.

These things understood, there remain only definitions and clarifications. The fish tonnage figures used throughout are metric tons (2,204.6 pounds). All distances are in nautical miles (6,076.1 feet, or one minute of latitude), unless otherwise stated. Ship tonnages are in gross register tons, which are actually a measure of space (100 cubic feet equals one gross ton). Applied mainly to merchant and fishing vessels, the gross tonnage of a ship is calculated by subtracting noncarrying from carrying space. Unfortunately, the formulas for determining which is which are very complex and not always the same.

The fishing industry makes a technical distinction between *factory freezer trawlers,* ships that process their fish into frozen fillets ready for consumption, and *whole-fish freezer trawlers,* ships that only gut (and sometimes behead) their fish prior to freezing. I have used "factory trawler" as a generic term for both, except where it seemed essential to differentiate them.

The transliteration of Russian names and phrases is old-style, not according to the International Slavicist, Library of Congress, or other such systems. The exactitude these provide for professionals is commendable, but I hesitate to render Yuri into Iouri or Jurij, or make Ševčenko out of Shevchenko.

Most important, all fish-catch statistics are based on what the fishing fleets of individual nations report to the Food and Agricultural Organization, which tries its best to verify and refine them. In the early years of factory trawling underreporting was quite widespread, not so much in total national catches as in regional breakdowns. (A nation that caught more fish than allowed in the Northwest Atlantic, for example, might spread out the overage among more remote world fishing areas.) Less of this is believed to go on today. Still, as with gross tonnages, the FAO catch statistics should be viewed as useful mainly for comparative purposes. In any case they are all that we have.

Cautiously, with apologies for the limitations of this work, I now hoist to the foremast the international signal flag known as the Blue Peter. I hope the reader will wish to respond to its call. Its meaning, universally recognized, is come aboard, ready to sail.

# Contents

# Distant Water

# ONE

# *Georges, 1976*

IT is a bright afternoon in early October of 1976. The trawler *Tremont* — one hundred and thirty feet in length overall, three hundred gross tons, and steel-built throughout — is leaving the Boston Fish Pier. Her departure provokes little notice. Although one of only four modern stern trawlers in the New England fishing fleet, the *Tremont* has become a familiar sight in Boston Harbor in her six years of service. Her lines slipped, she turns easily into the tidal stream of the inner harbor. Along her sides there is a suggestion of green paint, already sea faded and tinged by faint streaks of orange-red rust trailing from each deck scupper. Heavy diesels hum below her decks; a wavelet forms at the foot of her flaring bow. The *Tremont* picks up speed quickly and sets course for sea through the Narrows, between Great Brewster Spit and Georges, Lovell, and Gallops islands.

In four or five days of good luck, or seven or eight of bad, the *Tremont* will return early in the morning to her same berth at the Boston Fish Pier. In her fishhold will be anywhere from fifty to one hundred thousand pounds of gutted cod, haddock, and redfish, packed down in an almost equal weight of slowly melting ice. After helping to unload and swab down, the crew will go home. A little more than forty-eight hours later they will return to the *Tremont* for another trip. Another four to eight days at sea will follow, stretching to ten or twelve on difficult winter trips, then two more days ashore. Averaging in the annual haul-out and minor repair delays, the process will be repeated thirty-six times a year. Thirty-six round trips, out to the offshore bank called Georges.

As the *Tremont* twists through the tide-eddied Narrows, the lengthening afternoon turns very pleasant. Fresh northwest winds and a slanting October sun merge to create the brilliantly etched visibility that is the special joy of autumn on the New England coast. The men are in good humor. Some lounge on deck, sitting on piles of netting. Others crowd around the galley to cadge snacks from the cook, drink coffee, or offer comments on the supper menu. Young Norman Blake of Gloucester, the *Tremont*'s "twine man," or net-repair expert, and Lloyd Richards of Rockland, Maine, a rugged-looking substitute for a sick regular, are talking about the latest knifing in the Combat Zone, Boston's notorious night-life section. They are also carefully looking over an older crew member known as Old Mark or simply "the Frenchman," a Nova Scotian from a French-speaking enclave in Yarmouth County. Old Mark's eyes are red. He sits quietly at a narrow mess table, holding his head in his hands and sipping a cool beer.

"You going to be all right, Mark? You putting out the fires?"

"Oh, Jaysus, yes," Old Mark answers. "I be fine. I be fine."

The men seem reassured. Although genuinely sympathetic, they have an additional concern. Total earnings on this and all their trips rest firmly on the "lay," a time-honored system of sharing the proceeds of the catch. Mark is a shareman, like the rest of the nine-man crew, the captain included. To have one man sick can seriously affect the pace of deck work and, ultimately, the pay for the trip. Whether or not Mark will be fit for hard work early the next morning is what the younger men also want to know.

First Mate Dick Jellison, from the village of Minturn on Swan's Island, Maine, is telling of problems with his small-plane schedule in getting home. The way it was, with delays and all, he barely had twenty-four hours with his family and then it was time to turn around and come back.

"I can't answer why I do it," Jellison says. "I can't answer that question."

4

He shakes his head, continuing to wonder why he puts up with it. So many trips, one after another.

"My daughter's in college now," he adds, very slowly, speaking to no one in particular. "And, you know, I don't hardly know her.

"Well, so maybe we have a good trip this time," Jellison concludes. "Who knows? If we don't get dried up by the foreigners, that is."

The men immediately pick up on the new subject. Foreign fishing, or the huge international fleet of factory trawlers that has all but swept Georges Bank clean of certain valuable market fish, has long been their deepest concern and the chief conversational topic of nearly every trip. Soon, they have heard, the foreign abuses may be a thing of the past. All are aware of a bill passed by Congress the previous April, moving U.S. control of coastal fishing out from twelve to two hundred miles. The way they understand it, most of the foreign ships will be kicked out starting the first of March next year. It is true, as some point out, that a few foreign trawlers may be given licenses to fish inside the two hundred miles, but only for what American fishermen don't much take. Squid, hake, and possibly a little herring, that is. But even as they discuss these developments, many of the men cannot conceal a strong skepticism. It's all very well for the politicians to put together new laws, to make new promises. That has happened before. But how all these things will come to pass, far out at sea and long after all the speeches have been made, they aren't quite sure.

As I listen to the conversation, it is hard not to think of the completely opposite view and the high optimism the federal bureaucracy in Washington holds for the Fishery Conservation and Management Act of 1976, as the legislation creating the two hundred-mile fishery zone is officially known. At the Department of Commerce's National Marine Fisheries Service it is being hailed as the rebirth of American fishing and "a new order of government" in which rigid quotas of whatever fish may be allowed foreign vessels within the new zone will be jointly determined by the federal government and citizen advisory councils. The latest word from Washington, in fact, is that the foreigners already seem to be leaving. From a February peak of two hundred and twenty-six foreign trawlers, over one hundred of which were Russian, the National Marine Fisheries Service–U.S. Coast Guard inspecting teams have sighted only twenty-one in July off New England and the Atlantic states, a decrease of eighty percent from July of the year before. The NMFS officials are now speculating that the sharp drop may be due in part "to the interests of diplomacy," meaning hopes for favorable quotas after the two-hundred-mile act goes into effect the following March.

Remembering these statistics, I ask if we will still be seeing any of the foreigners.

"Seeing them!" scoffs Tom Kelly, a third-generation fisherman from Quincy, Massachusetts. "The bastards will be all over us."

"They're back for the fall herring," Dick Jellison explains. "The East Germans, the West Germans, the Russians. Maybe some Poles, too."

"They won't never leave," says Kelly. "The last trip, near where we're going now, at night it looked like the city of Chicago."

"They got big Jesus ships," adds Norman Blake. "And big Jesus nets."

"They'll never leave," Tom Kelly repeats. "I'll believe it when I see it."

The others agree. It is hard to believe. The foreigners have been around a long time; it must be a dozen or more years, as near as anyone can recollect. The Russians came first, sweeping up and down Georges with their ships paced out in long diagonal lines, plowing the best fishing grounds like disk harrows in a field. Mostly, in those early days, they fished for cod and herring. Then they took the haddock, when they realized what a good fish it was. You could look up what's happened since, the men say, in the *Tremont*'s records or the logbooks of any blue-water boat, as the offshore trawlers are called, from New Bedford to Rockland. The Georges Bank cod catch is down by half of what it was in the 1960s. And now the scientists at Woods Hole are calling the haddock "a seriously depleted stock," or possibly even endangered. But you didn't need the scientists to tell you, the men insist. It's all in the books. Haddock, which nearly always fetch the best price on the fresh-fish market, are way down. One third of what they were, all agree, before the foreigners came.

"In the old days, if I found spawners, I left them alone," Jellison observes. "I moved on. I tried to avoid them. The same with a run of small fish. Then look what the foreigners do! They take it all; they want the roe, the small fish, everything. I tell you, we are our own worst enemies."

"You'll see them all right," Norman Blake adds. "Germans, Russians, Poles, Spanish, even some Japs. They got big Jesus nets."

Like Tom Kelly, Blake thinks the foreigners are here to stay, law or no law. Too often he has been disappointed by promises of a better day. Everyone knows that not one thing has ever been done to give the offshore fisherman the slightest break. And, like all New England fishermen, he himself has seen the damage done by the big foreign ships. Nets lost in tangles, fixed lobster gear swept away, even some collisions.

"You can fill out some papers, put in a claim, and then wait," Blake continues. "Nothing ever comes of it, though. Not that I know of, at least."

It occurs to me to inquire about the International Commission for Northwest Atlantic Fisheries. ICNAF, as it is better known, is an international organization based on a treaty signed in 1949 to control offshore fishing in the Northwest Atlantic. Mainly at the insistence of its American and Canadian delegations, the European member states have recently and very reluctantly agreed to accept complete inspection of their big trawlers at sea, as well as a system of national catch quotas. Surely ICNAF's surveillance efforts, I ask rhetorically, have done something to curb the foreigners' overfishing.

A volley of expletives greets the question. ICNAF is a farce, the men all claim, not worth the paper its initials are written on. The foreigners still have plenty of ways to cheat, Dick Jellison maintains, and the catch statistics are too long coming in. Tom Kelly agrees. Most of the time, he explains, ICNAF spends over a year in compiling the total catch figures. By then, of course, it's much too late to do anything about the damage already done to fish stocks.

"And so what if the Coast Guard now boards and inspects?" Jellison adds. "If they find something wrong, what can they do about it? They write up their reports and then the ICNAF people send a note to the government of the ship that's in violation. It's like a tap on the wrist, a bad report card in school. You think that's going to stop them? It's true you can put them on notice, and later on maybe they seize a ship held in violation if it ever puts into an American port. But, believe me, that doesn't happen very often."

Lloyd Richards wants to make sure I understand that the U.S. Coast Guard does nearly all of ICNAF's inspection, even though the other countries are supposed to share the duty. "It's easier for them to inspect us," he says. "And we can get hauled in and fined."

"Oh, gorry, we try hard enough," Dick Jellison concludes. "But sometimes we get starved up pretty bad."

After supper the breeze stiffens and a quarter moon, waxing, hangs halfway up the night sky. Cables sway and the net gear shifts and clanks, tugging at stop lines, on the spray-swept steel of the main deck. To the south the distant flashes of Cape Cod lighthouses are easily seen on the horizon. Race Point, Highland, Nauset Beach — each conjures up its full share of summer memories. But the *Tremont* is hurrying along at twelve knots, pushed by quartering seas, and the lights fall off fast to starboard. Soon they are no more than smudged and irregular twinkles, frequently obscured by heaving seas. A pyramidal wave rises up in the dark, showing a large white crest, and slams hard against the *Tremont*'s side. Water explodes through the crack of a hinged scupper and hisses across the deck. It is reminder enough. We are going somewhere else. And summer is over.

Up on the bridge the rolling is pronounced. Captain Carl Spinney, fifty-four, is finishing out his four-to-midnight watch, after which he will be relieved by the first mate. Captain Spinney is a tall man, quiet of speech, with sandy brown hair and deep-set eyes that seem locked in a permanent squint. Although now a resident of Lynnfield, north of Boston, he comes from a Nova Scotian family that has seen three generations of its men go to sea. With him is his son Scott, a high-school graduate of the previous spring, who shares his father's height and has been glad to earn some real money working for him through the summer. Scott has just made a down payment on his first car, a secondhand Ford Capri. After his father gives him some advice on insurance, he heads below for his bunk. There is no need to tell him; sleep will soon be a precious commodity. Starting with the first tow of the net, the crew watches are four and eight, meaning four hours for food and rest followed by eight hours of demanding labor, around the clock. "It's savage," Scott says of the watch system, as he descends the bridge ladder. "Really savage."

"We're going to some hard ground about sixty miles southeast of the Cape," Captain Spinney explains. "Flat and hard, between seventy and eighty fathoms. It's called Jim Dwyer's Ridge, but you won't find the name on the chart. The foreign boats are there. I don't like to work too close to them, but the Poles and the East Germans have smaller side trawlers with a big load of plastic barrels for salting down the herring. They throw over the herring belly sections and that's good cod feed. So we occasionally tow around them.

"The sometimes we cross over the Channel, Great South Channel, that is, closer to Nantucket. But you have to be careful about the dogs [*Squalus acanthias,* the common dogfish or sand shark]. That's sandy ground over there, mostly, and the dogs are thick in the sandier parts. You don't want to get into the dogs."

The *Tremont* continues to make good speed. A migrating fall warbler is flitting in and out of the arc of the main-deck working lights. At times the tiny land bird darts close to a steel platform above the winches in the lee of the pilothouse, its small wings beating furiously to hold place in the wind. One wants somehow to communicate, to offer it a welcome aboard for a long and much needed rest. But the strong lights scare it away, back into the night.

It is four o'clock in the morning. Someone is waking up Tom Kelly in the bunk below me. His snoring stops abruptly. Groaning, he lights a small Italian-twist cigar, dresses, and goes aft for his oilskins. Presently there are metallic noises from far astern — muffled thumpings and rattlings — followed by a loud midships whirring. The whirring noise is rhythmic and cyclical, with vibrations that run through the ship. Five minutes later, engine speed is reduced and one last great shudder convulses the hull. Pitching and rolling noticeably diminish. The *Tremont* has made the first "set" of her net, having rapidly paid out some 1,500 feet of cable from her main winches. She is settling down comfortably to the work for which she was built.

Four hours later the watch changes and breakfast is on the table. The *Tremont*'s cook is Arthur Doyle, fifty-eight, a native of Conception Bay, Newfoundland. He is a short man of robust pink complexion, a balding head, and darting blue eyes framed by wire-rimmed glasses. Like many of his countrymen Doyle moved to the United States in the great depression years, back when Canadians took to calling the Boston area "Little Newfoundland." This morning he has laid out the usual fisherman's at-sea breakfast, which is to say various fruit juices, grapefruit halves, stewed prunes, hot porridge, cold cereals, small pancakes, fried potatoes, link sausages, salt cod, and hard-boiled eggs.

"Yes, the skipper wants hard-boiled this morning," Doyle says, winking. "We're towing to starboard so the eggs mus' be hard-boiled. That's the signal the skipper gives me; that's how he tells me."

Two hauls have been made during the night. Resting on chopped ice deep in the bottommost pens of the *Tremont*'s fish-hold is just over half a ton of assorted fish. But the men are not happy. The proportion of pollock is too high. Pollock, large and strong-swimming relatives of the cod, with handsome dark blue topsides, do not fetch much on the market. This is because the fish has some gray flesh, or "dark meat," which makes it look marbled when pressed and frozen into fish blocks. Although the pollock is firm fleshed and excellent tasting, American housewives and the restaurant trade tend to pass it by in favor of pure or all-white-meat species. As with wonder breads and bleached rice, in other words, so with fish.

"You're lucky to get ten cents the pound for it," Norman Blake comments.

"They eat it more in Canada," adds Dick Jellison. "It's called Boston bluefish up there."

Outside the wind has moderated slightly and shifted to the southwest. Only small white clouds drift low to the horizon across an otherwise clear sky. The cresting seas, so threatening at night, jump up and frolic forward invitingly in the patchwork sunlight. The *Tremont* responds, rising and falling to meet them smartly, as though exulting in the fine weather. Visibility is good and the clean air invigorates. It is a day to be at sea.

Birds define our position. Through the night land-based gulls have been dropping off from the crowded and noisy "tail" of sea-birds that fly in the wake of every fishing vessel. Now the gulls have given way in great numbers to true pelagic species, or "oceanics," as ornithologists call the ceaseless roamers of the open seas. Here, at this time of year, the greater shearwater is over-whelmingly dominant. It is a handsome black-capped bird with the hooked beak and the tube nostrils common to all "tubenoses," or the large family whose members range from tiny sparrow-sized storm petrels (the Mother Carey's chickens of sailor's lore) to the great albatrosses of the southern oceans. Given today's con-ditions, the shearwaters honor their name. They swoop stiff-winged into deep troughs, mere inches from the water, and then rocket up to triumphal heights off the faces of the larger seas. It is as though they, too, are responding to the good weather in what may well be a valedictory exercise, a final celebration of ideal au-tumnal soaring conditions. By November all will be gone on their long journey to the midocean islands of Tristan da Cunha in the Southern Hemisphere, which is their only known breeding site. As of this moment, however, the growing flock of shearwaters — at least two hundred have joined us — provides a good naviga-tional fix, marking our progress into a zone of transition. Their presence in such numbers is the surest sign the *Tremont* has crossed an invisible yet undeniable line. We have entered the realm known as "offshore." We are on the grounds, as the fishermen have it. Right on the hard and flat ground, in fact, of Jim Dwyer's Ridge, close to the southwestern corner of Georges Bank.

So, too, are others. Captain Spinney has called me up to the bridge to view our neighbors. "You wanted to see them," he says matter-of-factly. "Well, here they are."

Ships are all around us, near and far. I count some thirty-three, slowly scanning the full circle of the horizon with binoculars. All are foreign fishing vessels — modern in design and considerably larger than the *Tremont* — with hard, utilitarian lines that give a grim, or at least businesslike, aspect to the fleet at large. It is a sight to see: a floating metropolis, a city at sea, just as the crew had described it. One thinks immediately of the fish. How any schools can escape the hidden eyes of this armada, since every ship in the fleet is equipped with multiple underwater electronic fish-finders, is difficult to imagine.

At middle distance, or halfway to the horizon on our port side, is a Russian. It is a big ship, close to three hundred feet in length overall, with relatively short aft working space and a lengthy housing, or superstructure, rising from her main deck. The superstructure decks are punctuated by long rows of cabin portholes, which, along with an unnecessarily large, fat, and raked funnel, give to the ship the distinct passenger-liner appearance so characteristic of early Soviet factory trawlers. It is too far to make out her name. But painfully, by constant refocusing of the binoculars, the letters KB and numerals 0322 emerge in black from a dirty white panel painted squarely amidships on her hull. She is, according to the registry lists, the *Almaz*, a Mayakovksy class *Bolshoi Morozilni Rybolovny Traler* (literally, a "large freezer fishing trawler" or BMRT, as the U.S. Coast Guard prefers simply to say), home port Kaliningrad, 3,170 gross tons, stern ramped and factory equipped, with a crew of ninety. The *Almaz*, it appears, was built in 1960. Judged by the life span of modern factory trawlers, she is thus a very old ship, a seasoned veteran of many North Atlantic campaigns. Indeed, her age is beginning to tell. Rust predominates on her tired flanks, and there is a notable absence of fresh paint anywhere on her hull or superstructure.

Between us and the *Almaz* are three sleeker and thoroughly modern ships with jutting bows, twin black funnels, and black hulls broken only by very thin and neatly painted white cove stripes. Above their main decks, two boat decks and a bridge deck rise step by step to make castlelike superstructures, gleaming white in the sunshine. The three ships seem to be merely prowling the sea, scanning and searching by sonar, since none has any towing cables streaming astern. It is easy to guess their identity. Words like *Seewulf* and *Panzerschiff* spring to mind. They are unmistakably German. West German, to be exact, part of the crack Unilever-owned Nordsee fleet, known throughout the fishing world for exacting quality control and devastatingly high catch rates. Nearest to us is a fourth ship, the *Karlsburg* of Bremerhaven. She looks to be well over three hundred feet in length and has a handsome black and white hull. Shields with golden crowns and crossed keys, devices reminiscent of the ancient coats of arms of cities of the Hanseatic League, adorn her tall twin funnels. A thin red and white pennant snaps at her main truck. Appropriately, the *Karlsburg* is the flag and command ship of the Hanseatische Hochseefischerei company fleet, Germany's second largest and chief rival to Nordsee.

"They're herringing," says Captain Carl, who like many New England fishermen makes an intransitive verb out of whatever fish species one may be pursuing. "They do a lot of hunting like that before they set one of their big mid-water trawls. You'll see. They're so big, those mid-water nets, it takes them half an hour to haul back after the doors are up, at least. So they don't fool around until they are really on to some fish."

There is a great difference, Captain Carl goes on to explain, between what we and the Germans are doing. The *Tremont* is using a ground trawl — a bottom-hugging net shaped somewhat like a flattened funnel — that is continually dragged over the sea floor in tows lasting approximately three hours, night and day. Heavy wooden or steel plates, known as otter boards or doors, linked to the towing cables, open a ground trawl's mouth by shearing along the bottom with a paravane-like action; ponderous steel balls called bobbins and small aluminum floats rigged to the net's "ground-rope" and "headline," respectively, combine to keep the trawl snug to the bottom and give the funnel mouth its rise, or vertical opening. By contrast the Germans' mid-water trawls can be made to "fly" free of the ocean floor by a combination of airfoil-shaped doors, changing ship speeds, and weights on the towing cables. (See Appendix I) Mainly used to catch fast-swimming herring, mackerel, or other pelagic fish, the biggest of the mid-water nets are now one thousand feet, or more than three football fields, in length. Not only that, Captain Carl emphasizes, they have under-water sonars attached to their headlines which give remarkably clear recordings of both headline and groundrope depths, bottom depth and topography, and fish entering (or escaping) the net. It is these sonars, or "netsounders," which can scan ahead up to two miles when used in conjunction with the ship's sonars, that make mid-water trawling so deadly efficient. (The *Tremont*'s sonar works vertically; it shows fish only directly under the hull.) The only constraint on this form of fishing is that the big nets are extremely cranky and difficult to operate. Like the spinnaker of a sailboat, they may collapse from too sharp a course change, tricky currents, or, sometimes, for no apparent reason at all. This is why, Captain Carl repeats, the Germans don't go around making idle or chance tows. Rather, they hunt patiently until all their electronic devices "lock" and simultaneously record a big school of herring. It could be days before they make one of their quick sets, he concludes. But when they do, it's bound to be a big one.

Close to starboard is a smaller and seaworn vessel. Her name and number are easy to see: *Rudi Arndt,* ROS-410. The "Ros" prefix means she hails from Rostock on the Baltic Sea, the principal fishing port of the German Democratic Republic. The East German is bottom trawling, as we are, and measures just over two hundred feet, seventy feet more than the *Tremont*. But here any similarities end. The *Rudi Arndt* is beamier and deeper hulled, with 998 gross tons as against our 310. She is also much scarred along her sides, and various dents disfigure her rails. Drab gray, one supposes, was her original color, but it would be impossible to say now for sure. Rolling in the troughs she shows a foul bottom. Much of her hull seems deeply and dangerously rust pitted.

"That's one of the East German catcher boats," Captain Carl comments. "They got detachable cod ends [the reinforced final section of a ground trawl, where the fish collect]. They put extra floats on them, attach a radio beacon, and then drop the whole cod end off in the water. Then the big factory ship, the mother ship, comes along and picks it up. See her? She's laying 'way over there, on the horizon."

Again refocusing the binoculars, all I can see is that the mother ship is by far the largest vessel in our crowded quarters. She appears to be reasonably well kept and shines a silvery gray in the distant sunlight, in sharp contrast to her dull and rust-fouled daughters. Captain Carl is meanwhile explaining that with any kind of fair weather the big mother ship will take the catcher boats alongside for unloading, which is why they eventually get so banged up. He has heard it said that the East German catchers stay out for years on end, in fact, with crew replacements at sea.

"Yes, the foreigners are leaving us 'way behind," Captain Carl adds, trying to sum it all up. "They got all the best equipment — like you take this sonar we use, made in Norway — and they keep just about everything they catch. Squid, skates, dogs; you name it. We don't eat enough fish in this country. That's the problem. It's such a terrible waste; everything in these seas can be eaten. The Boston Fish Pier takes so little. Most of what they do handle comes in over the road in trucks, especially from Canada. Look, I can't come in the same day as the *Old Colony* [the *Tremont*'s sister ship]; we have to make sure of that. If we come in together, it's too much fish and the market can't handle it. Same with two or three of the little Gloucester boats. Say you got fifteen thousand pounds of medium cod. You come in the right day with nobody else around and the price is thirty cents a pound. The next day, if you got company, it can drop to ten cents. That's a three-thousand-dollar loss on the one item alone. Take the whole catch, and you can be talking of anywhere from ten to twenty thousand dollars' difference. It's crazy, but I've seen it happen so many times.

"Sure, like you say, a captain has the right to refuse to unload if he thinks the price is too low. But if you hold over, it's a gamble you seldom win. The buyers know your catch is a day older, and you got no place else to go. They don't need us. That's the real problem."

It is the evening of the sixth day at sea. We are back on Jim Dwyer's Ridge, once again surrounded by the foreign fleet. During the course of the trip the *Tremont* has periodically crossed Great South Channel to fish the tide-scoured sands of Nantucket Shoals and then returned to Jim Dwyer's or other areas on the southern tip of Georges, alternating between grounds known to be good by day and others that are more productive at night. One or the other of the *Tremont*'s two trawls has been laboriously set and even more laboriously recovered for a total of thirty-eight tows. Some of the days have been rough, with long swells and breaking seas caused by a hurricane named Gloria, down by Bermuda. ("That's good, hope it comes a little closer," Captain Carl had said when the warnings were first broadcast. "Maybe the smaller boats will run home and we'll get a good market.") Other days have been flat calm, with oily smooth seas. Far too frequently the nets have come up with large tears. The men have mended them patiently, without complaint, since "rimracks," as they call hangups on boulders or other obstructions, are accepted as a matter of course on certain parts of Georges. On occasion we have run into the dogs or sand sharks. One night it was over ten tons of them, in fact, over near the Half Moon Ground on Nantucket Shoals, which meant many hours of lost fishing time spent in hacking away at a swollen trawl to spill enough fish to ease the overload on the winches and then pitchforking the rest over the side, once the net could be fully recovered. But one way or another the catches have been improving all week. Not so much in quantity, that is, but by getting cleaner and cleaner, meaning more cod and haddock and fewer low-priced fish or the trash species that are thrown overboard. Scratching around, Captain Carl calls it, or searching here and there by the seat of your pants and the accumulated knowledge of years of fishing the same grounds. Add a little luck and you can come up with fairly clean haulbacks of one ton or more, rarely two tons. This is not what anybody would call good fishing, of course. But it's about all you can expect these days, he says, what with the foreigners swarming all over you.

Nevertheless, the crew is quite happy. Norman Blake, who in addition to being the *Tremont*'s best twine man also "hails," or keeps a running estimate of her catch, has made an announcement. Down in the cavernous fishhold, in the glare of naked light bulbs and the cold fog rising from pens of chopped ice, lie over fifty thousand pounds of fish. The men know; nothing more need be said. Fifty thousand is enough. Not only that, today the daily radio market report quoted haddock at sixty cents a pound and all three cod sizes — scrod, "market" or medium, and large — at over thirty. These are good prices. It is time to make for port.

Although Captain Carl has yet to give an official order, Arthur Doyle is celebrating the occasion with one of his best menus. For starters we have "Newfoundland turkey," meaning juicy oven-baked cod heads, which the men like as a relief from too many fried fillets or cod steaks. After that it's bean soup, porterhouse steak, baked potatoes, mixed salad, strawberry ice cream, and pound cake. The ice cream served, Captain Carl gets up from the table and returns to the bridge. Shortly thereafter he gives the long-awaited order over the public-address system. "Haul back, hose down, and secure all gear," he announces, quite casually.

Two hours later the last fish have been snugged down in ice and the decks thoroughly scrubbed. As night falls, the men turn to on the nets. Both trawls are carefully plucked and shaken clean of all weed and fish scraps, which would otherwise rot and weaken the twine, and then tied down securely. Up on the bridge Dick Jellison nudges the engines full ahead, to eight hundred revolutions per minute. Free at last of the heavy drag of her nets, the *Tremont* surges easily over coal-black swells. The lights of the foreign fleet, the city at sea, drop away fast to the southeast. We are bound home.

A sudden and pervading silence engulfs the *Tremont*. After six days, fourteen hours, and thirty minutes of continuous throbbing, our big General Motors diesel is throttled down to dead slow and stop. Tom Kelly in the bunk below agrees with me. Your ears pop in relief, as when emerging from a tunnel, and the quiet wakes you up like a cannon shot. "You miss the engine," he says. "It gets to be like a lullaby."

Out on deck Scott Spinney and Norman Blake are tightening our spring lines. Dawn has not yet come, and a thick, drenching fog obscures the buildings of the Fish Pier. All we can see, in fact, is the distressing presence of two other boats, crowding us out of the best berthing space at the end of the pier. They are small draggers, wooden-hulled side trawlers: the *Manuel F. Roderick* of Boston, a veteran of thirty-five years of service, and the *Santa Maria* of Gloucester, a mere youngster of ten. By the time breakfast is on the table, Dick Jellison has already been out to scout them, peering at their waterlines for a rough estimate of their loads.

"Jesus, I think the *Roderick*'s got as much as we do," he reports.

A wiry man in his midforties joins us for breakfast. "Good morning, gentlemen," he says. "How many of youse are working today?" Our visitor is the head lumper, the longshoreman who will be in charge of the *Tremont*'s unloading. He asks the question because the crew members may or may not help unload, as they choose. Those who do not get $42.00 docked from their trip share. Many will say it's not worth it, given all the frustrations. Sharp practices are a tradition on the Fish Pier, and the crew must constantly be on guard against a variety of lumper deceptions. Some are quite crude, such as putting more than the allowed weight of ice in the tractor-train carts that shuttle between shipside and the pier's weighing platform. Others are rather ingenious and take a watchful eye to detect. The tractor operator, for example, can drive the carts onto the weighing platform in a sharp turn. The torque so produced on the couplings can substantially reduce the cart's weight. Inevitably there are arguments. The fish, especially the cod, look old and flabby. Almost no skin color remains on those from the bottom of the hold that are already about a week old. Thus a lumper can place these fish prominently on the top of a cart, perhaps adding a few crushed specimens from the pier pavement, and try to have the cart condemned. But seldom do these attempts at condemnation succeed. All the fish will be sold sight unseen, with the same price for week-olds as for those at the top of the hold which were caught the day before. Quality is not paramount. Rather, you have to move your product fast, as they say on the Pier. Condemnation procedures mean too much time, too much hassle, all things considered.

By seven o'clock there is enough light at the end of the pier to see a grim brick and stucco building that would look more at home on the grounds of a state penitentiary. It is, in fact, the seat of the New England Fish Exchange. Inside on the ground floor is a large and echoing hall, into which buyers are now beginning to file. Near the entrance is a green slate painted with white horizontal and vertical lines which form boxes for the names of vessels and the weights of the different fish they have caught. A man is chalking in the *Tremont*'s hail: 6,000 pounds of haddock, 14,000 large cod, 9,000 scrod cod, 15,000 market. . . . The chalked postings move through the flounderlike species collectively known as flatfish, the spiny little redfish, the low-priced pollock and hake, and finally, in the column farthest to the right, 3,000 pounds of "cats," which usually means wolffish and goosefish, or two of the most grotesque of all groundfish, as anything caught on the bottom is called in the trade.

Lying on a table near a row of bank-teller windows is a worn copy of *Rules and Regulations, New England Fish Exchange,* published July 15, 1935. Prominent in the text is Article VII, entitled "Conduct on the Exchange — Notice of Sales by Signal." It reads in part:

No offer shall be made to any captain or seller of vessel fish until he is on the platform. All pushing and placing of hands on the captain and all ungentlemanly conduct in the Exchange is prohibited. Entrance to the hall must be kept clear. Buyers must not get on the platform. . . .

Exactly in the center of the hall is a low wooden platform guarded on all four sides by carved oak railings. At approximately seven-fifteen two middle-aged men wearing chest microphones, known only to most fishermen and buyers as Red Top and Funnyman, step up onto this platform. Quickly, they are joined by two younger men with clipboards and notebooks.

An auction, in a manner of speaking, is about to begin. By now the buyers have had ample opportunity to look over the board and chat among themselves over Styrofoam cups of steaming coffee. It is therefore most unlikely the auction will hold any surprises or even animated bidding. Nor is there apt to be much pushing or placing of hands on captains. Very little of such ungentlemanly conduct has been seen on the Exchange since the *Regulations* were first printed, when vessels two or three abreast around the Pier, and not trucks from Canada, were the objects of all attention. The buyers already know that today's three boats have more than enough fish to supply the restaurants and retail shops they serve in Greater Boston. There is no need to bid high. Perhaps, some buyers may decide, one of them could come in very low on a big lot and then divide and resell it to his colleagues after the auction, when no records need be kept. No collusion, of course, you understand. Just some friendly and essential conversations on the state of the market. After all, there isn't much time. You have to move the product fast.

"Two thousand haddock on the *Roderick*," Red Top intones. "I got two thousand haddock at fifty-two. Offered fifty-five."

In the back row a tall and stony-faced Italian American wearing a green alpine hat quickly raises his pencil.

"Sold at fifty-six. The *Roderick* haddock at fifty-six."

Funnyman picks up on the large cod. Captain Carl is listening intently, along with Norman Blake, who has momentarily left his unloading duties to get an early line on the prices. He is amazed, he tells Captain Carl. The large cod have dropped ten cents from the day before.

"Looks like everything is down a dime from yesterday," Captain Carl answers. His voice reveals not the slightest emotion. No one could have guessed the *Roderick* and the *Santa Maria* might sneak in this morning. But, then, of course, he has seen it happen before. So many times.

The bidding goes quickly. Having sold the top market species, one at a time and boat by boat, Red Top now moves on to smaller quantities of the lower-priced fish.

"Cart of hake from the *Santa Maria!* Fifteen hundred of hake open! No splits, Victor. I'm not cutting up no pies here; I'm just selling fish. Fifteen hundred hake. A cart of hake open!"

In less than half an hour the auction is over, as quietly and unceremoniously as it began. Tom Kelly has joined Captain Carl. Both are busily jotting down figures in soiled pocket notebooks, hoping to get a preliminary idea of their trip earnings. They begin with what is called the gross stock, the total value of the catch. By the terms of the just-completed auction the *Tremont*'s estimated 59,120 pounds of fish of all kinds are worth approximately $19,700. This figure they now divide by the traditional lay of 40 percent for the boat, which means the owners, and 60 percent for the crew, minus a confusing array of deductions. From the owners' share come the captain's 10 percent bonus (plus flat $50 trip bonuses for the first mate and chief engineer and $25 for the cook), wharfage, Fish Exchange commission fees, the in-port watchman's salary, contributions to the Fishermen's Welfare Fund, and, only in the summer months, the cost of ice. What is left is the net stock, an amount to be divided into equal shares among the nine-man crew, the captain included. But first, Captain Carl is patiently explaining, there are additional and heavier deductions. From the net stock you must subtract the costs of diesel and lube oil, food, groceries, drinking water, and, for most of the year, ice, all of which can mount up to $2,000 or $3,000 a trip.

Tom Kelly's stubby pencil is working fast; his concentration is intense. He hasn't quite finished his calculations, but he already knows that the $19,700 gross stock was not very good to begin with (winter trips, when many fewer boats venture out to Georges, often gross over $40,000) and that it is eroding rapidly under the combined assault of the lay division and the numerous deductions.

Two hours later the pandemonium of unloading is almost done. Tom Kelly has finished his figuring. A final settlement will come after all weights and prices have been duly recorded by the Exchange. But right now it looks like the *Tremont*'s 59,120 pounds of fish mean about $700 to each crew member. This is not necessarily bad, Tom says. But then again it might have gone over $1,000 without the *Santa Maria* and the *Roderick*. You never know.

The dockside areas of the Fish Pier are almost deserted. All the noise and confusion now shifts to the cobblestone truck parks and the buyers' offices and filleting rooms that line the two-storey stone buildings on either side of the pier. The more timid seagulls on the rooftops, who have been waiting patiently, now fly down to perch on carts and fight with others over fish scraps.

Arthur Doyle, dressed in a brown suit and gray fedora, is walking down the pier, looking for a taxi he has ordered. His gait seems hesitant and uncertain. Norman Blake, tired and suffering a headache from the lumpers' abuses, gets into a car his wife has driven down from their home in Gloucester and prepares to do battle with downtown Boston traffic. Blending into the crowd, both men suddenly look much smaller.

Back on Jim Dwyer's Ridge, at approximately the same hour as bidding began at the Fish Exchange, the Hanseatische Hochseefischerei's flagship *Karlsburg* might typically have been locking into a fine early morning rise of fish with various combinations of her four electronic fishfinders. Then, in less time than it had taken to finish the ritual auction, the *Karlsburg* would set and haul back her big mid-water trawl. With any kind of luck the cod end would come up filled with at least 120,000 pounds of sleek Atlantic herring, over double the weight of fish caught by the *Tremont* in six days at sea. Back home in Germany the herring would be much appreciated. Eventually, in fact, the single haulback would sell for the equivalent of $38,500, almost twice the *Tremont*'s gross trip stock.

# TWO

# *The Fish Killers*

THE middle of May is a time of hope in Newfoundland. The hope is that winter will at last disappear. Although snow may yet fall, alder and birch are beginning to bud in inland valleys. Out on the barrens the larch trees are still bare, but horned larks and buntings fly bravely, low to the ground, over wind-rippled clumps of tussock grass. Along the coast the first warblers — blackpolls, myrtles, and yellowthroats — begin to invade sheltered pockets of dwarf spruce on the lee slopes of towering headlands. In each outport, as the more isolated fishing communities are generally known, laughing troops of boys and girls eagerly clutch long bamboo poles as they strike out over the barrenlands in search of their favorite pond. If the wind drops and the sun comes on strong, insects will rise, birds will sing, and hungry little brook trout will fill their creels. But, of course, the gray clouds in the west can at any moment race across the moors, spitting wet snow or cold rain, and force the children to run home. It does not much matter, really. Tomorrow or the next day will do as well. Spring in Newfoundland is not a recognizable climatic season. Rather, it is a state of mind. Hope identifies and sustains it throughout, a sure hope that winter will inevitably relax, that children will soon be free to play long hours out of doors, and that men can return to the sea.

Once, some years ago, I stayed with a fishing family in a small outport on Newfoundland's north coast at just this time of year. For the men it was a busy period. Their rickety stages, or mooring platforms, each year mauled by winter ice, needed much repair. Inside the nearby twine lofts were miles of moldering long lines and gill nets to check for serviceability. Some of the fishermen talked of setting out the first cod traps, but others thought it too early. There was, after all, a big iceberg off on the horizon, not to mention some few pans of residual local ice. Might not the berg, before it grounded, drift down on a trap and carry it away? That was a serious question. A Newfoundland cod trap is in reality a large underwater pound net suspended from the bottom by an intricate combination of floats, steel chain, and heavy grapnel anchors. A fully rigged trap costs over $6,000; to set it in place takes two boats "with a good crowd of hands" working for four or five hours in reasonably calm weather. It is not, therefore, something that you can move around on a moment's notice. Taking all this very much into account, most of the trap crews thought it prudent to wait. In the meanwhile they could always put out a few lobster pots. Thus, every morning I either watched or accompanied the fishermen as they went off lobstering in their handsomely fashioned lapstrake trap skiffs. Often their work took them uncomfortably close to the bases of dizzying cliffs, where heavy ground swells exploded as booming surf on wet-black rock. In many places, just outside the churn of the surf, were rocky half-tide ledges — "sunkers," they call them in Newfoundland's lugubrious maritime vocabulary — on which the seas broke heavily. Those who set their pots as close as they dared to the sunkers, it seemed to me, got the most lobsters.

One Sunday morning, remarkably clear and warm, my hostess suggested we "ride out on the high road" to go visiting here and there by car. A vigorous woman in her late fifties, she had been active in local politics and was thus welcome in many places normally reserved only to men. Secure in this knowledge, she took me down to the village's main wharf. Here, as in every outport, older or retired fishermen gathered on any fine Sunday to watch the weather and retail the latest news.

The talk that morning covered many subjects. There was a new boat in the harbor, a big longliner just come up from St. John's.

Some of the men were very worried about her. They wondered if she would stay in local waters throughout the summer voyage, as they called their brief inshore fishing season, and thus be competing with them. Then there was the man that came ashore at Green Island Light, hadn't we heard? Just two days ago, it was. A handsome enough young fellow, most likely off one of the Norwegian seiners. It took me some moments to understand what everyone else took for granted; namely, that "to come ashore" in these icy north-coast waters meant as a corpse, washed in by the tide. Newfoundland speech can be disturbingly direct.

But the oldest men in the group much preferred to talk of the past, particularly of the halcyon days of the annual schooner trips to the Labrador coast. Their eyes brightened under the visors of their Irish-style cloth caps as they competed to tell me of this once-great vernal event.

"Yes, my dear, we fared well in those days. Down to the Labrador we went. Just this time of year it was, and you don't see us home until October month! A thousand cantles [quintals or hundredweights] we fished, and we were all in the family for crew."

"That's right, Captain Aaron. All in the family except one and, you know, I'm thinking that was the cook. Yes, it was a good share we got those times. We fared well."

Never, in fact, did the conversation stray very far from this single and sorrowful theme, or an almost rhythmically recited threnody for the better days of the men's youth, which few of them thought would ever return. Now, everyone agreed, the problem was mainly the squid and the capelin. Squid were nowhere as plentiful as before, and none of the men could ever forget the first dense shoals that moved inshore every summer. So thick they were that the whole town went out to fish them. You used little lead weights — squid jigs, you called them — painted red and crowned at their bottoms with twenty or more tines, bent upward and needle-sharp. You jerked a string of these weights up and down, attracting the curious squid, and pretty soon, sure enough, you hooked one on the tines. Sometimes, in fact, you even got two or three of the creatures on a single jig. And wasn't that great sport and a bright time for all!

Yes, the men kept saying, you filled your dory easily in the old days and always had more than enough bait for the season. (Squid has long been an essential cod bait in Newfoundland; today it is used mainly for long lining, fishing with a long central line to which hundreds or even thousands of hooked snoods, or drop lines, are attached.) It was a happy time, no doubt about it. There were many more scoffs and soirees, as the oldest men called the attendant parties and celebrations.

Then there was the capelin. With every mention of the subject the men's heads nodded in unison. The capelin, they insisted, were simply not coming ashore the way they used to. Their numbers were way down, and they had been that way for the last several years.

The Atlantic capelin is a small pelagic fish seldom exceeding eight or nine inches in length that swims in large schools in the coldest waters of the North Atlantic. For reasons not fully understood by scientists, one part of the Northwest Atlantic capelin population spawns far out at sea near the eastern edge of the Grand Banks. Another part comes close inshore — right up to any suitable sand or pebble beach, in fact — to cast their milt and roe in the roll of the surf. The "scull," or arrival, of the inshore spawners is an eagerly awaited event in nearly all Newfoundland outports. It can come very quickly at any time from the first half of June to the end of July, depending on slowly rising water temperatures. Suddenly, one day, the green wall of every wave will show itself dark with swarming fish. It is a dramatic sight and the word that "the capelin are rolling" travels fast. Men, women, and children run down to the beaches, since fresh-cooked capelin are a highly prized dish and the little fish also "pickle" well when salted in barrels. The men wade out into the waves, expertly throwing circular cast-nets, to be sure they get their share of the first runs. Behind them women and children soon do just as well with baskets or pails. Nearly always there will be a wave-sculptured hollow on the beach shingle; inevitably, many capelin strand in these hollows, unable to wriggle back in the draw of the surf. These fish need only be picked up, as fast as small hands can work. So it happened, the men told me, that the big runs of former years were another happy occasion, another time for the scoffing and the soirees.

There was, however, a more important consideration. Biologists, fisheries officials, and generations of fishermen could all agree about it. Soon after the capelin come the cod. Capelin and cod; the two go always together. Practically speaking, for Newfoundland's inshore fisheries, the one does not exist without the other. So important are capelin as a prey fish that draw cod inshore that they largely determine the success or failure of the smaller outports' fishing year. If the capelin run thick and strong, the trap crews, the gill netters, the long liners, and even the few dory fishermen who still row out to jig the cod will all have a good summer voyage. If not, they will sink deeper in debt to the buyers. The problem, as every man on the wharf that Sunday morning repeated again and again, was that "capelin is nowadays everywhere scarce." I had heard this opinion many times in outports extending from the Labrador coast to Newfoundland's south shore. The men were not sure why it was so, but many had heard the big foreign ships were beginning to take capelin and thought that probably had something to do with it.

When at last we left the wharf to continue our Sunday visits, my hostess turned to me and asked: "Now, you seen the gentleman with the gall by his neck? Well, he was a great fish killer! Yes, by deed, a great fish killer, he was!"

Unlike many Newfoundland localisms, fish killer is easily translated. It means what the rest of the English-speaking fishing world calls a high liner, a top-earning fisherman. I was to hear the term often in the next ten minutes.

As we followed a crooked street between the little cracker-box homes that are the trademark of Newfoundland outport architecture, my hostess identified each house's owner and told me in lengthy detail of his or her relative standing in the community. "You see the house all pretty yellow, with the blue trim?" she might ask. "Belonged my grandfather, on my dear mother's side. And wasn't he the great fish killer! Had two schooners going down to the Labrador. *Two* schooners, by deed, he did!"

Only when we passed the last house and the high road arched straight over the rolling barrens did she become momentarily quiet.

"Truth is they was all great fish killers, those days," she said after a pause. "A whole generation of them, you could say."

A week later I was in St. John's, the capital city of Newfoundland and the most frequented port of call for the factory trawler fleets of many nations. Fishing is the principal business of St. John's, and St. John's takes its business very much to its heart. Unlike other ports, which shunt fishing vessels to the most undesirable locations, hidden behind wastelands of rotting wharves, warehouses, and steel-link fences, the city offers foreign fishermen its best waterfront. Their ships berth comfortably alongside a long quay with park benches and a scenic parallel avenue, known as Harbour Drive. Walk a short block up from Harbour Drive on any one of a number of steep and narrow side streets and you are in the center of St. John's business and shopping district. Thus it may happen that a visitor dining in one of St. John's downtown restaurants can look out a harborside window and find a giant ship nudging up to the quay, directly at eye level and close enough to hear shouted orders from the bridge.

It was under exactly such circumstances that I first saw a modern factory trawler close at hand. First to glide into view in the frame of the restaurant windows was a huge flared bow. Painted on its side were Cyrillic characters that seemed to spell out, rather incongruously, the word *Rembrandt*. Next came towering kingposts, cargo masts of the type one more commonly associates with freighters, and a multiwindowed bridge painted fresh white and extending across the full width of the ship. Aft of the bridge was a boat deck with two large lifeboats hung on strong davits and a lengthy promenade that gave promise of cruise ship comforts. A large placard between the lifeboats repeated the vessel's name in the Roman alphabet. There was no mistake. The ship was named the *Rembrandt*. Uniformed officers, replete with gold braid and white hats, peered from the bridge wings. A large crew, including some women, lined the rails. All appeared stolid and impassive, yet it was clear they watched everything on shore with the utmost attention, like cautious visitors from another world. In a very real sense, they were. Towering above them, dominating the *Rembrandt*'s superstructure, was a large funnel painted with a wide red band. In the middle of the red band were a golden hammer and sickle.

Down on the quay, standing in the shadow of the *Rembrandt*'s high walls, I judged her length at over three hundred feet and her capacity at something beyond four thousand gross tons. Such dimensions are, of course, quite small by contemporary merchant and tanker fleet standards. But viewed against the backdrop of St. John's small fjordlike harbor and compared with anything most of us picture as fishing vessels, the *Rembrandt* looked every bit the *Queen Mary*.

Curiously, nothing in the ship's forward half suggested anything of her function. The foredeck resembled a freighter; the superstructure, a passenger liner. Only back aft did the *Rembrandt* reveal a more workmanlike character. Here large and heavily rusted steel plates — extra doors for mid-water trawling, I later learned — hung on the stern rails, just above where the ship's name was repeated, along with the name of her home port, Murmansk. Near the stern quarters rose a high two-legged gantry mast for heavy lifting. From it and a smaller mast at the forward end of the main deck hung many strong steel cables, each eventually leading to one or another winch. Most noticeable amid the clutter of gear, standing out by their very size alone, were the nets. Great mounds of them rested on the trawl deck or were jammed into odd corners in the lee of the superstructure. Each of the net mounds looked as large as the average Newfoundland outport home. In fact, it was easy to imagine them engulfing a dozen such homes or an entire small outport — as well they could in the case of the mid-water trawls, at least, when fully opened in a proper set. Almost as surprising was the view from astern of the *Rembrandt*. Here the dominant feature was the stern ramp. At a distance it seemed only a gash, an ugly wound that parted and disfigured the normally pleasing contours of a ship's stern. Up close it was a monstrous chute, plunging steeply from the main deck some twenty feet down to the waterline. One might understand the need for such a device to haul great whales up from the sea. But, like everything else on the *Rembrandt,* it seemed way out of scale or too gross a conduit for anything the size of ordinary fish.

Further up the quay were smaller vessels, some tied two or three abreast. Although not more than one hundred and fifty feet in length, they were in every way as unusual in appearance and as baffling to the novice as the giant *Rembrandt.* They bore such names as *Morebas, Uksnøy,* and *Garpeskjaer;* their home ports were invariably Ålesund, Tromsö, or Hammerfest. Sturdily built with high bows and elegant sheer, there was about them an extraordinary compactness. Odd assemblages of equipment — tripod lookout masts, large rubber-sheaved blocks, metal chutes, and bulbous suction pumps — crammed every square inch of their deck and superstructure space. Along their sides back aft were horizontal steel rods holding scores of steel rings, like jousters' lances heavy with trophies. Only a few of the boats carried their nets on deck. They were made of fine black twine, and of very small mesh.

A Canadian Fisheries and Marine Service inspector doing his rounds of the quay told me these boats were purse seiners, designed to hunt and encircle schools of fast-swimming surface fish. "They come over from Norway with a big factory ship for the spring capelin spawn," he added. "The factory ship's anchored way out. She converts the capelin to fishmeal, some three hundred tons a day, I'm told."

Were the reader to have a similar experience — that is, to pass rapidly from the rural outports to the harborside scene at St. John's — he might imagine that he had witnessed two worlds of fishing, perhaps centuries apart in methods, existing side by side in Newfoundland. If so, no well-informed scientist or fishing industry spokesman would ever dismiss such a thought as in any way exaggerated. Nothing less than a latter-day industrial revolution, the experts might claim, separates the outport fishermen with their longlines, traps, and other methods that are indeed centuries old from the multinational citizens of the electronically guided factory trawler fleets that pursue many of the same fish in much the same or at least contiguous waters. A revolution, some might add, that has radically altered the fortunes of nearly all fishermen, the seas where they fish, and, ultimately, the laws by which man governs the world oceans. To describe the effects of this revolution on its rank and file at sea — especially when two-hundred-mile fishery zones began to signal its end — is the main purpose of this book.

A ship like the *Rembrandt,* in the vocabulary of the trade, is correctly termed a factory-equipped freezer stern trawler. "Factory trawler" is the more commonly used short form; quite appropriately it emphasizes the fact that vessels of this type both catch and process their fish. Factory trawlers are thus distinguished from factory, or "mother," ships, which perform only the latter function, after obtaining their raw material from smaller catcher boats.

Common to all factory trawlers are four essential elements that set them apart from the generations of fishing vessels that preceded them. These are a stern ramp or slipway for the rapid recovery of nets from astern (rather than over the side), a sheltered belowdecks factory section with assembly-line machines to gut and fillet fish (as opposed to cleaning by hand on an exposed main deck), an ammonia or freon refrigerating plant for the quick freezing and frozen storage of fish (in place of heavy and space-consuming chopped ice), and equipment to make fishmeal (to utilize both the factory leavings and trash or nonmarketable fish).

The idea for a ship that might combine such advantages was born in the United Kingdom in the late 1940s. Not surprisingly, at least to those acquainted with the traditional resistance to change among fishermen and fleet owners alike, it did not originate within the fishing industry. Rather, it first took shape from whaling or, more specifically, from the concerns of a Scottish general shipping and whaling firm known as Christian Salvesen Limited. Although this company was at the time a world leader in modern factory-ship whaling, Captain Harald Salvesen, its chairman, was much worried about diminishing whale stocks. Captain Salvesen himself, in fact, had tried to do something about them as early as the 1930s, through industry or self-imposed quotas on certain species. But his industry colleagues were as yet in no mood to police themselves, and nothing significant in the way of whale conservation occurred for more than a decade, until the establishment of the International Whaling Commission in 1946. By that time, however, Captain Salvesen was convinced the initiative was already too late. The international control systems would be ineffective, company officials remember him predicting, and there were too many new entrants, most notably the Soviets and the Japanese, competing for stocks that continued to decline very rapidly. Rather than wait for the death of the whales and the industry, Salvesen's would use its whaling experience in new directions. The most obvious was fish.

Among the concepts borrowed from whaling was a ship with the size and the range to go for lengthy voyages, to be equipped with a large stern ramp to haul up the great quantities of fish expected to be found in new and more distant waters. The application of a stern ramp, so commonplace in whale factory ships, might not at first seem a significant technological breakthrough. But in the tradition-directed world of commercial fishing, it was no less. To understand why, one must first have some knowledge of how the side trawlers that then dominated world fishing went about their business. These vessels, as their name clearly implies, carry out all their working operations over the side. To recover their nets, for example, they must stop dead in the water, broadside to the seas. The forces of wind and current will then cause the side trawler to drift rapidly downwind and stretch out the gradually rising net abeam, perpendicular to the hull, where it will not foul the rudder or the propeller. The net is then brought in over the rail, an action that can become both wet and dangerous when high seas crash aboard during heavy rolls and flood the main deck. A stern trawler is spared this ordeal, since it can maintain some forward progress and a safer bow-to-the-wind heading throughout most of the haulback. As a consequence stern-ramp trawlers can continue fishing in heavier weather, when side trawlers must stop, although fishermen argue endlessly about the exact point in the Beaufort scale where this occurs.[1] Another consequence, about which there is no argument, is that stern trawlers can both set and haul back their nets faster than conventional side trawlers. Fishing time, in other words, is significantly increased. For those who first thought of applying stern trawling to large vessels, therefore, it seemed to have all the advantages.

All except one, that is, which critics were quick to point out. The collecting bags, or cod ends, of ground trawls would surely burst, the critics insisted, with every good catch. This was because any trawl hauled up a stern ramp would have to come aboard all of a piece or by continuous heaving; there was no way of dividing a large catch with the time-tested methods used by side trawlers, which we will examine presently. The dissenting critics' most serious objection — it later proved to have some foundation — was that no known netting material could stand the strain of such total-catch hauling. (Synthetic twine had not yet been introduced; at the time all nets were still made of manila or other natural fibers.) If nets did not burst, the detractors further claimed, crews would at the very least have to "cut in" or rip out panels of netting to spill fish and ease each load, thereby losing any time advantage. True, stern trawling was not new. It had long been practiced successfully by small wooden draggers and at least one experimental steel vessel in New England. But these boats simply hauled in their relatively small catches over a roller on the stern transom or up a short ramp, and they operated for the most part in calmer inshore waters. To bring in a cod end with thirty tons of fish over the waterline edge of a bucking and heaving stern ramp in the giant seas of open oceans was quite another matter. In such event one had to consider the powerful inertial forces generated by the extreme pitching of a large vessel.

On ships over 250 feet in length stern pitching was known to

1. A standardized scale of wind speeds and sea conditions. See Appendix III.

reach thirty degrees. The vertical acceleration forces so produced might mean that the 30 tons of a flat calm would become 60 in heavy weather. Even if a trawl were somehow successfully recovered under such conditions, the critics finally insisted, the fish would be badly bruised and crushed in the process. In England and other European countries, where fish quality is important in the marketplace, this seemed another very real objection.

By contrast the largest side trawlers of the day had none of these problems. If their crews were lucky enough to see a swollen cod end with thirty or more tons broach the surface in a boiling, heaving mass — always a thrilling spectacle — there was no need to worry about the strain of taking it aboard all at once. Side trawler crews first winched the mouth and foreparts of their trawl onto the deck and then used a rig known as a splitting strop or doubling becket to "split" or divide the contents of the sacklike cod end. The strop was simply a noose of cable laced into the girth of the cod end; by heaving in on another cable attached to it which ran along the top of the net, variously known as a bull rope or bag becket, the noose immediately tightened and cut off or cinched the fish in the rear of the cod end into a compact ball of four or five tons. After this ball was winched aboard, crew members quickly untied a slip- or purse knot at its bottom, let the fish fall out on deck, retied the knot, and then heaved the empty cod end back over the side. (During all this time, we must remember, the mouth of the net remains on deck, thus effectively closing off to the remaining fish any escape route.) It was then only necessary for the skipper to send his ship "slow astern" for a brief moment to collect more fish in the butt of the cod end, after which the stropping process could be repeated as many times as necessary. In this manner side trawlers were able — and are still very much able today — to bring aboard heavy catches in discrete amounts. This option, of course, would be impossible with a long net trailing well astern in the wake of a big ship with forward progress. Side trawlers might require a little more time to haul back, to be sure, and there was always a possibility a man might get knocked off his feet or even swept overboard by a boarding sea. But at least there was no danger of losing a whole bag of fish. For the owners of the conventional sidewinders, as side trawlers are called in Great Britain, this was reason enough not to try anything different.

"Yes, there was a great debate in those days as to the practicability of stern trawling, especially for a ship of the size we had in mind," recalls L. M. Harper Gow, a Cambridge graduate and army commando officer, known to his associates as Max, who began his career with Salvesen's on an Antarctic whaler and later served seventeen years as the company's chairman. "The majority thought it impossible, but we had at least learned enough from our experiments with the *Fairfree* not to be overly discouraged. So Salvesen's took the big leap forward. We decided to build a factory-equipped stern trawler from the keel up."

The *Fairfree* was the former H.M.S. *Felicity,* a minesweeper of the Algeria class purchased and rechristened by Salvesen's in 1947 to provide a floating laboratory for Sir Charles Dennistoun Burney, R.N., an enthusiastic yachtsman, aircraft engineer, and inventor of the paravanes used in World War II minesweeping. Sir Dennis, as he was better known, was mainly interested in a radically new design for trawl doors, or otter boards — "parotters," he called them, in obvious acknowledgement of their evolution from his experience with paravanes — which he hoped might lift ground trawls free of the bottom and permit fishing at various depths. The parotters, however, did not work. Try as Sir Dennis might, the *Fairfree*'s trawls either refused to budge from the bottom or at best took off for only brief bursts of mid-water flight. But even in failure Sir Dennis must be given due credit for his early vision of the great potential in variable-depth fishing. When mid-water trawls were finally perfected a decade later, they immediately took their place alongside electronic fishfinders as one of the most significant technological advances of twentieth-century fishing.

Meanwhile, although mid-water fishing would have to wait, Salvesen's gained considerable experience with stern trawling, which was the method used throughout the *Fairfree* experiments. As a result company officials came to believe it could be tried on a much grander scale. The plans for the stern trawler Salvesen's had in mind, in fact, ultimately called for a ship of 2,600 gross tons, with an overall length of 280 feet, and accommodation for a crew of eighty. Thus, by dimension alone she would indeed be a big leap forward. The largest British side trawlers then in use averaged 185 feet in length and 700 gross tons. Their normal crew complement was twenty.

Salvesen's placed the order for their new leviathan with J. Lewis and Son, a small shipyard in Aberdeen, early in 1953. Although the Lewis firm had never attempted so large a vessel, work proceeded on schedule and the ship was launched with appropriate fanfare in March of 1954. In a felicitous choice that honored both her immediate ancestry and her pioneering role, she was christened the *Fairtry*. Or as maritime historians later came to know her, the *Fairtry I*, since she soon spurred the construction of two sister ships, the *Fairtry II* and *III*.

Size alone, however, was not all that surprised the crowds that watched the *Fairtry*'s launching. There was also her unseemly appearance. As nearly everyone commented, she looked more like an ocean liner than anything ever built for fishing. To the layman's glance the *Fairtry*'s superstructure seemed almost entirely given over to living accommodation; there were no fewer than twenty-two cabin portholes on each side at the fishing-deck level and an equal number just below. All were well above the waterline, which meant the luxury, unknown on low-freeboard side trawlers, of being able to keep them open in all but nasty weather. Inside were comforts never dreamed of by previous generations of fishermen. A photograph in a special *Fairtry* issue of London's *Fishing News International* showed a typical four-man cabin in which contented crew members reclined in sturdy double-decker bunks or wrote letters at a common central table. The caption glowed:

> Individual lockers are given each man and there is an air of attractive roominess about each berth. Selection of mates is left to the men themselves. Officers have single berths, petty officers are in double berths, and other hands in four-berth cabins. Ample showers (hot and cold) are provided throughout the ship, and cinema is regularly shown in the crew's mess.

"The floating Ritz, we called her," a member of the original crew has told me. "Showers we never had before, and some of the old sidewinders had no toilets. Over the side you went, summer or winter. A shocking thing it was, but little the gaffers [owners] cared!"

"We planned the better accommodations, the movies, and such from the beginning," says Ted Sealey, a veteran Salvesen's official. "We were accustomed to handling problems of keeping crews out of mischief. After all, the whaling voyages lasted eight months, and we knew that an idle mind is an evil mind, as we used to say."

But the true test of the *Fairtry*'s future would lie more in the equipment concealed deep within her hull than in external design or creature comforts, although the latter quickly proved their value in attracting and keeping good crews. The most important single unit of equipment — central to all Salvesen's planning and the key to potential profits — was her quick-freezing plant. The reason for installing one was quite clear: at the time of the *Fairtry*'s commissioning British fishing had already reached a point of no return in searching out new and more distant grounds. This search, nearly always successful, had long been the particular pride and mainstay of the British high-seas fishing fleet. It had started as early as 1891, when a few steam-powered trawlers first fished the rich offshore grounds of Iceland. Not long thereafter the British fleet extended the quest for better fishing north of the Arctic Circle to the North Cape of Norway, Bear Island, Spitsbergen, and the Barents Sea. By the 1930s, as these Arctic grounds (especially Bear Island) began to supplant Iceland in importance, the term "distant water fishing" had become firmly established in British vocabulary and British fishermen had grown accustomed to the endless night of their winter trips to the Norwegian Arctic. After World War II occasional journeys to West Greenland — the round-trip distance was 4,500 miles — were not uncommon. British skippers and industry chiefs might be justifiably proud of these achievements, which other nations sought to follow. Nevertheless, two nagging problems remained. First, as distances increased, more and more ice had to be carried, until ice and not fish came to be the heaviest item in the fishholds of returning trawlers. The farther you went, in other words, the less was the absolute limit of fish you might expect to bring home. Second, the time expended in getting to and from the more distant grounds — "steaming time," as it is still called today — was seriously prejudicing and sometimes totally destroying the quality of fish. A typical trip to the Barents Sea will readily show why. Given a little luck, a trawler fishing the Barents could fill her hold in ten or eleven days. But five and a half to six days of steaming were first required to get there, as well as to run home, making a round trip of twenty-two to twenty-three days. This meant that the fish caught the first day on the grounds were already sixteen days old upon reaching port. Sixteen days, as it happens, is the generally accepted maximum-preservation period for iced fish, beyond which it is judged putrid or inedible. Even six- to twelve-day-old fish are considered by food technicians as "spoilage affected" in both firmness of flesh and flavor. Thus the "freshers," as ice-filled side trawlers are known in Great Britain, rarely brought home a truly fresh product. Their owners suffered accordingly on the marketplace, since British auctioneers, unlike their American counterparts, grade the catch of every vessel and sell it in lots, according to freshness. But far worse was in store for any trawler forced to heave to and lose precious fishing days riding out gales and storms, which on winter trips was more the rule than the exception. The added days meant that one third to one half of a catch might be condemned, to be sold, if at all, for fishmeal. Sometimes, in fact, total-catch condemnations might occur, especially on the West Greenland run. As C. L. Cutting, one of a small band of distinguished British fishing historians, said of the times, the ever-lengthening trips were sealing the doom of fish quality in Great Britain because "icing at sea has been carried up to and beyond its natural limits."

New methods of preservation, quite obviously, would be needed to go beyond these limits and to continue without risk the search for more profitable grounds. Salvesen's thought quick-freezing the only workable alternative. By fortunate coincidence frozen-food technology had advanced to the point where high-capacity freezing units small enough for shipboard use were being perfected at about the same time the plans for the *Fairtry* were taking shape. This was so largely because of the long and untiring efforts of the American inventor Clarence Birdseye. More than a quarter century earlier Birdseye had begun experimenting with frozen foods — with frozen fish, in fact, using New England redfish and not the vegetables for which he was later to become more famous — in a small laboratory in Gloucester, Massachusetts. After ten years of effort, Birdseye and his associates had invented in 1933 what is now known throughout the industry as the multiplate freezer, a device in which stacks of metal plates, through which ammonia refrigerant ran in small tubes or passages, could be opened to receive prepackaged foodstuffs and then closed to the desired pressure by hydraulic action. Originally developed to be mobile or at least capable of being trundled around without too much difficulty to follow vegetable harvests for "field-fresh" pickings, the multiplate freezer had a number of advantages over the quick-freezing methods that preceded it. The most common of the earlier methods was cold air or blast freezing, which required large "rooms," or freezing chambers, and was also much the slowest process of the time. Another was brine immersion, which many experts, Birdseye included, disliked because of the flavor changes it inevitably produced. The multiplate freezer effectively solved these difficulties. But it was not until after World War II (industry historians usually cite 1946 as the turning point, or critical year) that frozen foods gained widespread public acceptance in the United States and multiplate freezers became a standard of the industry. Public acceptance was much slower abroad, but word of Birdseye's imaginative advertising campaigns — he is as well remembered in the industry for his perseverance in marketing as for his inventive genius — eventually trickled across the Atlantic. Cautiously, a number of European countries began to inquire about licensing arrangements for the manufacture of Birdseye-patented freezers.

One of the first was England. Salvesen's had itself begun experimenting with a freezer designed by Sir "Dennis" Burney — he seems to have enjoyed working in many different directions at once — aboard the *Fairfree* in 1947. Dubbed by him the "Fair-freezer," it combined both blast and contact-plate freezing. Once again, however, his invention had only theoretical and not practical merit. After sharp scrutiny Salvesen's engineers found it too big to carry its weight, so to speak, or to allow of economical operation within shipboard confines. Much more to their liking were the weight- and space-saving features Clarence Birdseye had worked out for on-site vegetable and fruit freezing. From orchards and truck farms, therefore, the multiplate freezer went to sea.

The third essential element in the *Fairtry*'s planning, the idea of using automated filleting machines, had not been previously tried on the *Fairfree*. As usual, many experts thought it impossible. Such fish processing machinery as then existed in shore plants depended on delicate and accurate pre-positioning of fish in guides or holding brackets. Thus the conventional wisdom was that at sea fish would be constantly slipping or slithering out of the guides with any kind of ship motion. There were troubles enough in high-seas fishing, the experts maintained. To add to them with a roomful of complicated machines that might spill fish with every pitch or roll did not make sense.

"Yes, here again there was much debate," Max Harper Gow remembers. "The big question we faced was whether to fillet or simply to freeze whole fish. But since we were going to make long voyages, we thought it most economical to bring home a maximum tonnage of fillets and also to use the offal for fishmeal. We wanted no waste."

"No, you didn't want to go to all that trouble just to be storing bones," Ted Sealey agrees. His remark is well put. The yield from machine-cut fillets is approximately one third the "round," or whole weight, of a fish. But the remaining two thirds of the carcass, bones and all, may be ground into fishmeal of good quality. The decision to do this — to use all parts of the fish, as well as to fillet at sea — seemed doubly advantageous.

To make it a reality Salvesen's turned to Nordischer Maschinenbau Baader, a small firm in Lübeck, West Germany. During the thirty-five years of the company's existence its founder, Rudolf

Baader, had invented about a dozen machines for gutting and cutting fillets from cod, herring, and a few other fish of comparable size and shape. Ingenious as they were, the machines had not, however, had a great success with land-based processors. The weight of tradition — in this case a strong preference for hand labor in the cleaning of fish — was as heavy in Germany as anywhere else. Nevertheless, among Baader's early wares was the Model 99 *Schwanzlaufer* — the "tail grabber," most fishermen now call it — a complex filleting mechanism that was finding some clients. The machine was so named because in its first action it grasped cod or similar fish of about two to four feet in length by the tail in a viselike clamp. In the next step the holding brackets or guides measured the fish for size and transmitted the information so obtained to the internal elements of the machine. Then, in a split-second sequence too fast for the eye to follow, the fish was pulled into the machine's central section, where revolving knives sliced out fillets along both sides of its backbone. Water shot in jet streams to cool all cutting edges, and loud shrieking noises might occasionally emanate from the machine's innards when knives sawed into the vertebrae of carelessly positioned fish. But in the end, most of the time, out came neatly cut fillets, forty-eight to the minute. Simultaneously, fish with only their heads, vertebral columns, and tails remaining — indeed, they looked like they had been eaten by discriminating cats — dropped from the machine's nether parts onto conveyer belts to be ground into fishmeal. In short, the Model 99 *Schwanzlaufer* was precisely the kind of mechanical wonder that would have transported the late Rube Goldberg into ecstasies of delight. More to the point, however, it caught the eye — with cautious approval, if not transports of joy — of Salvesen's far-searching engineers.

Still, there were problems when the *Schwanzlaufer* went to sea. It proved rugged enough, but salt water caused many of the moving parts to seize up. For this reason, in fact, the machine had to be almost totally redesigned.

"But I was satisfied the Model 99 was reliable," Max Harper Gow recalls. "Although there were many difficulties in the beginning, the rolling of the ship, curiously enough, was not one of them. We found the freshly caught fish had much firmer meat than fish brought back after long trips to be processed on shore. The firmer meat prevented slipping. In time we worked out all the problems and added new machines, including skinners and a special line for redfish. The key to success was that Baader sent their mechanics to sea to work with us. We had a real hand-to-hand partnership all through the early years. In fact you could say we gave Baader their future."

The statement is no exaggeration. The Baader firm went on to become the IBM of automated shipboard processing, training operators afloat or ashore, and selling, renting, or licensing its machines to all the world's fishing fleets. Today the complete Baader line includes over sixty machines, both general and specialized, and their work speed has increased dramatically. Not forty-eight per minute, but two fillets per second now shoot out from their fastest units.

The objective of no waste through using the remains of filleted fish for meal (and also incidental or by-catch fish species normally thrown overboard) was much more easily realized. Ever since the 1920s, when the fishing nations of northern Europe began to discover the great efficiency of fishmeal as a growth agent in chicken and livestock raising, "industrial fishing," the capture and conversion of herring or other abundant small fish to meal and oil, developed rapidly, especially in Norway. The machinery to do this — it consists essentially of dehydrating presses, grinding mills, and drying ovens — is not complex and may readily be designed for a wide variety of capabilities. Salvesen's, therefore, simply went to the best of the Norwegian manufacturers and ordered a scaled-down unit to fit a convenient space on the *Fairtry*. Other than exercising strict precautions against fire — fishmeal, like flour, is extremely combustible — there were no special problems. Thus equipped, the *Fairtry* and all the factory trawlers that were to follow her became "the vacuum cleaners of the sea," as envious small-boat fishermen say of them, using all the fish their trawls swept up from the sea bottom.

Stern ramps, multiplate freezers, Baader machines, and a compact fishmeal plant. The *Fairtry* incorporated all of them and in so doing proved to be the complete factory trawler. Of all her remarkable attributes none stands out more clearly than the fact that practically speaking she allowed of no further evolution. The *Fairtry* inspired generations of factory trawlers; all followed her basic design and all included the four key elements she first took to sea. Naval architects and engineers might later experiment with many different systems of rigging, superstructure configuration, and deck layout. But belowdecks all the succeeding generations had the same essential features (often with equipment of identical manufacture) placed in approximately the same relative position as in the *Fairtry*'s original design. This is as true today as it was thirty years ago.

But advanced design and the *Fairfree* trials notwithstanding, the *Fairtry*'s first months at sea were not easy. Unanticipated problems broke out everywhere — on deck, in the factory, or back aft in the curious little second bridge or pilothouse, perched above the stern ramp, that was first used to steer the ship during the setting or hauling of nets.[2] Meeting these problems with great patience and perseverance was the late Captain Leopold Dixon Romyn, the *Fairtry*'s first captain. In no way typical of British fishing skippers, Romyn was a public-school-educated man widely regarded in the fleet for his knowledge of engineering and general erudition. ("He keeps up-to-date by reading technical magazines of many countries in the original," *Fishing News International* said of him, "but he never lets up in the search for fish.") In addition, Captain Leo, as he was best known, had a gift for command and was very popular with his men, although some are said to have objected to the Sunday morning church parades he occasionally held at sea, in best public-school fashion. He was also a good writer. His graphic logbook entries and special reports on the *Fairtry*'s initial difficulties

2. This structure was originally thought necessary because the *Fairtry*'s long superstructure blocked any view of fishing operations astern, but in practice the officers of the watch found it easier to steer from the wings of the forward bridge, with shouted guidance relayed from the crew aft.

are required reading for anyone who would understand the early trials of stern trawling from a large ship.

Ironically, the first and most serious problem was that the *Fairtry* caught too many fish. Bags of twenty or more tons regularly inched up her stern like swollen sausages too big for their skins, as photographs in Salvesen's archives painfully attest, only to get stuck in the rampway. If, that is, they had not already burst, just as the critics had predicted, or caused damaging strains on winches or other gear.

"No method of splitting the bag has been found; consequently all the fish has to come in with one heave," Captain Romyn wrote rather wearily in one of his first reports. "This is possible with new gear and fine weather up to a weight of about twelve tons, but anything more than that is a source of great anxiety and often damages the gear severely, even if it does not tear it clean off . . . and slither cod ends, fish, and all down the ramp into the sea to disappear forever. Nothing is more provoking than to see this happen or the cod end burst and the sea covered with dying fish. Especially is it vexing to have an accident of this kind while a side trawler is heaving in a similar amount of fish safely, bag after bag, alongside one's ship."

But in time remedies were found. The *Fairtry* was fortunate in having as her first mate Jim Cheater, a native of Twillingate on the rugged north coast of Newfoundland, who had fished in England after the war and had married a Grimsby girl. Cheater (pronounced *chay*-tor) had what is called in fishing "a pure nose," the unfailing, seat-of-the-pants instinct to know where the fish are, which, although impossible to define, is enviously acknowledged by all skippers and fleet owners. He was also a seasoned fisherman, skilled in the art of jury-rigging, making on-the-spot solutions to gear problems. Between Cheater's practical knowledge and Captain Leo's technical expertise, the *Fairtry* was blessed with a formidable command. One by one, the vexations gradually vanished.

"We done a thousand things, learning from experience," Cheater says of the process. "First we learned to cut down on tow time. You let your net down one hour and it was more fish than you could handle. That's how it came about we made tows of twenty or thirty minutes, no more. Even so, the trawls were loaded! These times it's hard to believe the fishing we had. Then we fitted out the winches with springs and hauled back very slow, with slack wire. That way there was no surge [sharp rise and fall] of the cod end in heavy weather. And then we found ways to stop the fish from squatting [being too much crushed]. We made a double-wing cod end. The net was double-tailed at the end, same as your trousers."

On her maiden voyage and nearly all subsequent trips, the *Fairtry* went to the Grand Banks of Newfoundland. The choice was obvious. In the 1950s, in spite of having been intensively fished for the salt cod trade by the sailing fleets of many nations for over four centuries, the Banks were still one of the world's most productive fishing areas. Its best grounds, however, required round trips of over five thousand miles from England. For ice-provisioned side trawlers this was too far, the barrier beyond which they could not profitably fish. To be sure, a few British "freshers" periodically attempted the trip after World War II, but optimum fishing and steaming time frequently combined to more than thirty days, and too many of the Newfoundland catches were condemned. For the *Fairtry,* of course, with her freezing units and seventy-day cruising range, the Newfoundland barrier did not exist (nor any others, for that matter, in the world oceans), and she thus enjoyed some remarkable fishing. Some of her first-year trips produced such astounding results as six hundred and fifty tons of cod fillets (from two thousand tons of round or whole weight fish) in thirty-seven days of fishing, a catch rate that makes present-day factory trawler captains shake their heads with envy. Occasional side trips to West Greenland for the highly prized Atlantic halibut, which were then abundant there, did almost as well. Seldom, in fact, did the *Fairtry* need to use her full seventy-day range. As often as not she crossed the Atlantic, filled her fishhold, and was bound home in half that time, without any provisioning calls at North American ports.

Among other factors contributing to these early successes was the relative absence of competition, not only from rival British trawlers, but from all other sources as well. For a limited time, in fact, the *Fairtry* had the field pretty much to herself. The few other fishing vessels then on the Grand Banks — the side trawlers that Captain Romyn enviously watched bringing in their catches safely while he was sometimes losing his — mainly carried the flags of France, Spain, and Portugal, nations that had fished there more or less continuously since the discovery of the Banks in the sixteenth century. The ships they employed were large "salters," designed especially for Newfoundland service, with cavernous holds that entombed mountains of salt to make the split and salt-dried cod so much esteemed in those countries. These ships, well designed and sea-kindly, represented the ultimate in the evolution of conventional side trawlers; a number of them measured over two hundred and fifty feet and were thus only fifteen feet shorter than the *Fairtry*, although only half her tonnage. The Spanish, for reasons no one can remember, called them *bous*. To the French, much more logically, they were *chalutiers terre-neuvas* or "Newfoundlander trawlers"; to the Portuguese, *arrastoes* or simply "draggers." In addition Portugal had her "great white fleet" of about fifty dory schooners, which arrived in April and left in October, and Spain was beginning to have great success with her lethal pair trawlers, small twin vessels that towed a widely stretched common net, of which we will learn much more later. Like the Portuguese, many went home for the winter months. The offshore reaches of the Grand Banks were, in fact, a rather lonely sea, with far fewer fishing vessels than in the great age of sail.

All this changed, and very rapidly, beginning in 1956. As the *Fairtry* fished in solitary splendor on the ground known as the Tail of the Bank on a fine July morning of her third summer, Acting Captain Jim Cheater got the surprise of his life. A large vessel suddenly appeared on the horizon. She was totally different from any of the company the *Fairtry* occasionally kept, yet there was something strangely familiar about her general outlines. As she came closer, the mystery cleared very quickly.

"I couldn't believe my eyes," Captain Jim recalls. "The ship was the *Fairtry* exactly! Only the name was different. She was called the *Pushkin!*"

Captain Cheater's startled reaction was all too accurate. The Soviet Union was making its debut in distant water fishing. It was doing so, moreover, with a ship that naval architects would later describe as a "slavish copy" of the *Fairtry*.

As with all things in the Soviet Union, the debut was the result of years of careful planning, both to obtain the *Fairtry* blueprints and to secure fishing rights to the offshore Canadian waters, which were already internationally controlled (loosely speaking, some would insist) by ICNAF. For the latter purpose, unknown to the *Fairtry*, a sister ship named the *Sverdlovsk* came over later that summer and put in at St. John's. Aboard her were Alexander Ishkov, the U.S.S.R.'s minister of fishing industries, and a host of lesser functionaries and fishery biologists. The *Sverdlovsk*'s visit was fully authorized. More than that, it was in fact a second and reciprocatory event in a government-to-government exchange aimed at possible fishing industry cooperation. A year earlier Canada's minister of fisheries, James Sinclair, had been invited by Ishkov for a grand transcontinental tour of the Soviet Union. Now Sinclair was returning the favor. "I'm looking forward to showing the Russian visitors how fishermen in a democratic country such as ours live," he is quoted as telling the *Canadian Fisherman*. "I think it will be an eye-opener for them." The tour would take Mr. Ishkov from St. John's to Vancouver, the *Fisherman* added, and include "everything from champagne to Cadillacs."

The visit of the *Sverdlovsk* became front-page news in St. John's, especially when after some hesitation the Russians allowed both public and press to come aboard. Reporters marveled at her modern deck gear, the ingenious Baader machines, and, in one case, at least, "the plentiful washroom facilities . . . including the luxury of Turkish baths."

Throughout the visit Minister Ishkov and his aides stressed two points, one in private and the other very much in public. Privately, the Soviets expressed great interest in becoming a member in good standing of ICNAF (in which Canada, as much as the United

States, played a dominant role) and then carrying out some experimental fishing from which "both countries can learn much from each other . . . [through] an exchange of scientists, fishermen, and periodicals," as minister Ishkov put it. In its public utterances, however, the visiting Soviet delegation repeatedly held out the lure of a new export market, thus touching on the raw nerve of the Canadian fishing industry's long-standing concern over heavy dependence on sales to the United States. "Unlike Canada, nearly all our catch is used on the home market," Ishkov's deputy, Igor Semenov, is quoted as saying. Although the Soviet Union was second only to Japan, with an annual catch of two and three-quarter million tons, he further explained, it still had to look to imports to supply the fish needs of its two hundred million people.

As the initial excitement of the visit subdued, one reporter thought to ask the *Sverdlovsk*'s captain if the U.S.S.R. was building more such vessels and, if so, where they intended to fish. The captain, described as speaking excellent English, replied without hesitation that the Soviet Union was indeed building more factory trawlers, but that they were designed primarily for Russia's rich home waters, north of the Arctic Circle, although some few might be sent to the South Atlantic for sardines. Similarly, when asked if the Soviet Union might not want to intensify its fishing efforts on the Grand Banks, Minister Ishkov was equally reassuring. "No, we can catch all the cod and haddock we need in many other fishing grounds," he answered. "We are, however, interested in the ocean perch [redfish] that can be caught here."

Even Minister Sinclair joined the chorus. There was no need for concern; he felt sure the Soviets' intentions were mainly experimental and research-oriented, as they had repeatedly stated. "It is more economical for Russia to fish in waters nearer home," he told the *St. John's Evening Telegram* at the time of the visit. "The Grand Banks is a long way from Russia."

That autumn the *Pushkin* and the *Sverdlovsk* went home with a catch of 3,000 tons of cod and 12,900 of redfish, about one thirtieth the combined catch of the Portuguese, Spanish, and French salter fleets. Perhaps, after all, there was no need to worry.

But the very next summer the *Pushkin* and the *Sverdlovsk* returned with several sister ships. Two years later there were 35 Soviet factory trawlers on the Banks, or all but one of 24 Pushkin-class ships and twelve of a newer and larger class. Six years later, by 1965, the Soviet fleet in the Northwest Atlantic — now fishing north to Greenland and Labrador and south to Georges Bank — numbered 106 factory trawlers, 30 factory or mother ships, and 425 side trawlers of assorted size and vintage.[3] Its total catch for the year (the fleet now fished winter and summer alike) was 886,000 tons, one third more than the combined catches of Spain, Portugal, and France. Within this total, moreover, were 278,000 tons of the cod and the haddock Minister Ishkov had declared to be of no interest. Still, this was only a beginning.

How the Soviets managed to replicate the *Fairtry* is another story and one almost as deceptive as Minister Ishkov's assurances had proven to be. As early as 1951 a resident Soviet trade delegation incorporated as the Anglo-Soviet Shipping Company of London had begun buying British distant water side trawlers from the well-regarded Brooke Marine yards in Lowestoft. A small scouting force of these vessels and some Polish-built copies had in fact been used to conduct tests on the Grand Banks, scarcely noticed, two years before the appearance of the *Pushkin* and the *Sverdlovsk*. But by 1953 the events taking place at J. Lewis and Son in Aberdeen were of much more interest to the Anglo-Soviet Shipping Company. Late that year, but still well before the completion of the *Fairtry*, Lewis officials were surprised to receive a tender from the Soviet government for the construction of twenty-four factory trawlers of the *Fairtry* design. As an aid to speeding negotiations, the Soviets inquired, might not a set of the Fairtry's plans be sent in advance for preliminary study?

"I remember strongly advising them [the Lewis yard] to make the Russians pay a substantial fee in advance," states Max Harper

---

3. Although relatively few in number, the 106 factory trawlers accounted for over 70 percent of the fleet's gross tonnage. Soviet trawlers first extended their operations to U.S. offshore waters in 1961; four years later 60 percent of the Soviet Northwest Atlantic catch came from Georges Bank alone.

Gow. "But they kept telling Lewis their business regulations prevented them from providing any advance. 'We merely want to make a prior study of the plans and will settle such other matters later' was in effect what the Russians said."

Gordon Milne, a thoughtful and hardworking Scot who was then managing director of Lewis, well recalls the consternation the Soviet inquiry caused. "We were a small company, the *Fairtry* was the biggest ship we had ever built, and I wasn't prepared to book up the yard to the exclusion of all our other clients," Milne remembers thinking. But there was the satisfactory precedent of the Brooke Marine side trawler sales, and Britain's Conservative government was much interested in expanded trade with the U.S.S.R. "Yes, you could say I was urged," Milne says of this. "The government said: 'At least talk to them.'"

The plans of the *Fairtry I* were sent to Moscow.

Milne himself followed within a year. He was pleasantly surprised with the technical professionalism of his Russian counterparts, but not with their requisites for doing business in the Soviet Union. Contract terms, it appeared, would have to be written according to Soviet law. All Milne's suggestions for outside or third-party arbitration in case of dispute — the Hague Court, for example — were rejected. These and other preconditions, along with the burden the large order would place on the Lewis yard, ground the negotiations to an inflexible halt.

Milne returned home, thoroughly discouraged. The plans of the *Fairtry* did not. The Soviet authorities were too busy shopping for their soon-to-be-born distant water fleet to bother with so trifling a detail, much less such troublesome capitalist niceties as patents or the determination of naval architects' fees.[4] Very soon thereafter, in fact, Minister Ishkov and colleagues succeeded in placing their order for their twenty-four Pushkin-class ships with the Howaldtswerke yards in Kiel, West Germany.

4. Patent infringement suits were never seriously considered. Expert opinion usually holds that only parts or features (for example, the Baader machines) and not the total concept of a new ship are patentable. Besides, the Soviet Union at the time still had an ambiguous view of patent law in general and did not establish its first permanent patent office until a year later.

Thus occurred what was probably one of the most important and certainly the fastest transfers of technology in the history of commercial fishing. With virtually no prior tradition of high-seas fishing, the Soviet distant water fleet was off and steaming.

"The Lewis people weren't cute enough," Captain Jim Cheater has commented on the incident in retrospect. "It was all right they talked with the Russians. But they should have left the plans at home."

Well might he say so. The rush was now on. Not surprisingly, West Germany was next in line. In the summer of 1957 or one year after the debut of the *Pushkin* and the *Sverdlovsk,* the *Heinrich Meins* — the Federal Republic's first experimental stern trawler — appeared on the Grand Banks. Although small and equipped for whole-fish freezing rather than complete factory processing, the *Meins* was the forerunner or test ship of what soon became a highly efficient fleet of about thirty factory trawlers much envied for their electronic fishfinding wizardry and over fifty large fresh-fish stern trawlers which made a specialty of fast trips to Iceland and East Greenland. A year earlier, far away in the Pacific, Japan commissioned her first experimental stern trawler, the *Umitaka Maru,* "following closely the design of a European stern trawler and a study of European stern trawling techniques," as one Japanese authority has diplomatically acknowledged the *Fairtry* influence. Thereafter, relying heavily on ever-larger factory trawlers, Japan rapidly built up the world's leading distant water fleet.[5] Soon other major European fishing nations followed the British and West German initiative. Although some might hesitate or adopt a wait-and-see attitude before investing the heavy sums necessary to factory trawler construction — the *Fairtry* had required a capital expenditure of £1,000,000 — the strong demand and steadily rising fish prices in European markets along with the decline of fish stocks

5. In volume of catch, that is, averaging ten million tons a year by the 1970s. The U.S.S.R. developed a considerably larger fleet, but remained a constant second to Japan in world catch rankings, by about one to two million tons. One of the reasons for this is discussed farther on.

in home waters made the factory trawlers, costly as they might be, an economically viable alternative that was hard to ignore. As the 1960s drew to a close, Poland, East Germany, Rumania, Spain, Portugal, and France all had sizable fleets of the new leviathans, fishing mainly on the Banks or other Northwest Atlantic grounds. Waiting a little longer or only building smaller freezer stern trawlers primarily for use in other or nearer waters were Norway, Italy, the Netherlands, Belgium, Iceland, and Denmark. And, paradoxically, the United Kingdom. In England the sad truth was that the brilliant successes of the *Fairtrys I, II,* and *III* at sea found no counterpart at home on the marketplace. So strong was consumer resistance to frozen fish — stemming largely from the introduction of poorly made supplies to the armed forces during World War II — that ten years elapsed before other companies followed Salvesen's lead and cautiously began to build their first "filleters," as the British commonly call factory trawlers. Nevertheless, overall, the factory trawler — the big leap forward — was fast coming of age.

Nowhere, however, was the growth process so spectacular as in the Soviet Union. By 1974, in what some experts have called the most rapid and successful development of a specialized fleet in the history of merchant shipping, the U.S.S.R. had by far the world's largest fishing fleet. Within its ranks were 2,800 side trawlers and other smaller fishing vessels of all kinds, 103 factory or mother ships, and 710 factory trawlers. The latter, as always, were the heart of the fleet, accounting for seventy percent of its tonnage and approximately two thirds of its catch. Sustaining this armada, moreover, was a large train of fleet support vessels. Like the trawlers, many had been purchased abroad and even greater numbers had been built in the Soviet Union. They included not only the giant factory ships, but also refrigerated fish carriers for offloading at sea, oceangoing tugs with well-equipped repair shops, research and scouting ships, food and fresh-water supply ships, tankers, and, ultimately, combined tanker–fish carriers. All were considered necessary because the Soviet government wanted its fishing fleet to be completely self-sufficient at sea, since it was unwilling to spend hard-earned foreign currencies for provisioning or repairs abroad or, for that matter, to have its trawler crews with too much time on their hands in foreign ports. By 1974, in fact, the worldwide fleet support train had grown to 510 ships of 3,000 tons or more.[6] By this time, too, the efforts of Soviet fishermen completely encompassed the world oceans. Although the North Atlantic remained the area of most intense fishing, large deployments of the distant water fleet also ranged the incredibly rich grounds of the Northern Pacific and the almost equally productive coasts of South Africa. Smaller detachments went even farther — to the South-western Atlantic, the Southwest Pacific, and Antarctica. Only in tropical latitudes did the big factory trawlers suffer failures. As early as 1962 the Soviets had attempted expeditionary fishing in the Gulf of Mexico and the Caribbean, only to find too many different kinds of fish and not enough of any one for efficient factory processing. The problem, we will see, remains, not only for the Soviets in one particular area, that is, but for all factory trawlers in almost all tropical waters.

In two decades after the *Fairtry I*'s launching, in these ways and by such shipbuilding programs, factory trawlers had moved to a dominant position in world fishing. What this single fact meant was that for the first time in history fishing vessels of one nation might steam to the shores of any other in the world within two or three weeks, remain there indefinitely with either crew or vessel replacements at sea, fish in all but the worst weather, and be rewarded with an hourly catch rate that surpassed the best efforts of conventional side trawlers by twenty-five to fifty percent.

Equally important, the new fishing leviathans soon found themselves freed from the restrictions of fishing only along the bottom. For a number of years their owners had watched with mounting envy as purse seiners rapidly increased their catch rate tenfold,

6. Fishery statisticians, lacking any better yardstick, measure fishing efficiency by comparing total fleet tonnages with catches. The Soviet Union's numerous support ships have customarily been added to her fishing-fleet tonnage; this is one of the reasons why the Japanese, who use a very small support train, have always been considered as "catching more with less" or "most efficient."

making record hauls of herring, mackerel, and other surface-swimming fish, all as a result of a single invention known throughout the world as the Puretic power block.[7] But factory trawlers suddenly acquired the ability to catch these fish, too, when in 1969 the West Germans perfected the mid-water trawls described in the previous chapter. Once armed with the new free-flying nets, moreover, the factory trawlers immediately held one significant advantage over purse-seining vessels. Since the latter make their catches solely on or near the surface, their skippers are often frustrated by tantalizing views on their sonars of great schools of fish swimming placidly along at depths just below the "hang," the vertical reach of their nets. (Or, worse, by frightened fish that dive for the bottom before encirclement is complete or the purseline at the bottom of their seines can be drawn tight to prevent downward escape.) Fishing with mid-water trawls has no such problems. Properly trimmed and handled, the nets can be made to tow anywhere from a few meters off the sea floor, where they may take bottom fish hovering over grounds too rough for weighted trawls, up to the light-filled waters of the surface, where they will easily overtake pelagic species in direct or straight-line pursuit.

Factory trawlers, in other words, became all-purpose. As their mid-water nets grew ever larger, they found they could take the coveted herring in bigger hauls than the purse seiners. Or, for that matter, any other fish in the oceans, with the single exception of the fastest-swimming members of the tuna family.

The cumulative effect of so many technological advances coming within so short a historical span created problems, of course, not all the problems that now plague world fishing, that is, but many crucial and long-lasting ones, the exact nature of which it is important to understand. Contrary to the complaints of many American and Canadian fishermen, factory trawlers were not the

7. Named after its inventor, Mario Puretic, a Yugoslavian-born fisherman of San Pedro, California. Before it was patented, the large seines used in the southern California tuna fishery were pulled in hand over hand through one or more blocks (pulleys), a process that normally took five or six hours. Puretic applied hydraulic power to the rotating internal element, or sheave, of a much enlarged block; the block was thus transformed from a static load point to a dynamic mechanism, which itself transported the net back into the boat, in minutes instead of hours.

sole cause of the depletion of fish stocks in the North Atlantic. Rather, what the factory trawlers did do was to place an additional or extra burden on stocks that were in many cases already being fished close to the maximum sustainable yields by vessels far smaller. (In the case of the Atlantic halibut in New England waters, the species had long before been commercially fished out.) That this additional burden soon became intolerable is mainly due to the factory trawler fleets' remarkable ability to mass their force very quickly, to "target," in the language of fishery biologists, on specific fish in specific areas. Factory trawlers could focus their efforts very efficiently, in other words, on the often precise localities where fish gather seasonally in greatest number. To give the reader some idea of what this meant or how elements of a large fleet might be deployed in the actual practice of massed or highly targeted fishing power, we must go to the eyewitness accounts of those who first monitored the factory trawlers in the Northwest Atlantic. To the time, that is to say, when free fishing, meaning either the nonexistence or the nonobservance of international controls, was the order of the day.

"I remember flying surveillance out of North Carolina in the winter of sixty-eight, flat-hatting in a Grumman *Goat* three hundred feet above the water," says Charles Philbrook, a veteran National Marine Fisheries Service enforcement official. "Often you could count as many as two hundred Communist-bloc trawlers within a twenty-mile area off Hatteras Island. Every one of them would be wallowing — filled to the gunwales, you might say — with herring."

What Philbrook saw was a good example of what came to be known as pulse fishing. Simply defined, pulse fishing means the calling together of all ships in a given fleet — even those at some distance, that already might be enjoying fine fishing — to combine their efforts on a particularly good find. In the above case the find was late-winter or prespawning schools of Atlantic sea herring and two species of anadromous herring that would soon enter the Chesapeake Bay or the North Carolina Sounds (where they are the object of important local fisheries) on their way to fresh-water spawning creeks. In this as in all examples of pulse fishing, the strategy was to keep fishing until the schools were wiped out, after which the trawlers might disperse in more random patterns. Special scouting ships then took the pulse, so to speak, of other waters until new concentrations were found and all ships again called in.

The sad result in the example reported by Philbrook would be that a month or two later the Chesapeake Bay watermen who fish for herring with pound nets might find their annual spring runs greatly reduced. "Herring is everywhere scarce," the watermen would then say. And wonder why.

Not two hundred, but a much smaller number of factory trawlers might have the same effect on a particular year class, as scientists call the crop and the year in which fish are born. Dr. Wilfred Templeman, dean of Canada's fishery biologists, remembers one such case from a cruise in July of 1960 of the Canadian government's veteran research ship, *A. T. Cameron,* to a Grand Banks ground known as Southeast Shoal.

"The *Cameron* was fishing thirty thousand pounds of haddock in thirty minutes, at the height of the capelin spawning," Dr. Templeman recalls. "They were mainly small fish from the 1955 and 1956 classes, the last good year classes of Grand Banks haddock. The *Cameron*'s skipper, the late Baxter Blackwood, was much given to radio chatter, like most Newfoundland captains. Excited, he started shouting the news to all his friends. The next morning the *Cameron* was surrounded by eight Soviet factory trawlers and four Spanish pairs.

"The new Soviet effort that followed, added to the already existing Spanish and Canadian haddock fisheries, was," Dr. Templeman ruefully concludes, "the start of our most serious haddock decline."

For many years after the first factory trawler invasions, Canadian and American fishery management officials clung to the hope that the fishing fleets of both countries — large in number of vessels and fishermen employed but small in tonnage — could somehow keep pace with the big visitors from abroad. At times, in fact, there was reason to believe that the patient work of the U.S. and Canadian ICNAF delegations in strengthening that body's conservation measures might reverse the tide of overfishing. Or that the United Nations' Law of the Sea Conference, then trying to settle all problems of extended national jurisdictions over coastal-shelf waters for offshore oil drilling, seabed mining, and fishing, might eventually succeed in its visionary effort to construct a rational worldwide fishery-conservation scheme. Time, however, seemed to be running out. The haddock was down to an all-time low throughout its Northwest Atlantic range, so low, in fact, that fishery biologists feared the end of a commercially viable fishery, if not species extinction. Even the bountiful cod — the sacred cod of America's first industry and the chief sustenance of Newfoundland for over four centuries — was showing serious declines. So, too, were the redfish, yellowtail flounder, and many other prime market fish.

The year 1974 marked the turning point. In that year alone 1,076 Western European and Communist-bloc fishing vessels swarmed across the Atlantic to fish North American waters. Their catch of 2,176,000 tons was ten times the New England and triple the Canadian Atlantic catch.[8] For anyone who cared to analyze this catch figure or compare it with previous years, moreover, a picture far more disturbing than sheer volume would emerge. Huge as the total catch might seem, the catch per vessel was down and the fish were running generally smaller than before, even though the foreign vessels fished longer hours with improved methods over a larger range for a greater part of the year. In fact, the foreign catch had been better for five of the preceding six years — slowly declining from a peak of 2,400,000 tons in 1968 — with fleets of equal or lesser size. When this happens or when the yield per unit of effort starts to fall off, as management experts prefer to say, it is

---

8. These and all other catch figures are for fish only and do not include crustaceans, mollusks, and other invertebrates, which by 1974 formed 16 percent of the New England catch and 10 percent of the Canadian in the Northwest Atlantic. The latter term, as defined by ICNAF and here used, means all waters north of 39°, the latitude of Cape May, New Jersey, and west of 42°, the approximate longitude of Cape Farewell, Greenland.

nearly always an early and sure warning of the general decay of major fishing areas. First observed in the Old World with the herring and sole of the North Sea and the cod of Norway's Arctic grounds, the phenomenon now seemed to be repeating itself in the Northwest Atlantic. Everywhere the factory trawlers went, in other words, more were fishing for less.

Back on the Grand Banks a new fishery was developing very rapidly to satisfy a worldwide boom market for fishmeal. Because herring was scarce on both sides of the Atlantic, power-block purse seiners accompanied by mother ships and factory trawlers equipped with the new mid-water nets were now zeroing in on the little capelin that came each spring to spawn far out near the edge of the Banks at Southeast Shoals. In 1974 their catch was 300,000 tons and rising fast. As yet Canada's fishery biologists could not detect any effect from this offshore catch on the inshore or beach-spawning capelin. The two populations, in fact, were considered separate stocks.

But to the Newfoundland fishermen the signs were already there. By 1974 you could hear the refrain in every outport. The capelin sculls were not as before. Nor the cod, of course, that followed them in. This was a serious matter. In over 270 Newfoundland outports with no other employment than fishing, the fishermen's average annual income was down to $4,500. If things got any worse, the men told you, a man just couldn't make it on the summer voyage.

A new generation of fish killers had come across the Atlantic. In twenty years in North American waters, they had by their own account taken over 72,333,000,000 pounds of fish. Very few among them could see that this was too much or that they had fished too well for their own future.

## THREE

# *The Best*

I<small>T</small> was on Georges Bank in 1976 that I first heard about the Germans. "If you want the best, go with the West Germans," Dick Jellison, first mate of the *Tremont,* had said. "Most everything in modern fishing starts with them."

Not long thereafter, I heard some surprising testimony from a Canadian fisheries management official on how rival foreign captains view West German proficiency. "They can't understand it," the official said. "Why, I've had Soviet skippers come in here and tell me they watch the Germans pull in one bag after another while they get nothing, fishing almost side by side. They think the Germans must have some mysterious new electronic gear."

Then came Captain Earl Demone of Lunenberg, the veteran fleet captain of Canada's largest integrated fishing and processing company. "Now, you take the West Germans and their ice fishing on the Labrador, that is something to see," Captain Earl counseled. "In comparison, everything else is a piece of cake."

So comes the advice. And so, too, one makes first choices.

*Thursday, January 20, 1977* [Aboard the Federal Republic of Germany's Fishery Support Vessel *Frithjof III*. St. John's, Newfoundland] All day in port, storm bound, in the fullest sense of the word. Acting Captain Scharfe has posted 11:00 A.M. sailing time, but since severe storm is predicted, he decides to radio Hamburg for instructions. Barometer skidding fast, but no need to look at it, really. The signs are clear enough. Morning started unseasonably warm with brief moments of sun, then rain, then wet snow.

By lunch it's much colder, with lowering black clouds and rising winds. You feel it in your bones. A big change, coming fast.

Use time to explore ship further with able young Third Mate, Jürgen Lorenzen. *Frithjof* is 250.8′ in length, 1,637 gross tons, crew of thirty-seven, and the most modern West German *Fischereischutzboot*, literally "fishery protection vessel." Painted black and battleship gray, she somewhat resembles a scaled-down destroyer escort, but with fairer lines and a distinctive ice conning tower (really a second bridge, completely enclosed, with all essential controls) rising high above forward superstructure. Meteorological station has all the most modern equipment, including teleprinter weather-map recorder. Same goes for hospital section, which boasts operating room better than many you see in major hospitals ashore, one six-bunk general ward, two small isolation wards, and one private room for serious accidents. Latter has extra large bed hung on gimbals. Lorenzen tells me current trip began in Cuxhaven just after New Year's, going first to Norwegian coast to deliver set of plate glass windows to trawler which had bridge smashed by big sea, then Greenland, then directly to St. John's. Also learn that Captain has been put ashore in hospital here. "No, nothing serious, a nervous condition you might call it," Lorenzen says, politely and quite casually.

*1530:* Much colder, snowing harder, winds thirty to forty knots, gusting to fifty. A true cyclonic disturbance, Force 12 or hurricane strength, is now the prediction. We remain on standby. Acting Captain Wilfrid Scharfe explains that *Frithjof* is fully equipped for towing, with three diesel-electric motors of 1100 h.p. each. So if word comes any trawlers are in trouble, it's out to sea for us. "If duty calls, we must go," Scharfe says. "For that we are here."

The above is the first entry in a personal log or journal of a trip taken to follow up on the advice that was impossible to ignore — of the first stage in a long journey, that is, to see the best in action. The choice, as it proved, was a good one. Anyone interested in the ultimate challenges of modern fishing does well to start with the West Germans, in winter and on difficult grounds.

All the next day the *Frithjof* remained in port as a hurricane-intensity storm with maximum wind speeds of 120 miles per hour ravaged St. John's, causing a power plant to explode and dumping a foot and a half of fast-drifting snow on the city's steep and narrow streets. The following day, with the storm barely passing to the east, the *Frithjof* put smartly to sea. Two days later she reached the main body of the West German fishing fleet off the Labrador coast at ten o'clock at night during the height of a strong gale. Nevertheless, her deckhands went promptly to work "servicing," supplying the needs of the various trawlers. Using remarkably sea-worthy air-inflated outboard launches, they delivered everything from spare gear and luxury food items to late Christmas packages and packets containing licenses and regulations for fishing inside Canada's new two-hundred-mile zone to one ship after another. (Canada had begun enforcement of her two-hundred-mile zone only three weeks earlier.) This work continued through the night.

To describe the above event and all that followed, first impressions may be best. The operation of a large factory trawler, the lives of the crews of distant water fleets, the rigors of fishing off Greenland and the Labrador in midwinter — all these are subjects so far removed from other forms of seafaring and indeed from all normal human experience that they are perhaps most easily understood through the fresh or innocent vision of a neophyte observer. What follows, therefore, are further excerpts from my logbook. Also included are explanatory passages and technical exegesis, wherever required.

*Monday, January 24:* Hans-Joachim Heinemann, our conscientious young meteorologist, tells me that early this morning we entered another big depression, Force 9 Beaufort. But, again, one scarcely need be told. Morning dawns gray, on all points of compass, with occasional snow flurries. Seas are capped by tumbling, angry-looking breakers; troughs in between are streaked with patches of spray. During breakfast one big slammer wave breaks a good portion of the galley china. Dishes and plates jumped right out of their holding racks, making dreadful mess. But Herr Doden, our paragon of a steward, doesn't bat an eye. *"Bitte sehr, ein bisschen mehr Kaffee?"* he asks. And stands ever watchful, ready to fill your cup to just the right rough-weather level.

*1200:* Noon position is 53° 20′ W., 54° 05′ N. We are getting up there, near eastern edge of Hamilton Bank or about one hundred and twenty miles east of Labrador mainland, where chart shows two little outports named Black Tickle and Domino. Have a feeling fishing fleet must be close, since seabird population is suddenly enormous. Not just the little kittiwakes that are always with us, but great numbers of fulmars. They keep hanging in the wind very close to ship, stiff-winged and motionless except for quick snaps of the head to inspect us with quizzical look. Puzzled, no doubt, not to find fish on deck or scraps in the wake. One of the sailors says, yes, there do seem to be more birds, but we still have some fifty miles before estimated fleet rendezvous.

*2215:* The fleet is in sight! It's a wild and black night, the gale winds moan in the rigging, and the cold is numbing. But there they are, a dozen or so huge factory trawlers in a single glance, all brightly lit and calmly maintaining the necessary sea room. After so many miles of dark and empty seas, it is like a grand *son et lumière,* a truly festive illumination. There are the glares of powerful afterdeck working lights, the green over white ("we are fishing") and red over white ("we are hauling") masthead lights, the Christmaslike twinkle of red and green running lights, even the pale orange dots of long rows of cabin portholes. One has a sense of having arrived, of reaching, at last, a friendly place.

Up on the bridge the VHF channels are crackling. Greetings pour in, one after another.

"*Frithjof, Frithjof!* This is the *Stuttgart.* Good to see you! Welcome back to the grounds!"

"Yo, *Frithjof!* It's the *Regulus* here. Where have you been so long?"

Willi Scharfe very busy acknowledging them all, thanking, trading jokes, etc. Then general conversation suddenly stops. It is replaced by incredibly ho-hum or back-to-work dialogues with individual ships. Typical example, in rough translation:

"*Julius Fock, Julius Fock,* we have you in sight. We will come up on your port quarter."

"Okey-dokey, *Frithjof,* we are standing by. You know about our problems? You will be sending over the chief engineer and the radio officer?"

"That is correct."

"Listen, *Frithjof,* we didn't have it on the list, but how about two kilos of pastry flour? Our cook is frustrated."

"Pity! Can't have that. We will look for it, two kilos pastry flour. Now, how about the sick list?"

"We have it right here. One shoulder injury, one intestinal, two with bad colds, and one of our gallant deckhands has, how shall we say, a strong case of *Kavalierschnüffeln* ['man-about-town sniffles': i.e., gonorrhea]."

"[Laughter] Sorry to hear that! We will do what we can for the *Kavalier* and the others. Coming to you. Over."

Can it be that we are starting to "service" at this hour and with such seas? Yes, it can. Back aft on main deck an electric crane has lifted one of the outboard launches — *Schlauchboote* or "bubble boats," Germans call them — snug to starboard rail. It is about sixteen feet long, with two fat air-inflated cylinders of heavy fabric reinforced top and bottom with steel rods. Cylinders come to a point at the bow, which is decked over and has small spray shield. Boat is hung — better said, perfectly balanced — on four-point bridle fastened to single safety-catch hook. Bolted to stern transom is thirty-horsepower Johnson outboard, warmed up and ready to go.

Two coxswains get in. They wear lightweight oilskins and snug vest-type life preservers, which permit maximum freedom of movement. One holds walkie-talkie radio and goes forward; other sits down snugly in stern, hand on engine throttle. The radio officer and chief engineer climb aboard, very calmly. Then crane operator lowers boat a few feet. Suddenly a great swell of pitch-black water surges high up the *Frithjof*'s side, reaching the hanging boat. "Now!" shouts the stern coxswain. The bow man pulls on a lanyard; click goes the safety catch. The bubble boat slides down and away, engine churning.

Rush up to bridge to watch progress. Bubble boat is just now getting out of our lee, Scharfe having nudged *Frithjof* forward as close as is prudent to *Julius Fock*. But two ship-lengths of rough and open sea still separate us. No matter, the *Schlauchboot* is doing fine. A strong yellow strobe light, blinking cheerfully from little mast on her bow, traces her erratic advance. Helmsman keeps on course much of the time, slicing diagonally up the face of the seas, but turns at last moment to meet big wave crests head-on. Up and over goes the "bubble." Then, readjusted to course, she slips down into the troughs and disappears from sight. Have my nose squashed against bridge window, watching all the way. Sometimes the out-of-sight intervals seem too long. But always the little boat reappears, blinking away and easily topping the breakers. Soon she is alongside the *Julius Fock*, bobbing up and down at a large open port halfway up the ship's side. Through binoculars you can see men silhouetted in light of port. They are our patients, waiting turn to be helped down a short rope ladder.

Soon the *München,* close to starboard and next in line, is calling to ask if we brought her five sacks of new potatoes; it is time to go over her order list while second bubble boat being readied for launch. Off to port the *Karlsburg* is anxious about marine electronics expert, sent out especially to fix her radar. Further away the *Wiesbaden* says surely she has time for another tow. ("There's no money waiting around with the nets on deck, you know," her captain protests.) Then *Julius Fock* comes back again, wondering why we have to keep one of her patients. Don't we know they are already short-handed, so why not strap the man up, give him supply of painkillers, and send him back?

Scharfe answers them all, patiently and politely. A consummate diplomat, he tells *Wiesbaden* please, no, do not take another tow, since this would probably cause major alterations in servicing schedule, to general inconvenience all other ships. At same time he summons ship's doctor to argue with *Julius Fock.* All the while Scharfe must also keep weather eye on *Frithjof's* position relative to other ships and make sure we maintain steerageway. Helping him do this are two seamen. One keeps constant track of bubble boats and the bearings of nearest trawlers. The other, who has rating of master helmsman, is at the wheel.

During brief lull First Mate tells me this is all in day's work, nothing unusual, for the *Schlauchboote* and their coxswains, who are specially selected and trained. In emergencies they have operated in Force 11. The big secret, he says, is that bubble boats have underwater ballast tubes. (Indeed, I had not noticed.) You can pump in water ballast, up to one ton of it, as sea conditions require. For this reason they are said to be unsinkable or at least impossible to flip over.

"Unless, of course, the coxswain falls asleep," Scharfe adds, smiling.

At the launch point two coxswains are getting out of their boat for a brief between-trips rest. One has to brush and stamp a thin glaze of ice off his oilskins. Other has icicles in his moustache, which he doesn't bother to wipe. They sit quietly in storage room, drinking hot coffee and staring at nothing in particular with red-rimmed eyes.

Way down the line some ship is complaining about the *verdammte* Canadian regulations. The captain has some questions. Scharfe thinks of waking Lorenzen, who has best knowledge of English, but doesn't. Some other time, he decides.

The bubble boats keep working, long into the night. Back and forth they go, over the dark and empty spaces, linking the friendly lights of our little trawler metropolis.

"It is our duty," Willi Scharfe repeats. "For this we are here."

At eight o'clock the next morning the *Frithjof* was ordered to break off from the fleet and steam to West Greenland to pick up fourteen extra hands flown there from Germany as replacements for injured crew members of the trawlers fishing off the Labrador. Two days later, after a passage slowed by bad weather and occasional ice, she called at Godthaab, the capital city (population 10,000) of Greenland, where the crew loaded supplies and enjoyed a twenty-four-hour revel with the native girls who swarm aboard every ship visiting that port. The following morning, somewhat wearily, the *Frithjof* put to sea again. She thereupon remained on station off the West Greenland coast, servicing a few vessels fishing Fyllas and Banana Banks. She then refueled at the lonely port of Faeringehavn, and, finally, ran down the coast of southwest Greenland to Cape Farewell to pick up the crew replacements, who had been put to work temporarily on a trawler fishing there. These tasks done, the *Frithjof* returned to the Labrador fleet exactly eleven days after she had left it. The journal continues.

*Saturday, February 5* [Aboard the Fishing Motor Vessel *Wesermünde*]: Long and busy day, starting with bubble boat transfer at 0730, amid snow flurries and what seem like mountainous seas. But for most of crossing, praise be, there is undulating carpet of gray-white slush ice and small pancakes which completely smothers all breakers. The scramble up rope ladder is mercifully short, thanks to high-surging seas and coxswain's carefully timed instructions. Nevertheless, manage to squeeze my toe in rung and get bootful of icy water.

Entry port on this and similar ships takes you right into factory section, which is to say sudden wave of noise, glaring lights, and all the old familiar fish smells, the "perfume" of every fishing vessel large or small. Scene is one of barely controlled confusion. Men are working fast to unload and reload the bubble boat, with much attention focused on hapless crew member with broken leg, strapped down in wire stretcher and obviously in great pain. I stand around waiting for luggage or some indication of what to do next. Hop around on one leg would be more accurate, trying to restore circulation to numbed foot.

But presently it's up to bridge to meet captain and two of three *Steuermänner,* as deck officers are called. Then comes whirlwind tour of ship. Learn that *Wesermünde* is one of four "third-generation" factory trawlers, West Germany's largest, built for Hanseatische Hochseefischerei, which is part of Rudolf Oetker conglomerate or one of many companies built on original success of famous "Dr. Oetker" brand puddings.[1] She measures out at 3,567 gross tons and 311.6′ in LOA, has cruising range of 78 days, and provides crew accommodations for 73, although total complement is now 60 or less, for reasons of economy. Most remarkably, *Wesermünde* has six tenths of an inch plating and strong vertical frames spaced every two feet from stem to midships and, up at the cutwater just below waterline, an extra-heavy bulbous bow which not only reduces pitching but also helps break ice. Thus armored and with 5,000 h.p. diesel engines, she and her sister ships have structural strength and power equal to most icebreakers. Even so, my guide tells me, *Wesermünde* had her hull buckled on maiden voyage to West Greenland by big growler [an iceberg fragment, awash or nearly all underwater] and had to go limping and leaking back home.

*1200:* Heavy luncheon of pork chops with thick gravy, mashed potatoes, creamed celery, and bland vanilla-flavored pudding. Conversation mostly about weather or, more specifically, what has so far been a relatively warm winter, but with more than usual number of storms.

"Last year you could have traveled better with a sled and eaten nothing but seal meat," says First *Steuermann,* or chief mate, meaning that at this time and place the heavy pack ice was already well developed and migrating harp seals were everywhere on the horizon. This year by contrast there is as yet no heavy pack; it appears to be what merchant shipping calls a "good" ice year. But it's no good for Germans, who count on penetrating edge of pack for their best winter fishing.

*1300:* Woken from nap by strange noises from main deck and some sort of command booming out over P.A. system. A haulback, apparently, is about to begin. Go up to bridge, where large rearview windows afford excellent view of all the action. Directly below, two huge winches, each holding a mile and two thirds of three-and-three-quarter-inch wire, are

1. One of the world's largest privately held corporations. Its assets include banks, insurance companies, hotels, and publishing firms, in addition to food products and both fishing fleets and fish processing.

slowly winding in heavy towing cables. Water drips off them for the length of their run above deck and they crackle as they snap into place on winch drums. Deckhands are walking calmly to their posts, smoking cigarettes or drinking coffee as they go, even though pitching and rolling is considerable. Occasionally, large seas lift stern skyward. Then it drops like an elevator and buries itself in troughs with great convulsive shudder felt throughout ship. Seawater thereupon crashes up ramp, exploding in stern sheets and flooding deck almost knee-high. But deckhands anticipate every time; split seconds before each explosion they hop over protective coamings on each side of net runway and huddle in the lee of nearest piece of machinery, like bullfighters tucking behind *barrera*. Or, if caught in middle of deck, run like hell clear over to ship's rail, coming to halt much like baseball players fetching up against outfield walls.

Second *Steuermann* watches intently and manipulates complex array of switches and levers. "Playing the piano," he calls it, on a ten-foot console which extends almost full width of rearview windows. It has no fewer than twelve separate controls for two main and eight auxiliary winches, not to mention about twice that number of warning lights, alarm horns, and voltage meters. Meanwhile First *Steuermann* — "Jupp" Merkler is his name — reduces power by signaling "ahead, very slow" on engine-room telegraph. Even so, great inertial strain of pulling in net causes ship to slip backward: i.e., actually make sternway.

After about ten minutes tape marks appear on towing cables. They are warning indicators. It is time to slow winches down — way down, in fact, until last few feet are brought in inch by inch with frequent hand signals from men at stern stations. Gradually, with eggshell touches of winch levers timed to rise and fall of seas, Second lifts big oval-shaped doors up out of water until they clang into place against the gallows frame. Then he quickly locks them there with winch brakes. Doors weigh 2,100 kilos each, he tells me, and have replaceable bands of extra-hard high-alloy steel called "shoes" or "soles" running along their bottom edges. Replaceable, that is, because despite hardness soles wear down fast from constant abrasion or bumping and grinding of doors' spreading action on the bottom.

Now two men walk aft pulling "messenger" cables off auxiliary winches. At same time others at stern struggle to uncouple slack independent wires from main towing cables. This done, they quickly shackle them to ends of messengers. Then, in rapid succession, slack taken up by auxiliaries, tail ends of independent wires unhooked from backstraps or towing bridles behind doors, and, presto, first phase of haulback is complete. Now nothing to do for moment until the long sweeps or cables running from doors to net — Germans call them *Jaeger* or "hunter wires" — are wound in. Crew can relax.

But not for long. In three or four minutes bulging cod end heaves up in ship's wake like a shallow-broaching whale. It is studded with fish heads popping through the mesh, and a dense cloud of fulmars and kittiwakes dip and wheel above it, screaming with excitement. Moments later wings of net and headline grind up the ramp. Then come first *Kugeln* or bobbins: i.e., the huge steel balls that keep groundrope snug on bottom. "Rope" in this case, however, is a misnomer. Rather, what emerges is giant, ponderous necklace, the "lace" being in fact doublestranded steel chain and the beads some thirty-five heavy bobbins.

Work tempo now gets rather frantic. More cables come into play, pulling horizontally, vertically, and diagonally. Men literally dash around deck. At one moment they are helping ease wings over big mound made by second or reserve net. (Must always have one at the ready because of frequent tears on these rocky grounds, Merkler says.) At the next they are working feverishly to free section of headline caught underneath groundrope, which if left unattended would foul the next set, or "shoot," of the net. Meanwhile, to add to confusion, Merkler has brought ship around broadside to seas, which makes for extreme rolling and much shifting and crashing of gear. Nevertheless, groundrope is somehow safely lashed down, after which all hands concentrate on bringing in the trawl's long extension piece, the tubular section between mouth and cod end. It is hauled in high, section by section, from blocks hung on steel span between *Wesermünde's* twin funnels, and then fleeted, laid down zigzag on deck. (Necessary because total length of net is about three times that of working deck.) At height of this operation — I cannot believe my eyes — deckhand holding cup of coffee *runs* up and over piles of netting, comes to a neat stop, and gives cup to friend, without spilling a drop.

Eventually, approximately thirty minutes after winches first started winding, the heavily reinforced cod end eases up the ramp and plops on deck. Steel safety gates swing shut to close off ramp. Men now move about in what is noticeably more relaxed fashion. One is loosening purse knot at tail of cod end — it looks like oversize hangman's noose — while others attach cables from tall two-legged gantry mast found near stern of every factory trawler. All now ready for closing act. Big bag is hoisted high up gantry; its underbody trails Medusa-haired streams of black-rope baggywrinkle and pieces of dripping oxhide, without which it would chafe apart from abrasion of dragging over sandy or pebbled grounds. Then, very suddenly, there is loud whooshing noise. Tons of fish tumble through deck hatches down into the factory.

"Not so good, not so good," says Jupp Merkler, who has been watching intently. "About twelve tons, mixed cod and redfish."

To the casual observer any trawl net on deck looks like a formless lump of cording to which loops of cable, pieces of chain, floats, and other items of hardware appear randomly attached. The whole seems a shoddy piece of work, more the product of jury rigging or improvisation than any careful plan. Yet just the opposite is true. In the water the various parts will come together to form a harmonious and efficient unit, the shape of which is determined by minutely calculated gradations in both mesh size and twine diameter and the careful study of stress points. A net such as the one used by the *Wesermünde,* known as an Engel 250, is in fact the end product of a precise engineering science supported by frequent testings of models in flume tanks, computer monitoring, and lengthy sea trials. The Engel 250, so named for the export trade because its groundrope measures 250 feet, cost the equivalent of $16,800 in 1977 ($21,000 today) and utilizes over thirty-five miles of multidimensional synthetic twines, twenty to forty bobbins weighing from 175 to 550 pounds each, and at least 150 brightorange plastic floats, about the size of junior league soccer balls, that are built to withstand pressures down to five thousand feet. Given moderate weather and good fishing, an Engel 250 can bring up fifty to sixty tons of fish with no trouble at all.

Not only net design, but also rigging, an essential part of the art of making nets flow through the water as efficiently as possible, has seen many advances in recent years. The most significant of these has been the placement of the doors well forward of the net. With this location, modern net makers theorized, the doors' shearing action might be given fuller scope and thus effect a wider opening of the net mouth. (In the age of sail ground trawls were held open by thirty-foot beams lashed to the headline; the first nonrigid spreading devices, introduced around the turn of the century and originally known as otter boards, but now more often simply as "doors," were for many years rigged right at the mouth of the net.) The new theory proved correct, the effective span of the older trawls was doubled, and fishermen were quite happy with the results. It is now therefore not uncommon to have the doors riding like bottom-bumping kites as much as six hundred feet ahead of the net, with approximately three hundred feet between them.

But neither fishermen nor net designers were at first fully aware that the lengthened sweeps running between the doors and the net were having another equally important effect, although the Germans seem to have been on the right track in calling them "hunter wires." Beginning in the 1970s underwater television cameras and intrepid scuba divers proved what had previously been only dimly suspected: namely, that the sweep cables dragging along the bottom cause curtains of turbulence or clouds of mud, sand, or gravel through which fish will rarely swim. Fishermen now generally recognize or at least argue about this "herding effect," and many tend to think of the true span of their trawls as starting up at the doors, which, of course, themselves produce not clouds but veritable storms of turbulence. One thing, though, is certain. In many subsequent underwater viewing experiments fish consistently behave as though the water roiled by the sweeps were a brick wall. Time and again bottom fish idly grazing near the inside of the sweep cables have been seen to dart away at right angles and then peacefully resume grazing midway between them. Little do the fish realize, in other words, what is coming next or that they are in effect caught between the narrowing legs of a long isosceles triangle by their own mistrust of turbid water. What comes next, moreover, comes very quickly. Pioneer scuba divers have been surprised to observe that fish swim along without apparent fright as the wings of the net advance alongside them or even as the headline silently draws a canopy of netting above them. But, calm as they may be, fish cannot thus swim or keep pace with the mouth of the net for very long. Ten minutes, at two or three knots, is about the maximum staying power of cod and similar fish. After that they tire very quickly and start falling back down the long tube of the extension piece. From here on there is no possible escape. Unless, that is, there has been some human failure in the set of the net, such as forgetting to retie the purse knot at the butt of the cod end. This last, incidentally, is the most grievous error a crew member can commit. Certain New England fishermen call it "making a Boston tunnel."

The hazards of towing or hauling huge ground trawls in heavy weather have been much reduced by such modern innovations as tension bollards on the towing cables, which register danger signals up on the bridge, and hydraulic-pressure brake shoes on the main winches, which act like the drag of a fishing reel in the event of snags. Still, the essential ship maneuvers first discovered by trial and error on the *Fairtry* remain today as hard-and-fast rules. In towing, for example, skippers prefer to go downwind or downcurrent, whichever is greater, so that their trawls will "sit" more calmly on the bottom or be less subject to flattening and lifting forces. But at Force 6 or higher the rule is to round up and tow into the wind, regardless. If this is not done, a bad hangup of the net will in effect anchor the ship in a vulnerable stern-to position. Following seas may then overwhelm the after part of the ship and crash full force the length of the trawl deck. During haulbacks in heavy weather it is for much the same reason that the helmsman must pay constant attention to the ship's heading and fall off, beam to the wind, at the critical moments of net recovery. If he does not, excessive pitching from meeting the seas bow-on can plunge the stern to such an extent that heavy seas will come up the ramp and carry away the men who at certain stages must work right at its edge. The rolling that follows from taking the seas abeam creates new problems, of course. To the lay observer, in fact, it seems almost a Hobson's choice. Cables and heavy hooks swing wildly; the big bobbins transform the deck into a demonic bowling alley as they roll and crash athwartships. But if the mate of the watch operating the levers and switches of the bridge's rearview console does his job skillfully, he can do much to dampen this confusion. If not, fouled gear, delays, and crew injuries will surely result. And even a few injuries, as fishing captains are frank to tell you, are much to be preferred to green seas charging up the ramp. Thus the choice.

The kind of work which fishermen routinely perform in bad weather has no parallel in the world of seafaring. On a merchant ship such feats as leaping to catch wild cables or ducking out of the way of objects shifting around on deck are normally required only in emergencies, but aboard trawlers they form part of nearly every shooting or hauling of the nets. Thus all fishermen (and especially deckhands) develop their remarkable balance and timing as a matter of everyday survival. They also make one minimal concession to safety — a private vow or rule, that is, which they try never to break. "One hand for me and one for the ship," is the way most like to express it. This does not mean, of course, that they go about their work one-handed, but rather that they make sure there is always something near to grab, as ship motions make necessary. Some British fishermen claim they carry the rule one step farther. "Do you know what we say in the bad times?" a Yorkshire trawlerman once asked me. "It's two hands for me and fook the ship."

*Sunday, February 6:* We bagged forty tons — mostly cod, some redfish — early this morning during Merkler's watch. Wish I had seen it come aboard. Now (6:30 A.M.) the big cod end remains half full, hanging high from aft gantry, since hatchways down to factory still clogged with fish. Meanwhile, crew has set out second net, another Engel 250.

Sunday breakfast special is *Schokoladesuppe,* a watery chocolate pudding (another famous "Dr. Oetker" product?), followed by eggs to order and cold Westphalian ham. Jupp Merkler is unhappy, in spite of his big catch. Keeps banging fist on table, saying "No good for production." The cod were either too small or too varied in size for efficient machine processing in factory, he claims, and the redfish are now a by-catch, or incidental species, under new Canadian regulations, not to exceed 10 percent of any foreign vessel's total catch. And, if that weren't enough, adds Karl Jürgen Blum, the *Wesermünde's Fischmeister,* or factory boss, Labrador redfish are often infected with parasitic cysts, which make dark spots in flesh. Also learn from Blum that factory hands on *Wesermünde* and nearly all other German trawlers are Portuguese. Like deckhands they have watch schedule of six and twelve (i.e., twelve on, working the machines; six off, for sleep and recreation; then twelve on again) and that for some years now no Germans can be found to do this kind of demeaning belowdecks labor. "The Portuguese, they know how to handle fish and they work harder than the Spanish," Blum says. "But you have to watch them all the time."

Big news this morning is that many trawlers in vicinity — not just other West Germans, that is, but Russians, Poles, and Portuguese — plus Canadian fishery patrol vessel *John Cabot*. Apparently last night *Cabot* apprehended Norwegian longliner and is escorting to St. John's. Rumor is Norwegian drifted over from Greenland, no license, no documentation, nothing. At first skipper resisted, claiming ignorance and disputing position, but *Cabot* threatened to call in navy for armed escort.

"My God!" says Captain Ernst Hörhold, who is not yet used to this sort of thing. "It's Chicago on the high seas."

Spend most of morning on bridge, determined to learn more about all the winch controls, not to mention mystifying electronic gadgetry. (*Wesermünde* has no fewer than four fishfinders, which work either singly or in concert, plus about twice that number of navigational aids.) Captain Ernst is glad to explain their functions, but does so rather deprecatingly. Wants to be sure I know that helpful as new technologies may be, there are other things that enter into the equation. "Better you should start over there," he says, pointing to chart table and bookcase, which is crammed with multiyear logbooks and his personal fishing notes.

First impression of Hörhold is one of hard-driving skipper, all gruff and no nonsense. His every feature — big head, bull neck, walrus moustache, well-trimmed beard, and piercing black eyes — suggest power and authority. But looks disguise his lighter side, which pops out occasionally in terse jokes or sharp little satirical thrusts, most often directed at himself. Although only forty-three, hair and beard already graying. In course of twelve-hour watch (he and *Steuermänner* do twelve on, twelve off) he smokes great many roll-your-own cigarettes and drinks prodigious amounts black coffee. Wears same outfit every day: namely, turtleneck sweater, tasseled woolen ski cap, nondescript gray trousers, and jogging sneakers. Overweight, or at least getting a little thick around the middle (keeps promising himself to go on regimen, but never does), he nevertheless goes around ship with lithe and easy step of an athlete. Started at age nineteen aboard small cutter, crew of four, fishing Baltic and North

Sea. Made captain at thirty-one and has had command of *Wesermünde* since her commissioning in 1973.

"What would we do with our hands if it weren't for these cigarettes?" he asks, as he dexterously shapes another roll-your-own in the middle of a lengthy discourse on electronics. "I'd like to be done with the damn things, but of course they are the secret of our delicate touch." As if to underscore, he changes depth setting of cathode-tube fishfinder, which means hairline tuning of two of its five control buttons, and gives me first lesson on how to interpret its flashing green signals: i.e., distinguish between plankton or shrimp layers, the false "bounce back" or echo of very hard bottoms, and fish. Next he shows me echograph recordings from previous trips (one is quite spectacular, with clear picture of how *Wesermünde* took one hundred tons of large cod in two hours of mid-water trawling over foul grounds off Norway), plus local charts for Hamilton Bank, on which he and *Steuermänner* have accurately plotted every bad hangup or rocky patch, not to mention hot spots. Then spend most of morning looking over fishing logs, year after year of them, and asking occasional questions. This produces wealth of esoterica on fish behavior and tricks of gear handling. For example, where do you make best tows on Nantucket Shoals? Answer: along the lee of its parallel sand ridges, where fish rest from strong tides. Off Norway and Iceland? Do just the opposite, since there fish prefer tideward side of ridges, especially during ebb flow. How is it that few bother to trawl for redfish at night? They scatter vertically, at too many different levels. (Except off Labrador in winter, where for some reason they don't.) Why is fishing generally poor during northeast winds? The groundfish grow restless and disperse far and wide, though no one knows why. What does it mean if you are getting good signals on a hard bottom, but not many fish? The bobbins on your groundrope are bouncing too high and fish escaping underneath. What do you do about it? Let out more scope and put on some "ponies" [a small second pair of doors, rigged at the mouth of the net], which stop the bouncing. On and on it goes.

Putting it all together, begin to see what Captain E. means. Superior as West German electronics may be, there is no substitute for experience, for thorough knowledge of grounds and patient years of record keeping. These, perhaps, are true secrets of the best.

*1155:* Studies suddenly interrupted. Ship shudders, cable wrenches violently off main winches, and loud alarm horn is squawking. Needle of

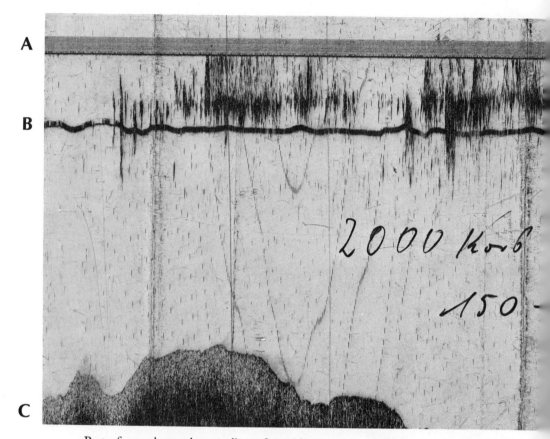

*Part of an echograph recording of a mid-water tow made by the* Wesermünde *over rough grounds off Norway. Line A shows the headline to which the net-sound, or underwater sonar, is attached. Line B shows the groundrope. The black smudge in between represents schools of fish. C is the rough bottom. At D there is a break as the net is lowered to catch fish passing under the ground-rope. The legend reads, "2,000* Korbe *[fifty-kilo 'baskets': i.e., one hundred metric tons] in two hours, large cod, 150 to 170 meters [in depth]."*

tension gauge jumps into red danger zone and stays there. It is a true *Hake,* a bad hangup or rimrack of the net.

Captain Ernst swears, orders full stop, and moves quickly to rearview windows. *Bestmann* [bosun] indicates by hand signals that trawl is probably firmly anchored on one of big boulders that make Hamilton Bank so difficult to fish. Bosun's mate is ordered to climb up on spare nets stored on top of stern gallows frame, the better to see and signal direction of cables.

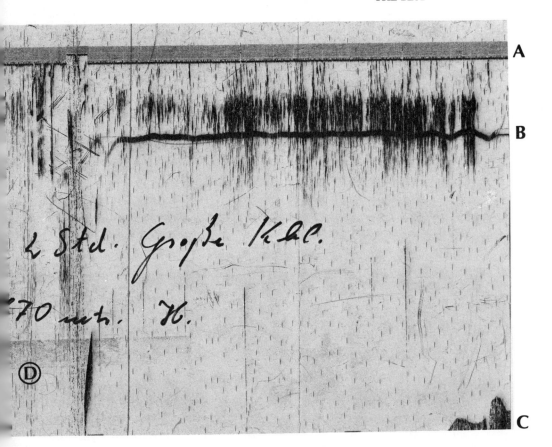

A

B

2 Std. Große K.u.C.

70 mtr. N.

Ⓓ

C

*Wesermünde* is slowly backing down to net. Task complicated as we slide completely out of protective calm of pancake ice and into rough open water. Soon short and amazingly steep seas start pounding up ramp (we are, of course, in dangerous stern-to position), and much of yesterday's chaos is with us again. Captain Ernst spots one deckhand who forgets to secure vital cable; it quickly starts to ride up gantry like loose halyard traveling up mast of sailboat. Instantly, Hörhold opens window and roars out command that easily carries length of deck. But in a moment he is back on P.A. system calmly reassuring men with a "steady now" or "stand fast" every time he anticipates boarding sea. Clearly, Captain Ernst has both attention and respect of crew. And they all know, of course, that he was once down there on deck, like themselves.

After long time (fifteen minutes?) towing cables hang straight down ~

from their heavy blocks. We are over the net, more or less. Hörhold now orders series of intricate maneuvers — forward, backward, this way and that — which in spite of wild scene are not much different from trout fisherman trying to pull his line in every possible direction to dislodge fly caught on midstream rock. Finally, main winches begin to wind steadily and easily. The net is free. And, as it soon proves, with only minor tear and five tons of fish.

"Luck!" says Captain Ernst, smiling. "*Rasmus*[2] was kind to us. Very kind, considering it's Sunday."

*2200:* Have friendly chat with Second *Steuermann* Theo Hermann, whose cabin is across from mine. Tells me he was deckhand with Captain Ernst on various ships earlier in their careers. (Seems older, however, with bald spot and remaining hair all gray.) Eventually worked up to captain and had command of *Roland* (one of Hanseatische Hochsee-fischerei's early side trawlers) for some ten years. Quiet, very considerate, spends most of his free time writing long letters to his wife and two grown children. Became grandfather during previous trip, as matter of fact. (Says this very casually, but note of pride creeps through.) Saw action in World War II, or rather was drafted at age fifteen for mine-sweeper duty, of which he prefers to say little except that those were very hard times.

Although long recognized as leaders in electronic fishfinding and other sophisticated shipboard technologies, the West Germans are almost as superstitious as other fishermen. One of their principal concerns is Sunday, a day that is widely held to bring ill fortune. So firmly rooted is this belief that some authorities think it accounts for the origin of a special countervailing weekday, supposed to redress the balance. This is the so-called *Seemann Sontag* or "seaman's Sunday," which falls on Thursday and is celebrated with tasty stews, freshly baked bread, and other better-than-average foods. The custom, in fact, is quite widespread, extending also to the merchant marine.

West German fishermen also retain a strongly traditional nautical vocabulary, which their merchant marine counterparts have completely let pass. The first or chief mate and second and third

2. The "god of the winds," as Neptune is of the deep.

officers of merchant marine practice invariably carry the title of *Steuermann* on trawlers. Literally translated, the word means "steersman" or "helmsman." In German, at least, it has a fine archaic ring. Similarly, the *Bootesmann,* or chief bosun, of other ships becomes simply the *Bestmann* on a fishing vessel. His assistant is the *Netzmacher.* Both are very appropriate terms for the bosses of the rough-and-tumble fishing deck, where strength, leadership, and net-repair proficiency are prime requisites.

All West German trawler captains work their way up from the deck, without which experience they could not possibly understand the gear-handling seamanship that is an important part of their job. Much given to mild ridicule of the merchant marine ("Imagine, just steaming from one place to another, back and forth; I would go out of my mind! *Das ist nicht Seefahrt!*"), they have very high earnings in good years, fully comparable to those of corporate executives. But their tenure, if indeed it can be called that, gives them much anxiety. Possibly one and certainly two trips per year with poor catches means replacement. For this reason one often finds former captains among the *Steuermänner.* They are content with what is still good pay. And none of the worry.

*Monday, February 7:* Gets much colder in afternoon, and we are back in dense field of pancake. From distance other trawlers look to be stuck or held motionless in firm, unyielding matrix of pure white, which stretches far as eye can reach. But up close you see they glide through ice with relative ease, leaving long lanes of open water behind them. Wind screams down the narrow lakes thus formed and turns them into little oceans, each with complete wave system of its own. Up at windward ends or in immediate lee of ice, water is merely ruffled with tumbling wavelets. Here glaucous gulls, fulmars, and even dainty ivories, rarest of gulls, happily bathe and preen. But midway down lanes fast-curling breakers and even mini-rows of spindrift begin to appear. So, too, do ghostly wisps of sea smoke — the "breath of the ocean" that always vaporizes in very cold air — blown along by the racing seas. Down at far ends, where ice comes together again, longer and higher waves crash into field of white. Spray flies, ice blocks jumble, and seas rear back in pyramids. Here no birds rest.

How does an ocean freeze, right before your eyes? Well, first it's patches of gray slush, somewhat resembling oil slicks at a distance, but without any sheen. Ship makes pleasant hissing noise passing through. Germans call it *Eisbrei,* "ice porridge"; Newfoundlanders rather onomatopoetically refer to it as "sish." More technically, good old British Admiralty *Arctic Pilot* defines as "ice spicules and thin plates about one-third of an inch across, known as frazil crystals" and notes, quite accurately, how they blanket wave crests and reduce swell. Next, this frazil freezes into small, roughly circular masses which break up and bump into each other. Water sloshed up in bumping action quickly freezes, making raised edges or rims and changing color to snow white. Thus "pancakes." Finally, given continued cold and moderate seas, pancakes begin to stick together in sheets, which then alternately thicken, break, and freeze again until they eventually commingle into many varieties pack ice. This just beginning to happen this afternoon. Later on the bigger pieces of "brash," or broken pack, grow three to four feet thick and "shine blue," as boys say, exhibiting that inner glow of deep emerald-blue exactly like wave-washed icebergs. And then, of course, you can stop ship, climb down onto pack, and have a nice walk. Hope cold weather continues.

*1930:* Nice visit from *Bestmann,* who has heard of my interest in sailing from Captain E. and comes all prepared with drawings and notes on gaff-rigged larboard sloops used in Baltic herring fishing when he first went to sea as lad of fifteen. Name is Hans Baltrusch. Oldest member of crew by far. Born 1916 in small fishing village near Königsberg, formerly capital of East Prussia, now Kaliningrad, U.S.S.R. Had four years in navy during World War II, plus three in French prison camp after V-E day. But hardest of all for him is memory of how Soviets subsequently ravaged his homeland. ("It seemed to me the world was turned upside down," he says of this, very quietly.) Sometimes, of course, thinks about retirement. Especially, he adds, after a few more good trips.

*Tuesday, February 8:* Another big haul of forty tons, more or less, during early morning hours. So far all big catches seem to come then, or during Merkler's watch. Have started kidding Captain Ernst about this. He doesn't seem to mind.

"Ah, yes, it is true," he says at breakfast, bowing his head and feigning embarrassment. "Merkler, he has the golden touch."

After short visit to bridge, put on oilskins and head straight for factory. What a chaotic and deafening scene! Hatchways still jammed with fish, as happened yesterday, long after haulback. Ditto eight big sorting pens, each holding 800 pounds, plus almost equal amount of fish spilled over onto catwalks and steel gratings of factory deck. Portuguese factory hands and all Germans not needed on deck watch are attacking this overflow, making initial sort. Cod heaved onto one conveyor-belt system leading to machines; incidental catch of spotted wolffish, Greenland halibut, and redfish, which must be hand-cleaned, to another belt which goes to wooden cutting tables on starboard side; skates, eelpouts, sculpins, and other "trash" species to still another which takes them down portside to fishmeal factory one deck below. Some Portuguese singing, others shouting, joking, or trading obscene gestures with Germans. Much camaraderie, much excitement over big catch. *Fischmeister* yelling head off trying to have instructions heard over clamor. His responsibility alone to decide on sorting and best, most efficient use of Baader machines. Smaller cod can go to model 38 or 338 *Rundlaufer* [horizontal revolving cutting table], spewing out 80 fillets per minute, or 181 *Kopflaufer* [vertical, receive whole fish headfirst], which accommodates greater size range. Larger cod go to Super-99, fantastic device which grabs fish by tail and pulls them right side up through continually adjusting fillet knives, 24 fish per minute.

From here onward, fillets go to battery of skinning machines, five abreast, which remove cod epidermis with amazing precision, leaving only small sheen or trace of skin on outside each fillet. (Blum says this is called a *"Spiegel"* [mirror] and that it improves flavor and helps hold meat together.) Next, they are whisked by conveyors to plastic-topped inspection tables — some are transparent just like photo lab light tables — where men trim any ragged edges or remove tiniest bits of bone by hand. Thus manicured, fillets are then weighed and packed in lots for two different sets of freezers. One set is of horizontal plate variety, to receive trays that will emerge as blocks weighing between seven and eleven kilos; other has vertical slots lined with cardboard, into which approximately twenty-five kilos of fillets may be pressed down very tightly. There are three of former, each capable of receiving sixteen trays, or slightly more than one ton of fillets, and five of latter, with total of ninety slots. After two hours at −24° C. for trays and a little longer for slots, all is ready. Frozen trays are warmed by hot air injections and their contents "knocked out." Similarly, vertical units are removed whole, cardboard and all. Stripped of cartons, blocks look exactly like slabs of fine white marble. Ashore in processing plants these will be sawed into fish sticks and fishburger portions so popular in U.S. and Canada. But for moment, slabs are stacked in elevator — they clunk like cordwood as they fall in place — and taken down into the *Kuhlraum,* the frozen fishhold. Tray packs merely shoved down metal slide. There both remain, permanently frozen at $-28°$ C. for duration voyage.

"So there you have it," Blum says with obvious pride. "That is how we keep the production flowing." Tells me herring, for which there is separate line of machinery, always give highest production. *Wesermünde* used to process 60 tons herring fillets in twenty-four-hour period — from 180 tons whole fish, that is — back in good old days on Georges Bank. But such amounts were "maximal" or "record production," as Blum puts it. With cod and other groundfish half that tonnage is a very good day's work. Happen to notice there is yet another idled assembly line. Blum says this special for redfish. "We would be using it now if it weren't for the damned regulations," he says, rather pointedly.

Conversation interrupted by Portuguese worker, who says one of machines is jammed. Feel need of exercise and so start aft to help sort fish. (Blum says O.K., but be careful, leave it at that, and don't touch machines.) Have to inch my way through deep layers of wolffish backed up near cutting tables. Some are still writhing slowly. Disquieting, since boys say healthy specimens can bite through oar handle. My thin Topsider boots not made for this sort of thing.

Sorting proves more than good exercise; i.e., it's also only way to get close look at the fish on this or any other factory trawler, where everything falls straight from net into factory. First thing you learn is not to grab indiscriminately. Redfish have sharp dorsal-fin spine, wound from which so painful some fishermen think it is venomous. Ditto dogfish, although fortunately they are very rare up here. Most skates or rays have thorns and rough knobs on backs and tails. By contrast, hake are flabby fleshed, and some flatfish, especially witch or gray sole, so slippery you can't get a good hold. But *Gadus morhua,* the sacred cod, is a delight to handle. Flesh is reasonably firm, skin not particularly slippery, and all ten fins are what ichthyologists call soft-rayed, meaning there's not a prickly spine in any of them.

Some of by-catch species quite another matter, however, or so grotesque you shrink from touching them. Most prominent, since we have been fishing deep (approximately 2,500 feet), are the grenadiers, better known to all fishermen as "rattails." Have strange, almost fossiloid appearance. Blunt head, oversize eyes, thin body tapering to whiplike tail. Fresh caught, their eyes glow fiery red, then eventually fade to color and consistency jellied consommé. Blum says grenadiers' raspy scales so sharp and tough species cannot be used for fishmeal. So overboard they go, where, I have noticed, even the gulls pass them up.

For the rest there are brilliantly colored little lumpfish (from which cheap caviar taken), odd looking spiny tapirfish, soft-fleshed blue wolffish or "jelly cats," a great variety of skates, sea robins, pouts, sand eels, goosefish, cusk. . . . The list is long. They all go below for "reduction" to fishmeal, as industry calls it. Surprisingly, so, too, do gray sole, dab, winter flounder, and other fine-tasting flatfish.

*1135:* P.A. system booms out familiar monotone call, always twice repeated: *"Hieven, hieven, an Deck, einhol'; hieven, hieven, an Deck einhol'!"* Deck watch returns topside. Another haul is beginning. Where will new fish fit, since pens still half full? Soon chains rattling and big bobbins rolling and bonging on steel deck immediately overhead. Add this to factory noise, and it's strictly the anvil foundry, the devil's workshop.

How grand to reemerge in daylight! Wind is up, sky is one great mass of low and ugly clouds with color and texture of fine steel wool, and snow is flying here and there. But a lone shaft of sunlight bursts through far to the west, a promise, perhaps, of better weather. Grab rail stanchion and watch fascinated as fulmar soars calmly in ship's updraft not four or five feet away. There's that quick snap of the head and that silent inspection again! Evidently bird very interested in my struggles to maintain footing and keep camera dry. Have curious feeling. Who is observing whom?

Before the start of two-hundred-mile fishery regimes, cod and redfish were the target species most favored by foreign fleets in the colder waters of the Northwest Atlantic. (And also the haddock, in the slightly warmer waters from the central Grand Banks southward.) The redfish was the small fish first successfully frozen by Clarence Birdseye in Gloucester, Massachusetts, in the 1930s, before which time it was considered trash by both American and Canadian fishermen. Its color, ranging from pink or rose to flaming red, sets it apart from all other fish in gray northern seas, like a cardinal in winter woods. Among its other distinctions, the redfish bears its young alive and may be one of the longest-lived of all marine fishes. Sexually mature individuals, weighing about two pounds and measuring fifteen inches, may be as old as eleven or twelve years; whoppers of over thirty pounds and forty inches are believed to be over fifty. Unfortunately, redfish are not much to look at by the time they are hauled up from the deeper waters they seem to prefer for much of the year. In addition to a rapid loss of skin color, their large sounds, or swimbladders, often rupture, forcing out internal organs and further swelling naturally protruded "goggle" eyes, which is why the redfish is seldom seen in fresh-fish shops. Its flesh, however, is firm, pure white, and more tasty and richer in fat than the cod's. Long a favorite in a number of European countries — it is, in fact, the highest priced of all market fish in West Germany — the redfish was first heavily exploited on Icelandic grounds. After Birdseye renamed it "ocean perch" and promoted it with great flair, the species grew increasingly popular in the United States, where it is now much used as a prime constituent in the frozen "heat-and-serve" fish sticks, fish pieces, and miniature cocktail fishballs found in every supermarket. One consequence of its more widespread popularity is that the redfish has lately suffered some serious declines in the North Atlantic that are exacerbated, of course, by its extremely slow growth or recovery rate. The heaviest losses have occurred in the Gulf of St. Lawrence, on the Grand Banks, and off the Labrador. It is for this reason that Canada wisely made the redfish one of its first by-catch-only species for all foreign trawlers.

Canada also put other market fish under a complex system of time and place controls, allowing so many "fishing days" for this or that type of vessel in one or another sector of her two-hundred-mile zone. Known in the fishing industry as "limited entry," such systems are considered the most effective of all conservation efforts. By-catch regulations, however necessary, are not. They remain, in fact, the most vexing single problem in fisheries management, since their enforcement is fraught with practical difficulties. The difficulties arise in the first place because there is no such thing as ground trawling for one fish alone. Fish everywhere intermingle, especially on the bottom, and species that may be prohibited or under low quotas are bound to come up with others. Once the prohibited or over-quota fish are caught, furthermore, the next question is what to do with them. Most regulations require that the proscribed fish be sorted and returned to the water as quickly as possible. But, except in the case of short tows made on shallow grounds, 90 percent of the returned fish will be dead or dying, the victims of either changing depth pressures, which crush internal organs, or crowding in the cod end, which squeezes gill covers shut and results in suffocation. Nevertheless, imperfect and wasteful as they are, by-catch regulations have at least a deterrent effect. Fishing captains like neither to litter the sea with dead fish nor be burdened with the time and trouble of having crews sort out heavy catches of incidentals. Captains may sometimes therefore move to new areas of their own accord in hopes of finding "cleaner" catches of allowed species. To encourage this tendency, many regulations require such moves. They ask, at least, that "demonstrable efforts" be made to minimize the catch of regulated species. And that, in ground fishing, is about all that can be done.

Any attempt to describe all other incidental species caught in ground trawling, even scientists will admit, can be heavy going. Worthy of special mention, perhaps, are the odd-looking *Macrouridae,* or grenadiers, that both the sea gulls and the *Wesermünde*'s *Fischmeister* turned down. These fish belong to a family of almost worldwide distribution, some species of which, once their tough scales are removed, produce tasty fillets. For this reason Canada initially pushed the "rattails," offering foreign fleets liberal quotas within her new fishery zone. (None but the Soviets and East Germans took advantage of them, however.) In so doing, the Canadian authorities were undoubtedly still influenced by the siren songs about inexhaustible fish resources and the importance of underutilized species so common during the great oceanographic-sciences boom of the late 1950s and early 1960s. During those heady days, the reader may remember, oceanographers assured us that the living resources of the sea were largely untapped and the obvious answer to protein deficiencies in a hungry world. Prominent in their repertoire of underutilized species were the grenadiers — indeed, few of their global marine-productivity estimates ever failed to mention the "rattails" — which they described as one of the most abundant of all fishes both on the continental shelf and in deep waters. This assessment, however, had one serious flaw. Grenadiers are fairly abundant on the slopes or dropoffs of our continental shelves — not the easiest place to fish, incidentally — but their presence on the deep sea floor is now recognized as extremely rare.

In this the grenadiers symbolize a worldwide fishing problem: namely, the great bulk of commercially exploitable fish tend to crowd together on continental shelf and slope waters, whereas the deep or abyssal waters that make up 85 percent of the world oceans increasingly appear to be vast deserts, fish poor and biologically impoverished in general. This was not always so clearly understood. Scientists, however, now no longer argue the point. Approximately 85 percent of the world's marine fishes, nearly all agree, are denizens of the coastal shelves or relatively shallow seas that constitute but 15 percent of the ocean's total surface area. Also not clearly understood (and still the subject of much debate) were the possible limits or maximum yields of both these fish and the pelagic species that crisscross the open or deep oceans. At the height of the oceanographic-sciences boom in the 1960s, for example, Dr. Milner B. Schaefer, director of the prestigious Scripps Institute at La Jolla, California, concluded that "at a conservative estimate, the world fishery production may be increased to 200 million metric tons per year with no radical developments such as fish-farming or far-out new kinds of fishing gear." Especially promising, Dr. Schaefer thought, were the fishes of the open ocean and underutilized species in general. A Scripps colleague, Dr. John Isaacs, went even higher. Dr. Isaacs saw no reason for a protein-hungry world if commercial fishing would concentrate on the smaller and more abundant prey fish and invertebrates one link from the top in the oceanic food chain. At the level of herring, anchovies, sardines, and squid, Isaacs predicted, a yearly production of 350 million tons of fish protein was quite possible. Against these estimates the United Nations' Food and Agricultural Organization's first global productivity assessment, made in 1960, seems rather conservative. Rather than attempt total oceanic biomass projections with all things from plankton soup to edible fishmeal concentrate seriously considered, the FAO's Fisheries Divison (which was then and remains today one of the most active specialized agencies in U.N. history) used as its data base its own patiently gathered catch statistics, which had risen by a steady 8 percent per annum in all the years following World War II. Since there was then no sign of diminishment, the FAO confidently predicted that "with appropriate international controls and management of resources, we could take 60,000,000 tons of fish each year without impairing the viability of stocks or drawing on new resources."[3] Subsequent FAO bulletins somewhat qualified this estimate, but only to add that the sixty-million-ton level would probably not be reached until 1980.

By 1977, however, the FAO was issuing some surprising new data which the distant water fishing powers scarcely heeded in their general concern over the lengthening shadow of two-hundred-mile zones. The sixty-million-ton world catch, it appeared, had been reached in 1974, six years early. Not only that, it had remained at about that level on a well-defined plateau through the succeeding years. This had occurred, in fact, despite a greatly intensified world fishing effort, which the FAO itself had done so much to encourage.

*Wednesday, February 9:* Some time last night Captain Ernst called it quits and we heaved to. This morning storm winds in excess fifty knots assail us, and all the sheltering ice has receded far to west. Watch in uneasy fascination as Russian, Polish, East German, Portuguese, Spanish, and French trawlers (our little international community has been growing by the day) start to disperse in search of sea room. They wallow and plunge toward distant horizons, taking full seas over ice-lacquered bows. All are laboring, or pitching and slamming hard, as they struggle merely to stay up in wind. And so are we, it seems, as storm intensifies. Every

3. The quotation is from a statement made by Dr. D. B. Finn, then director of the division, in connection with the U.N.'s Freedom from Hunger Campaign. References to this projection are often found in contemporary studies and Five-Year Plans of the Soviets, who were greatly influenced by it in their decisions to build up their distant water fishing capability. The same is true to a lesser degree of many other countries, both developed and underdeveloped. It is impossible, in fact, to overemphasize the FAO's role in promoting world fisheries.

third or fourth sea produces great hollow bonging noise. Then come quivers running through entire hull. The big ones literally explode on impact, sending sheets of spray clear over bridge and down full length of ship. Don't know why, but looks much more appalling when you see other ships going through motions. Then slowly dawns on you your ship not doing much better.

Quiet chat in P.M. with Captain Ernst as we watch *Junge Welt* — the big East German mother ship first seen on Georges — and two of her catcher boat "daughters." Latter are having hard time of it in storm, sometimes disappearing hull down in the troughs. Ask Captain E. if he ever has friendly radio conversations with East Germans, as he does endlessly with his *Bundesrepublik* colleagues. Says some years ago he did, when there was older generation captains, but now it's a younger lot who have grown up under Communism, know nothing else, and consider idle VHF chitchat frivolous, decadent. "I tell you, I can't stand to listen to them," he says. "Occasionally they do joke among themselves, but it's so childish. You hear them announcing some little gift, some trinket like a lapel pin or a pennant, for a good catch or going over a quota, just like they were kids in school. Can you imagine? And there's a commissar on the *Junge Welt* for monthly political meetings at sea. Then they send out announcements. Maxims, they are, straight out of Mao's little red book. I don't want to listen to it, it disturbs me so."

Conversations with Russians equally rare, he adds, although sometimes Soviet skippers will inquire about fishing conditions, especially when off alone on scouting trips. Tells me funny story about how last year one of his colleagues in Nordsee fleet actually succeeded in getting Soviet master with fair knowledge of German to talk about women on board. Captain Ernst's friend kept asking what it was like living so many months at sea with lusty young fisherwomen. Soviet captain, highly embarrassed he ever got drawn into topic, kept stammering *keine Problem, keine Problem,* all his *Mädchen* had excellent *Disziplin,* etc., etc. Captain of *Bremen,* listening nearby, got so fascinated he tangled his trawl with Russki's. (A serious business, incidentally, which can lead to lawsuits, just like collisions.) This, of course, was the story of the year, throughout the fleet.

Captain Ernst grudgingly admits Russians catch fair amount of fish (how could they not, he implies, with so many ships), but says they are atrocious seamen with total disregard rules of the road. "They think they own the sea!" he grumbles. "*Tigerziege* [billy goats], that's what I call them."

There comes a time when all fishing vessels, even the largest of factory trawlers, must halt normal operations and concentrate solely on the weather. When the wind rises to unsafe velocities, smaller side trawlers sometimes save fuel by lying to the seas with dead engines. They simply roll broadside to the wind, a most uncomfortable experience. But sooner or later, if the weather worsens, it becomes necessary to restart the engines, round up into the wind, and keep up sufficient power to meet the seas head on. British fishermen call this "dodging"; Americans and Canadians, "jogging." When to begin doing so is, as previously suggested, a point of much argument. Prudent side trawler skippers will usually stop fishing at Force 8 ("fresh gale, winds 39 to 46 m.p.h., moderately high waves . . . , edges of crests begin to break into spindrift"). But many often go higher, especially when they feel pressured to make up for lost time on a poor voyage already plagued by too many storm or nonfishing days. Serious risk, however, attends all who try this. A heavily laden vessel that keeps fishing too long will be unable to round up — she is held a downwind prisoner by sheer force of wind and wave — and has no choice but to run before the seas and search the lee of some friendly land, if indeed there is any on her forced heading. This can be a dangerous and sometimes fatal practice.

Factory trawlers usually forgo lying ahull and go directly to dodging somewhere around Force 10 ("whole gale, winds 55 to 63 m.p.h., seas take on white appearance as foam is blown in dense streaks"). There are good reasons for doing this. Like many merchant ships, factory trawlers have greater windage, meaning a much larger lateral surface area to present to the wind, than low-freeboard side trawlers. Thus, although factory trawlers can fish safely bow-to-the-wind in worse weather than side trawlers can, the bigger ships roll too much if left to drift abeam in heavy weather. Not only that, the moment of rounding up, when it comes, can be particularly difficult for them. Having just stopped fishing, they will most often have several tons of fish sliding and shifting high on the trawl deck. One deck below, but still well above the waterline, the factory will be busy processing catches for some time to come. This means that a considerable volume of water — rapidly accumulating from the knife-cooling jets of every Baader machine and the giant hoses used to rinse fish — sloshes back and forth on the factory deck. This water quickly creates the "free-running surfaces" that accentuate rolling and build up the momentum that naval architects consider the greatest threat to stability. Then, too, unlike merchant captains, fishing skippers never have the security of knowing exactly how much cargo they carry. Their cargo — fish — is constantly being augmented, and they must trim their ballast accordingly. ("Mind your ballast!" a large sign wisely placed on the *Wesermünde*'s bridge reminded all watch officers.) At the critical moment of rounding up, therefore, given the above circumstances and a skipper who neglects his trim, a factory trawler in a storm can be very vulnerable. She can lay over, as fishermen put it. And, sometimes, not come back.

*Thursday, February 10:* Storm continues. Still dodging. At breakfast "Big Mosquito" Heinz, our estimable and spheriform young steward in officers' mess, is dreaming about exotic drinks he used to sample when on Hamburg-Amerika Line tropical cruise ships. *"Ach, ein echtes Bacardi Collins, das schmeckt so gut!"* he says, pursing and smacking lips. Tells me there was quite a party up forward last night and appears to have mild hangover.

This morning heard violent argument between fishmeal foreman and unidentified crew member in forward passageway. Then, at lunch, *Fischmeister* complains long and loud about insufficient help. Says owners reduced factory hands disproportionately this trip. He can't maintain optimum production; it's not right to expect it, etc.

Long chat in evening with radio officer, who claims he is very lonely. "I thank you for your company, since nobody on this ship speaks to me," he says right off, pouring himself stiff belt Scotch. "I tell you, from the birth this ship does nothing right. Mr. William, perhaps you think I will be crazy, but I believe every ship has a *soul,* and this one is bad from the birth."

"But the captain, he is okay," he quickly adds. "He knows how to catch fish. He will never get fired."

Are we losing our *Geist?* Are nerves beginning to fray? *Wesermünde* has now been at sea 64 days; self, about three weeks. Wouldn't be surprised.

Morale generally runs very high on West German factory trawlers. Initially, crews welcome the opportunity to rest and catch up on their sleep at the beginning of bad weather. But not for long. The flare-ups and complaining moods noted above were unique to that day and undoubtedly reflected the restlessness that soon comes with the prolonged inactivity forced by unrelenting storms.

Unlike the Russians, the Germans do not bother with special recreational programs or other morale-building activities for their crews. One of the reasons for this, as the Germans explain it, is the relative shortness and variety of their trips. Russian factory trawler crews remain at sea for exactly five months, often going repeatedly to the same grounds, after which they are usually, but not always, flown home for three weeks' leave. Thus their shipboard chess tournaments, periodic pep rallies or songfests, and the much-noted presence of women crew members presumably play some part in forestalling anomie. By contrast the West German fleet, which fishes pretty much as a unit, makes four separate seasonal-geographic area trips averaging less than three months each in the course of a year. The usual schedule is the Norwegian coast in spring, Georges Bank and other New England or Nova Scotian waters in summer, the North Sea, the Hebrides, or Spitsbergen and the Barents Sea in autumn, and Greenland and the Labrador in winter. The ships return to home port between trips for a week to ten days, during which all but a skeleton maintenance crew takes short leave. Wives of German officers may accompany their spouses on any given trip. The winter Greenland-Labrador trip is not popular.

Although individual ship rules may differ, some drinking at sea is permitted on all West German trawlers. On the *Wesermünde* crew members were allowed to buy one bottle of schnapps and one case of canned beer a week. In the view of most captains, crews self-regulate drinking or other social problems. So strong is the motivation to keep fishing or make a quick and profitable trip that a man whose drinking interferes in any way with his work is quickly singled out and dropped by common consent before the next trip. So, too, of course, with born troublemakers.

At the heart of the high morale of distant water fishermen of many nations is what is relatively good pay. This is especially true of the West Germans, thanks to a complex system of tonnage "premiums" or bonuses, which begin to accumulate with the first ton of fish to be brought aboard and processed. Thus, although apprentice deckhands and beginning factory workers on West German distant water trawlers receive no more than the equivalent of $270 a month in base pay, they may easily double or triple that amount through a wide array of bonuses, ranging from 55 cents for each ton of fishmeal to $1.17 for bone-free butterfly-cut herring fillets. Similarly, a middle-ranking bosun's mate or factory section foreman may get a monthly base of $650, while an experienced First *Steuermann* will receive $1,200. But in the course of a good year (assuming three trips, although many crew members take four, deferring annual leave) the premium for top-grade boneless cod fillets alone means an additional $6,000 to the middle ratings, $12,000 to First *Steuermänner*, and a whopping $60,000 to captains (1977 prices and wages; 2.31 DM to the dollar).

Much the same motivation, of course, is provided by the percentages or the shares of total catch proceeds received by many other fishermen; in each case, the amount of fish caught determines to a significant degree the pay the fisherman will ultimately receive. But nowhere is the difference between trip or base pay and the tonnage bonuses so great as with the West Germans. So important is this difference to all hands, in fact, that there is a little rhyme about it, often repeated. *"Die Heuer,"* the fishermen say, *"sind nur für die Steuer* [The base pay just goes for taxes]."

*Saturday, February 12:* Force 6, barometer falling, and seas building up again. We have been fishing since early Thursday morning, when storm somewhat abated. But no sooner did we start than entire cod end lost to bad rimrack. Then yesterday it was broken idler, which meant dragging door up ramp, plus large tear in bosom of net. Jupp Merkler, of course, banged his fists (or head!) against bridge windows. Captain Ernst, his usual calm self, simply kept saying *"Rasmus* did it." Or sometimes, *"Der liebe Gott im Urlaub ist* [God has gone on vacation]."

*0800:* We have lots of company again. Last night I counted twenty-two large trawlers in sight and spotted some twenty more on radar. This morning the crowd is still very much with us — a veritable international parade, a *Who's Who,* you could say, of big-time fishing. Spanish, whose biggest effort usually further south on Grand Banks with smaller pair trawlers, up here now with nice-looking new factory trawlers: *Esquio, Dianteiro, Arriscado,* all La Coruña. Poles represented by rusty old *Lacerta* and *Libra,* both about 2700 tons, out of Gdynia. Mixing old and new, Portuguese show such extremes as *João Fernandes Lavrador,* a 235′ salter in her thirtieth year, and *Santa Isabel,* a splendid ultramodern factory trawler built in 1973. Snappiest of all are the French. ("Oh, you know how it is with France," Captain Ernst says of them. "All is design; all must be beauty.") In sight are *Joseph Roty* and *Pierre Pleven,* St. Malo; *Victoria,* La Rochelle, *Islande IV,* Bordeaux, all factory trawlers or whole-fish freezers with forward-raking gantry masts, slim twin funnels, and white hull stripes which taper to a sharp point on bow. Soviet presence, however, is overwhelming, dwarfing all the rest. Nearby are *Nakhodka,* one of old and now-rare Mayakovskys; *Polotsk* and *Krasnoputilovets,* two Polish-built B 26's out of Kaliningrad and Leningrad, respectively; huge *Aktinia,* Kerch, which captain says is one of new Super-Atlantiks built in East Germany (336 feet LOA, 3930 g.t.'s) and *Povolzhye, Pamir,* and *Nokuyev,* all Murmansk and all of Altai class, largest factory trawlers designed and constructed in U.S.S.R. Plus many more, too far away to make out their names.

Love to listen to the general Babel of their radio chatter on separate VHF set which Captain E., not entirely in jest, calls his "spy radio." Most of the time, however, his ear is glued to West German channel on another set, listening to his countrymen. Their conversations drone on for hours, night and day. The reason for this, bridge officers all insist, is the need to exchange essential fishing information. But in truth all their radio dialogues are a continuous verbal joust — a tournament of wits, to be more precise, rules and protocols of which make it impossible for any of contestants to score a clean win or even much of an advantage. Rule number one is to give just enough plausible fishing information (but never the whole story) to hope your neighbor will feel obliged to give you something useful in return, which must then be discounted to the degree you know he, too, will not be telling whole truth. Rule number two is never to indulge in complete radio silence, no matter how tempting, or refuse to answer properly framed inquiries. Apart from being considered bad form, radio silence simply doesn't work. Others will always interpret it as hot new discovery, the men tell me, and then rush over to where you are.

Joust takes on added spice when ships fishing close together. All captains and bridge officers will then grab their binoculars and focus on stern ramps of every other ship in sight. Information so obtained — rough estimates of weight of haulbacks, that is — is subsequently used in radio exchanges, usually as opening thrust. Results sometimes quite amusing. We had a dilly this morning, freely translated as follows:

NEARBY CAPTAIN: "Hello there, Jupp, that was a fat bag you just hauled. How much did you get?"

MERKLER: "It was nothing, my friend. About forty grams, I would say."

NEARBY CAPTAIN: "What a pity! Forty grams of big rocks, I suppose."

MERKLER: "No, no. Just forty grams of fish, without the rocks."

NEARBY CAPTAIN: "*Ach, du, Merkler!* How is it that I see such a crowd of sea birds in your wake?"

MERKLER: "Well, the chief engineer just flushed all the toilets, and the galley is dumping garbage. You know how the birds like our stuff."

NEARBY CAPTAIN (signing off): "Sorry you're doing so poorly, old friend. My heart goes out to you."

Communications with home offices in Bremerhaven have separate set of rules or, better said, safeguards. The other night Radio Officer Ernst Schmiedeberg told me each of four big West German fishing companies has secret code for all radio traffic with fleets concerning daily catches, moves from one ground to another, or how rivals are doing. If one of companies seems to be doing badly, owners immediately suspect their code has been broken and order it changed. For this reason, Schmiedeberg said, Hanseatische's flagship, *Karlsburg,* has two or three alternate codes which can be sent around to other ships and be put into effect immediately.

What a bother! No doubt average catches would be higher for all if everyone agreed to teamwork approach and full exchange, as Soviets reputedly do in pulse fishing. But, of course, that wouldn't be private enterprise.

*1830:* Daily wireless news bulletin tonight says European Economic

Community has agreed to total ban on herring fishing in North Sea. Then comes item about how more and more countries are accepting principle two-hundred-mile zones or, as in case of Norway and U.S.S.R., thinking of establishing their own. Oddly enough, no one seems to react much to the news. No doubt boys half expected herring ban anyway, aware as they are that North Sea stocks reduced almost to vanishing point. But what about rest of the picture? The U.S. has already withdrawn from ICNAF,[4] and the word is there will probably be no foreign quotas at all for cod, haddock, redfish, possibly even herring in the new American zone, starting March 1. And Canada has announced foreign quotas will be reduced progressively, year by year. Add Norway's prime grounds, Russian half of Barents Sea, and rich Icelandic waters, already long off limits. You begin to wonder. Where will big boys go?

Captain Ernst says there may be some hope in joint ventures which German government has negotiated with Canada. *Wesermünde* and other Hanseatische ships, for example, are under contract to deliver 600 tons frozen cod blocks to Canadian processing company in Harbour Grace, Newfoundland, and then keep remaining 300 tons of frozen fishhold space for home market. Similar arrangements have been made, he thinks, for rival Nordstern and Nordsee company fleets. All this has meant relatively good quota for West Germany this year. Perhaps there will be more of this everywhere in the future, he adds, but not with great conviction.

Fishing secrecy and encrypted messages, it must be emphasized, are not a unique practice of the West Germans. Fishermen the world over, whether aboard the smallest inshore draggers or the largest factory trawlers, constantly engage in the hide-and-seek game that goes under the name of fishing strategy. Underlying it all is the undeniable advantage that accrues to any skipper who first finds rich concentrations of fish and is then able to enjoy them for a day or two without the disturbance of competition. All fishing captains dream of such ideal circumstances. With experience, or to the degree they have enjoyed them, therefore, they grow very secretive.

Cautious optimism was the prevailing mood among distant water

---

4. The U.S. action, concluded five weeks earlier, at the close of 1976, ultimately caused ICNAF's collapse.

fishing nations during the time when many coastal states abandoned the U.N. Law of the Sea approach or other international alternatives and rushed to follow the U.S. and Canadian lead by establishing two-hundred-mile zones of their own. Joint ventures, such as the West Germans first negotiated with Canada, were seen as especially promising for both traditional and newly developing grounds. As an example of the former, many European fishing powers thought that surely Canada and the United States would be eager to have foreign fleets fish the offshore reaches of their newly-declared zones and then let the catches be sold to domestic processors, since practically speaking American and Canadian fleets did not fish those waters. (A 1976 Canadian government survey showed that 95 percent of Canada's 40,000 fishing vessels were "under 25 gross tons and generally stay within a day's journey of home port"; much the same was true in New England, especially in winter, to the point that foreign fishermen often claimed they never saw Americans out on Georges.) As for other parts of the world, the FAO saw joint ventures as an essentially healthy and desirable development which might well shift the focus of world fishing from overworked Northern Hemisphere waters to the promising grounds of the subequatorial developing nations. (The FAO's Fisheries Division, in fact, pronounced itself ready to serve as the facilitating agency, the "marriage broker," for all such cooperative enterprises.) Elsewhere, of course, there were the relatively unexploited but known-to-be-productive waters of Australia, New Zealand, and the Patagonian Shelf. Or the excellent test fishing already under way for the small shrimplike krill of Antarctica. And, finally, as the FAO had so often said, the time was ripe to concentrate on the legions of underutilized species in all the world's oceans. One had only to search and adapt to new circumstances, it seemed, and distant water fishing might continue to be profitable. That, in 1977, was the common belief.

*Sunday, February 13:* Miserable day. Gray, smoky cold, fairly high seas. We had a dreadful hangup before breakfast. Net almost completely torn off midway down extension. Nothing but few strands of Perlon synthetic twine saved us from losing it all. Jupp Merkler says he has never seen this happen before.

*2300:* We are steaming full ahead south to Sundial or Ritu Bank. Captain Ernst has had it with Hamilton, with all the rocks and the big *Konkurrenz,* as he likes to call the crowd. Also suspect his decision strongly influenced by report received earlier from *Frithjof.* She has six Canadian inspectors on board, plus two or three instructors from St. John's Fisheries College sent out by Canadian government to learn about winter ice fishing from Germans. Captain Ernst very disturbed about latter, although he is well aware previous history of instruction, especially by Nordstern fleet. "What do you think," he asked me, quite seriously. "Perhaps these 'teachers' are the true inspectors?"

*Thursday, February 17:* [Ritu Bank] The fishing goes on. Ten tons here, fifteen tons there. Cod, at least, are running larger, but we haven't had any of those whopping forty- or fifty-ton hauls for some time. Nevertheless, much to Captain Ernst's displeasure, largest part of *Konkurrenz* (the rivalry) has followed us down here. One day, if it's calm, they are all around us. The next, if it's foul, they scatter God only knows where. God and our skipper, I should add, since Captain E. seems to have remarkably clear grasp of where Russkis and all the others may be at any given moment, thanks to his spy radio, in spite of language difficulties.

The ice, too, comes and goes. At times it reaches way out to where we are now — approximately 180 miles from shore — and looks as though it's just about to firm up into heavy pack. Whenever this happens I go down to lower decks, well forward, to listen to weird cacophony shrieking and groaning noises as hull grinds through bigger pieces. Or up topsides, to scan eagerly for harp seals. But then weather changes, swinging around to east, and the ice all goes with the wind — cracking, jumbling, and shelving — far back toward land. It's constantly expanding or contracting, in other words, like folds of a concertina. Whether it's with us or not, it seems, is more of a function of prevailing winds than cold temperatures.

But, as crew keeps saying, we haven't really seen anything yet; true pack ice has still not arrived. When it does, they tell me, Germans line up in convoys, ten or twelve ships, go right into it, and then peel off to fish open-water "lakes" or leads. Sometimes, in absence of latter, trawlers create their own. Leading ship doesn't fish, that is, but serves only as icebreaker so that one or two may fish in her wake. This lead ship duty then periodically rotated, in order that fishing time equal for all. Similarly, should someone get stuck and require companion to come to rescue, rescued ship expected to be first to return the favor next time it happens to anyone else.

Everyone looks forward to ice fishing, I'm told. Not only does fishing improve, but it's always calm as a millpond, making work of all hands much easier. Possible exception, however, is captain, who must constantly worry about the weather. If strong east winds come up suddenly, you can get "nipped," or inextricably caught, in concertina squeeze. This, of course, is *sehr gefährlich*.

*1200:* Dull lunch of porkchops, mashed potatoes, red kraut, and, of course, Dr. Oetker pudding. (Why, oh why, do we so seldom have fish?) Ask Captain E. why ice fishing so much better. He says some say it's sharply defined water temperature layers, or thermoclines; others that fish gather under outer limits of ice before spawning. "When we first came here in the winter of 1955, there was no competition," he adds. "The fishing was excellent, but now it's way down."

Ask him how come, especially since Canadian fishery biologists call Southern Labrador–East Newfoundland cod stock largest in NW Atlantic and the great hope of Canadian fishing.

"*Ach,* the scientists and their 'stocks'!" Jupp Merkler chimes in, giving last word derisive twist. "What do they really know? I tell you they get most of their information on stocks from us, from what fishermen catch. And I can also tell you that every year we have to go deeper for the Labrador cod, ice or open water. Every year they are smaller. You know what that means."

Conversation then centers on spawning fish. From all that I can gather yearly rounds of West German fleet purposely scheduled to coincide with major spawning times and places cod and other market species. But certainly, I interject, this cannot be good for future of stocks.

"Surely by now you have seen that we fishermen are honorable persons and good conservationists who always speak the truth," Captain Ernst replies, making great pantomine of hurt feelings. "Well, the truth is we, too, would like to give the spawning fish a chance. But if we didn't take them, some other *Lumpenhund* would come along sooner or later and do the job for us."

*1500:* More trouble. This time it's broken ground chain and, consequently, long lengthwise tear in bottom square of net. Ugly SE wind rattles through rigging and snow is flying horizontally across deck. Topside work getting very dicey, as frozen slush accumulates everywhere.

Nevertheless, Captain Ernst orders second net out and puts crew to repairing first. Some are stringing up broken ground chain from aft mast, very near to slippery ramp edge, trying to immobilize big bobbins with stops or guy lines. In this weather! I don't want to look.

Today Canadian fishery management officials still consider the Labrador cod stocks the richest in the Northwest Atlantic, although the fish do run relatively small.[5] The successful winter ice fishery, biologists now generally agree, is explained by the urge of Labrador cod to mass in considerable number under the ice edge before spawning or to pre-position themselves, so to speak, in the right place well before the onset of their reproductive cycle. As the winter progresses, that is, they move from the shallow and colder inshore waters to the more comfortable and uniform temperatures near the coastal-shelf deeps. There both sexes mingle and wait for their spawning period, which comes in March or April and must occur in open water. (Cod eggs, like those of most sea fishes, float on the surface and depend on wind and current for dispersal.) After spawning the spent fish scatter in random patterns, and the West Germans, who have long understood the phenomenon, pull in their gear and head home.

The practice of exploiting concentrations of spawning fish is as old as fishing itself. It is based on the unfortunate habit of nearly all fishes to collect in their greatest numbers and in the most specific localities when they come together to produce young. For many centuries, therefore, the fishermen who first found these localities considered themselves blessed and fished them for all they were worth. The fact that at this stage the fish are also in their poorest condition — thinned and weakened from nonfeeding, the breakdown of muscle tissue to provide for rapidly growing sex organs, or a combination of both — has seldom bothered the fishing industry. Certainly it has been of little concern to factory trawlers, where high volume rather than quality is the paramount objective.

5. A stock is a mass or grouping of fish of the same species that stays largely within one geographical area, slight seasonal shifts or migrations to and from known spawning grounds excepted. The Labrador cod may run small not only because of overfishing, but also because they have a slower growth rate than cod of slightly warmer waters.

*Tuesday, February 22:* Another bad storm, Force 10 plus. Once again we dodge.

*1830:* Daily wireless bulletin carries news overall quota set by U.S. for Georges Bank herring next summer, or total allowable catch of 22,000 tons for all foreign fleets. This does shock one and all; only three or four ships size of *Wesermünde* could easily take this amount in course of season. As result Jupp Merkler, ever his perky self, is giving it to me. Says we have no conception abundance herring stocks off New England, which, to hear him describe, must be world's richest. Since we don't fish them, let others have good chance, etc. "It's hard enough, anyway, with your Coast Guard always coming at the wrong time," he says. "They're smart. They're not dumb, but they don't understand about *Pelagischenetze* [midwater trawls]. They see us steaming all over the place; they think we have gone crazy. Look, the herring, they swarm in a shape like a pencil. So you're hunting days and nights on end for them, watching with all the damned fishfinders turned on at once. You get red-eyed, you get a headache watching the instruments and steering the ship at the same time. It's a wonder we can do it! Then you find the herring and you lock on to them with the instruments. A half-hour set, towing at full ahead, and you've got enough for twenty-four hours' work in the factory. Then, of course, your Coast Guard wants to come aboard. They think, 'Ah, the Germans, they finally started to fish.' By the time they finish inspecting, the herring have gone to Canada!"

Captain Ernst agrees, says if we don't give foreign fleets better quota, herring will swarm up out of water and conquer the land. "You'll have to wade through the herring on that island you go to in the summer," he says. "You'll have to swim in herring oil."

"*Und Kap Cod!*" he finally snorts, lighting up another roll-your-own. "*Lieber Gott! Sie mussen den Namen auswechseln. Nicht Kap Cod. Kap Hering!*"

Later Theo Hermann quietly tells me how herring make whole year for West Germans. "The cod may tide you over, but it is really the summer herring trips that attract us," he says, explaining that these used to be two or three times more profitable than the others. "Now I don't know how it will come out," he adds.

Have heard much the same from various crew members throughout trip, come to think of it. They love to tell you about how it was on Georges in years past — in strictest confidence, of course, they always first warn. How in good years you usually made three or four quick trips to unload frozen herring at Saint-Pierre and Miquelon (plus maybe sell some to Danes at sea) in course of full July-to-October season. Then you filled up again for home journey. Or how Captain Ernst once got 157 tons in one haul, probably a record. Those were the days!

Mid-water trawls have both grown in size and improved their electronic instrumentation since they were first introduced by the West Germans in 1969. Awesome as their fishing power may be (the largest now measure a half-mile in mouth circumference and can easily take 500 tons of fish in a single haul), these nets nevertheless have the potential to be one of the greatest of all aids to fishery conservation. This is because they can effect what is called precision fishing, all but eliminating the disturbing problem of incidental catches. When the West Germans use them for herring, for example, they regularly catch 98 to 99 percent of what they are after. Their catches are almost totally "clean," in other words, without the great amounts of unwanted species that plague other forms of fishing. Moreover, although mid-water trawling originally concentrated on herring, mackerel, and other pelagic species, the West Germans and others who practice it have since found that almost as clean catches may be made when they use their mid-water nets for groundfish over bottoms too rough for conventional trawling. Many groundfish tend to rise as a unit when they ascend short distances up off the bottom, or so it appears, and the fishermen who catch them there will have very little of the intermingling of species so common on the bottom itself. For this reason, difficult though it may be, mid-water trawling should be vigorously encouraged.

*Friday, February 25:* Damn! Gotten very warm overnight. Now −1° C. Light SE wind, but with heavy cloud banks in distance. Ice gone again. Barometer falling. Another big storm brewing, no doubt. Must start thinking about how to get home, especially since *Frithjof* is long gone and her relief ship, *Poseidon,* said to be diverted elsewhere. Let's face it. My ambition to walk around ship on heavy pack ice (or see harp seal migration) may not be realized.

But no matter. For the moment this A.M. we have clear skies, calm seas, and the gang's all here again, working very close. Make laborious ship count; forty-one visual and dozen more on outer settings radar! This, plus fact nearly everyone concentrating on one particular hot spot, makes for constant traffic jams. Most annoying is Soviet trawler *Nokuyev,* Murmansk. She sticks close to us all morning and at one point decides to pass between us and new Portuguese stern trawler less than a ship's length away while we are both hauling back. Captain Ernst shakes fist, shouts *"Tigerziege!"* and keeps blasting two longs, one short on horn, which means "we are heaving." *Nokuyev* disregards, but slips through without tangles. Captain Ernst, still muttering, returns to his perch on bridge wing, where he has been gazing through his binocs all morning on what everyone else is hauling. He's congenitally incapable, I have decided, of resisting this most basic form of intelligence.

Just before lunch we spot two new arrivals. They are *William Wilberforce* and *Boston Comanche,* out of Grimsby. Both are old British "freshers": i.e., ice-filled side trawlers. They have nice traditional lines, but are so small and so low to the water they seem out of place in this big boys' neighborhood. Bows and midships heavily layered with ice, dangerously so, it seems to me.

Boys on the bridge stare in surprise and pass uncharitable comment. ("And they say England won the war!" "I've been to Grimsby. Good God, it's all *Dreck* and they've got rats running on the streets!") But Theo Hermann tells me he feels sorry for our new companions and that the others forget they all did time on similar boats. "Perhaps the British have no choice," he adds. "Norway doesn't give them much, and Iceland is out, as it is for us."

"Let's listen on the spy radio," Captain Ernst interrupts, only half joking. "You can interpret."

Catch two dreary voices, difficult North Country accents, using a familiar swearword so often it ceases to have any meaning. One is complaining about Canadian "fishing days" regulations. Other evidently has engine trouble:

"Och, Gordie, it's the fookin' Communists, the fookin' Rooshian Communists, they got all the time on the ground. We got twenty days. There's no fookin' use in it."

"Yah, Albert, and what with this ducky [crazy] engine of mine! We got the spare parts, you know, but I can't see fixing it at sea. Way she is, she only does a fookin' eleven knots."

"And the fookin' Germans, Gordie! They take all the fookin' fish!"

Make my report to Captain E.: to wit, doubt we will learn much from this pair.

*1500:* Weather changing, closing in very fast. Wind veering. Sight fine old Portuguese side trawler, hauling. Although large, she rolls sickeningly. Men having hard, wet time of it "drying up," bringing in net's midsection over rail.

*1750:* Black and stormy. It's a strong gale, blowing down from north. Temperature has dropped to $-15°$ C. On deck ice coats men's oilskins. Aloft wind shudders the rigging, and flying spray carries back to funnels, where it immediately freezes in fingerlike striations. Slowly we overtake some neighbors. To port is new French ship showing two red lights on aft mast. She is badly hung up and will wait until we pass before trying to free herself. Ahead is another large German, toiling away, plowing the sea. Tail kicks up white now and then with seas boiling up ramp. Altering course, you can briefly glimpse in glare of searchlights her great bulbous bow lifting clear of giant wave.

Spend long time gazing numbly through bridge windows rapidly being obscured by frost. At times like this you wonder. Why? What are we all doing here? This is, after all, such a woebegone, bone-cold spot on the globe, exposed in the case of Ritu Bank to full sweep of the Atlantic. Then you look at all the port lights, the cozy lights right down to lowest cabin deck, row after row of them. They make each ship look like a little city — much more so at night, anyway — within the bigger floating metropolis. Inside you know is warmth. The Portuguese coming off watch may play a round of cards, swigging their jugged red wine. The Germans will mutely watch a television cassette, wolf down a Holsten beer, and flop exhausted in their bunks. The British, still complaining, may be waiting for the nightly football scores broadcast; the Russians, if they have had a good day, for a songfest. Outside, our deck watch is once again repairing a broken groundline, cutting the heavy chain with blowtorches and trying to control bobbins on a rolling, icy deck. The men pause to flap their arms, fighting off the cold. *Bestmann* kindly allows some to take a break, for brief huddle by stove in the bosun's locker. But then the loudspeaker drones again: *"Hieven, hieven, an Deck, einhol"* . . ."

*1830:* After supper, while we are alone in mess, Captain Ernst makes interesting remark. "Perhaps you are writing at just the right time," he says. "In ten years all that we saw today may be gone."

# *FOUR*

# *Pairs*

You can distinguish them at sea, even at great distances. They appear on the horizon as two little specks which never change relative position. At night it is the same. The pinpricks of light from their swaying mastheads are as twin stars low to the horizon, traveling their determined courses, but always the same distance apart.

By these signs you will know they are pair trawlers, fishing together. But merely to say "together" is not enough; their true function must be expressed in stronger terms. What they are is two boats acting as one, firmly bonded by the towing of a common net. How well they fare in this difficult union depends on the closest cooperation, on complete coordination of every move. Above all, the two boats must maintain their fixed distance apart — a quarter- to a half-mile is the normal span, depending on water depth and the character of the bottom — as they search and scour the sea floor in tows that may last as long as ten hours. Not to do so is to twist or tumble the net, or court more serious troubles.

In port the twinned boats come together. You will always see them lashed one to the other, although the dockside may be empty and there is all the room in the world to berth in single file. There is no paradox here. For long months at sea, however much they work in unison, the crews of pair trawlers cannot communicate with each other except for shouted greetings during the brief moments when the two boats come close enough to pass lines for hauling or shooting. It is almost the same with the officers and their VHF communications. Of necessity their radio dialogue is mainly confined to the staccato of commands, numerous and terse, so necessary to coordination of maneuvers. Thus it is that after coming to land the pairs bind themselves together, so that officers and crew alike can climb over the rails on endless exchange visits. They swarm over each other's decks, inspecting damaged gear and chatting about the price of cod, letters from home, or other subjects of similar import. And so the boats remain, locked by their spring lines in the closest possible union, for as long as they are in port.

Such is the way, at least, a casual observer might have seen the Spanish pair trawlers *Terra* and *Nova* in St. John's harbor at eight o'clock on a clear June morning of the first year of Canada's extended-fisheries jurisdiction.

The *Terra* and *Nova* are at an oil dock in an area of fish plants, storage tanks, and ship chandlers known as "southside," across the harbor from the city. The scene is peaceful, even lighthearted. Alongside on the dock pavement the shaven-headed bosun's mate of the *Terra* is leading a procession. Slowly and with great effort he coaxes a mournful dirge from a homemade *gaita,* a Galician bagpipe. His friends, all draped in blankets in imitation of monks' cowls, try their best to accompany him with a toy accordion, a tin flute, tambourines, and cymbals. Their step is slow and one of them holds a coffee mug aloft as though it were a chalice in the moment of consecration. The men, it should be understood, have been carrying on all night and now it is time to seek penance with a proper processional. Various bystanders, including some young ladies coming off the early shift at a nearby fish plant, are much amused by the spectacle. One among the penitents asks a young Newfoundland mother if she and her small daughter will pose with the group for a photograph. Demurely, but with a smile she cannot hide, she accepts. The men are delighted and shower little trinkets on the child. Cameras quickly appear, the men rearrange their costumes, and there is an orgy of clicking shutters. The bosun's mate is very pleased with this.

All is not well, however, aboard the *Terra* and the *Nova*. One of the *Terra*'s younger crew members and two from the *Nova* are missing and long overdue. Both boats finished fueling the previous afternoon, and sailing time was announced for four o'clock. Now over sixteen hours have passed, and there has been no call from the harbor police or any other clue to the miscreants' whereabouts.

"*Ay,* what brutes the young ones are!" says Manuel López Muñiz, captain of the *Terra,* as he nervously paces his bridge. "In these times the kids have no sense of responsibility, no sense of obligation." Captain Manolo, as he is known to all, is not so much worried about the celebrants on the dock. "If that's all the damage this time, then we are well out of it," he says of them.

It is the missing crew who weigh especially heavily on Captain Manolo. In the dual command system practiced on all Spanish pair trawlers — there is both a fishing captain, the *patrón de pesca,* and a ship's or "nautical" captain on each of the two trawlers — it is the nautical captain who is in charge of all matters except fishing operations, including, of course, crew discipline. Not only that, the *Terra* is the "first" or command boat of the pair. Accordingly, Manolo is the *capitán náutico primero,* meaning that in situations like this he is in effect the supreme arbiter and personnel officer for both crews. If real trouble is afoot, it is he who will have to search out the Spanish consul, hire a lawyer, and possibly even appear in court.

"It is the worst, waiting like this! One can do nothing, not sleep, not even do busy work. *Ay,* how it makes me nervous!"

Manolo is addressing José Antonio Larruskain Errazquin, the *patrón de pesca primero,* or fishing boss of the *Terra,* searching him out for guidance or at least some sympathy. Other Spanish pairs have left crew members ashore all too often, Manolo explains. He is afraid the port authorities will lose patience and St. John's may soon be denied to all of them.

José Antonio Larruskain is not very concerned. He is a hardheaded Basque, not nearly as excitable as the *gallegos,* the Galicians, who constitute about 70 percent of the *Terra* and *Nova* crews. Joseán, they call him for short, and his reputation as a successful *patrón* is almost a legend in the fleet. He has seen this sort of thing happen before, of course, many times.

"*¡Qué va!*" he answers. "Some of the others here have gotten into knife fights ashore. Yes, I know it is so! And nothing happened to them."

At noon a luncheon of boiled lobsters, cod stewed in "green" garlic sauce, Spanish sausages, tomatoes vinaigrette, and freshly baked bread is served in the *Terra*'s tiny wardroom. Father Joseba Beobide is giving his opinion on the topic of the day, the question of what to do about the delinquents. Father Beobide is priest-in-residence to the Spanish fishing fleet. As such he is required to hold a special mass for fishermen every Saturday in the *Hogar del Marino,* the Spanish seaman's home in downtown St. John's, which also provides pair trawler crews with such luxuries as hot showers, washing machines, and private telephone booths to place calls back home. In addition Father Joseba is chaplain to the Christian Brothers community at Brother Rice College, one of two secondary-level parochial schools in St. John's. For today's visit he has brought a large Atlantic salmon to sell to the *Terra*. The price is very reasonable for such a fine fish, he explains, and his brothers at the college will greatly appreciate the little help it may bring. José Antonio buys the salmon, as Father Joseba fully expected. The transaction completed, he is invited to stay for luncheon, as he also expected.

Father Joseba does not believe those responsible for the delay should be punished. They are very young, he points out, and spend all those long months at sea away from their loved ones. Then, too, the work is hard, and each watch has the right to a full twenty-four hours of well-earned rest and recreation.

Manuel Soage, the *jefe de máquinas* (chief engineer) of the *Terra,* does not agree. Barely containing his anger, he tells Beobide he is confusing rights and responsibilities. He himself has been ashore for only twenty minutes, to send a telegram.

"What about me and my engine room gang?" Soage asks. "And what about the cook and his helper? We have rights, too, but we stay aboard. We stay aboard because you want electricity from the engines to have lights and to play your radios! The cook stays aboard because you all want food. You do like to eat, it seems to me!"

It is time for José Antonio to intercede. Joseán is ever the peacemaker.

"Well, sometimes you can't help it," he says very casually. "You can get detained for the most trifling things. I remember one time we were held up for twelve hours because the *sindical* [the crew's union representative] said we were short a dozen eggs."

Manuel Soage can barely wait to reply. He is the *Terra*'s master of logic, superbly endowed with the great Spanish gift of seizing the abstract, of getting quickly to the heart of the matter.

"Begging your pardon, José Antonio, but it is not the same thing," he says. "However unimportant they may have seemed, the dozen eggs were a matter of *derecho,* of rights according to ship's articles and the bill of stores. We have no lack of eggs, but what we have seen today is a total lack of responsibility, a total lack of respect for all who understand the need to work together. Is it a right of one degenerate to make the others wait all day?"

Chief Manuel has triumphed. The conversation turns to matters of greater moment, such as the ladies of St. John's or the new Canadian catch quotas.

After lunch it is decided that Captain Manolo will go to the chief of police. There is no other remedy. I am to accompany him, to help as needed in interpreting.

As we prepare to leave, the errant crew members appear on the dock. They lurch to the gangplank with uncertain step.

A crowd immediately assembles on the *Terra*'s small poop deck. Voices are raised. Some are for leaving the latecomers ashore. The consul can ship them home by air, they say, and then their shares can be reapportioned. Others favor a fine. But the younger deckhands, who are in the majority, say the *Terra*'s command was at fault. The sailing time was not made sufficiently known, they claim.

"Great host of the sacrament!" shouts Captain Manolo. "Must I hold everyone's hand like a nurse? Must I deliver to each a personal invitation?"

"Leave them ashore!" shouts one group.

"Douse them with cold water!" shouts another.

"*¡Que nos vamos, que nos vamos!*" chants a third, louder than the other two.

Agreement has been reached. The decision on what to do about the three, it seems, can be postponed to another day. If, that is, there will be any decision at all. In point of fact, the most important requirement of the controversy has already been satisfied, since every crew member has had full opportunity to voice his opinion. It is ever so. Spanish pair trawlers do not run by strict chain of command. They run on almost daily applications of catharsis, or the deep sense of fulfillment and relief that can come only from a compromise reached by all after a good argument, a good *escándalo*. We have had our dose for the day.

Pilots are obtained. Lines are triced and decks made clear. From deep down in each boat's engine compartment there come two or three loud and sibilant puffs of irregular beat, followed quickly by a more steady chugging. The *Terra* and the *Nova* put to sea.

Much is expected of José Antonio on this campaign, as the Spanish call the five-month trips of their pair trawlers. It is his first aboard the *Terra* and *Nova,* and the pair has heretofore not done very well. Neither, in fact, has its *armador,* or owner, José Ignacio Serrat of Pasajes in the Basque port of San Sebastián, whose fortunes are now at their lowest ebb. Less than a year earlier the *Ráfaga,* one of a modern stern-ramped pair that was the pride of his small fleet, had been lost to fire. Although the other boat of the pair, called the *Ciclón,* brought the fire under control and rescued all but one of the crew in a daring maneuver, the *Ráfaga* subsequently sank in a storm while under tow. Then, last autumn, it was José Antonio's turn. He was at the time serving as *patrón de primero* of an older and smaller pair, the *Isla St. Pierre–Isla Miquelon,* fishing Fyllas Bank off West Greenland in November. Fire struck again, and the *Isla St. Pierre* was burned beyond repair. As a result Expes Incorporated, as José Ignacio Serrat's company is more formally known, must now face the costs and frustrations of laying up the surviving *Ciclón* and *Isla Miquelon* indefinitely, since it is a peculiarity of pair trawlers that unless both boats have identical engine ratings and approximately similar design, they cannot work well together. With the exception of some smaller pairs fishing home waters, in fact, the *Terra* and the *Nova* are all that Expes Inc. now has. And José Antonio.

"I had to give it much thought," he says of his return to sea. "I have changed a lot in the last two years and now see things differently. You must know that all the effort of a long campaign, it builds up, it accumulates within you. It used to happen that I always got sick — a touch of the grippe or the flu it was — after every campaign. Now I make it a rule not to receive anyone for the first two weeks when I am home. I stay quiet, seeing only my family. Yes, I gave it much thought before taking this command."

We are finishing supper in the *cámara de oficiales,* as the *Terra*'s cubbyhole wardroom is grandly designated. It is about ten feet long and so narrow that a man standing in its middle cannot raise his arms without touching either bulkhead. Seated at its table, one has the feeling of being inside a shoe box. Only four persons regularly eat in the *cámara:* José Antonio, Captain Manolo, Chief Engineer Manuel, and the First Mate. Even so, given all the plates, silverware, wine bottles, and napery that the Spanish consider essential to their four- or five-course meals, the fit can be tight.

"It is difficult to rid one's mind of such things," José Antonio continues, referring to the loss of the *St. Pierre.* "But I always try to think of the good this world has to offer. I think of today and tomorrow, not the past. We have a special advantage this trip and perhaps we will do well."

Mounted on a small shelf in the forward starboard corner of the wardroom is a plastic statuette of the Virgin Mary. A tiny scapular hangs on a golden cord from the Virgin's outstretched hand. It barely moves as the *Terra* goes through some twenty-degree rolls, serving in effect as the indicator needle of an inclinometer. The same is true of a large Spanish sausage — it has grown a fine gray mold — hung by a string from the handle of the forward porthole.

"Oh, I am so happy, so content with the prospects of this campaign!" Captain Manolo is saying. "Ay, Joseán, do not die on us now! Do what you wish after we get back home, but stay alive for this trip. I have the feeling we will have a great good luck."

Captain Manolo is explaining that the *Terra* and *Nova* have been given the lost quotas of the *Ráfaga* and the *St. Pierre*. This is indeed, as José Antonio so concisely expressed it, a special advantage. Nearly all other ships in the Spanish fleet — the side-trawling *bous,* the factory trawlers, and the pairs — will have to go home this year with half-empty holds, since Spain's total allowable catch in the new Canadian two-hundred-mile zone has been reduced by over 60 percent from the year before, down from 85,000 to 29,000 tons. The *Terra* and the *Nova,* however, can load their salt-filled *bodegas* to the top with five hundred and fifty tons of cod. Over one thousand tons for the pair, that is, just as in the good old days.

"I don't like all this good luck wishing," José Antonio replies. "It is better not to talk about it all the time. The French do it right. They tell you '*bon voyage* and shitty fishing.' This is an absolute rite, *de rigueur,* with them. It wouldn't do to say anything else."

José Antonio is serious as he speaks. He is a strong man of short and stocky build, with certain very noticeable contradictions in his general appearance. Cheerful and young looking for his age, he nevertheless gives the impression of being disheartened, of having already experienced too much in his forty-one years. He wears his brown hair short, almost in a crew cut, but also sports long and elegant sideburns. His blue-green eyes are friendly and receptive, but they are at any moment capable of changing focus very quickly into a transfixing gaze of remarkable intensity. At such times they seem to be saying that here is a man holding back great passions, a man struggling to suppress something he very much wants to say. This may be, as the crew has already told me, that he has had more than enough accidents and personal misfortune to turn his back on the sea. Or that, more simply, José Antonio is not a person to cross. A man who says what he means, whose word, as the Basques like to say of themselves, is his honor.

"You see, he doesn't exteriorize himself," Manolo comments. "Joseán, it is so natural to wish good luck, or to be happy when things go well."

Captain Manolo is eleven years José Antonio's senior. Although a Galician by birth, he has the dark hair and darting black eyes of a Spaniard of the south. As he says of himself, it is in his nature to be happy. More than that, he is in reality possessed of an almost continual exuberance. There is no doubt, he is now telling me, that pair fishing is the hardest, the most difficult, *la pesca más bruta que hay*. But the life of a fisherman — any fisherman or even a merchant seaman, for that matter — has its satisfactions. Take, for example, what mothers in Spanish seafaring communities tell their daughters about marriage. It is an ancient rhyme that his maternal grandmother, a true saint of a woman, taught him as a boy. And all the girls know it, too:

| | |
|---|---|
| *No te cases con un herrero;* | *With a blacksmith do not wed;* |
| *¡Tiene mucho que lavar!* | *so much washing will there be!* |
| *Cásate con un marinero;* | *Marry a seaman, a sailor, instead;* |
| *¡Viene lavadito de la mar!* | *he comes home laundered from the sea!* |

"It is true!" Captain Manolo exclaims. "We come home and our very souls are purified by the sea!"

The *Terra* is now rolling more heavily, presenting her beam ends to fog-saturated winds from the southwest that have swallowed up the nearby *Nova*. Aft of the dining table, jammed behind the wardroom entrance door, is a small cabinet. It is filled with wine and cognac bottles and heavy glasses, which now clank loudly with every pitch and roll. This cabinet, a hissing radiator, and the dining room table are the sole utilities of the *cámara de oficiales;* its only decorations include the statuette of the Virgin, a certificate of Apostolic Benediction for the *Terra* signed by Pope Paul VI in 1968, a primitive painting of a mountain village in Galicia, and a discreet girlie calendar on which someone occasionally crosses off the days since the trip began. There is not much more to say about the *cámara,* except that it is located at a low point on one side of the *Terra's* superstructure, only three feet inboard from the starboard rail. This means that it is constantly buffeted by boarding seas in heavy weather, when the steel-plate covers of each porthole must be dogged down tight and all doors clamped shut. The effect inside is then very gloomy, more like a coffin than a shoe box.

"Well, we have passed the midfield line and now approach the zone of attack," says José Antonio, who is an avid football fan. "Perhaps tomorrow we can kick in the first goal. We are going east of Whale Deep, away from the others. I prefer to fish alone and keep quiet. You will hear the others asking on the radio, 'Where is that bird?' Sometimes I break in just to say good morning. Then the others say to themselves: 'If a Basque says good morning, he means just the opposite.' So they stay away."

"He doesn't exteriorize himself," Manolo repeats. "But we Spanish know the Banks like the palms of our hands, and none better than José Antonio! I tell you, Joseán, don't die on us this trip!"

After the others leave, José Antonio remains seated, telling me more about the loss of the *St. Pierre.* He doesn't mind talking about it, he says, since sometimes it is well to bring these things out. To exteriorize, as Manolo would say.

"You cannot imagine how quickly the flames spread," he says. "I was a long time in the water, trying to save a young deckhand who had jumped off the stern to escape the flames. He was caught in some folds of the net and was crying out to me to save him. I tried to give him *ánimo,* the will to hold on until help came. But it was no use. He was too long in the cold water. I could feel the life flowing from his body, even as I held him in my arms. Then when my younger brother, Vicente — he who is now *patrón* of the *Nova* — came over in a raft from the *Miquelon,* I was all swollen from the freezing temperatures, and my fingers were like steel hooks in the net. I tell you, Vicente wept like a child. He cried and cried to see me as I was."

We are interrupted by Captain Manolo. He is calling down from the bridge asking José Antonio for more precise bearings on to-morrow's "zone of attack."

"Well, soon you will see," José Antonio says as he leaves. "You will know why they say *Las parejas son las que más pescan, las que más rinden* [The pairs catch the most, yield the highest return]." His eyes are bright with expectation and he is suddenly smiling.

"It is to be seen if you will bring us good fortune," he adds, pausing at the hatchway. Gone for the moment, it seems, are all his disclaimers on luck and well-wishing. He speaks the words slowly and seriously, and the intense gaze has returned.

Early the next morning the *Nova* moves in very close on our port beam. A wet and chilling fog has reduced visibility to less than three ship lengths, but this is more than enough to provide that rarest of opportunities, or a chance to observe closely how the vessel one is aboard looks at sea. A true copy of one's vessel, rather, since the *Nova* is an identical twin, down to the smallest detail.

First to pierce the fog is the *Nova*'s jaunty bow. It angles up sharply from the waterline in a stern with pronounced forward rake and it is crowned with two large steel rollers. About forty feet behind, on the main deck, is a strong three-legged steel mast. Many cables hang from it, like vines from a tree, as well as four large and three smaller blocks. From here aft there is a clean or uncluttered sweep of the main deck until midships, where two large barrel winches are firmly bolted. Immediately behind the winches is the *Nova*'s two-level superstructure. It thrusts forward with pleasing boldness, almost repeating the angle of the bow, and is surmounted by a bridge that, although very small, is nicely faired and has eleven windows. One may, in fact, lean down from any one of these windows and hand something to someone standing by the winches. Similarly, standing on the main deck in the narrow passageway outside the wardroom, you may, if you wish, reach up to one of the side porches aft of the bridge and pull at the trouser cuffs of anyone standing there. Or, once on the porches, you can easily grab the roof of the bridge and hoist yourself up for inspection of the radar masts and radio direction finders that crown it. Everything about the *Terra* and the *Nova,* in short, is small in scale and close at hand. For those wanting more precision, it is only necessary to add that both boats measure 158 feet in length overall and twenty-eight in width; that their working capacity is calculated at 579 gross registered tons, and that they draw twenty feet when light in the water. Or that they are *clásicos,* meaning they haul their nets over the side in the conventional manner and have sensible and sea-kindly lines. Small, lively, and able is the cumulative impression, as they roll easily in the swells.

There is no more time for undistracted observation. Deckhands have taken station on both bows, and the two boats are coming closer together, alternately moving now slow ahead, now full astern, as they carefully test the wind, current, and ground swells. When they are less than half a length apart, at such a proximity that all who see it for the first time are thoroughly unnerved, one of the *Terra* deckhands picks up a *tirador,* a light heaving line. At the end of it is an eight-ounce slug of lead which fishermen call the *piña* (pineapple). Since the *Nova* has already set her net in the water — it is on her opposite side and cannot be seen — tradition decrees that the *Terra* must now throw over the small line that will eventually grow thicker and yoke the two boats like oxen to the drawing of a single net. The *piña* whistles through the air, but falls in the water considerably short of the mark. The *Terra* deckhand quickly tries once more with a second line, but again he is short. Up on the bridge José Antonio is both mad and a trifle edgy, since every *patrón* wants the dangerous moments at close quarters to be as brief as possible. Both crews shout *maricón* (pansy), *sinvergüenza* (shameless one), and other commonplace insults at the hapless deckhand, who will not be given another chance. Up on the *Nova*'s bow a short and stocky man wearing a leather cap —later I learn he is one of the best line throwers in the fleet — picks up a spare *tirador.* In one split-second motion, he sweeps his right arm back and then shoots it forward, stiff as a board, in a nearly flat plane. The lead slug parts the air with what seems like a rifle trajectory, and the men on the *Terra* jump clear as it wraps itself high in our rigging. Instantly the *Nova* backs off and a young deckhand begins to recover the heaving line hand over hand, stringing it through one of the big *rolines,* the rollers on her bow. Since the line is only one eighth of an inch thick, it looks ridiculously small as it passes through the heavy roller. But the *Terra* is now crossing the *Nova*'s bow and paying out the light line very quickly; it is soon followed by a three-quarter-inch rope and then a heavy green hawser, thicker than a man's wrist, which fits the roller very snugly.

Within seconds the *Nova* drops back astern and is lost to the fog. I can neither see nor fully understand what happens next. There are various sharp turns, the constant grinding of winches, much shouting by the crew, and, up on the bridge, a rapid punctilio of commands and acknowledgments on the VHF. After about fifteen minutes the main towing cable that was once passing through a roller on our bow has somehow been taken aft and attached to a solid post — it is called the *disparador* ("shooter") and is fitted with a trip-hammer release mechanism — located at the geometric center of the *Terra*'s rounded poop deck. Now, as José Antonio explains, there will soon be nothing more to do than "pulling the big rag and finding the fish."

The cross fire of radio communications with brother Vicente on the bridge of the *Nova* is slowing down. Rather than exchange commands, the two *patrones* now engage in a quiet antiphony of mutually reassuring observations, to make certain both boats are proceeding on parallel courses with equal engine power or that they are paying out cable at the same rate and watching for the exact moment when the proper scope relative to water depth is reached.

"A quarter to port and ten more rpm's?" one asks.

"A quarter it is and ten more from the engine," the other replies.

"I read two hundred fathoms and a clean bottom."

"Agree. Two hundred and clean."

There follow some moments of silence. The winches on both boats stop. Each has laid out 250 fathoms of cable, which is about seven or eight times the depth of the water, more than double the scope used in conventional trawlers.

"Well, now, that rag of yours is well set? All is in order, don't you think?" It is José Antonio again, and his questions are purely rhetorical.

"*Vamos bien*," his brother answers.

We are fishing.

The origins of pair trawling are the subject of much conjecture. Many Spanish fishermen believe it started with them. There were sailing pairs in the Cantabrian Sea and the Mediterranean at the end of the last century, they say, or even earlier, in times no one can remember. Then, with the introduction of steam, the Spanish were the first to take the little pairs down the African coast or up to Ireland, the Channel Islands, and the North Sea. Right up through World War II, in fact, when both the Allies and the Axis powers strafed their boats until they looked like Swiss cheese. A veteran *capitán náutico* who fished off the Irish coasts during the war years once told me that the Spanish pair fleet was, of course, explicitly warned by both sides to suspend fishing, no question about it. "*Pero, sabe, el español es egoísta*," he went on to explain. "So the more you deny us, the more you challenge us, the more we persist.

"Besides," he added, "the price of fish was then very high."

Be such matters as they may, pair trawling as a method of fishing in its simplest or pristine forms must have evolved independently in many different places over a wide span of time. If it is true, as has been suggested by some fishing historians, that a primitive fisherman wanting to get his line farther out in the water of a great river used a board shearing against the current and so discovered the paravaning effect by which today's trawl doors spread their nets, similar inspiration born of the same need may have seized other early fishermen wading in the water and pulling the first haul-seines along beaches or lake shores. It must have occurred to them, that is to say, that they could take their net out to deeper waters, and with less effort, if it was hauled by two boats rather than themselves. That some such event did occur in antiquity can be ascertained by visiting the Cairo Museum. There, amid the splendid collection of royal yachts and cargo boats found in an undisturbed chamber in the tomb of Mehenkwetre, a prince of the Theban dynasty who died about 2,000 B.C., is an extraordinary model of two fishing boats. Those who have followed Thor Heyerdahl's recent adventures will instantly recognize them as reed boats, similar in form to the *Ra,* made of papyrus-reed bundles with boldly rising bow and stern sections. The boats are perfectly matched, and eleven swarthy Nubians comprise their joint crew. Two of them on each boat are stationed fore and aft with long dagger-bladed paddles; the remaining hands are in the act of hauling in a net strung between the two boats. Although the net is crudely made of rough cordage, it is funnel shaped and has small wooden floats on its headline and stone weights on its ground-rope. At the narrow end of the funnel, moreover, is what appears to be a reinforced cod end, with the mesh heavily tarred to withstand bottom chafe. Unmistakably, the net is a ground trawl. Similarly, the boats are without doubt pair trawlers, employing a net with certain appurtenances not too far removed from those in use today. The question of whether these Egyptian boats gave birth to primitive Spanish pairs in a purely Mediterranean diaspora or there were indeed many other independent origins we may leave to the scholars. For further verifications, as they like to say.

What the Spaniards did do, nevertheless, is develop modern pair trawling to a high art and take it across the Atlantic in what they style — the phrase has a noble ring — *pesca de gran altura,* meaning true distant water fishing. This occurred on the Grand Banks in 1948. José Antonio is sure of it. He had an uncle on the first pair, the *Virgen de Lourdes–Virgen de Almudena,* he insists, although others on the *Terra* say the *Lince* and *Linabea* — or was it the *Rande* and *Rodeiro?* — were first by a few months. At that time, at any rate, the Spanish fleet consisted mainly of steel side trawlers constructed especially for the Grand Banks fishery and modeled after the French *chalutiers terre-neuvas.* These side trawlers, the *bous* of Spanish nomenclature, started fishing the Banks in the early

1920s and originally had French captains, bosuns of the deck, and net specialists on loan to help them, since the Spanish, unlike the French, had suffered a long gap on the Banks between the age of sail and the advent of steam trawling. In time, or at least by 1930, the once-great but now defunct Spanish fishing consortium, Pesquerías y Secaderos de Bacalao de España (PISBE), built up a respectable fleet of twenty or so of these large side trawlers. But after World War II, although more *bous* were being built, the pair trawlers took over. From a handful of wooden vessels in 1948 and 1949, smaller still than those in use today, the *parejas* (pairs) grew to seventy-eight boats by 1959 and 144 by 1968, at which point they constituted 70 percent of Spain's Northwest Atlantic fleet. It was during these same years, too, that the Spanish catches in the area climbed sharply — they exceeded 200,000 tons for eleven years, from 1961 through 1972 — leaving such old friends and rivals as the French and Portuguese far down the list.

Spain's heavy commitment to pair trawling, however, did not alone account for her worldwide catch increases, which also rose spectacularly during the above period, especially in waters far removed from the North Atlantic. These more distant catches had their origin in 1961, when the Spanish government, after taking due note of persistent shortages in animal protein, enacted a law for the strengthening and renovation of the fishing fleet and embarked on a factory trawler construction program that almost equaled the Soviet Union's in sudden enthusiasm and the extent of state planning and support. Thereafter, the great shipyards of northern Spain began churning out bold new designs of factory and whole-fish stern trawlers at such a rate that Spanish frozen-fish production rose from 4,000 tons in 1961 to approximately 500,000 tons in 1972, in what Spain's fishery management officials now refer to nostalgically as "the golden age of Spanish fishing." Firmly bolstering this endeavor were generous government loans and other forms of subsidy which one out-spoken government authority has described as "total, with no possible risk to the large fishing companies who were the beneficiaries." Or to the shipyards, he might have added, which by the early 1970s had built the third largest fishing fleet in the world, after the U.S.S.R. and Japan, and, for a short time, had been world leaders in fishing vessels for export, with satisfied clients ranging from such old hands as Iceland and Portugal to newcomers like South Korea and Cuba. But through all these years Spain's big new factory trawlers concentrated mainly on the rich *merluza* (hake) fisheries of South Africa and, to a lesser extent, on new species off South America.

Meanwhile, the *parejas* were left largely to fend for themselves. For the most part they were owned by small companies — Expes with its original fleet of three pairs is typical — and they received no government assistance other than a percentage rebate on the fuel oil they purchased. Nevertheless, the pairs continued to make high catches and significant contributions to the "golden age." In 1968, for example, Spain's peak year in the Northwest Atlantic, some seventy-two pairs brought home 239,000 tons of a record 341,000-ton catch; this was 16 percent of Spain's estimated world catch for the same year and about double the frozen-fish catch of her bigger ships in South African waters. Even as late as 1971, by which time a significant number of Spanish factory trawlers had moved to North American waters, there remained some surprising indices of the greater relative efficiency of pair fishing. The foreign catch of cod, the most sought-after species, then totaled 778,000 tons in the Northwest Atlantic. At the time Spain's pair trawler fleet accounted for only 4½ percent of the gross tonnage of all foreign vessels fishing the area, but it nevertheless managed to take some 28 percent (218,000 tons) of the cod catch. Even in the era of factory trawlers, it was evident, there was still a place for the little pairs.

There are reasons. Chief among them — and one that argues most forcibly for the inclusion of pairs in a work otherwise concerned with bigger and more modern fishing vessels — is the net with which these boats fish. There is no larger ground trawl in existence. Not even the world's largest factory trawlers — the Soviet Union's *Natalya Kovshova* at 420 L.O.A. and over 8,000 gross tons, for example, or the only slightly smaller *Tenyo Maru* of Japan's worldwide Taiyo Fishery Company — can successfully tow a ground trawl of the size customarily used by the Spanish *parejas*. As the reader may have deduced, this is because a pair trawl needs no doors, the boats themselves providing the lateral spread. Doors are, of course, the heaviest single pieces of equipment on a conventional ground trawl; they may account for up to one third the total tonnage drag of a bottom net. What the Spanish did in adapting pair trawling to distant waters, therefore, was to take advantage of the savings in weight and horsepower requirements from the elimination of the doors to design nets of extraordinary length, width, and circumference. In general or all-around dimensions, the largest pair nets are more than double the size of the *Wesermünde*'s Engel 250, to cite but one comparative example. In terms of total capacity they can bring aboard — in average sea conditions, in a single haul and without undue strain — an astonishing 180 tons of fish. Adding to their efficiency, of course, is the fish-herding action of their long towing warps. Under optimum conditions, which is to say very smooth and shoal grounds, the towing cables will extend aft some two or three thousand feet in the form of a long isosceles triangle, with a base, the distance between boats, of as much as half a mile.

"It's a lot of ground they drag," you will hear American and Canadian fishermen say, as they watch the pairs go about their work.

Not infrequently, a small concentration of pairs can sweep a fishing bank almost clean.

"There ought to be a law against them," other fishermen may then be moved to say.

We have fished for two days, in continuing fog. The catches have been fair, working out to about fifteen tons a haul. José Antonio, however, is not satisfied. Too many of the tows have come up "dirty," without a high enough percentage of cod, the only fish the *parejas* keep for salting, and with too many incidentals or by-catch species, all of which are returned to the sea. The fog is such that unless one is on the bridge looking at the radar or listening to the radio, it is easy enough to imagine the *Terra* as steaming alone on an untracked sea. Then, when you least expect it, after both boats have turned around and almost finished the long task of hauling in the towing cables over their forward rollers, the *Nova* will suddenly reappear. Standing on her bow as it rises and falls to the swells is a lone deckhand, isolated by the swirling fog. He is there to point and shout out the direction of the cable, so that it will come up on the roller straight and true, just as good crews on a yacht will station a man up forward to help their skippers run down a long anchor rode. For a fleeting moment the pose is heroic. The solitary deckhand looks like an ancient Viking helmsman, leaning forward and straining for a sight of the alien shores that the *Terra* and *Nova* now honor by their names. But presently other men join him, trudging up the deck with their shoulders bent forward inside their jackets against the damp chill. Then the *piña* whistles through the air once again. It is the signal, of course, to begin one more hour of frenzied cursing and difficult deck work, one long and dangerous hour to recover one net and set another.

"Do you remember that cook's helper on the last trip, the one who kept throwing all the plates and silverware overboard rather than wash them?" Manuel Soage is asking the question at a magnificent Sunday luncheon of cold lobster, baked halibut steaks in tomato and onion sauce, fried potatoes, salad, and vanilla ice cream. Chief Manuel is pleased that on this trip, at least, we have a good *marmitón,* or *chou,* as the cook's mate and wardroom steward is called, one who does his assigned work well and can also help out on deck.

"Oh, yes, I remember that other bird," José Antonio answers, laughing readily. "He hid his own knife, fork, and spoon, but everything else disappeared little by little, until we were almost reduced to eating with our hands, right out of the pot!"

"I don't think he did it with malice or bitterness," Chief Manuel observes. "He was born of bad milk. He did not have the proper formation for this kind of life."

Chief Manuel goes on to explain that strange things will always happen to those who are not strong enough or mentally prepared for the close quarters and long voyages of the pairs. Or to almost anyone, as a matter of fact, if the trip is a poor one, lasting six months or more, with a crew that doesn't especially get along. His own method of predicting trouble or deteriorating morale is to observe how the men react when they squeeze by or bump into each other in narrow passageways.

"At the beginning of a campaign you will actually hear the men say 'pardon' or 'excuse me,' " Manuel continues. "But three or four months out and it's *'cabrón* [studgoat, lecher]' or *'monte de mierda* [pile of shit]!' Then, on a poor trip, this in turn can lead to blows."

José Antonio and Captain Manolo cannot wait to tell of other incidents, wilder or still more improbable. The reason is clear. Other fishing nations, most notably the U.S.S.R., both Germanys, and Poland, conduct extensive research on mental illness among their distant water fishermen; the results in some cases are then published in annual reports for the guidance of fleet doctors. Similarly, the designers of modern factory trawlers give considerable attention to comfortable living quarters and other crew morale factors. But the Spanish pair crews have no such consolations. They live in cramped accommodations no one would ever call comfortable, nor do they have doctors at sea, much less the reassuring concern, if indeed it would be so received, of psychological investigations. Their only recourse is to talk and to joke about the strange and unfortunate by-products of *la pesca más bruta que hay.* It is, once more, the balm of catharsis, the necessary exteriorization.

"Oh, I remember a cook we once had who was in love, don't ask me why, with a prostitute, a common whore," Captain Manolo begins when his turn comes. "Every time he got home he would propose to her, but she paid him no attention. Well, at the start of one campaign — we were just leaving Pasajes in thick fog — he jumped overboard with a knife and a bottle of cognac. The knife was to kill his *enamorada* and the cognac was to keep him warm as he swam. Fortunately, the other boat found him and picked him out of the water, miles from shore. But, do you know, the swim brought him back to his senses! He worked hard, there was no more trouble from him, and the campaign proved a good one for all of us. As I have said before, sometimes we are purified by the sea!"

"That's nothing," Chief Manuel interrupts. "Do you remember the sailor who liked to collect copper? He developed this mania for stealing and hoarding bits of copper. Well, once in Saint-Pierre he somehow managed to find the main transatlantic telephone cable and cut himself a good piece, leaving the islands incommunicado. I tell you, we had some problems getting out of there that time!"

The stories go on. Some are very strong, José Antonio claims, involving knife fights and killings that have delayed trips or forced returns to home ports, causing all manner of troubles. He believes the root of such problems lies with the *armadores,* the owners. When a boat is a man short, too often they will pick up any drunkard on the street who happens to have a *libreto* (a "ticket," seaman's papers), rather than spend a few hours to find a qualified fisherman-deckhand. These pickups are the ones who can't stand up to the work, who inevitably become the troublemakers. Chief Manuel agrees and remembers all too well one such case from a recent trip. The man drank continually, got in arguments, and eventually hit the cook over the head with a wrench. Why, the cook almost lost his right eye, such was the force of the blow! Then he began menacing others with a knife. Since Spanish maritime law forbids the use of handcuffs, the crew had to subdue him with ropes and throw him in the chain locker. But back in Spain the *armador* paid a thousand-peseta fine to get the man out of jail and secure the return of his *libreto.* Then, of course, Manuel claims, the owner sent him right back to sea on another boat.

Oh, yes, that's about what you can expect, the others agree. *Cosas del oficio,* they say, or the hazards of the profession.

In the afternoon the wind changes and a hole in the fog bank off to the northwest becomes larger and brighter. Many birds now find us, and soon we are in full sunlight. José Antonio has decided that after eight or nine hours the tow has been long enough, although the sonar indications have not been very promising. On this occasion the *Terra*'s net is in the water, and it will be the first opportunity to watch a complete haulback sequence in clear weather.

"Well, what do you say, my friend?" José Antonio asks brother Vicente on the VHF. "Time to veer, perhaps?" Again the questions are rhetorical, since he scarcely waits for an answer.

"Let us stop the engines," Vicente immediately replies.

Both boats continue forward, gliding of their own momentum. José Antonio is watching for the moment when they will be barely maintaining way and the strain on the warps will be much eased.

"All right, *now!*" says José Antonio, with somewhat more authority. The moment has come to give clear orders, to make sure of synchronized actions.

Back aft a deckhand yanks out a steel tholepin on the *disparador* post and hits the handle of its release mechanism with a sledgehammer. A chain linking the post to the towing cable explodes in a small cloud of rust flakes — the "shooter" is well named — and flies out over the *Terra*'s rounded stern. The heavy cable cuts back and forth in the surface water, vibrating for some instants like the plucked E-string of a giant double-bass. The same, of course, is happening on the *Nova*'s stern, at exactly the same time.

"Ahead, full!" José Antonio snaps out. "And port all the way, port all the way!"

Both boats leap smartly into fast turns, free now from the full drag of their trawl. They heel over sharply as they circle around 180 degrees to port. Large flocks of shearwaters hover over the broad and glassy wake each boat makes in turning, searching for morsels in the smooth water. The maneuver is very well timed; the *Terra* and the *Nova* are tracing tight and perfectly matched parabolas. It is a pretty sight and one you do not see very often, unless, of course, you have watched destroyers as they wheel around to chase down the first signals from a hidden submarine. Unlikely as the comparison may seem, the two actions are not entirely dissimilar. To fishermen, what the *Terra* and the *Nova* are now chasing down is almost as exciting and fraught with suspense as a prowling submarine. Such is especially the case, at least, if a huge and near-to-bursting cod end floats up from the depths in a boil of bubbles and then wallows at the surface, thrashed by breaking seas. The men will cheer loudly, just as destroyer crews might when a wounded submarine breaks the surface. Which, in fact, is what a rising cod end very much suggests.

But first both boats must travel down the full length of their towing warps. This was the reason for their turns in the first place, or to be able to haul in the cables over the big bow rollers straight back to the winches with steady forward progress. Meanwhile, the net hangs quietly on the bottom; the boats come to it more than it to them. Unlike other ground trawls, a pair net has a cone-shaped funnel hung inside its deep-throated *gorlón* (extension piece) to keep fish from escaping at this stage, when it is barely moving.

In fog the exchange of orders and exhortations between José Antonio and Vicente would now be almost continuous. But on this fine afternoon the boats are in clear sight of each other and the dialogue is only occasional and sotto voce. The two brothers routinely sound out the cable markings — so many meters wound on or so many still to come. With this knowledge José Antonio suggests minor course changes or tells Vicente to slow down or speed up, as the case may warrant. The object, of course, is to keep the boats evenly matched as they come closer together down the sides of the long isosceles triangle of their towing warps.

"Take care, take care!" José Antonio suddenly shouts. "It's coming hard."

At almost the same instant two ponderous steel weights — they look like toy spinning tops, upside down or with their pointed ends forward — break the water close to the stems of each boat. These are the leading bobbins, attached by wire bridles to the wings at either side of the net. The *Terra* and the *Nova* are again at close quarters; each hauls in the last few feet of cable until the bobbins are almost at the rollers. A man on the *Nova* is leaning over her bow with a gaffing pole trying to hook a piece of cable ending in an eye splice. This can be a very wet and trying experience in heavy weather, but today he quickly snares the splice and hangs it on a small *disparador* mounted on the rail near the bow. Now the bobbin can be eased down a bit and left to hang on the eye-splice cable, while it is being unshackled from the main towing cable. The same is also being done on the *Terra*, except that, with the aid of block and tackle, the bobbin and bridles are hung farther aft, astern of the lowest part of the rail, where the net will eventually be brought aboard.

There follow the now-familiar protocols of passing the lines — the *Nova*'s tosser continues to demonstrate his superiority — until our big green hawser, fully paid out, reaches the *Nova*'s bow. Here it is secured to the bobbin-and-bridles assembly, called the *calón* in Spanish, which remains hanging on the bow shooter. The deckhand then knocks the shooter's release mechanism with a marlinspike. The heavy *calón* drops to the water with a splash.

Both ends of the net are now in the control of the *Terra* alone. The *Nova* immediately backs off. Her work is momentarily done, except, possibly, to think about readying her net for the next set. If there is no twine repair or anything else to fix, she can stop her engines, roll with the swells, and give all hands a much-needed rest.

Pandemonium, by contrast, now begins to take hold of the *Terra*. It is to some degree controlled, to be sure, and almost ritualized in the way it gathers force, but pandemonium none the less. The wings of the net have already been hoisted high up the three-legged mast, where they sway like soggy curtains, showering water and dropping small fish and seaweed on the men below. Meanwhile, the *calones* are being dragged across the deck with the help of a capstan, to get them out of the way. But one of the bridles catches on an obstruction. It tightens almost to the breaking point, and then snaps free.

"Big lump of shit!" José Manuel Rua shouts at the capstan operator. José Manuel, better known as El Morocho, "the Moorish one," because he is from the south and has dark hair and complexion, is the acknowledged leader of the younger deckhands. As such, of course, he cannot let the incident pass without comment. "Don't you screw us up any more," he adds for good measure.

"*¡Gran hostia, le doy hostia!* [Great host of the sacrament, I give you the host!]" the capstan operator shouts back quickly, but almost indifferently.[1]

And now the other *calón* is snagged. It has fallen through a broad deck hatch, not properly closed, knocking the cover askew and jamming itself in a corner of the hatch. Also, someone has let go of one of the mast's hoisting falls. It swings wildly with every roll. If not soon caught and secured, it will either ride up the mast out of reach or hit someone in the head with the heavy hook at its end. Men are running about, perhaps more than necessary. The cursing increases, freshly flavored:

"*¡Cabrón!* Slack off, slack off!"

"*¡Mala leche, vos* [Born of bad milk, you are]!"

"Mother of God! What a way to begin!"

"*¡Jodida la cosa* [All is screwed up]!"

Up on the bridge José Antonio is very disturbed. "What you see is not normal," he mutters. "This crew is still very green."

As he has done before, José Antonio quickly runs down to the deck, quiets the shouting, and gives the crew a patient lecture on the fine points of gear handling. Even as he does so, he goes about fixing things with deceptive ease, here unhooking a nasty snag or there seizing an errant cable. José Antonio is as strong and nimble as any of the crew; the men respect him accordingly. He throws himself fully into their work, being careful only not to get fish slime on his new sandals or his "O.K. Corral" blue jeans, made in Barcelona.

Now the action shifts to an L-shaped pit in the main deck at the port rail. It is cursed by some fishermen as the "swimming pool" because, being at the point of lowest freeboard, it often

---

1. Some fishermen believe this expression, of common use, originated in the manner of Marie Antoinette's let-them-eat-cake. During the famines of the Civil War, they allege, a Spanish priest once said, "What, no bread? Let them come to mass and eat of the host."

gives them unwelcome seawater baths. The *Terra*'s pit is smaller than most, only twelve by seven feet in its largest section and not more than three and a half feet deep. In it the big net must somehow be contained.

Vicente Domingo Pineiro, the *Terra*'s *contramaestre* (bosun of the deck), makes the sign of the cross as he descends into the pit, much like a bullfighter stepping into the ring. He has his reasons. Although an experienced hand, Pineiro is new to the *Terra* on this trip. Minor accidents and more confusion seem to be the rule when he is in charge, whereas the work flows more smoothly and is almost trouble-free when he is relieved by Fructuoso Pineiro Sendón, the shaven-headed bosun's mate of the dockside processional and no relation, who is very popular with the deckhands. It is quite possible, of course, that the men are still testing their new leader rather severely before they entrust him with their full confidence. (Or their lives, in a very real sense.) The practice is common enough, in truth, among deckhands of many nations.

El Morocho, who is also in the pit, now leans out over the low rail. He is trying to throw a strop — a continuous or spliced loop of heavy rope — around the column of netting suspended from the mast. On the third try he succeeds. Vicente, the bosun, catches the other end. The two men then quickly wrap it around the net, twist or dogear the loop ends, and hang them on a hook coming down in a fall from the mast. The hooked section is winched up as high as possible and halted, while El Morocho and the bosun throw another strop around a lower section of the netting that is now down on the rail. Then, in a coordinated action, one winch operator lets down the upper portion while the other hoists up the lower. So the big net inches aboard, like a caterpillar climbing the mast.

Strop and hoist, strop and hoist. The process is repeated ten times before the long headline — it carries no fewer than two hundred floats — is all safely aboard. Simultaneously, the first bobbins of the groundrope begin to appear. It is now that the bystander cannot help but worry. The smaller bobbins weigh 154 pounds; the larger ones used near the center or bosom of the groundrope, called *diablos,* 240. They dangle precariously right over the pit. The men working underneath them become noticeably nervous. You can tell by the way they steal quick upward glances or offer a steady torrent of advice to both the winch operators and the extra hands who are trying to control the swing of the big "devils" with guy lines.

"*¡Vira, vira* [Heave away, heave away]!"

"*¡Arría, arría* [Let fall, let fall]!"

"*¡Cornudo* [Prick]! Mother of God, watch what you are doing!"

The tempo, the shouting pick up again. The last of the larger bobbins are overhead. Spreading out on deck like a giant and high-crowned mushroom is the pile of netting, which has now far out-grown the pit. The men have to climb over it as they run about, stumbling frequently.

Back aft the winch men continue their patient work, unmindful of the general commotion and deliberately ignoring every bit of advice. They are stationed at two small "gypsies," or running winches, universally considered the most dangerous items of equipment on any fishing vessel, and thus cannot permit themselves the slightest distraction. The gypsies work very simply, by the winding of more cable turns around the constantly revolving winch drums in order to hoist, less to slack or let down, and just the right number to slip on the drum surfaces and hold a load stationary. The work is tiring — the cable alone, without the effort of pulling, weighs about fifteen pounds per yard — and requires constant attention to both the run of the wire and the rolling of the ship. If the latter is ignored while lowering, for example, a cluster of the big bobbins may swing into the mast, jump the hook, and fall to the deck with a crash. Or, should the operator take off one turn too many, the cable either runs completely out of control or slips for a distance and then catches again, creating recoils and whiplashes that cut down any men or machinery in its way. Then, too, there is a special inferno, a separate category of dangers, for the operators themselves. Winch accidents are many, but the worst of them occurs when a man catches his fingers or even the tips of his rubber glove under a turn of cable he has just wound on. By this very act the cable has better purchase, and the man will nearly always "be taken around," as British fishermen say, or yanked about by the full length of his arm and repeatedly slammed to the deck before someone else can get to the winch motor and turn it off. This accident, needless to say, is sometimes fatal.

"All running gear is dangerous," José Antonio is telling me. "But the two men we have on the *muñones* are good. They know their trade."

*Muñón* is the Spanish word for a gypsy winch. It also means the stump of an amputated limb.

"Look, there it comes!" Captain Manolo suddenly shouts. "Look how it boils!"

After some twenty strops, the end is in sight. A great froth of bubbles — a veritable boil, as Manolo keeps repeating, emanating from the ruptured swimbladders of thousands of fish — is now roiling the surface. Seconds later, the big *saco,* the cod end itself, shoots up into sight. It heaves up and down, almost bouncing at the surface, and then settles low in the water. Waves now break over it as though it were a small island in the sea, and the shear-waters soon home in on it, fairly screaming with excitement. All work stops. The men line the rails to study the bag or look for subtle indications of the size and composition of the catch.

"It is very dirty!" shouts one. "Look at all the *platuxa.*" He is using the Galician and Basque word for flounders and other flat-fish.

"It is too soon to say," José Antonio observes from the bridge porch. "There may be big cod inside."

"Joseán, you are right!" says Manolo. "Look how low the bag is in the water. That is the sign of big fish, of quality fish! If they were small, the bag would float higher."

Presently the splitting strop that will close off the rear part of the cod end is within reach. It is hitched to heavy cables running from double blocks at the masthead and wound around the port-side gypsy winch, this time with extra care and some spare hands to tail or help pull the cable end. Slowly a compact ball, packed tightly with about eight tons of fish, comes up over the side. Men immediately grab it by the mesh and attach lines to control its swing. Young José Francisco Carames, the best of the winch operators, gently lets the ball down close to the edge of an open hatch. El Morocho darts under it, watching it carefully for any slight movement, and snatches a loop in the purse line at its bottom. The line is tied with a series of loops in the *nudo de cadena,* an ingenious chain knot. It will never give under pressure, but a sharp pull on any one of the loops will untie it all. This El Morocho now does; eight tons of fish cascade down to the deck below. Immediately other deckhands begin to retie the knot, since there are more fish to haul up from the forepart of the cod end and the extension piece still in the water. Some of the fish can be seen through the mesh, gently finning the water or swimming in confused circles. They are quality fish — big cod of thirty or forty pounds — just as Manolo predicted. Twice more the emptied cod end goes overboard. Twice more the eight-ton balls are carefully hoisted.

It is all done. After one hour and ten minutes, the haulback is finished. For one more time, the largest ground trawl used in fishing has been taken aboard one of the smallest of deck spaces.

"It is twenty-four tons easily," says one of the deckhands. "And maybe eight salted down." The others agree. It is a fair catch, not at all bad for the time and place.

"You know, you really haven't brought us any bad luck yet," José Antonio says to me very suddenly. The intense look is there again and his tone is serious, as though he fully expected I might.

The mood at the supper table is exuberant; the talk is all of a short campaign. The *Terra* and *Nova* left Spain on the thirteenth of April, the men are telling me, and then, in the usual trip pattern of the pairs, fished for a month off Norway before coming to the Grand Banks. The normal expectation would therefore be to return to Spain by mid-September or October. But now a four-month campaign seems at least possible, given a little more fishing like today's. Even as we are talking Ignacio ("Ñaqui") Leceta Echebeste comes down from the bridge to report that the *Nova*'s net is already well set on a smooth bottom and that our sonar echograph and cathode-tube fishfinder are both showing very good signs. Ñaqui Leceta is a youthful-looking Basque, thirty-five years of age, who serves as the *timonel,* or first mate, of the *Terra.* He is already dreaming of getting home by late August, he claims, in which case the first thing he will do is go to the beach with his family. "I will simply lie in the sun and let my children throw sand all over me," Ñaqui says. "I tell you, there is no greater joy in this world than to watch the little ones at the beach, making their cakes and castles in the sand."

Chief Manuel is not so sure about an early return. He has seen too many moments of fleeting euphoria and knows better than to make predictions based on a single day of fair fishing. But he will go along with the spirit of the occasion. If the *Terra* and the *Nova* get home before September the thirteenth, which is his birthday, he will treat all hands to a party.

"Fine with me," replies José Antonio. "You know I don't like to put dates on things, but let us drink anyway to an early return." He lifts his glass of the bottled spring water that is part of the diet and health program he has pledged to observe on this campaign, along with a personal supply of fresh fruits and some dumbbells for exercising.

"And what are you doing drinking water at a time like this?" Manolo asks both José Antonio and Chief Manuel. As a matter of principle, Manuel drinks very little at sea. "You know what I say about that?"

Captain Manolo lifts his hand as though calling a meeting to order. He recites another verse.

| | |
|---|---|
| *¿Agua clara y cristalina?* | *Water so clear and crystal?* |
| *Madre de ranas y sapos,* | *It is the mother of frogs and toads,* |
| *donde se lavan los trapos!* | *a place to wash old clothes!* |
| *¿Quieres que la beba yo?* | *Do you wish that I should drink it?* |
| *¡No! Aguardiente y vino puro* | *No! Rather, strong spirits and fine wines,* |
| *de ese que beben los reyes.* | *Like those that are fit for kings.* |
| *El agua es para los bueyes* | *Water is for the oxen,* |
| *que tienen el cuero duro.* | *oxen with thick hides.* |

"A pretty verse, but here is the truth of the matter," Manuel replies. "Here is what we say in Galicia about drinking, in our own language: *'Eu bebo para afogar as penas, mais as condenadas vienen aboiar* [I drink to drown the sorrows, but the damnable things float right back up]!' Now that is a truthful saying!"

But tonight both the *patrón* and the chief engineer will make an exception to their regimens, given the occasion. Quickly searching in the clinking cabinet, Captain Manolo finds a bottle of sparkling wine — *Carbomas Vino Gasificado–Reserva Especial,* the label reads — and pours glasses for all, including Paco, the *marmitón.* There follows much joking about Manolo's endless store of poetry, songs, and fable. What about *"Terra Nova,"* Ñaqui Leceta asks him, or the song of his own composition? Manolo is reluctant. It is a small thing without great merit, he protests, which simply came to him one night on a lonely watch.

"But if you insist, here it is, original music and lyrics by Nautical Captain Manuel López Muñiz," he finally says, laughing. Then, becoming more serious and using the style of the *cante hondo,* he sings:

| | |
|---|---|
| *No sabemos cuando es fiesta o domingo;* | *Sundays or holidays pass all the same.* |
| *Terra Nova no se trata de disfraces,* | *Newfoundland is not for costumes or disguises,* |
| *como algunos que en España se divierten* | *as of those who in Spain amuse themselves* |
| *alternando por las boites y esos bailes.* | *in a round of dancing and pubs.* |
| *¡Marineros, pescadores,* | *Seamen, fishermen!* |
| *que no saben lo que es vivir,* | *You who do not know what it is to live,* |
| *hay que venir aquí!* | *here you must come!* |

A burst of *ole*'s and exaggerated applause greet Manolo's rendition. José Antonio and Chief Manuel lift their token glasses. All hands drink to a short campaign and to the seas where men must come to learn about life.

One deck below, neither poetry nor inhibitions about drinking form any part of the crew's supper. The *Terra*'s total complement numbers twenty-four persons; twenty of them dine in the crew's mess at two separate sittings. The deckhands usually eat first, very quickly, washing down their meals with wine and cognac. The wine is dispensed from a 4,000-gallon tank. The men fill their leather *botas* at its tap, and the cook, who traditionally gets a percentage from all alcoholic-beverage sales, keeps their accounts on a small blackboard hung near the galley entrance. Cognac, by contrast, is bought in turn by the different crew members who like it. One bottle, at least, is always in a holding rack on the table; it is invariably capped with a pouring spout of the kind used in bars. The latter is both for hygiene and ease of consumption, since the men shoot the cognac in a stream into their open mouths, just as they do with their leather wine bags. Not so hygienic is the between-meals snack box, a battered aluminum baking tin containing long-opened cans of sardines and anchovies, leftover bread, cheeses, and pieces of *chorizo,* the ubiquitous Spanish sausage. It is also the home for various forms of insect life — fruit flies, roaches, and a hardy strain of the common housefly — which have defied all the cook's efforts at extermination.

After supper most of the deckhands will take a short break in their quarters before returning to the chores of cleaning the day's catch. (Spanish pair trawlers have neither a factory nor a separate category of workers to handle the fish.) Tonight, as is his custom, Fructuoso Pineiro Sendón stretches out full length on the hard floor of his cabin, still wearing his oilskins. Fructuoso, who takes heroic drafts of both wine and cognac with every meal, says he does this not to fall completely asleep, since others have complained that he is impossible to wake up once he gets in his bunk. The younger men go to the "rancho grande," a six-bunk cabin, the largest on the *Terra,* to play their latest tape-cassette selections of Elton John, Pink Floyd, and *Seemon y Garfunkel,* as they pronounce it. And, perhaps, as their mood dictates, to smoke a little grass.

No bell or loudspeaker announcement signals the return to work. After ten or fifteen minutes the men's aching bones will tell them. The faster they get the work done, they all know, the sooner they will gain the soothing balm of true rest and sleep.

El Morocho and his gang get up first, stumbling heavily from their bunks. They turn off their tape players, shake Fructuoso and other dozers awake, and stop by the galley to refill their wine bags and stuff their pockets with snacks. Thus provisioned, they file wearily into a long, low-ceilinged, and noisy room under what is almost the full length of the main deck. This is the *Terra*'s "factory," the place where most of the crew spend their longest hours. Ironically, in vocabulary that seems to borrow from the Soviets, it is officially called *el parque de trabajo* (the park of labor) in the ship's plans. But the men have forgotten this full designation. To them it is simply "the park," and they often complain that it should be much better provided with work-saving devices to merit its name. What it does have are three early Baader machines; the first is a nobber, or beheader, the second is a machine to remove the cod's spine for what is known as a butterfly or lapped cut, and the third is a water-sprayed tumbling barrel to give the fish a final cleansing before they go to the salters. For the rest, the *parque* provides space in its forward half for receiving fish through two deck hatches and in its after section for a large wooden table with various holes cut in it. In these two areas most of the men are occupied. The *tronchadores* (cutters), stand forward, waist-deep in the fish, pushing them back toward the big table, culling out the trash species and deftly splitting the bellies of the cod. They then heave the split cod on to the table, where two or three *destripadores* (gutters) stand like jack-in-the-boxes in the small holes cut in its surface. (Indeed, these men must crawl under the table on their hands and knees to reach their stations.) The *destripadores* yank out the fishes' innards with one great downward tug — large fish, however, may require two or three — and then slam them down on the table near two men working the machines. The two machine operators keep their positions throughout the campaign, although their jobs require much less lifting and muscular strain. No one begrudges them the lighter work, the others will tell you, because both are recognized as having "the fastest hands." This means they can double-load the machines, putting two fish in revolving brackets or guides intended only for one. To speed up the work is the paramount objective, all agree, and thus it wouldn't do to suggest a change.

This evening the *parque* is still three or four feet deep in fish, although the crew worked the catch for two hours before supper. The men are discouraged. It is not so much that they know they are in for a long night, but rather because a careful look at the remaining fish suggests that the normal three-to-one ratio of tons in the net to salted cod in the *bodega* will not obtain tonight. Big cod there are in quantity, but there are also too many flatfish — good yellowtail flounder, witches, even some dab — which, of course, will all go overboard. Subtract this incidental catch and the cods' loss of weight during curing and it will be four tons of dried cod, rather than the expected eight, when the fish are unloaded for market. This at least is the opinion of Norberto ("Polo") Beceiro, the veteran *jefe salador* (chief salter) of the *Terra,* and on such matters the men never dispute him. Polo has been examining catches and calculating their dried weight for some thirty-five years. Ever since the age of twelve, in fact, when he was orphaned and first sent to sea.

"Look at all the *platuxa!*" says José Francisco Carames, the winch operator, as he alternately throws the cod to the gutting table and the flounders onto a waste-disposal conveyor belt. "What a crime, with all the hunger in this world!"

"If we only had a small freezer, like some of the *bous,*" adds El Morocho.

It is a common refrain. For many years Spanish fishermen have shown far more sensitivity to the wastefulness of the pairs than either their owners or the Spanish government, who should have been the most concerned. There are good reasons for this. The fishermen know what the fleet owners and government officials do not: namely, that many other ships have watched them for a long time. Too often Spanish pair trawlermen have seen their colleagues of other nations shake their fists in silence as their ships passed close in crowded waters, while the *parejas* left their telltale wake of discarded flatfish, pollock, redfish, and even the prized haddock. There is not one among the *Terra*'s crew, in fact, who does not harbor the uneasy feeling that someday soon such practices will work to their prejudice.

José Antonio believes the time has already come. He sighs as he thinks about the closure of New England waters. The northern tip of Georges Bank was the favored winter ground of the pairs, a place you could count on for big cod, but now the Spanish have no quota for cod or any other market fish on Georges. Instead, Spain's total allowable catch in all American waters is a mere 1,500 tons of butterfish, a small and little-valued species, and 5,000 tons of squid. To be sure, José Antonio explains, squid commands a good price in Spain, but it requires different gear or, if one is to be really successful, the specialized new squid trawlers some owners have recently built. That is the reason, he thinks, why the Spanish government may push for some kind of joint venture with the Americans for New England squid. But, as usual, no one is doing anything for the pairs.

"And look what is happening here!" José Antonio adds. "You can see for yourself how empty are the horizons. Right now there are only twelve other Spanish pairs fishing the Grand Banks. It's nothing like times past, but already the Canadians are talking about reducing our quota by another thirty percent next year! And who knows what the Norwegians will do?"

But, of course, José Antonio admits, the owners have not had much incentive to do anything about the wasteful practices of pair fishing. Dried *bacalao* remains a delicacy in Spain with high market value; the current rate for large and well-cured cod is up to seventy-five pesetas: (approximately one U.S. dollar) a pound. With prices like that, José Antonio insists, there is not much reason to bother with freezers for flounders and other species that command little favor on the market.

Then, too, José Antonio believes that Spanish underreporting of catches has been just as damaging as the dumping. He is quite frank about this, as are other *patrones* and nautical captains, describing it as chronic and widespread. There are various explanations, to be sure. Some *patrones* say the owners don't want them to radio back accurate estimates when the fishing is good, since both the domestic and international competition will always be listening. Others point out that their income taxes are computed on the estimated tonnage of each trip, rather than what the dried and boxed fish may later fetch on the market. This being so, they add, to make "high" and more realistic estimates is simply to cut one's own fingers, as the saying goes.

"The other countries do much the same," José Antonio says, as we talk alone on the bridge. "But all the Spanish — the pairs, the *bous,* and the big stern trawlers — have lied so much about their catches for so long that the ICNAF officials caught on to it years ago. And now the Canadians will remember this."

"Please try to understand," he adds in afterthought. "In such matters I do not consider myself Spanish. We Basques are more direct, more bound to our word. I do not volunteer information, but if someone asks me how much fish I have, I tell them truthfully."

It is a fair statement, confirmed by my own observation and that of the crew, who speak of their *patrón* as one of few but honest words. Even as José Antonio says it, however, his face darkens and the steely gaze returns. He is thinking of his Basque homeland and the current troubles there.

"Look," he says very slowly, "we Basques are a united people. If some among us have needs, we share what we have. We are not like the Galicians, who have more lawyers than any other province and will go to court for a cow. We have been given no institutes, no university, but we know what it is to work. I tell you, we Basques are willing to remain under the flag of Spain, but only if we have autonomy. A true economic autonomy, that is, which gives us all we deserve for supporting the rest of the country.

"And for this hope our people suffer," José Antonio concludes. Once again I have the impression of something held back, of someone trying to keep stronger emotions in check. But that is all he will say.

Polo Beceiro, the chief salter, comes up to the bridge, doffing his leather cap deferentially. José Antonio asks him what good news he brings, slapping the older man on the back and playfully rubbing the stubble of his short and graying hair. José Antonio respects Polo and welcomes his ritual visits to the bridge.

"Four sleeping, boss, four sleeping," Polo replies. It is his standard form of reporting. By this he means that all of today's cod have not only been cleaned, but also carefully "buried" or "put to sleep," as he likes to say, in the salt of the *bodega,* and that their dried weight will indeed be no more than four tons.

Outside the last of the flounders from the *parque*'s discharge port float away luminously on the dark swells, now dimpled with a hissing rain.

The next day the fishing improves. The *Nova*'s early-morning haulback produces a commendable thirty tons, and now, with our net out, the echograph is tracing a series of fish signs in the form of jagged peaks just above a fairly smooth bottom. The signs are "mountains," "a veritable *cordillera*" to Ñaqui Leceta, who is beside himself with excitement. A number of the peaks, he is eager to point out, have little white spaces or hollows in their centers. These are the surest signs of great masses of fish, since they appear only when the fish are so densely concentrated that the echo signals cannot fully penetrate the mountains' interiors, but instead, so to speak, ricochet off their outer slopes.

But although the fishing has improved, it has taken us into more rocky grounds. *Embarres,* as the Spanish call rimracks or hangups, are becoming annoyingly frequent. They shake the *Terra* from stem to stern — most pair trawlers have no tension bollards or other devices to absorb the shock — and in the worst of cases they can force both boats to stop, turn around, and steam down the full length of the towing cables so that a freeing tug can be applied in the opposite direction from the tow. Although this maneuver has not yet been necessary, we have had a number of severe jolts, very worrying to Ñaqui. Further, the weather is puzzling. Last night's rain has given way to overcast and a totally windless sea, disturbed only by a few storm petrels delicately plucking minute food particles from the placid surface. Large rafts of shearwaters float by on the oily swells; nothing, not even the rich effluvium of the *Nova*'s *parque* discharge, will inspire them to attempt flight without the help of any wind. But the calm sea may be deceptive. The barometer is falling slightly. Before dying out, the wind was from the northeast, an unusual quarter. Even the most experienced hands are not sure what to make of it.

By midmorning the echograph tracings continue strong, but so, too, do the jolts of momentary *embarres* or hangups, any one of which can mean a torn net. Ñaqui Leceta cannot stand it any longer. He sends a man below to wake up the *patrón de pesca*. José Antonio listens patiently to Ñaqui's report and then quickly makes his decision. We will haul back our net, although the tow has not gone three hours.

As the haul nears completion, the men pause as usual to look for the surging "float" of the cod end. It does not appear. Then, as though a further portent of troubles to come, much of the net is fouled with pieces of *trasmallo,* the gill netting of fine twine which the Portuguese set over rocky grounds. José Antonio is annoyed, not so much because it will require a little time to cut the netting away, but rather because he wishes the Portuguese would stay up at the Virgin Rocks. The latter are among the loneliest sentinels in the North Atlantic: a low-tide outcropping of rocks, the only such on the Grand Banks, one hundred miles due east of Cape Race. Beginning in the late 1960s the Portuguese began converting their dory schooners, shorn of masts and supplied with better engines, to carry motor launches for the setting of gill nets around these rocks, where the bottom is so foul as to preclude any possibility of ground trawling. (The largest of these ships, some newly built for the purpose, may have as many as five or six launches, each one with one hundred nets.) I had heard Canadian authorities describe this as a model fishery in which the Portuguese tended their nets night and day and were always careful to take them in before bad weather. As a result, the experts said, the Portuguese were rewarded with large and very clean catches of big cod, in good condition. But not one of the *Terra*'s crew believes this. All too frequently their trawls have come up with Portuguese gill nets that have gone adrift in stiff weather. Sometimes it is a whole net or a curtain of drowned cod and other fish — white, swollen, and still imprisoned by their gills in the twists of the mesh — not to mention murres, puffins, or other diving birds, which can be similarly entangled. On other occasions a ground trawl will pick up the heavy grapnel anchors by which these nets are moored, which, of course, cause bad tears. And, as the evidence before us now suggests, the Portuguese over the years have extended their gill netting far and wide from the Virgin Rocks, from which we are now one hundred and fifty miles distant.

After a few strops and heaves, the men's worst suspicions are confirmed. The groundline of the *Terra*'s net is parted in two and a long tear extends deep down the belly and into the extension piece. In the twisted and collapsed cod end there is not even a ton of fish.

"Oh, my heart is going *tric-trac, tric-trac!*" Ñaqui Leceta confides to me, adding that he feels the mishap was probably his fault. He might have called José Antonio or himself ordered a haulback much sooner.

"What a disaster!" says Captain Manolo, who has been aroused from his morning sleep by the commotion. "What disillusion! What have we done to deserve such bad luck?"

"Listen, there are no such things as misfortunes or bad luck in this trade," José Antonio replies very sternly. "Events happen and one must confront them."

He sets the crew to net repair and orders both boats to stop their engines. It will be many hours before the *Nova* can finish with her thirty-ton catch, and it would be too much for her crew to interrupt their labors, set their net, and then possibly have to deal with another large catch before the first one was processed.

In the afternoon the rain returns and surly little whitecaps begin to stir the surface. I have been given the bridge watch with orders to keep an eye on the radar — a few other pairs and one or two Russian factory trawlers have entered the area — and to consult with the *Nova* in case anyone appears to be bearing down on us. Or call José Antonio, who himself is out on deck leading all available hands in the repair of the net.

The *Terra* rolls heavily, dead drift to the swells. Both the wind and the rain are mounting — the latter is now almost horizontal—and the visibility is poor. Vicente, the *contramaestre*, who has suffered an arm injury, joins me on the bridge. He has come to listen to the Spanish fishermen's hour, one of a number of foreign language programs broadcast especially for the Grand Banks fleets once a week by Radio Saint-Pierre and Miquelon. But today the Spanish hour carries a melancholy note. Earlier in the week, as we had heard it, a man named Suárez on a neighboring pair had slipped in the pit and had his chest crushed by a swinging cod end. Now, the resident Spanish priest at the Stella Maris Seaman's Home brings the sad news that he has died in the St. Pierre hospital from his injuries. The priest suggests that all who knew the deceased write to his family in Spain. Then, requesting a moment's silence of all his listeners, he recites the classic Spanish seaman's prayer, so moving in its brevity and simplicity:

| | |
|---|---|
| *Tu que dispones de tierra y mar,* | *You who rule the sea and the shore,* |
| *haces la calma y la tempestad;* | *making the calms and the tempests, too,* |
| *ten de nosotros, Señor, piedad.* | *grant us thy mercy, O 'Lord.* |
| *¡Piedad, Señor! ¡Señor, piedad!* | *Thy mercy, O Lord! Lord, mercy!* |

The prayer is followed by verses from Rosalía Castro, a nineteenth-century poet revered almost as a saint in her native Galicia, against a background of regional music. The verses are in Galician or that strange confluence of two languages, as much Portuguese as Spanish, which on this occasion seems to have been especially created for the poetry of sorrow:

| | |
|---|---|
| *Non m'olvides, queridiña,* | *Do not forget me, dear one,* |
| *si morro de soidás . . .* | *if in solitude I die . . .* |
| *tantas légoas mar adentro . . .* | *many leagues distant, far at sea . . .* |
| *¡Miña casiña!, ¡meu lar!* | *Oh, my home! Oh, my hearth!* |
| | |
| *Airiños, airiños aires,* | *Gentle breezes, gentle winds,* |
| *airiños d'a miña terra;* | *winds of my native land;* |
| *airiños, airiños aires,* | *gentle breezes, gentle winds,* |
| *airiños, leváime á ela!* | *carry me there!* |

Outside the rain slants harder. Vicente the *contramaestre*, a gruff and heavy-set individual who worries continually about his problems with the younger deckhands, is staring through one of the "clear-viewers," the motor-driven circular panes of glass installed in all bridge windows to spin off ice or rain. Rosalía Castro's verses roll on, to the cadence of soft drumbeats and the soaring wails of Galician bagpipes. The heavy lurching of a ship without way continues, rhythmic, monotonous, and uncomfortable. The clear-view pane, which is not operating properly, contributes a high-pitched whine.

Five or six hours later Captain Manolo is taking over the late-night watch from José Antonio. This is normally Manolo's happiest hour, when he plots the *Terra's* course with professional pride, tidies up the logbook entries, and, if his mood is especially buoyant, gives discreet bits of fishing information by radio to other pairs on which he has close friends or relatives. But tonight he shares the general gloom, which has run through the *Terra* like a deadening virus. He talks first of the high losses among pairs, citing the fact that he, José Antonio, and Chief Manuel have all endured shipwreck, fire, or sinking. And as for Ñaqui, the *timonel,* only a chance or temporary assignment teaching the Canadians pair trawling saved him from going down with the *Beizama,* his last boat before the *Terra,* which sank twenty miles from St. John's from rust-weakened plates and a lack of adequate pumps. But of course, Manolo emphasizes, it was even worse in the old days, as, for example, when the aftermath of the Civil War forced him to sea at the age of fifteen.

"I was eleven when the War began and you cannot believe the hunger there was in the north," Manolo is saying. "My family says that I was a true *señorito,* a young boy of endearing appearance. So, while others had to go into the fields to rob, I went about barefoot in short pants and got gifts of food from the older people who were sorry for me. I always shared these, of course. My mother died in 1938, and two years later my father, who was a stoker, told me to go to sea. He said fishing was the only remedy, the only way out. I seldom saw him, since he was away so much. Just to show you how it was in those days, he lived through seven shipwrecks, three times long in the water. But I took his advice."

Captain Manolo believes he was very fortunate in having as a friend a rich lady in San Sebastián who gave him some tutoring as a boy and later, during his military service in the navy, a captain who took a kindly interest in him and gave him the most thorough professional training.

"I have always had the desire to learn and advanced very rapidly," he continues. "This is how it came about that I was once *patrón* on a small boat on which my father was fireman. When I whistled down the speaking tube to the engine room he would ask '¿*Qué mande, Señor* [your order, sir]?' I would plead with him to stop it. I would cry 'Papá, it is me, your own son!' But he would always answer, 'Here there is no "papa"; there is only one who knows his duty and carries out orders.' I supported him in his later years, when he was not well, and he died in my home. Perhaps he was not happy in those years, being a proud man, but I know that he was very pleased with my advancement.

"Well, our time is short, and it is true that we pass quietly enough through this world," Manolo concludes. "Think of it this way. If this boat sinks and we all die, my wife and children will weep. Your wife and children will also weep. Save for those few, we pass unnoticed. But consider the death of some third-rate *politico!* The nation mourns him and the press is full of platitudes about his presumed virtues. But are we not just as good men as he? And is not a pine box just as good as cedar or mahogany?"

"There it comes!" shouts Ñaqui Leceta. "I knew it would be so. The *lupita* has been going *pla, pla, pla* all morning, making the strongest signs!"

"Most holy Mother, look at the froth, look at the bubbles!" Manolo is exclaiming. "It is like a purgative from the deep, a giant biocarbonate of soda!"

"Bread of our children!" says Chief Manuel. "I have not seen such a float since times long past."

Another huge bag — over sixty tons for sure, both José Antonio and Polo Beceiro agree — is coming to the surface. Nearly all the crew is watching at the rail. Although most have been on their feet for over twenty-four hours, they are cheering loudly in Spanish, Galician, or Basque. As the final strops draw the cod end closer, it is easy to see that the male cod have gorged on capelin and the females are heavy with roe.

Up through a skylight on the poop deck, through all the shouting, comes the voice of Juan Castro, the *Terra*'s masterful cook. Although pots and pans slide back and forth in the galley and some flour sacks have broken loose and spilled all over his pantry, he is singing brisk *pasos dobles* and Argentine tangos at the top of his lungs. A hard-working man whose best efforts approach true *haute cuisine* (handicapped, however, by the use of olive oil for cooking everything from breakfast eggs to dessert pastries, since the *Terra* carries not an ounce of butter), Juan Castro is seldom seen anywhere except at his galley stove or asleep in his bunk. But within minutes, this morning, the excitement of the haulback is too much. Juan Castro makes a rare appearance on deck.

"*Sí, Señor,* we have come to good fishing," he says to me. "But the boys will have much work and soon they will be hungry. *Sí, Señor,* in the galley we also serve!"

The latter is one of Juan Castro's two most repeated statements, apart from observations on the daily menu or the state of supplies in his tiny pantry. Like many other ship's cooks, he has been a deckhand in his time and wants it clearly understood that galley work is as hard as any. The other, which he pronounces much more frequently, is that he feels sure that this will be his last trip. He has worked hard all of his life, he will tell you, not wasting a centavo on drink or other bad habits. Now he has two apartments purchased as investments in his native city of Ponte Vedra, owns a good automobile, and is building a vacation home — a *chaletecito* he calls it, always using the diminutive — high in the mountains of Galicia.

"Oh, yes, I think this will be my last voyage," he now repeats. "If the Good Lord permits us more such fishing, I will go home and finish my *chaletecito*. *!Sí, Señor!*"

"Great mother of whores, what big fish!" says one deckhand. The cod end is now alongside, and the segmented hoisting of its contents has begun.

"I told you Joseán was right to move here after the rain," Captain Manolo whispers to me in conspiratorial tones, as though somewhere in the empty sea competitors might somehow be eavesdropping. "At this time the fish are not quiet as in winter. They are restless, waiting for the capelin, and even a slight change in the weather can set them moving. All this Joseán knows better than any."

Here is the Platier, a small ground known only to the older Grand Banks fishing nations. Two days earlier José Antonio, growing restive with the frequent *embarres* and the arrival of more trawlers, had decided to abandon our former position east of Whale Deep. At the time he complained he could "go only by the loran in my head," meaning that he sorely missed his carefully compiled notebook of good bearings, seasonal fish movements, and other vital observations, lost to the fire on the *Isla St. Pierre*. Nevertheless, he is telling me this morning, something far back in his memory convinced him it was time to steam sixty miles east to the Platier. Something, he adds, that was perhaps stirred by a small chart still in his possession entitled *Région du Platier — Office Scientifique et Technique des Pêches Maritimes,* made by the French in the 1930s, which he now constantly studies. A marvel of detail, the small chart not only delineates the nature of the bottom, from mud to sand to dangerous rock needles, but also shows the benthic fauna with little schematic drawings — *étoiles de mer, éponges de pain d'épicier, coques noires,* and *holothuries patates* are especially prominent — wherever they exist in sufficient concentrations to clog a trawl. Surprisingly, these bottom-dwelling invertebrates seem to be almost exactly where they were forty years ago, when the chart was made, and it has proved very useful in avoiding them. Especially is this true of the heavy *holothuries patates,* the sea cucumbers (the Spanish, like the French, call them "potatoes," which they much more closely resemble) that can crowd together in great agglutinated masses, big enough to burst a cod end.

The result, in consequence, is a fisherman's dream. We have found the first schools of offshore spawning capelin and not another vessel is anywhere in sight or radar range. Now, for the third day, cod are coming together from every point in the compass, homing in on the greatest of their seasonal delicacies. So, too, do great humpback whales in surprising number. Although the humpbacks are toothless baleen whales, they readily ingest the little capelin in gentle surface glides or easy dives, occasionally breaking the water with startling acrobatic leaps in ecstatic celebration, one supposes, of feasting on such easy prey. No more dead flounders foul our wake. As yet only the cod are chasing down the capelin, and our catches are ninety-nine percent clean. All the signs attest to it. We are in the right place at the right time.

Minor ancillary problems, nevertheless, seem to be developing. Some are merely amusing; others, potentially troublesome. One is that my presence on board has come to be regarded as a force for good. Earlier, Captain Manolo had counseled me very carefully about the rigid codes of superstition among Spanish fishermen. There were words never to be uttered — "priest" being the worst,[2] followed closely by "snake" and "fox" — and actions or initiatives to be avoided at all costs, such as spilling olive oil, which causes some captains to return to port, or predicting the weather, which most often brings a turn for the worse, with all blame attaching to the prognosticator. But now he throws all caution to the winds. "You have brought us great fortune and you must stay with us for all the campaign," Manolo is the first to cry. Everyone else, from engine-room greasers to José Antonio, heartily agrees. I am the talisman. The men may joke as they say so, of course, but there is an undertone of sincerity, of true pleading, in all the requests that I remain.

A more serious problem is that the almost endless hours of work are now producing small signs of stress and tension, underneath the soaring morale and the cheers for swollen cod ends. The reason is not hard to discern. Properly speaking, Spanish pair trawlers have no watch system at all (except for the bridge and the engine

---

2. A carryover from earlier years when fleet chaplains went to sea, circuit-riding from one vessel to another. Spanish fishermen never liked this practice — for them priests were too often associated with last rites — and they therefore coined substitute words or phrases to avoid referring to the visiting *padres* as such.

room, where at least one man is always on duty), and their crews work as much and for as long as is necessary, which on occasions like the present may extend to an unbroken forty-eight hours. And in every capacity. There is a tacit understanding that anyone temporarily idled will pitch in with the job at hand, without loudspeaker announcements or the summons of the bosun. On the *Terra* this means, for example, that Paco, the *marmitón,* will replace José Francisco Carames at the gypsy winch when the latter is dangerously tired and must go below for a snack. Or that greasers and salters do a turn in the *parque* when not occupied with their normal duties. Even José Antonio, model *patrón* that he always is, will go down and slice cod bellies as deftly as anyone, when the fish lie too deep in the hold.

The tension comes during the long hours, therefore, when rightly or wrongly some begin to suspect that others are coasting or making less than a full effort. On the *Terra* such suspicions most often arise between the two age groups. Last night, for example, Captain Manolo was twice called down to the *parque* by some of the older men, who complained that the younger deckhands were yelling their heads off from too much wine or marijuana, throwing fish at each other, and generally making tomfoolery of the work.

This morning, as if in direct challenge to the elders, El Morocho and his gang in the *rancho grande* have a new sign on their cabin door. *El Pub,* it proclaims in huge letters, along with such standard storefront advertising slogans as *¡Hay de todo!* (we have it all!) and *Tenemos surtidos* (wide assortment). Dominating the sign is a realistic sketch of a hookah or water pipe, with a smoking tube labeled for each of the cabin occupants, who are also listed as "proprietors."

Captain Manolo and Chief Manuel do not like this, but José Antonio, although aware of the younger men's habits and their occasional mischiefs belowdecks, is not much concerned. All such things are merely the excesses of youth, he insists, which can be conquered by setting a good example or working alongside them. And, of course, knowing when to stop, before driving the men to the point of perilous exhaustion. After all, José Antonio points out, there has not been a serious accident thus far in the campaign, which in itself is a considerable achievement. Nor have the deckhands ever balked at turning out, even after only two or three hours of sleep, as is now more and more the case.

As the days and nights roll by, José Antonio's work ethic is sorely tested. But, true to his self-imposed standards, he is out on deck for every set or haul and down in the *parque* for every big catch. Sometimes, as in his own words, he will indeed "know when to stop," ordering both boats to lie to the swells for four or five hours of rest for all hands. At other times he pushes the men hard. Most often this is for a reason they well understand, as when an exceptional haul fills the *parque* to the brim before all the fish have been emptied from the net. In such event the deckhands must stop their work and go below to help. Meanwhile, if the ground is at all shoal, sections of the huge net will be dragging and chafing on the bottom. Should this continue for more than an hour, the fish that remain inside will be much bruised and *patrones* will begin to worry. Severely bruised fish will have such soft flesh that they will not cure well in the salt; they may even spoil the curing of other fish stored near them. Rather than incur this risk, *patrones* will reluctantly order the bottom-dragging net hoisted and its contents dumped overboard.

More than once in the last few days the men have labored feverishly to avoid the loss of a dumping, going for long stretches with neither sleep nor rest. At such times the piercing shriek of the de-spining machine is more and more heard, as tired operators position the fish improperly and the machine's rotating blades cut through rather than around backbones. It is like the noise of a sawmill, reaching every part of the ship.

Food is provided when the men need it, at any hour, and they no longer know or care whether they are sitting down to breakfast, luncheon, or supper. Coming straight from the *parque,* they have clots of dried fish blood on their faces and are too tired to remove their oilskins or the gauze bandages around their wrists, which protect them from sand and other irritants in the cod bellies or the constant chafing of their oilskin cuffs. As they wait their turn to be served in the narrow passageway leading to the galley, the men bend over so that their hips rest on one bulkhead and their heads, cupped in their hands, on the other. It is a posture of defeat, a warning sign of the dangerous exhaustion José Antonio seeks to avoid.

But the great floats of the cod end continue, attracting so many shearwaters that their high-pitched cackling now gets on the men's nerves. Occasionally one of the deckhands will hurl a mangled fish at the birds in sheer annoyance. But this only increases the tumult.

Down in the *bodega* Polo Beceiro and two helpers are carefully salting the fish. Their work resembles brick-laying; the bricks are the cod, laid lengthwise in neat rows, and the salt is the cement, applied with a broad trowel. Unlike bricklayers, however, Polo and his assistants cannot employ equal or uniform amounts of their matrix. Rather, they must first judge the size of each fish and then ration the salt accordingly. A half kilo of salt for every kilo of fish is ideal, other things being equal. Too much salt causes the fish to lose too much weight in drying. ("*El pescado chupe sal* [the fish sucks up salt], as much as you give it," Polo likes to say.) Too little will result in what Spanish fishermen call a "sweet," or malodorous, fish, the market value of which may fall from one hundred to fifteen or twenty pesetas per fish. Seasonal variations must also be kept in mind. Very lean spawning fish do not lose so much weight in curing as nonspawning "fat" fish, and each must be treated accordingly. Nor can the *bodega*'s temperature be neglected. Ideally, it should not exceed four or five degrees Centigrade. Anything higher will result in fish that seem to be curing very nicely, but in reality they are not absorbing the salt properly at the warmer temperatures and will be ill-smelling and soft by the time they are unloaded. And a boatload of such "sweet" fish, the chief salters can never forget, may mean a loss of hundreds of thousands of dollars. Not without reason do *patrones* compete for men like Polo Beceiro, salters who have a good nose and a fine eye for the curing process.

The fish come tumbling down from the *parque* on a plastic slide which can be moved about to be as near as possible to where the men are working. Apart from the faint hum of the engines and the gurgle of water rushing by the hull, the steady plop of the fish falling in little wet pools in the salt is the only sound heard in the cavernous and dimly lit *bodega,* which is lined with insulating layers of cork and wood paneling to help preserve cool temperatures. After the din of the *parque* and other noisy quarters, the quiet is almost startling. So, too, is the immensity of the task awaiting Polo and his helpers in the form of the two hundred and sixty tons of salt loaded in five transverse compartments of the *bodega.* The salt's texture is not unlike firm beach sand; to reach the sternmost compartment where the men are working one must climb up and down great white dunes or balance on planks spanning hard-packed cliffs. But before the campaign is done Polo and his small crew, occasionally helped by extra hands, will have hacked down all the cliffs and leveled all the dunes. They will have rearranged, in other words, the entire lading of salt so that it individually blankets anywhere from three hundred thousand to a half million fish.

The salters work quietly and never complain, although many suffer chronic backaches from the posture their work requires. Some will tell you that the sound of the falling fish is music to their ears, or that they pass the time by translating each plop into current market prices: 1,800 pesetas (U.S. $24.00) for the heavy splash of a ten-kilo *grande;* 130 pesetas (U.S. $1.70) for the lighter sound of a smaller *coscorro;* and so on, through all five of the standard marketing sizes (1977 prices; 75 pesetas to the dollar).

It is easy to understand why the men do this. Like the Germans, Spanish pair crews have a premium or, more accurately, a percentage increase over and above trip pay for what every ton of salted cod will eventually fetch on the market. The percentages start at one-third of one percent for novice deckhands or greasers, rise to one half of one percent for middle ratings such as chief bosuns or watch helmsmen, and reach a peak of 2 percent for nautical captains of first or command boats. At first glance they do not seem very high. But they add up very quickly on every bonanza "fifty tons salted" day such as we are now experiencing. ("Just think, tonight I am richer by one thousand of your Yankee dollars!" Captain Manolo will say whenever the occasion warrants.) On these days the beginning deckhands will pocket the equivalent of U.S. $280, even with *barajillas,* the smallest of cod sizes; a middle-rated bosun, or *timonel,* will get $400 for the same-size fish. Apply these percentages to the combined 1,100-ton fishhold capacity of the *Terra* and *Nova* and assume two good trips a year with the holds filled with medium-sized cod at $2.00 the kilo. What results is not inconsiderable — the only answer, Captain Manolo says, to why men put up with the hardest fishing there is.

For respected *patrones* like José Antonio the rewards are even higher. Often their pay goes beyond the percentage system altogether to some form of partnership with the owners. Since each campaign may gross approximately $2,000,000 against expenses ranging between $500,000 and $700,000, even a limited partnership can be an enviable arrangement.

Strangely, neither the high pay of the top officers nor the comfortable profit margin of the owners is much resented by the crew. With respect to the former, as Captain Manolo sees it, this is because the men view the way up to captain or *patrón* as entirely open to themselves. As indeed it is, he will always add, witness his own career. There is bound to be some grumbling against the owners, of course, but it is mainly directed at what the men consider inadequate outfitting or provisioning for sea. The owners' profits, by contrast, are often spoken of with stubborn pride; crew members will cite them as proof of their constant claim that pair trawlers are the most efficient of all fishing vessels, yielding the highest return on investment. Yes, the big factory trawlers may fish much faster, the men will admit. But in the end it is *las parejas que más pescan, que más rinden.*

Thus the bitter complaints about owner profits or pay scales that hold sway on other ships are not dominant conversational themes on Spanish pairs. Rather, the men will talk much more of luck; the luck of the draw in bringing together a good crew, the luck of certain *patrones,* the luck — most important and elusive of all — of being in the right place at the right time. Then, as the trip progresses, luck gradually gives way to calculations. To talk of expectations, more correctly defined, as the men begin to consider such matters as the possible trip gross or homecoming dates.

This has now begun to happen on the *Terra*. As a consequence crew members go down to the *bodega* with increasing frequency for a quick look at the progress of the salters. From long practice they need only glance at the steadily rising walls of split cod and salt to calculate very accurately the tonnage of fish necessary to fill the *bodega* and the days it will take to catch it. (If, that is, no streak of ill luck upsets their equations.) Toward the end they will more willingly lend a helping hand, as the work of Polo Beceiro and his salters becomes more difficult. In time, in fact, the latter will be forced to work on their hands and knees and even flat on their stomachs in order to top off the *bodega* compartments right up to the scuttles. When at last the time comes to head home, the *Terra*'s plimsoll mark will be deep underwater and her main deck awash in all but light airs. Some of the crew admit to anxiety about such overloading, which is standard practice on Spanish pairs. "On my first trip home I was afraid to look out on deck at night, so low was the hull," one confessed to me. "I would say my prayers and then, when everyone off watch was asleep, I would open all the drinking water faucets. We had plenty of wine, so it seemed the least I could do to lighten ship."

But for most of the crew so great is the joy of being homeward bound that worries about the ship's trim or anything else are easily forgotten. The danger of starting across the Atlantic hull down is after all only temporary, they will explain if asked, since the cod lose half their weight in drying in the course of the journey and the hull will rise accordingly. All one has to watch out for, therefore, is bad weather at the start. Thus do campaigns end, with a small risk as well as a fortune, deep down in the hold.

A week has passed on the Platier and, to the incredulity of all, the fishing so reminiscent of earlier times continues undiminished. José Antonio is pacing the crew carefully, watching for signs of excessive fatigue. My solitary bridge watches, as he orders more rest for all hands, grow longer and more frequent.

Not only birds and whales, but Soviet factory trawlers and some Norwegian purse seiners now also pursue the capelin. The purse seiners pass by bow down and foredecks completely awash from the weight of their catch ("You see, we are not the only animals out here," José Antonio invariably says of them.) But, unlike the Spanish pairs, they do not have far to go in their overloaded condition. The *Norglobal,* the world's largest fishmeal factory ship, is just over the horizon. The seiners shuttle back and forth, guided by a huge and pungent cloud of white steam emanating from her six tall smokestacks.

Other pair trawlers have also joined us. Large and remarkably clean concentrations of cod are still feeding on the capelin, and the word, in spite of José Antonio's best efforts at radio silence, is getting around. By the quick estimates of Captain Manolo, who this week has had the duty of reporting Spanish catch estimates by radio to the Canadian authorities, all pairs known to be in the Northwest Atlantic are in our general vicinity or soon will be.

Among the recent arrivals are the *Lasaola* and the *Lasaberri,* a pair wallowing very low in the water. A quick radio call confirms what their waterlines already make quite clear. They plan to fish for three more days and then steam to Saint-Pierre to refuel for the homeward passage. Coincidentally, José Antonio is beginning to grumble about the competition. It may be time to go elsewhere, to follow the cod that will soon be moving northwest. The loran in his head is telling him so, he claims, as it did before.

José Antonio understands the potential convenience of the *Lasaola* and the *Lasaberri.* Much as he would like me to remain, he agrees that it might be a matter of weeks or months before another opportunity to start home presents itself. Meanwhile, he will have just enough time to finish a belt he is weaving for one of my daughters, whose twenty-first birthday I have set as the latest possible date for my return. The belt is made of small beads of red, white, and green, *las rayas vascas,* the colors of the Basque nation, as he never fails to mention. Skilled in knots and fancy tatwork, José Antonio has worked hard on it at every spare moment, all through the days of heavy fishing.

"Alexandra, that is a pretty name," he now says. "Do you think that she will like to wear the Basque colors?"

I say that surely she will.

"I have a daughter," José Antonio continues, after a brief silence. "She is doing well in school and will soon complete her *bachillerato*. And my three sons, what a joy they are to me! I tell you, I think they will grow to be the bicycle champions of Spain."

There is another and longer silence. The steely gaze is once more in José Antonio's eyes and his body tenses. Both are the now-sure signs of suppressed emotions. "Do you know what it means if we continue to have good fishing and get home early?" he suddenly asks. "It means the owners will send me right out again to make an autumn trip to Norway. And that I neither need nor want! I tell you, we *patrones* go through life like bullfighters."

I ask if by this he means that the higher he reaches in his risk-filled profession and the better he does, the more is expected of him. José Antonio says, yes, that is surely the problem.

Porpoises are circling the *Terra,* playing lazily in rolling white-caps gilded by faint rays of early morning sunlight. Surprisingly, no other ships are in sight except the *Lasaola* and the *Lasaberri,* now standing close by. The moment is at hand. Bobbing precariously at the foot of a short rope ladder is a small boat which Captain Manolo grandiloquently refers to as the *Terra*'s launch, although it is of the same size and shape as a yacht dinghy. El Morocho, I, and my luggage fall into it, in that order and at the top of successive swells. At the last minute José Francisco Carames decides the occasion demands an additional escort and jumps down to share the stern seat. Captain Manolo, worried, advises me to stay quiet and *enganchado,* all curled up, in the bottom of the boat. There is not much freeboard, he shouts, in final and superfluous advice.

Fortunately, the humor of the situation tempers the deep emotions of all such leavetakings. There is, after all, something totally bizarre about paddling around in an overcrowded dinghy on the broad Atlantic, some one hundred and fifty miles from the nearest land. The crew, all lined at the rail, is making raucous comment about El Morocho's struggles with the oars or yelling at me to watch out since he will surely screw up and capsize the boat *en pleno Atlantico*. El Morocho and José Francisco like this — clearly they view our little excursion as a lark — and return the commentary in kind. And so we exchange well-wishes, jokes, and curses, shouting far across the water. We shout out everything, in short, except, perhaps, what we most want to say.

Five minutes later, the *Lasaola* is setting course for Saint-Pierre, engines full ahead. From her throbbing deck the *Terra* and the *Nova* recede astern very quickly. A little boat, now no bigger than a speck of flotsam on the crests of the long swells, is inching back toward them. There is nothing more to see, all around the horizon.

# FIVE

# On the Grounds

THE sea is often spoken of as infinite and featureless. To Milton it was "a dark illimitable . . . without bound." William Cullen Bryant, we may remember from "Thanatopsis," mourned "old ocean's gray and melancholy waste." James Russell Lowell, in a more prosaic declaration, said he understood why there were pirates. It was, he claimed, because "there is nothing so monotonous as the sea."

It has never been so to fishermen. To them the sea offers an endless progression of small clues — small heralds of things to come or of transition from one zone to another — which they watch carefully and study with great attention. There is, to be sure, some boredom in fishing, especially if one makes repeated voyages to the same area. But to the factory trawler crews who cross and recross the width of the Atlantic, fishing many different places along the way, life is made interesting by constantly changing seascapes and a multiformity of clues to master. Some of the clues may be important as indications of danger — the "ice blink," or cloud reflection, that warns of pack ice over the horizon, for example, or the giant swells that precede summer hurricanes dying out on the Grand Banks — while others might simply mark the passage from one fishing ground to another with signs so subtle they go unnoticed by the layman. Fishermen, however, have always been quick to observe and interpret them. Although factory trawlers may spend long months at sea out of sight of land, all elements of their crews — bridge officers, engineers, deckhands, factory workers — grasp at every possible means of orientation. They want a sense of being somewhere, of knowing exactly where they are. One of their most remarkable attributes, in fact, is that they nearly always do.

"Kap Møsting and East Greenland!" a German captain exclaims. *"Was für ein Steingarten* [what a rock garden]! And there are no rougher seas in this world. I tell you, you have to be a sportsman to fish there."

"Ah, the Bear Island ground," sighs a British winch operator. "Now that is a different kind of fishing! We call it the deckie learner's pitch." In British fishing parlance, a deckie learner is a young apprentice; the meaning here, therefore, is that Bear Island is a very easy place to fish, winter gales aside, with the kind of smooth and rock-free bottoms all deckhands dream about, but are seldom vouchsafed.

"Do you remember how we split the rocks in the Westmanns, at the Back Way and the Iron Foundry?" his colleagues may ask, referring to the excellent fishing that daring British skippers used to find under Iceland's towering cliffs. "Aye, many a dangerous pitch there was, in by the Foundry or out at the Haystack. If the wind changed on you, you dragged around and said your prayers until you hit a fastening [a hangup or obstruction]. That was your sea anchor. That was what saved you."

"Oh, the herring of Jeffreys and Cashes Ledge!" a Russian mate says, pointing on a chart to two small grounds in the Gulf of Maine. "I have never seen the equal."

On it goes. Veteran distant water fishermen know all the grounds along their transatlantic routes. They know and talk about them as familiarly, in fact, as if they were streets or squares in their own home towns.

Linking them all together, these grounds form a great semicircle, a broad archway spanning the North Atlantic. The arch begins near Cape Cod in the New World and bifurcates as it approaches the Old, with one arm dropping south to the British Isles and the Bay of Biscay and the other going north around Norway's North Cape and east into the Barents Sea. All along its way, never separated by more than a day's steaming, are myriad ledges, tide rips, banks, and coastal-shelf slopes that are home to a great many fish.

The waters of this great arch are generally shoal, interrupted here and there by deep channels. In temperature they range from cool (11° C.) to very cold (−1° C.). Running just below and eventually fusing with them are the warmer waters of the Gulf Stream and its three most prominent extensions, or the Mid-Atlantic Drift, the Norwegian Coastal Current, and the North Cape Current. For much of its length, therefore, the archway is a transitional zone between contrasting climates, where colliding weather systems create fog, storm, and, occasionally, the freezing condensations so dangerous to all ships. Under the surface there is a similar zone of conflict in which shifting masses of water of markedly different temperatures shear against each other, producing turbulence and vertical mixing. This action, among others, has helped to make the arch an extraordinarily productive marine province. Within its borders, in fact, are some of the richest fishing grounds in the world oceans.

"It starts right here," New England fishermen will often say. "To the south and west you don't get any redfish. And not many cod or haddock either, except in winter."

Here is Nantucket Shoals. You can almost sense the line of demarcation standing atop Great Point Light at the northern tip of Nantucket Island. At your feet is an eastward-trending shoal — Point Rip, it is called — well marked by crashing seas in any northerly breeze. About six miles to the northeast is another shoal, less clearly defined, where strong tides racing over sand ridges often make for boisterous and confused seas. This is Great Round Shoal, a part of the vast Davis Bank–Nantucket Shoals sandy grounds, where a seemingly endless series of parallel ridges make echograph tracings of the bottom that look very much like profile maps of the Appalachian valley and ridge province. The wind from Great Round always seems damp and cold, as indeed it usually is. This is because it has traveled over Georges Bank, fifty miles to the east, and across Great South Channel. Winter or summer, deeper and colder waters from the Gulf of Maine flow out across Georges into the abyssal sea. Some of this cold water also courses through Great South Channel and spills over onto Nantucket Shoals, where it keeps summertime temperatures down to approximately 13° C. Water as cool as this is what cod and many other groundfish need at the upper limits of their tolerance. Anything warmer is not to their liking.

At the other extreme of the arch there is an almost equally precise boundary. "You don't find much east of Skolpen Bank," European fishing captains say of it. "That's about as far as you can go."

To get a similar feeling for this dividing line one would have to journey to the Soviet Union and stand at the tip of a peninsula some 140 land miles north of the Arctic Circle. There, at latitude 67° 30' N, is Cape Kanin, a low and boggy headland devoid of human habitation, which guards the eastern approach to the White Sea. Could we do so — it seems unlikely in view of Soviet travel restrictions in those parts — we might immediately note some similarities with the hydrographic factors of Nantucket's Great Point Light, albeit for different reasons. Any northeast or easterly winds at Cape Kanin would also be cold, having first traveled over the ice pack of the Kara Sea and then bowled down the glacier-capped slopes of the large crescent-shaped island known as Novaya Zemlya — the "new land island" — that all but blocks off the western approaches to the Soviet Arctic seas. Even in summer these winds might be cool enough to dispel the swarms of mosquitoes that, I am sure, must then infest the Cape. Winds from the north and northwest, on the other hand, would feel relatively warm all through the year, although they might often bring rain or wet snow. These would be moisture-laden sea winds blowing from Skolpen Bank, a large ground well known for autumn-spawning cod 130 miles to the northwest, and a scattering of small outpost banks immediately north of the Cape, among them Kanin Bank, Hildred's Ground, the Parson's Nose, and Ganse Bank, as they have been christened by British, German, and Norwegian fishermen.

Close examination of any detailed nautical chart of the area will reveal the reason. Look hard and you will find wavy-arrow lines, usually printed in light blue, bearing such legends as "Murman Warm Stream (strength up to one knot)" or "Kanin Current (weak, variable)." Incredible as it may seem, these lines represent currents that are the last faint manifestations, the last weak tendrils of the Gulf Stream. There are, in fact, at least three and possibly four of these Gulf Stream traces, as oceanographers prefer to call them. The strongest of them, known as the West Spitsbergen Current, is merely a continuation of the Norwegian Coastal Current, which meanders north at one knot or less as far as the Spitsbergen (Svalbard) Islands, where it makes possible the world's northernmost fishing and human settlements. Another, the Kanin Current, carries Gulf Stream traces to their most easterly limit. Current, however, hardly seems the right word for it; the Kanin might better be described as a broad and gentle flowage, never attaining more than half a knot, that courses slowly eastward over Skolpen Bank and the small outpost grounds north of Cape Kanin. Nevertheless, weak as they are, both these warm currents have enough force to keep the annual average seawater temperatures of the areas they affect at approximately 3° C. Some oceanographers hold that the warming influences of the West Spitsbergen Current may reach farther east after it curves around the top of the Svalbard Islands, whereupon "it submerges below the less saline waters of the Arctic and continues clear across the Polar seas where traces of Gulf Stream water of temperature slightly above 0° C. are found north of the New Siberian Islands." If so, it is of no importance to fishermen. For cod and similar groundfish, temperatures just above freezing are not sufficient, especially during spawning. (The freezing point of the blood serum of most North Atlantic fishes ranges between −.5° C. and −2° C.; those at the lowest end of the scale manufacture their own antifreeze.) The fish find them on the chill side and rather disagreeable, at least for a steady or year-round regime.

Cape Cod and Nantucket Shoals, Svalbard, Skolpen Bank, and Cape Kanin. In between lie all the historic grounds of the North Atlantic — grounds that through the centuries have provided more fish for man's consumption than any others in the world oceans. But from the mid-1950s onward these same grounds held a new and very special attraction for factory trawling, quite apart, that is, from their known productivity or the advantages of beginning with what was already familiar. Scientists speak of it as the species diversity coefficient, or the ratio of the number of species in a given area to the size of their individual populations. The reader may know of one of the more obvious manifestations of species diversity with reference to land in the high Arctic latitudes where what few species there are are there in huge or almost incalculable numbers — the lemmings among rodents, for example, or the caribou among quadruped ruminants.

The same phenomenon exists in the sea. Exact comparisons may be difficult, but broadly viewed the waters of the North Atlantic arch have their closest terrestrial counterpart in the extensive belt of sub-Arctic spruce forest — a life zone, that is, where some variety of organisms may be found, but only a few exist as dominants or in overwhelming numbers. Going south from this belt, first to more temperate and then to tropical latitudes, a reverse phenomenon comes sharply into focus. The closer one gets to the equator — from either pole, that is, or equally in both the Northern and Southern hemispheres — the more do the number of organisms or different species proliferate. But the populations of the numerous species are relatively very small. This, too, occurs in the sea.

The dominant species of the North Atlantic archway may be divided into two broad groups. The first, representing the groundfish, are the codlike fishes, what British fishermen call "codstuffs"; the second, representing the pelagics, are what the FAO world catch statistics categorize as "herring, sardines, anchovies, *et al.*" Among the first, *Gadus morhua,* the Atlantic cod itself, is undisputed champion. Its range extends throughout the arch, to all its extremes, in numbers that have traditionally exceeded all other marketable groundfish combined. Also important, of course, are other members of what is loosely termed the cod family. They include the haddock, the pollock (also known as saithe or coalfish in Europe), and some species of hake, each of which, although not as widely distributed as the cod, is found in more than enough quantity to sustain valuable commercial fisheries. In the second group, among the pelagics, *Clupea harengus,* the sea herring, and *Mallotus villosus,* the capelin, are the dominant species, by far. Many other small prey fish inhabit various segments of the arch, of course. But, like the lesser members of the cod family, their numbers and range scarcely match those of the herring and capelin.

What these two kinds of fish meant to the factory trawlers is easy to understand. As the designers of the *Fairtry* clearly foresaw, the big new ships could be profitable only if they caught great quantities of relatively few species of fish — species of more or less similar body form and predictable size ranges, that is, which would conveniently fit their processing machines. In the North Atlantic the cod and its closest relatives first clearly met this requirement. Later, or when factory trawlers began mid-water trawling, the herring and the capelin, successively, played the same key role.

Not to take advantage of these dominants, factory trawler fleets soon found, was a risky proposition. The few skippers who didn't or who yielded to the temptation to depart the arch for more benign southern seas found that to the degree they probed southward the more trouble they had in finding dominants, in finding the right kind of fish in the right kind of volume. But other skippers, the majority who resisted and stayed on northern grounds, had further and more convincing arguments to sustain their conviction. In fact, they needed only remind themselves of the early failures of large-scale Soviet experimental fishing in the Gulf of Mexico and the Caribbean. There, the Soviets discovered, not even the ingenious Baader machines could keep up with the rich array of tropical fishes. In those waters, in short, the diversity coefficient was all wrong.

For these reasons the major factory trawler fleets worked the familiar byways of the North Atlantic arch. Initially, they followed much the same routes and fished many of the same grounds as earlier generations of side trawlers. They did so, however, with a new sense of mission. This was because at the time a worldwide chorus of scientists, fishery management experts, and fishing journal editors constantly encouraged them to think that by concentrating on such abundant groups as the cod and the herring they would, of course, be doing most to relieve global protein shortages. Such encouragement, the reader must understand, then had and still today has much truth, since practically speaking the two groups are to world fishing what wheat and rice are to agriculture. Annually, in fact, they account for approximately 40 percent of all fish taken from the sea. From 1970 to the present, for example, the cod family catch has averaged about eleven million tons. "Herrings, sardines, anchovies *et al.*" annually weigh in at from twelve to fifteen million tons. Alongside these quantities the total catches of other fishes familiar to the reader may seem relatively minuscule, as indeed in some cases they are. Thus, although it is true that the entire tuna family catch (principally yellowfin, skipjack, and bigeye) occasionally peaks at a respectable two and a half million tons a year, many other well-known fish do not fare nearly as well. All flatfish species, from the delicious Dover sole to the giant Atlantic halibut, annually flounder — the pun is too apposite to resist — at just over one million. Farther down the list are all the world's salmon, which rarely account for more than five hundred thousand tons a year. Near the bottom is the much-prized swordfish, at thirty-five hundred and dwindling.

But yet another factor, beyond abundance or the relief of world protein deficiencies, impelled the factory trawlers to concentrate on the cod and herringlike species. It was purely economic: these fish have always had a relatively good market in Europe. (The United States, by contrast, prefers high-priced specialty seafoods; the annual catch of shrimps, crabs, clams, and other "shellfish" exceeds all marine finfish in dollar value.) Until very recently fresh or frozen cod and codstuffs have provided much the same boon in many European nations as salt cod did in past centuries — namely an inexpensive and highly nutritious meat substitute for the working classes. The same is almost as true of the herring, especially in those northern European countries where it is highly valued as a table delicacy and not only for reduction to fishmeal.

In time, as has been suggested elsewhere, the factory trawlers themselves would make these fish much scarcer and more difficult to catch. The economic answer to this problem was twofold. First, owners quickly raised prices. Second, more slowly, captains began to extend the traditional limits of the North Atlantic arch both geographically and seasonally. In a relentless search for more fish, they pushed northeast to East Greenland, previously neglected because of very foul grounds and notorious weather, or north to the Labrador, where many followed the West Germans in the practice of ice fishing in winter. Southward, they pursued migrating cod and herring well below Georges Bank, to the offings of Cape Hatteras.

For crews, this search, the extension of the archway, brought little hardship. If anything they welcomed it for the variety it provided and the additional clues that had to be learned. In some cases crews applied old clues which seemed to be right for new grounds; in others they learned new ones from scratch. But whatever the circumstances or wherever they went, distant water fishermen followed their customary practice of seizing every means of orientation. They continued subconsciously, that is, to seek out all possible guideposts, whether from sea or sky, wind and weather, or what came up in their nets.

One may cite many examples. The relative number of seabirds, as they come and go from distant breeding islands at different times of year. Whale concentrations, most notably of the humpback, which are remarkably consistent in time and place. The new or first-year icebergs, so sharply sculptured, that course slowly down the Labrador coast in summer, like a majestic parade of floating Matterhorns. Old second- or third-year bergs, sea-worn and rounded, against which winter storm waves crash and resound, like rolling thunder. The distinguishing character of ice fields ("Your East Greenland pack is there all year and it's got those big old floes drifting down from the polar ice cap, but the Labrador ice, it builds up fresh each winter"). Subtle differences in catches of the same species, which inspire experienced factory hands to boast they can tell exactly where they are by the heft and the look of the fish ("For sure, the Faroe cod have that big shoulder and give the best fillet yield, but the stinker cod of Bear Island and Spitsbergen are all lean, low-yield, and full of iodine from that weed they eat"). Or the masses of sluggish bottom-dwelling invertebrates — starfish, holothurians, sea urchins, and coralline algae — that can literally carpet the sea floor, causing gear damage or bursted cod ends for all who ignore their precise locations. Sometimes, even, there is the very appearance of the sea or the manner in which one wave follows another, as when the long surges of the deep ocean begin to shorten and steepen over shoal reaches of the continental shelf ("Do you mark the seas? We're right on the edge!"). All these things — birds, fish, whales, ice, wind, weather, and wave forms — contribute to the fisherman's sense of place. They give him the comfort he wants of finding something familiar, something definable in the limitless space of the sea.

As a result of their constant observations, quite naturally, most distant water fishermen become excellent empirical biologists, "finely attuned exponents of probability theory," as one very astute scientist has so accurately described them. Nevertheless, sensitive as fishermen undoubtedly are to all the signs of the natural world around them, it would be wrong to assume that they view them with as much fascination as the works of man. The latter, it must be said, are of much more interest to factory trawler crews during their long months afloat. They are, in order of importance, the nearest port, other fishing vessels, and other ships of any kind.

Like the invisible strands that draw seabirds to their particular breeding islands, fishermen constantly feel the pull of the nearest port city. The pull is very strong. It exists even when crews know their ship is not scheduled to make a call. The men will talk of the city anyway, recalling the shore leaves of former voyages. The pull also shifts and changes in subtle but perfect harmony with a ship's passage from one major ground to another. A good example of this was the conversation aboard the *Frithjof* in the course of her various shuttle trips between different elements of the German fleet off West Greenland and the Labrador. For all the time the *Frithjof* was off Greenland, the talk abroad was entirely of Godthaab.

"Wait until you see the *nuk nuks* swarm over us!" a deckhand might typically begin. "All they want is a few drinks and a good time. No money, you understand."

"Oh, yes, it is true," another would reply. "We call Godthaab the polar paradise, the Paris of the Arctic!"

"Yes, the *nuk nuk* girls are like little angels dropped from heaven, but it seems as though they all fell on their noses," someone would always add, in what passes for German humor.

"Who cares about the noses?" a fourth might answer. "That's not what I look at."

And so forth, throughout the course of many long watches. But when the *Frithjof* was suddenly ordered to leave Greenland and return to the Labrador, all talk of Godthaab ceased. It was quickly replaced by St. John's, which proved rather less interesting.

Although many nations fish the North Atlantic, the opinions of their crews on the ports most frequently used by fishing vessels are remarkably uniform. Halifax, for example, is considered too big and impersonal, though it ranks high for shopping purposes. Its harbor is the most ample in the Canadian Maritimes, but trawlers are usually crowded together alongside a lonely wharf without floodlights, on which sits a huge and half-empty shed sometimes used for tallow and vegetable-oil storage. In the immediate area are only railway yards or grain elevators, and it is a long walk to the downtown shopping centers. The walls of the storage shed are decorated with the names and home ports of many trawlers, crudely hand painted by their crews in the spirit of "Kilroy Was Here," a sure sign of boredom. But for those fishermen who do venture downtown there are the good stores, at least. And farther up the harbor, in the vicinity of a naval depot, the solace of massage parlors and like establishments.

Saint-Pierre and Miquelon, France's two tiny islands off the south coast of Newfoundland, are by contrast held to be very friendly. Spanish captains speak of them as *las islas de lo posible,* the isles where all is possible, and this is probably as good a characterization as any. Certainly their population of 5,600 — 98 percent of whom live in the principal town of Saint-Pierre on the island of the same name — has done everything possible to welcome outsiders. Historically, the St.-Pierrais have been extremely hospitable, for example, to the annual invasions of the great French salt-cod fleets of three hundred or more dory schooners that used Saint-Pierre as a base during much of the nineteenth century. Or, earlier in this century, to an almost equal number of American rumrunners, who found the small islands a convenient operational center for other purposes during the Prohibition era. More recently, factory trawlers of many flags have been drawn to Saint-Pierre like a magnet by moderate wharfage fees, tax-free ship's stores, bargain shopping, and permission to do on-board repairs. (Many ports prohibit on-board ship or even net repairs, in the questionable belief that they take away the rightful business of local ship chandlers.) But, what is most important, distant water fleets like the fact that the St.-Pierrais "ask no questions" and never bother them with nosy inspectors. Not only the West Germans, therefore, have called at Saint-Pierre to drop off their spectacular herring catches, as mentioned previously. Soviet, French, Spanish, and Portuguese factory trawlers have also crowded the port to effect quick trans-shipment of their total catches. The temptation to do so is very strong, in fact, since after each call the trawlers return to sea (and possible future inspections) with innocently empty holds.

Nevertheless, popular as Saint-Pierre may be for these reasons, foreign fishermen do not usually speak of it as a particularly attractive place. The island is bare, but for a few trees transplanted from France, and its approaches are studded with fog-shrouded shoals and menacing half-tide ledges with names like L'Enfant Perdu, Basse Bataille, and Caillou au Chat. But once inside the small harbor's man-made breakwaters, crews begin to relax and brighten with anticipation. They know, at least, that they will be welcome, as in few other ports of their call. Accordingly, after a long time at sea, their land-starved eyes quickly transform the small town rising up before them into a busy metropolis of great interest. Contributing to this transformation are brightly painted wooden houses and neat backyard gardens, ascending the hills on twisting and narrow streets. Down on the flat of the waterfront are impressive stone buildings that bespeak some official function, plus a sprinkling of small pubs and good restaurants. Near them, here and there, are iron-fenced parks — the Place Joffre, the Place Général de Gaulle — with scrubby grass, gravel paths, and beds of wind-stunted flowers.

Best of all, no customs or burdensome declarations delay the landing of foreign trawlers in Saint-Pierre. Once lines are made fast, therefore, officers usually head straight for the waterfront Hôtel L'Escale, which has a cozy bar adorned with nautical bric-a-brac and a proprietess, herself the widow of a fishing captain, who is attentive to their every need. Crews hit the streets with shopping bags that are soon filled with bargain-priced wines and liquors, perfumes, Bayonne hams, and French woolens. As the day progresses, the men happily compare their purchases and stop with increasing frequency at the Bar Le Caveau or the Club Stella Maris. Some, however, may be kept on board doing repairs or mending nets. But even crew members who draw port duty watches have their pleasant moments in Saint-Pierre. On a fine summer day the men will stretch out their trawls on the main wharf for easier mending. Here they can be sure strong young girls working in an adjacent fish plant will come out to watch them during their break, exchanging cigarettes or a joke or two. That evening, if the weather holds fair, the same girls dressed in their best slacks and windbreakers will stroll endlessly around one of the town squares, two by two and holding hands. Some may bring along a brother or a boyfriend for added security. The girls pretend not to notice the foreign fishermen, of course. Nevertheless, liaisons are made, especially with the younger and more handsome men. These may be no more than an acquiescence, a brief nonobjection to strolling together and laughing over monosyllabic attempts to break language barriers. Even so, a favored fisherman will treasure the moment. Later, at sea, he will tell and retell his companions every detail of the encounter, enlarging the dialogue and imbuing it with greater significance on each occasion. And, of course, dream about doing better on his next visit.

Other ports along the path of the North Atlantic arch are so small or inhospitable that many crew members will not bother to go ashore. There is Isafjördhur (Icy Fiord) on Iceland's rugged northwest peninsula, which is no more than a long pier, a fish plant, and some small houses clustered under brooding cliffs of black basaltic rock. Isafjördhur has a population of 3,500 and, most regrettably, no easy sources of alcoholic beverage. (There are no bars in Iceland; wines or liquors may be served only at restaurants as accompaniments to bona fide meals.) In such a small town, the presence of fifty to one hundred carousing foreign fishermen is like an army of invasion. The locals come to resent these invasions, of course, and fishermen quickly sense they are not wanted. Torshavn in the Faroe Islands, much used by the British during the cod wars with Iceland, and Honningsvåg, a town of 5,000 tucked behind the North Cape of Norway, are similarly stressed. In such places captains scarcely need hoist the Blue Peter, the traditional signal flag announcing intention to depart, or blast away on the foghorn for stragglers. As likely as not, all hands will already be aboard — tired, bored, and hung over — after the first twenty-four hours. When at last they leave, in fact, many look forward to the refreshment of returning to sea.

> North America's oldest city has a history of wars, pirates, and fire . . . yet she still stands, a monument to the proud past, looking forward to a bright future. From the majestic hills surrounding St. John's harbour the visitor to our city can see "The Narrows" through which John Cabot sailed in the "Matthew" on St. John's Day, 1497. From this vantage point he can see a modern, efficient harbour development where ships of all nations tie up to take on provisions and seek shelter from sudden Atlantic storms, just as they have for centuries. . . . Stay a while, friend, we'd like to know you better.

So reads the introduction to a free brochure and city map put out by the Tourist Commission of St. John's, Newfoundland. Insert the word "possibly" somewhere in John Cabot's discovery, substitute "fishing vessels" for "ships of all nations," and it is both accurate and free of all hyperbole. Even the invitation to know you better, which is extended to visiting fishermen as much as anyone else.

There is good reason for this. Whether they like it or not, sooner or later, all transatlantic fishermen visit St. John's. By any reckoning it is the nearest port to the major grounds of the Grand Banks and the Labrador. Thus, as it was in the dawn of the salt-cod fishery, St. John's in this century again became the busiest fishing port in North America. Accordingly, the provisioning and repair of fishing vessels have been the foundation of the city's commerce. Visiting fishermen, moreover, have played almost as important a role for its merchants. Given these circumstances, a state of watchful truce or a cautious mutual tolerance has evolved quite naturally between the two groups. Foreign fishermen may not rate St. John's very highly as a liberty port, but they at least appreciate the cheery "good mornings" with which sanguine shopkeepers occasionally greet them, the absence of curious stares when they lumber into restaurants, and the freedom from excessive police surveillance that is often their lot in other ports. For their part the citizens of St. John's generally agree that the visiting fleets do after all give the city some distinction or "a touch of local color." They enjoy rating the crews according to nationalities, in fact, almost as much as crews like to rate ports.

"Oh, they're not a bad lot," a taxi driver tells you. "I likes the Portuguese best. They're the merry ones, you know. And isn't it a bright time when the great white fleet [the Portuguese dory schooners] comes in! The flags flying, the men singing, and some are after playing football right on the dock!"

"The Russians are the most polite, no problem at all," a storekeeper observes. "Always on their best behavior, you can be sure, and very careful shoppers."

"Well, now, some do give us a little trouble," a shipping agent confesses. "The British crews think they have to tear up the town.

It's a tradition, like, with them. And how the Norwegians can drink!"

"Yes, and you can't imagine the problems we have with some of the stragglers and no-shows," his office colleague answers. "Do you remember the Faroe side trawler that came in a couple of years back? The captain put it to me straight. 'I want a bus to take all my crew to a good bar outside of town,' he says to me. 'That's all they want to do, so let's rent the place for twenty-four hours, get them all good and drunk, and then have the bus bring them straight back to the ship.' Well, you know, that's just what we did.

"Come to think of it, it was a damn sensible arrangement," he adds in afterthought. "I wish there were more like that Faroe skipper."

The approach from the sea to these and other sensible arrangements is both spectacular and inviting, but much too brief. This is because St. John's is what seafarers like to call a hole in the wall. The first landfall is always an unbroken line of cliffs. As far as one can see, to the north or to the south, there is not a semblance of protection — not even a sheltering bight, a baylike configuration — in the wall of rock. The only sign of man's presence is the headland of Cape Spear, the easternmost point of North America, crowned by a solitary lighthouse. But at about seven miles out on a clear day, one begins to distinguish a rocky knob, standing apart from the cliffs and rising abruptly five hundred feet above sea level, on top of which sits a small stone castle. This is Signal Hill, so named because its summit marks the point where, in 1901, Guillermo Marconi received his first transatlantic wireless message. Then, approximately three or four miles farther in, a small chink appears in the rock wall. Engines are slowed, the ship adjusts course, and suddenly the view through the chink opens up like a fan to show church steeples, drab gray stone and red brick buildings, long docks, warehouses, cranes — a city of one hundred thousand, in short, crowding the hills around a pear-shaped body of water. This is St. John's harbor, measuring no more than a snug mile and a half from end to end and a mere half-mile at its widest.

The rest comes very quickly. The Canadian pilot swings aboard smartly and sets the course to split the middle of the Narrows at the harbor entrance. (Well named, the Narrows are in fact less than eight hundred feet wide; more than once in St. John's history a stray iceberg has grounded in their mouth and effectively sealed off the harbor.) Within minutes the rocky fastness of Signal Hill towers close to starboard. Equally close to port, at the foot of a plunging ridge, is Fort Amherst Light, its foghorn wailing on all but the clearest of days. But there are no special dangers, and the Narrows are easily passed. Then, almost before anyone is ready for it, there is the long wharf and the bench-lined promenade of Harbour Drive.

The transition is jarring. At one moment a fishing vessel is rising and falling to the long swells of the open Atlantic, its only home for many months. Fifteen minutes later it is tied up in the center of a noisy city. Inevitably, the fishermen will line the rails, staring blankly. They can look at eye level through the back windows of office buildings and watch people at work. They see automobiles whizz by. They hear horns blare and heavy trucks rumble. Here is a policeman whistling down a driver. Is he going to give the man a ticket? There is a pretty young girl parking her car in a waterfront lot and walking briskly up one of the narrow side streets. Is she late for work or merely going shopping? To the staring fishermen such questions assume great importance. They are not idle or foolish, and one must try to understand them or give a token answer. Always, during the first moments in port, a struggle is taking place. The fishermen are straining hard to project themselves into the conventionalities of normal, dry-land existence. But all the associations of this existence, all the reference points — half forgotten during the nine or ten months of each year spent at sea — are rushing in pell-mell on them. The signals are too numerous; they impinge too quickly. It is hard for the fishermen. They are disoriented, in a way that no landsman ever experiences.

But not, usually, for very long. The Russians soon crowd down their gangplanks in groups of three or four. They carry cheap suitcases or empty string bags, the better to do their careful shopping.

The Spanish go to their Hogar del Marino, conveniently located on Water Street in the heart of the downtown shopping district. Here they play cards, drink strong coffee, and exchange news from home in rooms with tile floors and ornamental grillwork. Rare visitors like the Rumanians or the Cubans stand on the corners, utterly confused. ("They think they've come to a place called America," a professor at St. John's Memorial University once explained to me. "They have this image of Miami Beach or Disneyland, so the reality is quite a shock.") The West Germans, especially the older officers, seem a little tentative as they explore St. John's, or at least careful in their choice of which establishments they frequent. Perhaps this is because everywhere they turn there seem to be monuments to World War I and II dead, as befits a city that contributed more than its share to both those conflicts.

By the end of the day, however, nearly all deckhands or factory workers will head for the El Tico restaurant or the Stardust Club, the only two bars in St. John's which cater especially to foreign fishermen. Here they crowd around tables by country — there is not much international fraternization — to drink hard and listen to jukebox music in dimly lit rooms heavy with tobacco smoke and the smell of stale beer. (Notably absent are the Russians; the rules for conduct of Soviet seamen abroad prohibit visits to public bars or taverns.) At the Stardust Club the scene is sometimes enlivened by the presence of Newfoundland girls who come in from out of town "for a bit of a change, something different, don't you know," as one of them once explained it to me. Occasionally, they find what they are looking for. Some interesting liaisons may result.

"Oh, yes, I once met a very comely lass at the Stardust," a British first mate has confided to me. "I simply asked her for a dance. 'Oh, thank you very much,' she says to me, very polite. Well, now, I still can't believe what happened next. She ups and asks me if she and five of her mates can visit the ship! 'For sure, love,' I says, so they move right in with us. She organizes her troupe, pairs each one off with one of us, and tells who to do what. They made our beds, did our laundry, and helped us cook up some grand meals.

Now that was a jolly time, I tell you! One of the lasses did it in the shower with the fourth engineer — he was very conservative — after catching him by surprise there. And didn't we have a great laugh over that!

"I forgot to say we were in port waiting for engine parts. They stayed with us five days. They were very good to us, those Newfoundland lasses. When it come time to sail, they made up some diplomas and give us prizes, little souvenirs, like, from the local gift shops. One for the best in bed, one for the best cook's helper, one for standing the most drinks, things like that. I still have mine. It's some kind of little doll made of sealskin.

"Aye, it's the good times you have to remember," my informant concluded. Without them, he added, he would find it hard to continue, to sign up for one trip after another.

It is very seldom, however, that a night at the El Tico or Stardust Club ends in the above manner. A more common scene is fishermen weaving their way back to their ships through icy and deserted streets, since downtown St. John's is a dead city by night. It may be that you will see the younger men singing to themselves or laughing as they slip and slide in their high-heeled dress shoes down the steep side streets leading to Harbour Drive. But many others will be grim-faced and silent. Or drunkenly cursing the end of a joyless excursion.

A similar scene, of course, is played out in fishing ports around the world, and mixed emotions everywhere color fishermen's attitudes about shore leave. They must have it. Few would sign any ship's articles without provision for at least one or two breaks in the sea routine. Not since the great age of whaling have men stayed at sea for such protracted periods, it is necessary to remember, and no whaler ever suffered the continuous and exhausting work schedules of the modern distant water fisherman. Yet, when shore leave is done, few are ever happy or satisfied. This is because, unlike all other ships, a fishing vessel does not measure its journey by miles logged along a fixed course. Rather, it is the degree to which the fishhold is filled. Any interruptions in the filling process, therefore, mean a delay in the total journey. Here, of course, lie the roots of the fishermen's ambivalence about port calls. The men may look forward to going ashore, but they also know that they will be entering a hold pattern or that every day spent in port is a day more away from home. Tension builds up proportionately, and relief comes only with a return to fishing. Seldom, therefore, is general morale so high as in the first few days following shore leave. Ship's doctors worried about the mental health of some of their patients know this and look for signs of improvement during this period. Captains know it, too, and often steam fast to the nearest ground to take advantage of it by putting their men to work as soon as possible.

Once crews are back at sea, talk of other fishing vessels and how they are faring becomes almost as ubiquitous as the adventures or misadventures of the last port. It begins as soon as the first rival trawlers appear on the horizon. Officers of the watch will immediately seize their binoculars, carefully focusing on any haulbacks that may be in progress, and comment accordingly. *El gran vicio de la puente,* the great vice of the bridge, the Spanish call this, meaning they recognize the practice is overdone and that it takes much time that might better be spent on charts and fishing notes. Still, the Spanish do it as much as anyone else. The vice, in fact, is universal.

Deckhands, too, have a lively and constant curiosity about other ships in their area. An outspoken breed, they are also quick to express their displeasure if a nearby trawler seems to be making better hauls than they. No words are spoken. The deckhands simply stand with their backs to their catch, hands on hips or pointing to the other trawler, and glare up at the bridge. This, of course, unsettles the captain. Although he would probably do so anyway, he is now goaded into making discreet inquiries among his colleagues or to vessels of another flag he considers friendly. Thus begin the endless radio dialogues, the subtle exchanges that are so carefully contrived and yet so seldom successful in eliciting fishing information. This, too, is a universal vice.

But nothing stirs more general interest — especially when shipboard life settles into predictable routine — than the sudden appearance of a new class of fishing vessel. Officers and crew alike will crowd the rails to scrutinize the new arrival very carefully and make instant critiques. The more so is this true if the ship is of a strange flag or one rarely seen in the distant water community. In this event the men will memorize every feature of the ship's configuration, as well as where and for what it is fishing. Thereafter they never forget it and will look for the ship at the appropriate season and place in years to come. If they find it, it becomes, of course, another kind of guidepost or one more familiar item to fill out the horizons.

"Oh, yes, I have seen the *Pierre Vidal,*" a Soviet bosun once told me, in what proved to be a good example of the experienced fisherman's remarkable memory for ships. "How strange she looked and how odd that she both salted and froze her fish." He thereupon described the debut of France's first large factory trawler on the Grand Banks in 1966 as though it had occurred the day before, though he had not seen her since. Using an occasional rough sketch, he explained her delicate airfoil-shaped funnels, her canted gantry mast, and her hybrid fish processing in the most accurate detail.

Or, as many other fishermen will claim, no one could ever forget the surprise of the *Seafreeze Atlantic,* the United States' lone entry in North Atlantic factory trawling. Built at a cost of $5,300,000 in 1968, the *Seafreeze Atlantic* was the joint inspiration of the National Marine Fisheries Service and the American Export–Isbrandtsen Line, who thought that the best way for American fishing to catch up with the foreign trawlers was to beat the foreigners at their own game. Plagued by union-rule coffee breaks in the middle of haulbacks or other vital operations, the *Seafreeze* fished unsuccessfully from the Grand Banks to Greenland and Norway, guided by a frustrated West German "advisory captain" and manned largely by a green or nonfisherman crew. ("I thought it a big queer," a British trawlerman who remembers seeing the *Seafreeze* off the North Cape has told me. "With all the fish the Yanks have on Georges Bank, I asked myself, why would they be after coming here?") As time wore on, moreover, her original crew began to jump ship in alarming numbers, forcing the *Seafreeze* to wander disconsolately from port to port — like Herman Melville's *Rachel* looking for lost children — in a desperate search for replacements. Add to this the fact that the *Seafreeze*'s owners forgot the cardinal rules that had brought foreign trawlers across the Atlantic in the first place. These were, first, a reasonably prosperous and steady home market and, second, not enough local fish to supply it. Neither of these circumstances obtained in the *Seafreeze* experiment; it thus flew in the face of all fishery economics. Not surprisingly, therefore, the experiment was mercifully short. The *Seafreeze Atlantic* was mothballed after two years of highly intermittent service. A sister ship destined for the North Pacific, the *Seafreeze Pacific,* fared even worse, suffering retirement in less than a year.

In later years, of course, the ship watchers of the older fleets continued to be surprised or in some cases concerned by more and more new arrivals. There was the much-feared competition of the Japanese, masters of the North Pacific, who had penetrated the Gulf of Mexico as early as the 1950s and by the 1970s became a presence in the North Atlantic. Or the sudden appearance of the *Norglobal* in 1972, with her highly efficient satellite fleet of purse seiners, bent on supplying capelin for Norway's ever-hungry fish-meal industry. Occasionally, too, there might be a handful of handsomely designed Italian factory trawlers — the *Airone,* the *De Giosa Giuseppe,* and the *Tontini Pesca III* and *IV* — forsaking traditional waters of the South Atlantic to take squid on Georges Bank in the summer months. Or, similarly, the hardy Faroese who sometimes steamed down to the Grand Banks when fishing was slack in Greenland.

Finally, if the above weren't enough, there was the supreme entertainment of watching the ultimate greenhorns, the Rumanians, Bulgarians, South Koreans, and Cubans, who started late in the game with both big ships and the highest available technology for both ground and mid-water trawling. The remarks that greeted these parvenus were not always charitable, of course. Veterans either doubled over in laughter or stared in numb disbelief as the newcomers broke gear, crisscrossed their trawl doors, banged up expensive net sonars, or committed other follies long associated with the learning process.

The Cubans, however, were shown some sympathy. They were a friendly and hospitable lot, nearly everyone agreed, eager to please and grateful for any advice. Older hands seemed to sense that Cuban fishermen had been pushed into distant water trawling well before they were ready for it, as was indeed the case, by a 1962 Soviet–Cuban fishing agreement which gave Cuba trawlers and fishing instructors in return for a well-equipped base for the Soviet fleet in Havana harbor. At sea, therefore, the veterans sometimes gave the Cuban crews helpful hints, especially when their Soviet captains were asleep. But few could imagine what really went on, day after day, aboard the latest Cuban supertrawlers that Fidel Castro eventually acquired from East Germany and Spain at a cost of over $5,000,000 each. For this, a textbook case of the mistake of beginning too quickly with too much, we must rely on an eyewitness report of one of the first Canadian observers to be placed aboard a 353' Cuban Rio-class factory trawler. The observer, an experienced Nova Scotian fisherman, made his report in the form of a terse daily log which, although somewhat short on syntax, nevertheless speaks volumes on the hospitable Cubans, their constant frustrations, and what must have been staggering daily operational losses for Castro's eleventh-hour fleet:

*April 6*

Left Halifax at 1430 hrs. aboard the *Río Hanábana* as observer.

*April 8* sunny

Had a meeting with the captain and the fleet commander. They issued me with clothing because they didn't think my cloths were heavy enough. They found the weather very cold. They gave me a parker, pants to match, socks, heavy underwear, sweaters, boots and a woolen face mask. They tried out their net, they hauled back about 30 lbs. mixed fish and ate them right away. When they brought back the net it was in perfect shape but they tore it up on deck by getting it caught.

*April 9* strong winds

Working on the net.

*April 10* sunny

First tow about 2000 lbs mostly silver hake. Second tow lost complete trawl, all they brought back were the doors.

*April 11* sunny

Still working on the gear. Lat. 42 49 59 N. Long 62 53 57 W. [Near the edge of the Scotian Shelf, south of Sable Island.] Two Russian ships here at this time, can't see their names. They have music on the intercom at all times in our rooms, in the galley and in the processing room hot coffee's served while you work. The coffee is very strong. A steward cleans my room every day. I can't get used to their food so they made different things for me. They have closed circuit TV color tonight a western movie, Kojak etc. in spanish language.

*April 14* strong winds

We lost our lifeboat today. We transported supplies to another ship. When [the crew] returned . . . the lifeboat was tied alongside, the sea hit and overturned it. It stayed afloat so the boson put on a wet suit and went over the side after it. He could not get back so the captain went down the ladder after him and put a rope under his arms. We almost lost both of them, they are not used to the temperature of these waters.

*April 17* sunny

No fish today, a small shark crabs and cohogs.

*April 25* strong winds

Started blowing hard around midnight. Hauled back at 1000 hrs. They lost another net. Blowing too hard to fish now. Waiting for transfer to Fisheries patrol boat. Allmost had a longer stay because of the weather. Came home on the *Cygnus,* arrived in Halifax, April 27.

These people are wonderful people but know little about fishing. Its a shame because they have the very best of equipment. I will never know what it is like to be a king but I will always feel that I have been very close.

G. D. Norman<br>Observer, Bridgewater Office

One may appreciate Mr. Norman's closing note and wish the Cubans well. But, unfortunately, goodwill and friendliness are not enough. It is one thing to enjoy the high spirits and the novelty, as all crews do, that go with assignment to the newest or largest ships, to serve, as it were, with the pride of the fleet. It is quite another to face the continual challenges of distant water fishing or to return year after year to the moments that severely test all men.

The challenges and the critical moments come most often in one season, which announces itself very clearly. First, there are more rapid changes of weather from day to day. Then come snow flurries and heavy blasts of boreal air. The barometer falls fast, rising waves send defiant plumes of spray high in the air, and certain species of seabirds disappear quickly over the horizon. These are the signs, of course, that winter approaches. With it will come a steady and inexorable procession of great storms, in frightening number. It cannot be otherwise, in fact, as all the older fishermen know. This is because the path of the great archway and what meteorologists call the winter storm track of the North Atlantic are virtually one and the same.

Winter comes, the daylight hours grow short, and fishermen must face the storm track with no place to go. (Only rarely are they near enough to land to run for shelter.) Sooner or later, a giant sea will engulf all but the pilothouse of the smaller vessels, while every man aboard silently wonders if the ship will "shake it off," shuddering in protest, in time to meet another. Similarly, shrieking winds may lay over the largest of factory trawlers to hang for what seems like an eternity at an angle of incline well beyond normal. All hands dread these moments and the winter trips in general, although they seldom say so. Outwardly, they meet them with courage, confidence, and unrivaled seamanship. But, tragically, sometimes even their best efforts are not enough. On every major ground and in all seasons, the sea makes her claims. Inevitably, ships go down.

Sinkings are not a subject most fishermen like to talk about, especially while at sea. If at all, they may be briefly mentioned as sequels to discussions about which grounds have the worst weather. In this event every fisherman will have his own opinion, strongly influened by the degree of danger to which he has been exposed on this ground or that. But in the end there is usually close consensus. The grounds of Denmark Strait — more exactly, the contiguous grounds between East Greenland and the northwestern peninsula of Iceland — are the worst. The weather recordings patiently kept by support ships while on station with the fishing fleets fully support this contention. In this area, in the winter season, slightly more than one day in three will have gale (Force 8) conditions or higher. But such statistics are not what seasoned fishermen mention. Rather, they remember all "the worst winters" over a long span of years. Again, as with ships, they can describe them as graphically as if they occurred in the present. There is not an older fisherman among the traditional nations, in fact, who cannot recall the dreadful ravages of the winter of 1954–1955.

French, German, British, and Icelandic side trawlers all suffered. Ironically, the winter was the *Fairtry*'s first at sea, the full baptism, so to speak, of the world's first factory stern trawler. But although the *Fairtry* passed it without trouble, the remainder of the British fleet was racked by the cruelest losses of all. For them the winter began badly all along the North Atlantic arch. On New Year's Eve, for example, a small Fleetwood trawler with twelve hands went down in home waters, bringing the total of British fishermen lost in 1954 to forty-one. Up at Bear Island the next day, the *Arctic Scout* of Hull saw the New Year in with the loss of five deckhands, swept to instant and icy death by a giant wave. At about the same time the *Gypsy Queen* of Lowestoft, believed to be fishing nearby, went down without a trace with her crew of twenty-one. After the customary waiting period of two or three weeks, she was officially declared "overdue and presumed lost." But worse was to come before the end of the month. Typically, it came off northwest Iceland.

There, about fifty miles north of the Horn (the tip of Iceland's northwest peninsula), at nine o'clock in the darkened morning of Sunday, January the twenty-third, rapidly rising gale winds began to buffet a scattered fleet of British, German, and Icelandic side trawlers. All ships routinely stopped fishing. Since the distance to shore was not great, most started running for a sheltered anchorage in the lee of the Horn, more often called the "North Cape" by fishermen. Among them were the Hull trawlers *Roderigo* and *Lorella*, keeping close company. The *Lorella*, known in the fleet as "Lucky Lorella" for her oustanding catches, had a malfunctioning radar set and the *Roderigo* would lead her in. It was not an easy run for anyone in the fleet. At ten o'clock the wind was approaching storm velocities and by noon the visibility during the two hours of daylight was described as between nil and fifty yards. But later in the day, as the *Roderigo* and *Lorella* approached the Cape, others in the fleet saw them turn around and put out to sea again in response to a distress call from the *Kingston Garnet*, which had a fouled propeller. By the next morning the *Kingston Garnet* had freed herself and gotten to the anchorage, but the *Roderigo* and *Lorella*, who had not found her, were themselves in trouble. There was now a full storm howling down from the north and the two ships were taking on spray-blown ice. Under the circumstances their skippers took the most prudent course. Agonizing as the decision always is, they judged conditions too dangerous to turn and run before the storm; both ships would have to dodge or remain offshore bow to the wind. Besides, as all skippers knew, full storms with freezing temperatures seldom lasted long. Or, conversely, the long periods of deep subzero cold usually came with quieter air.

Contrary to the lack of precise information surrounding the disappearance of many fishing vessels, there is not the slightest doubt of what happened next. Another British trawler, the *Kingston Zircon*, was also caught outside. Her captain, Robert Rivett, wisely decided to get as far away as possible from the field of pack ice close to the northwest, which was lowering the temperature of the winds racing across it. The seas in the lee of the ice would be short and steep, producing maximum spray, he also reasoned, whereas the longer seas farther away from it might provide brief but regular moments of wind shelter deep in their troughs. Immediately after the onset of the gale, therefore, Rivett steamed south and east as fast as conditions permitted. It was a brilliant gamble. Not until three days later did he find sufficient lulls to send his men out to chop ice. But by this tactic Rivett saved his ship. In the interim, he kept constant radio contact with the *Roderigo* and *Lorella* and logged all their messages.

On Tuesday, the twenty-fifth, two days after the beginning of the storm, the *Roderigo* and the *Lorella* found themselves facing continuing high winds with driven snow and subzero temperatures. The two ships were experiencing heavy ice accumulations — indeed, the ice on their shrouds was now the thickness of a man's leg — but in the course of the day both skippers decided that it had become too dangerous "to send the lads digging out." In the afternoon the *Lorella* radioed: "Weather very bad, having to go full speed to keep in wind, continuous snow and freezing." The *Roderigo,* now some distance away, replied to the same effect. Both skippers agreed to make radio checks through the night.

By Wednesday the winds reached eighty to ninety miles an hour. A true cyclonic disturbance with hurricane-velocity winds was now attacking the ice-heavy trawlers. At 1426 in the afternoon the "Lucky Lorella" radioed a short message — "heeling over" — and switched from voice to Morse code telegraphic transmission. For three minutes she tapped out the message "*Lorella* going down, heeling over, *Lorella* going down." Then came silence.

The *Roderigo's* turn was not long in coming. Less than an hour later, she issued a calling-all-ships plea for assistance. Her remaining moments, which included radio dialogue with the *Lancella,* a sister ship of the *Lorella,* which was also caught outside, and a patrolling aircraft from the U.S. Naval Air Station at Keflavik, Iceland, were tersely recorded:

1630  RODERIGO: Aerials now icing up. Will call from time to time.

1645  RODERIGO: Can anyone take a bearing on me on this frequency?

1649  LANCELLA to RODERIGO: Bearing as near as can say northeast.

1650  RODERIGO: We could do with someone up here now. Having difficulty in maneuvering.

1651  RODERIGO: Come to us. Position becoming serious now.

1652 LANCELLA to RODERIGO: We are coming to you.

1701 U.S. NAVAL PATROL AIRCRAFT 5301: Roderigo, Roderigo, transmit on 500 kilocycles.

1702 RODERIGO: Unable to transmit 500 k.c. Listing heavily to starboard now.

1703 AIRCRAFT 5301: Roderigo, Roderigo, what are your intentions?

1704 RODERIGO: No intentions. Going further over. No visibility. Still going over to starboard.

1705 RODERIGO: Still going over to starboard. Cannot get her back.

1708 RODERIGO: Still going over, going over.

After four minutes of repeating "SOS, heeling right over" by Morse code, Captain Bob Rivett noted on the *Kingston Zircon,* transmission ceased.

No intentions. Nowhere to go. No further measures possible. The forty-eight men on the *Roderigo* and the *Lorella* knew it well before the event. So, too, probably, did the eight men lost from an Icelandic trawler driven aground in the same storm.

In later years, despite all technological advances, similar last messages were to be heard again. And will be, inevitably, in the future, as long as man fishes the great arch of the North Atlantic.

# SIX

# Tiddly Bank

THE sea is a leaden gray, flecked with small whitecaps stirred by a cold east wind. The place is the Arctic or, more exactly, the western reaches of the Barents Sea. The date is Friday, October 21, 1977, a moment in time when many coastal states around the world were locked in obdurate dispute over the boundaries of their newly claimed two-hundred-mile zones.

Some eighteen British stern trawlers and nine older side trawlers are working a small Barents ground known as Tiddly Bank. In the afternoon, as daylight begins to fade, an unfamiliar ship appears on the horizon. All through the fleet British skippers momentarily halt their nonstop radio dialogues to wait and listen. Very soon, a heavily accented voice breaks in on one of the high-frequency channels.

"British trawler *St. Jasper*, British trawler *St. Jasper*," the voice intones, in the monotonous cadences of normal radio telephony. "This is Soviet patrol vessel *Icaro*. You are fishing in economic zone Union Soviet Socialist Republics. Please acknowledge."

The same terse announcement is repeated to one after another of the trawlers, each being hailed by name, as the patrol vessel steers a weaving course through the close ranks of the Tiddly Bank fleet. Aboard the British trawlers, radio operators frantically tap out messages requesting instructions from their company headquarters in Hull. In each case, however, offices are already closed for the weekend.

Tony Scannell, the veteran Irish-born radio officer of the one-thousand-ton factory trawler *Kelt,* is not unduly alarmed. "Just like the Soviets!" he remarks to his skipper, Captain George Renardson. "It was Friday afternoon that other time, if I'm not mistaken."

Scannell's memory is correct. Four weeks earlier, on Friday, September the twenty-third, another Soviet patrol vessel had steered its way through the British fleet for twelve hours, making the same announcement, and then finally boarded the Hull trawler *Loch Eriboll,* threatening her with seizure if all other British trawlers did not leave the area immediately. This action had been justified — or at least so the Soviets insisted — because Tiddly Bank lay deep within a pie-shaped wedge of the Barents that was (and still is today) claimed by both the U.S.S.R. and Norway. But after this incident the Norwegian government had promised Great Britain and other interested nations that it would continue to support the right of all duly licensed "third country" vessels to fish in the gray zone, as the disputed area was coming to be known. Thus reassured, the British fleet had returned to Tiddly.

On this occasion, however, the Soviet patrol vessel moves much more quickly from its general proclamation and calls for acknowledgments to direct threats of seizure. Flash bulletins, rumors, and pleas for help or advice race through the British fleet. Up at one end of Tiddly the freezer stern trawler *Swanella* reports that the *Icaro* is closing on her. Down closer to the *Kelt,* the radio officer of the *Ross Altair* says he cannot raise the Norwegian patrol vessel seen in the general vicinity two days ago. Nor, it seems, have other ships done better in repeated attempts to contact any source whatsoever of Norwegian authority. Then it comes. The definitive word. The big factory trawler *Coriolanus,* off by herself on the fleet's northeast flank, is about to be boarded. There can be no doubt. Her captain himself is speaking. He says the Russians insist they will escort his ship to a Soviet port if the entire fleet does not immediately depart the gray zone.

The British skippers must decide for themselves, as is their custom, by a fleetwide radio forum. Crowded VHF channels now stutter and crackle as nearly all captains join in to discuss the situation at their sardonic and blasphemous best, in strong Yorkshire accents:

"Fookin' 'ell, Barry, what do we do now?"

"I don't know, Tom, it's just another Christmas box from the Russians, if you ask me. They're giving it to us early this year."

"What do you think, Kevin? I aren't for having any of our lads spend the 'olidays in Murmansk, you know."

"Right you are, Jack! I say we get the fook out!"

The last motion, so to speak, carries. Within an hour, as the afternoon quickly surrenders to the long autumnal night, Tiddly Bank is totally deserted. The fleet is spreading out in a broad fan-shaped pattern, as each ship steers its private course out of the gray zone. Conversation among the captains now turns to the delicate business of sounding out each other's intentions. The *Cassio* is thinking of fishing around the *Scharnhorst* wreck. The skipper of the *Dane* says he will steam far to the north, to Bear and Horseshoe Islands, maybe even Spitsbergen. Many others, or a clear majority, do not choose to tip their hand. They will fish the nearby North Cape grounds for a bit, they say, and then make up their minds.

On the bridge of the *Kelt,* Captain George Renardson is talking with Tony Scannell and his second-in-command, Mate Desmond Hendrickson, about the background factors or the recent misfortunes to British fishing that have encouraged the Soviets and others to act so cheeky, as he puts it.

"We have naught!" he begins, almost shouting. "When the negotiations started with the Norwegians, there was no one in the chair for us. The Norwegians want to deal individually with countries fishing in their zone, but the E.E.C. says they'll do it for us, so we have nobody of our own in the chair. Now the same will happen with the Russians. It's a shambles! A great and scandalous shambles is what it is!"

Captain George, a man of great girth with an air of constant concern, is pacing the bridge like a caged bear. He is referring, of course, to the hard fact that ever since the United Kingdom joined the Common Market, the European Community headquarters in Brussels has insisted that it will negotiate *en bloc* for fishing quotas from other countries and then divide up the results among its member states in what it likes to call a common fisheries policy. Desmond Hendrickson agrees that this is a bad thing. The Norwegians know the British stick to the fishing regulations and catch quotas more than anyone else, he maintains, so England would have done much better one-to-one at the bargaining table. Tony Scannell is still smarting over the fleet's ousting — the second in a month, he cannot forget. An avid reader with a consuming interest in international affairs, Scannell makes the point that unless Norway shows more on-the-spot support in the gray zone, the Soviets will be able to prove a record of de facto control. "A terrible, fearful shame it is," he concludes, with a mild trace of his native County Kerry speech. "And meanwhile the Russians lord it over us like we were kids in school caught breaking the rules. I'm thinking it's like the new boys in the class pushing around the old."

By eleven o'clock at night, most ships have already slipped quietly over the gray zone line. It is the hour when skippers retire, turning over the watch to their mates, and the radio forum of the sea has all but come to a halt. Only one captain, in fact, seems to be wide awake and talking.

"Aye, jolly England; jolly, jolly England!" he says, slowly and with mock solemnity. "If you want my opinion, jolly England is walking fast, backwards."

Somewhere out in the dark, just before signing off, a friend agrees.

The Tiddly Bank fleet had every right to be bitter. Twenty-five years earlier, when many of its crew members were beginning their careers as apprentices, Great Britain could boast the world's largest and most efficient distant water fleet. At its core were over three hundred well-built trawlers from Hull and Grimsby,[1] fishing Ice-

---

1. Until very recently the two Humber estuary ports of Hull and Grimsby were home to approximately eighty percent of the distant water fleet.

land, Bear Island, Spitsbergen, and the Barents Sea the year round. Well before then, moreover, throughout the first quarter of this century, British side trawlers had themselves discovered many of the best grounds in these same areas. (And christened them with names still found on all fishing charts; witness Tiddly Bank itself, "tiddly" being one of many designations for small haddock in popular British fish nomenclature.) In the pioneering era of distant water trawling Great Britain had led the way. By the 1930s some nations, most notably Germany and France, began to follow the British trawlers to the newly discovered grounds; many more looked to Britain for the latest in nets, rigging, and trawling techniques. Or to purchase vessels accurately described as "a triumph of the best minds in naval architecture." Staunch and superbly designed side trawlers, that is, with the high whale-backed bows, deep stems, long sheer, and perfectly rounded sterns that made them the most able and sea-kindly ships of their size ever built. Hardships at sea aside, it was the best of times for British fishing and British fishermen. Michael Graham, England's foremost fishery biologist and historian, has called it a time to be proud of, when trawlers often filled their holds in twenty-four hours and their skippers earned "more than any other seamen, the most successful even outstripping masters of crack passenger liners, and admirals — men twice their age."

One generation later, by October of 1977, the twenty-seven trawlers so brusquely ushered out of the gray zone constituted slightly over one half of the operative British distant water fleet. The reasons for the decline to one twelfth of its former number are many. But the most instructive, without doubt, emerge very clearly from a simple historical comparison of government attitudes toward fishing. At one extreme was Great Britain, where both the government and the fishing industry were quite content to leave each other alone during all the long years of prosperity. At the other were Iceland and Norway, two nations unsurpassed in government concern and support for fishing, in both good times and bad.

Understandably, in a nation where fishing accounts for ninety percent of the gross national product, Iceland led the battle to force the United Nations to consider a complete restudy of the laws of the sea with respect to fishing. After a 1948 request to the U.N. General Assembly produced no practical result, the Icelandic government moved from the traditional three-mile territorial sea limit to four miles — this was for fishing and other economic purposes, not "territorial" or full sovereignty — followed by extensions to twelve miles in 1958 and two hundred in 1975. These moves, vigorously enforced by the Icelanders, ultimately found much popular sympathy and exercised a strong influence at the U.N. Law of the Sea Conferences. But for England they meant three difficult and humiliating "cod wars,"[2] followed by total loss of access to grounds that had long supplied from twenty to fifty percent of the British distant water catch.

In Norway fishing accounts for only two percent of the GNP, but as early as the 1930s, the Norwegian government began to invest in programs that eventually gave Norway world leadership in fishery research, a fishmeal industry second to none, generous fishing-vessel construction subsidies, and, finally, the development of many new overseas markets. Unlike other European nations, Norway also viewed the advent of the factory trawler with commendable caution and restraint. Government officials even went so far as to impose strict limits on the growth of a domestic factory trawler fleet primarily because they feared Norway's numerous small-boat fishing communities might be depopulated as their fishermen left for the steadier pay and greater comforts of the big ships and the big ports. Moreover, government and industry alike were aware that Norway's coastal grounds — Europe's richest — made unnecessary the development of a large or far-ranging distant water fleet.

Against such a background of social and economic concern, it is not surprising that fishing played a part in Norway's refusal to join the Common Market. Membership in the European Com-

---

2. The first was in 1958, as a result of the twelve-mile and point-to-point (enclosure of bays) limits; the second, in 1962, when the limits were moved to fifty miles, and the third in 1975, upon enforcement of a two-hundred-mile zone.

munity would have meant conformity with its common fisheries policy, which required all member states to permit fishing to within three miles of their coasts at catch levels to be decided in Brussels. To the Norwegians this provision raised the specter of continually playing host to all the E.E.C. fishing fleets, who would, of course, choose to concentrate their efforts on Europe's best grounds. The general sentiment was that Norway should set her own pace and not be overwhelmed by international dictates, whether in fishing or offshore oil development. Accordingly, the Common Market referendum vote was a clear no. Not long thereafter the Norwegian government acted quickly to establish an exclusive two-hundred-mile economic zone.

What happened in England was almost exactly the opposite. In their successful campaign for Common Market entry, British authorities had seldom if ever mentioned possible consequences to fishing. Rather, the Labour government, fired with a new zest for expanding trade horizons, viewed fishing as a small price for admission, inviting E.E.C. member states "to fish right to the beaches," as Common Market critics would later claim. Some government leaders, it is true, genuinely believed that such minor questions as preferences for host-country coastal fishing or adequate quotas for the distant water fleet could easily be negotiated later. The reality was to prove far different, however. Common Market entry in fact saw the Community turn a deaf ear to coastal nation preferences and marked the beginning of a *mare clausum,* a virtual closing down of all traditional seas for British distant water fishing. To the point, that is, as Tony Scannell had so aptly expressed it, where the cheeky Russians and other new boys in the class could push around the old, the once proud masters of the game.

It is my first full day at sea aboard the *Kelt*. Captain George Renardson is trying hard to make up for lost fishing time. Two days earlier the *Kelt* had been ordered to tow a disabled side trawler into Honningsvåg, the small port on the leeward side of the island that forms Norway's North Cape, where I had boarded her.

Because of the interruption Captain George is now fishing a small ground not more than one hundred miles due north of the Cape.

"I made up my mind before the trip I'd not go chasing about," he explains, as we have our first chat on the bridge. "The fishing being so thin, there's no gain in steaming about night and day. Normally, at this time of year, we'd be on Skolpen Bank for the autumn cod spawn, but Skolpen belongs to the Russians now and the gaffers [owners] say to stay out. Presently I may give it a go on Tiddly Bank, though, in the gray zone. The fish run smaller there, but there's plenty of them and the pitches [bottom surfaces] are all fair."

Down in the crew's mess Second Mate Roland ("Buster") South and some of his deckhand friends are playing a game of darts. Nearby, most of the factory shift and a few engine-room greasers are sitting at the tables drinking strong tea. As often happens, the two adversary groups — all those who work above decks and all those who work below, that is — are having at each other with easy banter.

"Where you going, Booster?" a factory hand asks, noting that South has his hair combed and is looking unusually tidy. "Waiting for the Piccadilly bus, are you?"

Buster South is ready with the right counter to this opening thrust. "I knows where the water is, at least," he says, as he continues to throw his darts. "I knows where the doors are."[3]

"You better watch out, Barney," one of Buster's friends adds. "We'll be having you deckie yet."

"A deckie, you say. Fookin' 'ell! It's you that's going out to the doors, not me, mate."

"I shan't mind going to the doors," the young deckhand replies. "It's better than fookin' around with the fish!"

"You wouldn't know," the factory hand snaps back. "A lot of fookin' you do with the fish!"

The last remark has an edge to it, just sharp enough, perhaps, to turn a time-honored conversational pastime into something more

---

3. Trawl doors, so frequently the cause of mashed fingers, broken arms, or worse, are often used by deckhands as prime symbols of their dangerous work.

serious. The young deckie is glowering, since the factory worker has, in effect, accused him of being slow to respond or not working hard enough when called down to the factory for extra help in processing a large catch.

Chief Engineer James Henry Pick, sitting aside in one corner of the mess, is thinking of intervening. But Brian Pepper, the *Kelt*'s youthful second cook, suddenly gets it into his head to declare his work the hardest of all, no doubt about it. Explosive laughter greets this statement, and all join in to answer him. ("Pooh, shaking a pan! Don't be daft, Brian, go take your pastries out of the oven.") Pick, a huge man with prematurely gray hair and an amiable disposition, decides that Brian's little blunder has dispelled any lingering ill humor. Besides, even if it had not, he knows that no one will make remarks about him or his engine-room gang, at least not as long as he is within earshot. Chief Harry, as he is better known, started out as a fireman in the age of steam trawling and has also gone "big boating," as British fishermen say of service on passenger liners or merchant ships. Along the way, he has worked both topsides and below. All the crew knows this and respects him accordingly.

Chief Harry, therefore, is settling back in his chair, telling me quietly how it was, this business of deckhands versus engineers, in times long past. "They was more against us back on the old sidewinders," he begins. "We ate at separate tables. You sit down with the deckies, and they'd say, 'I got a crow at my table.' Oh, yes, we were the black gang, you know. They still call us 'noncombatants,' as a matter of fact."

There will always be some form of rivalry, Harry thinks. The deckhands are the most tightly knit group on any trawler — the shock troops, they like to call themselves — and it's simply in their nature to make snide comments about the greasers, the factory hands, the galley crew, and the radio officer. "It's anyone who doesn't get close to the water, you see," he explains.

"Light work they say it is!" Brian Pepper is muttering to himself as he clears the tea mugs and plates. "Let them try it then!" Tall, thin, and lean-faced, Brian is going about bare-chested, because of the heat in the galley, he says. But he flexes his muscles and postures in such a way that it is clear he also wants to give proper display to the thirty-two tattoos that cover most of his torso. The ones he likes best, the ones that cost him forty quid each, are an oriental tiger climbing up his left arm and a war-bonneted head of an American Indian that occupies most of his back. And, of course, a small garland of flowers with an inscription, on his right forearm. "To My Mum," it says.

Up on the bridge Captain George is pacing again. He is trying to decide when to haul. The signs from the electronic fishfinders on which he continually concentrates are not very promising. But staring at him from above his chart desk is a trawl clock, a small wooden plaque with brass numerals and hands that must be moved manually. Similar clocks, devoid of any working parts, are found on almost all fishing vessels. Often given out free by chandlers or equipment manufacturers, they are merely mnemonic devices to remind skippers how long their nets have been in the water. Nevertheless, they play as vital a role as many of the instruments costing thousands of dollars each — radars, echo sounders, lorans, autopilots, track plotters — that clutter the bridges of modern trawlers. The monotony and exhaustion of long watches frequently blur the senses, especially of time, and the captain who cannot remember when he began his tow loses an important element in the constant round of calculations so necessary to good fishing. The trawl clock prevents this, provided, of course, the user does not forget to set it whenever he puts out his net. But Captain George never does forget, and now his clock shows our tow has lasted a little more than three hours — a little more than usual, that is. His mind, therefore, is made up. He picks up a microphone for the ship's public address system and presses the transmitting button.

"Hauling time!" Captain George announces. "Hauling time!"

Below in the crew's mess, Buster South and his friends utter a few ritual curses, break off their dart game, and make for the wet lockers forward of the factory. Here they put on their foul weather gear slowly and deliberately — the oilskins rubbing against each other make a low whistling sound — as they adjust suspenders and wrap tapes around their pant cuffs, the better to keep out icy water.

But once they emerge topsides, the deckhands move with speed and precision. Harold Norfolk, the *Kelt*'s senior winch operator, sings out the marks on the cable. As the last ones are called Buster South takes a firm stand near the edge of the ramp and gently guides the big doors up out of the water with clear and sure hand signals. Immediately thereafter the younger men struggle and swear as they swiftly manhandle the ubiquitous messenger cables, back-straps, and independent wires. Soon, no more than twenty minutes after the hauling time announcement, a dripping cod end slides up onto deck. Unfortunately, considering the effort involved, it is not very big.

"About twenty baskets, I would judge," Captain George says, frowning. "And there's some squatties in there, too." He is using the traditional measure of about ninety-three pounds — what the old baskets used to unload fresh fish normally held — by which all British fishermen estimate their catch. By squatties he means red-fish, which bring very little on the British market.

"When we first came to these grounds up here in the Norwegian Arctic, we used to call the fishing 'dip and fill,' " he continues. "That's the way it was — short tows and always a full bag. But you see how thin it is now. Sometimes I think we're getting too good for the fish."

Within ten minutes chains rattle across the deck and heavy trawl doors knife into the water. Captain George signals full ahead on the engine room telegraph. After three or four minutes, when he is sure the doors are spreading properly and the net streaming straight aft, he reduces the engines to half power or less. The *Kelt*'s trawl sinks to the bottom and continues its work.

At noon a chill east wind begins to buck the North Cape Current, making lumpy seas and bringing brief showers of wet snow. In every direction the cloud cover is a monochrome gray, low and threatening, without a single window or lighter-colored patch. Not many birds follow the ship's wake. The few that do are mostly juvenile or first-year kittiwakes. Their parents, wiser in the ways of seasons, have long before flown south.

Captain George heaves himself into his well-upholstered fishing chair and resumes careful study of the instrument panels that surround it, pausing only to rub his eyes or adjust his wire-rim glasses. He wears his standard uniform of the day — a small knitted wool cap, a faded brown Scandinavian sweater with tarnished pewter buttons, well-worn blue jeans, and either clog shoes or sealskin slippers, depending on how cold it is. Over the years George has become rather stout, the result, he says, of the lack of any strenuous work since he made captain. His step, however, remains lively and sure, and his hips are narrow. So narrow, in fact, that occasionally the low-slung belt of his jeans will slip down over them and reveal his shirttail or even a gap of bare skin around his waist. He will laugh or apologize whenever this happens and rehitch his jeans with a quick tug. What is more remarkable, he will also laugh a little about the state of his scraggly brown hair, which he once lost as a result of extreme hypothermia and shock. Like many British fishermen who are veterans of long service on side trawlers, George has "gone over the wall," as he puts it, or been swept overboard.

"It was up at Bear Island in the dark time," he says. "It was very cold, about two degrees below zero, and the bobbins were just coming up. I was in the water fifteen minutes. The skipper, a very decent chap, come over after me and helped me hold onto the net. He saved my life. That's a fact, that is. He got the bronze medal from the Royal Humane Society for it."

The echograph is tracing clusters of small black smudges, just off the bottom, and the cathode tube fishfinder flashes its green pulses in the shape of a Christmas tree. Both are very good signs. Captain George halts his narrative, tunes the necessary dials for sharper images, and says perhaps there is a nice little fish shop, a nice little fish market, under our keel.

"Well, after that trip my hair turned gray and then my head went bald," he continues. "So I took some jobs on shore for a bit. But you can see my hair is growing back. It's coming along nicely now, isn't it? And the gray hair, that's all gone now, isn't it?" He laughs as he asks the questions, rubbing his head and stroking his sideburns and beard, which are indeed no longer gray and growing back nicely.

Soon only the thick black line of the bottom appears on the echograph, and the cathode tube Christmas tree melts away into the flat scatter signals that indicate the empty "bounce" of an even and hard ground. Quite clearly the little fish shop under our keel has disappeared as fast as it came. Captain George is visibly distressed. The *Kelt* left Hull in mid-August, some two months ago, he tells me, which means that right now the trip should be well over the halfway mark. But the problem is, what with the fishing being so slack, that the *Kelt*'s 370-ton fishhold is barely one third filled. There are reasons enough for this, George thinks. After all, in his father's time the British fleet used to take over 80 percent of its distant water catch from the Norwegian Arctic alone. Then when you consider those who followed — the Germans, the French, the Spanish, and all — fishing hard ever since, you don't have to be a genius to know the grounds were bound to get exhausted. But just try and explain that to the owners, he adds. All the gaffers want is a fast trip — "Just give us a quick turnover" is all they ever say — and they're not about to give any consideration to the poor conditions every skipper must face at sea these days. Of that you can be sure.

"I put in full effort," he concludes. "I give it my best. But it's a daft business, this. You come in with a nice kit of fish and you're a great man. Everyone's fine with you, and they treat you like a hero. But one bad trip and they give you the sack! Sometimes I wish the gaffers would sit down with you and talk man to man and tell you what they really think. But they never do."

Darkness comes quickly, at three o'clock. It is a sudden reminder that we are in the high Arctic latitudes, corresponding to northern Greenland and Baffin Bay across the Atlantic, where the sea ice would already be thick. The dark time, the long night that lasts almost three months, is not far off.

Five hours later, after supper, Mate Desmond Hendrickson is

up on the bridge well before the beginning of his watch. Des, as he is better known, is looking over the charts with Captain George, who is discussing options or other places to fish. The choices are not many. You have to stay well up in the north, for one thing, George explains, since the foreign catch quotas Norway has allowed for her southern coast, south of 62°, that is, are so low that none of the bigger ships are bothering to fish them. Between there and where we are fishing are the offshore reaches of the Lofoten Islands, generally considered the richest cod-spawning waters of the continent. But the Lofoten grounds have been boxed off as a special prohibited zone.

"Oh, how well I remember the Lofotens in the old times!" Des Hendrickson says, smiling. "I was in high glee when we dashed down there every spring! George, do you remember that tight little bank where we had to queue up to get in — we, the Russians, the Spanish, everyone — for the big spawning cod? We called it the Mixed Grill because it had plenty of other fair-sized fish, too."

"Well, that's not for us anymore," George answers. "The fact is, we got no place to go. It's here, the top of Norway, or nothing. The Norwegians give us a little more than the others — about thirteen thousand tons, I think it is, until the end of the year. But that's nothing compared to last year. Last year it was ninety-eight thousand tons."

Captain George is pacing the bridge again, a sure sign he is warming to the topic.

"And it's not just Norway and Iceland!" he continues. "It's Canada, too. We used to fish the Grand Banks some, back in 1966 and 1967, that was. But then we stopped and now they won't let us back in." He goes on to explain that the owners pulled their ships out the moment the good fishing slacked off and their trip profits weren't quite what they used to be. Since the Canadians are now basing their quotas on what foreign fleets fished in the last few years, there is very little for England.

"Besides, I made up my mind at home, rolling it around in my head, that I'd not go chasing the winds just because the fishing is thin," he concludes, repeating his master strategy.

For all these and his own reasons, therefore, Captain George has decided we will stay where we are for the moment, fishing the North Cape Bank. He is pointing on the chart to some of the better-known hot spots on the Bank, which is in reality a large irregular plateau, measuring approximately 170 by 90 miles, that encompasses many different fishing grounds. For the most part the hot spots rise above the plateau in the form of flat-topped knobs, or small seamounts, undesignated on the chart, to which the British have given such names as the Octopus, the Footprint, or the Bicycle Seat, according to their shape. These are also the wrecks: a great many of them, in fact, the hulks of all the World War II convoy merchant ships that failed to round the Cape, that didn't quite make it "around the corner" to Murmansk, only 160 miles distant. And warships, too, like the H.M.S. *Edinburgh* or the *Scharnhorst*. The latter, George says, forms a major ground in itself, since the *Scharnhorst* was blown to bits and there are pieces of her scattered over a large area. The same is true of a ground called the Aerodrome — it is the wreck of one of many long-forgotten merchantmen that ferried planes to Murmansk — where you are sure to snag some aircraft parts if you work in too close. All the wrecks offer good fishing. But you have to mind your bearings and skirt them very carefully, George cautions. If you don't, you're sure to get a bad fastening.

"And here's one we never go near," George adds, speaking more slowly. He points to a small elliptical mark on the chart, with no name or any notations. There is no need to be told. I guess immediately that it is the wreck of the *Gaul*, a sister ship of the *Kelt*, one of four factory trawlers that were hailed as the most modern and best equipped in the British fleet at the time of their construction. The *Gaul* had gone down with all of her thirty-six hands in a February storm not quite three years ago, "with a sudden loss of radio contact," as the captain of another British trawler in the vicinity testified. But the matter is still very much in the news. The

Department of Trade inquiry has never come up with an explanation satisfactory to all its members. And the widows of the crew have brought suit against the owners for compensation. It is very difficult in admiralty law to establish negligence when there is no evidence, meaning no survivors and not a bit of wreckage, as was the case with the *Gaul*. But the wives still hope and the suit is still pending.

"There was no icing; it was not icing up like some of the papers said," Captain George continues, still not saying the *Gaul*'s name. "The captain got into a bit of good fishing, you see, and his bunker was low."

Translated, George is merely stating what most distant water fishermen believe — that the *Gaul* was probably overcome by the classic sequence of events that makes factory trawlers most vulnerable. First, the decision to stop fishing is always put off as long as possible when it is going well. The weight of the last haulback is shifting around on deck, and tons of fish-cleaning and machine-cooling water are rushing back and forth under the gratings and catwalks of a factory working to capacity. If in addition diesel tanks are low, there may be a significant loss of ballast. No other preconditions are necessary. The sequence closes when rounding up into the storm, when the wind comes abreast. Shrieking gusts and a few big seas may then easily lay a large trawler on her beam ends. And hold her there, while she quickly fills and sinks.

By eleven o'clock Des Hendrickson begins his solitary watch. It is always so on most British trawlers, where extra hands are normally called to the bridge only as lookouts and helmsmen under difficult conditions. The wind has risen to Force 7, the night remains starless, and the short squalls are passing more rapidly, sending drier and finer snow flying horizontally across the arc of light in front of the bridge windows. In the distance to starboard is an aging "fresher," an ice-filled side trawler, the *Kingston Beryl*, built in 1959.

Des Hendrickson is watching the *Kingston Beryl* closely in between the squalls, trying to determine her approximate course. "I've done plenty of time on old freshers like her," he says to me, apparently eager to have someone to talk to. "Iceland was the worst, with all the blows and the cold, and mending, too. I went over the wall there. It was on the *Arctic Cavalier,* while we were hauling. We were just throwing the belly beckets, with the winches running full speed, when the wire that goes to the pie-eye catches me and sends me sky high.

"Well, I said my 'Dear Father' to myself," he continues, arching his body to imitate the course of his midair trajectory. "I says, 'Desmond, old boy, you got yourself a widow.' But I was wearing tight pant cuffs, so when I hit the water my oilskins trapped a lot of air and I shot up to the surface like a Polaris missile. Then I grabbed the net, hung on for dear life, and said the words of 'Amazing Grace,' my favorite hymn. The lads hauled me in, all right. But, you know, I try not to think of the hard times like that. I remember more of the good and look to the future. That way I have to say that, all in all, fishing has been very good to me."

Des Hendrickson, forty-seven, has strong reasons to say so. Born in Cardiff of West Indian parents, he is, as he prefers to say, colored, one of only five of his kind to make mate in the British fishing fleet. There were some bumpy times along the way, he will admit, but none that ever seriously troubled him. He prefers instead to think of all the good friends he has made through fishing. Without their help and encouragement he doubts he would ever have gone to nautical college for his mate's license. Des is proud he passed the exams on the second try. ("Some do it five or six times, you know, and then chuck it in the end.") But the hardest test of all, he firmly believes, comes when you get your first ship assignment and have to prove yourself as a second-in-command. In his case this occurred quickly, only two weeks after finishing his studies. Des remembers the occasion all too clearly. Just as he was going up to the owner's office for an interview, a factory manager he knew slightly asked him, in what seemed like a friendly manner, if it was true he had got his mate's ticket all right. After

Des had said yes and walked on a bit, the factory manager told him he might as well wipe his ass with it, since he would never get to use it.

"Well, it turned out the owners offered me the mate's berth on the same ship as that factory manager," he continues. "So when I came out I told him what happened and said that if he didn't want to sail with me, now was the time to say so and get the hell to some other ship. Well, he sailed with me, all right, and there wasn't much trouble, just an argument about the hail at the end of the trip. But I hit it right and he was wrong."

Des smiles with quiet satisfaction as he pauses in his story. He stands tall and ramrod-straight near the instrument panels, his long legs adjusting effortlessly to the ship's roll. As always he is wearing an army beret, pulled down low on all sides so that it looks more like a large skullcap. Des calls it his favorite memento of some eighteen months of military service, which he rather liked, or at least found a refreshing change from the sea. The black beret and his neatly trimmed sideburns contrast sharply with the light color of his skin. So, too, do his dark and deep-set eyes, which now take on a new fire. There seems to be something else he would like to say, and for a moment, as he pauses in silence, Des looks very much like a Hindu mystic deep in meditation. He has to confess, he finally says, that he is thinking of his father. He was a stern man who worked both at sea and in the coal mines of Wales before dying of an accumulation of accidents. Des cannot help but think how pleased he would have been had he lived to see his son a mate.

Our conversation is interrupted by the *Kingston Beryl,* which appears to be approaching on a constant bearing. Des first checks the *Kelt*'s course and then walks quickly to the radar. A small religious medal dangles from his chest as he bends over the scope in deep concentration. After a brief gaze he decides there is no danger or need to alter course. The *Kingston Beryl*'s course is a trifle tight, but she will pass astern.

Soon the older ship is close on our starboard quarter, dead in the water and hauling. Her deckhands are at the rail bringing in the trawl's midsection in the old manner or hand-over-hand, pausing only to brace themselves when a curling sea breaks aboard. Their heaving motions have an ancient and universal quality, the same as for every net ever drawn from the sea. But when the cod end comes up there are not many fish, barely fifteen baskets by Des's quick estimate. Rather than shoot her net again, therefore, the *Kingston Beryl* steams off into the night, hunting. The *Kelt* is alone.

To the observer at such a moment, the Barents seems an alien and unfriendly sea. An exhausted sea, much scarred by men's misfortune, it is impossible to forget.

Five days later, on a rare fine morning, we are steaming abreast of the bold outer cliffs of the North Cape, which are freshly topped by a foot or more of new snow. Sea gulls join us, circling lazily over the ship's wake, as we round into Porsanger Fjord. Soon the welcome snuggery of Honningsvåg comes into view.

Down in the officers' mess Chief Harry Pick and Third Engineer Morris Stryman are slumped into their chairs, tired and dispirited. Spread out before them on the dining table are the main-winch brake linings, which have somehow come loose from their shoes to the point of dangerous slippage. The linings might have been easily reset, Harry and Morris believe, but for the fact that after a long search they have been unable to find the necessary spare parts. Even a few screws of the right size, they think, might have done the job.

"Think of it!" says Chief Harry. "Just a couple of bloody screws and this call wouldn't be necessary. That's management for you!"

Captain George, of course, is even more dispirited. He has already given orders that our visit to Honningsvåg will be "a quick in and out, with no fooling around." Now he is expanding on the general theme of lack of support, moving from missing screws or other replacement parts to medical attentions and rescue capability.

"We have naught," he says, again employing his standard opener. "Last year up at Bear Island a man on one of the Seafridge boats got his arm caught in a block and chopped clean off. The *Frithjof* was down south near Hammerfest, but she steamed full speed twenty-four hours to save him. Then near here the mate of the *Kurd,* I think it was, got a nasty scalp wound from a swinging hook. Well, a Russian factory ship with those big pumped-up fenders they use come alongside and takes him off by gangplank. They operated on him then and there and returned him right to his bunk. A week later they checked to see how he was doing. When he got home, the British doctors called it a first-rate job."

On other occasions Captain George and his colleagues will express considerable pride in the way the British fleet has always taken care of itself, without all those fancy hospital ships, rescue tugs, and the like. This pride can sometimes carry to extremes. An example older crew members will never forget was the reaction of their skippers to the triple loss of the *St. Romanus, Kingston Peridot,* and *Ross Cleveland,* all overwhelmed by a winter storm in 1968 on the same grounds where the *Roderigo* and *Lorella* had gone down thirteen years earlier. When in the aftermath the government offered to put a navy meteorological and rescue ship on station off northwest Iceland, forty-three British captains declared after a radio conference at sea that the proposal was "an insult to the skippers and men who were lost and a slight on our intelligence and powers to command." It is unlikely such an attitude would prevail today (skippers and crews alike have become much more safety-conscious), but the pride in self-sufficiency remains. It manifests itself most strongly when skippers reminisce about the old days, when you had to live on fish and potatoes cooked in cod-liver oil, and union and safety regulations existed only on paper. You could fish where you pleased, too, and had superior crews. Things were always done right then, veteran skippers invariably add, by men who snapped to your orders without complaint.

It is with those times in mind, perhaps, that George is cheered to see the factory trawler *Dane* tied up in port as we close on Honningsvåg. The *Dane* is skippered by his good friend Jack Lilly, president of the Hull Trawler Officers Guild and one of the fleet's highest earning captains. George decides he will have a bit of fun and surprise his old friend — they were deckhands together, some years ago — in a manner befitting a top contender for the Dolphin Bowl annually awarded the highest grossing freezer trawler, often presented by the Duke of Edinburgh himself. Very eagerly, George switches on his VHF set.

"Fishing vessel *Dane,* fishing vessel *Dane,* this is the British trawler *Kelt* calling!" he announces, doing his best to imitate an upper-class accent and using all the required protocols, Royal Navy style, by which one ship properly addresses another. "That's Kilo-Echo-Lima-Tango, British trawler *Kelt!* I say, Jack, is that you in there?"

Greetings and laughter come back from the *Dane.*

"I say, *Dane,* are you long at the quay?" George continues. "When are you going out?"

"There's no out in sight for me," Jack Lilly replies. "Our fish-meal plant is paralyzed. We got problems with the meal."

"My word! My word! Well, it's a quick in and out for us, Jack, just a few hours. But I'll stop off for a visit if there's time for a walkabout. Over."

"Right you are, George. We'll be looking for you. Roger and over."

Captain George is smiling. He is relaxed, in fact, and sits back comfortably in his fishing chair as he cons the *Kelt* into port with precise orders to the helmsman. Sensing his mood, the helmsman responds with snappy aye-ayes and clearly repeats each course heading and engine room signal. Up forward and back aft the crew has secured all working gear, chockablock and Bristol fashion, and made ready the mooring lines. The *Kelt* slides smartly into a tight berth.

Twenty-four hours later the *Kelt* is still at the same berth, the brake-repair job having proved more difficult than Chief Harry anticipated. Her bow points directly at Honningsvåg's "downtown," which is in fact no more than a tight cluster of fish plants, chandleries, shops, and warehouses, relieved only by a small park with a statue of a sou'westered fisherman standing in a heroic pose. Behind the downtown section brightly painted wooden houses rise a short way up the slope of a mountain that looms very close over the town; the slope is quite steep and studded with parallel rows of sturdy snow fences to prevent slides or small avalanches. The day is fine, a Saturday as it happens, blessed with dazzling sun. Much of Honningsvåg's citizenry is out for a stroll, dressed in neat parkas or overcoats, wool hats of Lapplander design, and fine boots that crunch in the new dry snow. Many people push and glide along in gracefully designed foot sleds, the front seats of which are used for children, shopping goods, or a combination of both. The strollers and sledders come and go all morning, nodding *god dag* and comparing their weekend purchases.

The crew of the *Kelt* also come and go — to and from the ship, that is — carrying crudely wrapped packages, the contents of which they make little effort to disguise. Tacked up on the bulletin board of their mess, should any of them care to notice, is one of a number of standing orders which would seem to suggest that what they are doing is against the rules. It reads:

> Circular Letter No. 28: Drink on Board. This is a strongly worded document. It is the intention of the Company to eradicate, once and for all, the bringing on board of unauthorized drink. The Ship's Husband and Shipping Master have been instructed clearly that they must not allow drinks on board, and skippers and other officers must vigorously support this action . . . , which applies not only to sailing from Hull, but also to any other port in the United Kingdom or abroad.

The only authorized drinking, Circular Letter 28 goes on to say, is the daily allocation of two bottles of beer and, during winter, "rum by the tot only." In neither case, it adds, should it be the practice to pass out total allocations all at once, at the start of the voyage, as has been sometimes reported.

"Pooh, there's not a ship would leave Hull if they stuck to that!" a young apprentice engineer with whom I am watching the dockside scene tells me. "The gaffers would have a bloody riot on their hands, that's what." Like every other ship he knows of, the *Kelt* long ago distributed the beer ration, at least. Now it is gone, of course, and that is why the men are stocking up.

At two o'clock by the ship's Greenwich meridian time, the afternoon turns into night. Many of the crew are already back on board. They have had enough, they say, of battling the long lines in front of the Grand Hotel and the Café Ritz, the only two places in town where a man can get a proper drink. One of the returned crew, a factory hand named Ray Rodgers, invites me down to his cabin, where he claims a smashing party is in progress. "Come along and see how it is with us," he urges cheerfully. "You can't get any lower than my place!"

"Sometimes I think I should have taken my father's advice," Ray Rodgers is telling his guests, who understand immediately that he is leading into the subject of why he first went fishing. There are some twelve persons packed into his small four-berth cabin, sitting tightly wedged in both the upper and lower bunks or jostling for standing room only. The newly purchased beer flows generously, and the cigarette smoke is so thick that the fire-prevention sensitizer on the cabin ceiling is periodically triggered, causing the ship's alarm system to blast away from time to time. This, however, disturbs no one, except to occasion a good laugh.

"I was fourteen when I went out as a deckie learner," Rodgers continues. "When my father heard I was on the Iceland ground, he gets on the radio and tells me to get the bloody hell out of it. He didn't want me to be a fisherman, to be what he was."

Others agree. The same thing or something very similar happened to most of them. The older hands, however, have a different story. Almost without exception they first went to sea on what used to be called "pleasuring trips" with their fathers. Their fathers wanted them to be fishermen, in other words, and invited them along when they were only eleven or twelve as cabin boys for the summer voyage during school holidays. Most of them liked this kind of introduction, so after the pleasuring trip there didn't seem to be any other way to turn. The middle generation, like Ray Rodgers and those in their thirties or early forties, also had fishermen fathers. But their advice to their sons was for the most part ambivalent. "Oh, they tell you to get the fook out of it, that it's no life at all," an engineer from this group says. "But once you get a little money in your pocket, once you got a rating, they say not another word."

In marked contrast the youngest crew members insist they have reasons that had nothing to do with their parents, unless it was that their fathers wanted them the hell out of the house. The decision was entirely their own, they claim. Their sole objective, most agree, was to make some quick money — to have a few good years of fishing, that is, and then chuck it for something else.

"I saw this advert in the papers from the Hull Fishing Vessel Association," young John Rose, who is a cadet, or bridge officer trainee, is now telling the party. "It said, 'Have you got drive and initiative and want command at twenty-one?' "

Raucous laughter greets his explanation. Captain at twenty-one is stretching things a bit, his listeners all know. But not impossible. No, not impossible, some maintain, at least if it were a broken-down old sidewinder or a little coastal snibby.

As the laughter subsides someone asks Terry Towle to tell how it was with him. Terry is the *Kelt*'s chief factory engineer, the person charged with keeping all the Baader machines running smoothly. He is very popular with all hands. They have heard his story before, of course. But it's an unusual one, and they know he can be easily persuaded to tell it again.

"Well, I got married, that was the problem, and had to start making a few quid," he begins. "I was an engineer, so I took a job with the Birdseye plant in Hull. I used to stand all day, watching frozen peas drop into polyethylene wrappers, the same like we use here on board for the freezer trays. The only thing I had to do was check the weight of the peas and change the roll of polyethylene when it got low. It was not bad pay, mind you. The canteen was good, too, but you had to eat there all the time. There was no other place. You had to spend the whole day in the plant.

"The worst of it was that every now and then some quality-control bloke would come along and say, 'Look here, these packs are two grams light!' Can you imagine? So what is there for me to do? Adjust the control valve, that's all, and watch the peas drop for the rest of the day!"

Terry Towle is standing, waving his beer can in imitation of the endless cascade of green peas tumbling down on him. He is working toward his climax. "Look, is it any wonder I went to the Baader school and then shipped out?" he asks his listeners. "I was starting to dream about those fookin' peas!"

No wonder, indeed, his audience agrees, laughing once again at the thought of Terry tossing and turning in his nightmare sea of green. Anything would be better than that. Even fishing.

At this moment there is an interruption, marked only by a slight diminution of the general noise level. Captain George is rasping out something on the public-address system, but no one can quite make out what. An emissary is sent to find out. He returns to report that the skipper is asking for any information on the whereabouts of two or three men still ashore, since the brake repair is finished and the *Kelt* ready to sail. No one seems to know, or, if they do, they are not saying. The party continues, noisier than before and with still more guests.

"Did you hear I went to see the Spaniards this morning?" a new arrival asks, referring to a Spanish pair berthed at a nearby pier. "I'm glad I did! I was depressed, but now I see how they live I'm all cheery."

Many heads are nodding in unison. Some foreign fishermen do indeed fare worse. Still, as the veteran hands are quick to note, no worse than what they suffered in the heyday of the sidewinders. The trips were shorter, about three weeks as compared to three months on the filleters. But the short trips were just what made the old days so hard, the elders say. The pressure to fill up before fish spoiled, to fish through dangerous gales, or to make up for lost storm time by working the crew night and day — these were the things that made ruthless skippers risk the lives of their crews.

Not all the younger men are convinced. Many of them, in fact, say they often think of switching over to the freshers. There are plenty of good ones still around, they point out quite accurately, and the longest possible trip is still only twenty-seven or twenty-eight days. That's a hell of a lot better than coming home after three or four months on a factory trawler to find your girl friend gone off with someone else. Or, as some claim, that your children ask who you are.

"And there's the money, too," Buster South says. The pay on the freshers is getting better all the time, he argues, what with the price of fish going up the way it is. On the freshers, after all, you get percentages of what your catch grosses at auction — £6.60 for every £1,000 in Buster's case — whereas the flat tonnage bonuses of the filleters often don't work out nearly so well. "Put it this way, the risks are higher, the work is harder, and you get paid according," Buster concludes. "That's life, isn't it?"

The debate continues. There is one point, however, on which young and old can all agree. No matter what you shipped out on, the fishing was so much better just a few years ago that there was more fun to it and the time at sea passed more quickly. Ray Rodgers thinks this made everyone more adventurous and high-spirited. "Like the way you always had a good bash in port," he says by way of example.

On this point, too, all agree. The shore parties and brawls aren't what they used to be. Soon everyone is competing to tell his best-remembered story. Many, I suspect, are especially for my benefit. Surely I know of the Battle of Honningsvåg, someone asks. Three years ago, it was, and it all started when Patrick Kelly, the most generous man in the British fleet and a great party giver, got arrested in the Café Ritz on a false charge of marijuana possession and was put in the jug. When the word got back to his boat, the *Coriolanus,* and a Fleetwood trawler that was also in port, every man jack on the two ships joined in the charge on the Honningsvåg jail. In the battle royal that followed the Norwegians literally had to call in their navy and air force, complete with helicopters, to help the local police. "Oh, no, they wouldn't let Kelly out of custody or the *Coriolanus* out of port until the gaffers promised to pay damages," someone explains. "Then the Norwegians took the

*Cori* out to sea, but with a fookin' gunboat, under armed escort, like they say."

"Oh, he's a great one, Kelly, he is!" a deckhand proclaims. "He's single, you see, and it's always open house at his place in Hull. A real connoisseur of blue movies, he's got that projector of his running at nine o'clock in the morning, and it's party time all day long.

"Once some neighbors circulated a petition to have him evicted," the deckhand adds. " 'What's that?' he asks one of them on the street. 'Oh, aye, I'll sign it myself!' he says. That's Kelly for you! He still takes a trip with us now and then."

And then there were those strange and fearful things, the things you wouldn't believe, others are saying, that used to happen all the time on the older boats. Like when a big sea might come right down the smokestack of the steam-powered sidewinders, scoring a bullseye and putting out the fires. What you had to do, and very quickly, too, was chop up furniture or packing cases and get the fires up again before another giant sea might put you under. Or take the case of old Andy Eade, someone says, who had a fainting attack that everyone thought was the end of him. So what did they do but lay him out on the ice in the fishroom and notify the company by radio that he was dead. But then Andy rose up like Lazarus twenty-four hours later, giving the crew the fright of their lives.

"I swear by me wife and me bairns if it's not true!" the speaker adds. "You can ask him. He's on this ship, working down in the fishmeal plant. Old Andy, he says he still gets the chills from it and he still looks sickly, but he'll tell you."

Yes, it's sad, several of the men are saying, the way fishing has been so hard on poor Andy Eade. And on so many of their shipmates, when they stop to think about it, down through the years.

"Oh, it's no life at all, no life at all," one man says very suddenly. "People at home, they don't know what it is. They don't understand us."

"You know what that is?" a second responds. "It's because when you get home you don't know all the news, so everyone thinks you're ignorant. And look what happens when you meet new people! They ask you what you do and if you say fisherman the conversation stops."

"It's true Hull looks down on her fishermen," a third volunteers. "Have you noticed how the papers is always saying 'Fisherman in Accident' or 'Fisherman Docked for Drunk Driving'? But they wouldn't be putting it that way about a barrister or a greengrocer, would they now? The fookin' bastards. You gives your life to this industry. Then the gaffers put you out to pasture, and you're no good for anything else."

"The worst of it is you never get to see the bairns grow," an older engineer says, very slowly. "My son, he's six feet now, but I think of him so." The speaker is stretching out his hand, about knee-high.

The mood of the party is changing. Terry Towle, who likes to keep things on the bright side, has a suggestion. "Let's move up to my place!" he says. "I'm thinking this may be my last trip, so everyone enjoy!" Terry has a cabin up on the boat deck, the same as the bridge officers or the chief engineer. His suggestion meets with tumultuous acclaim.

"Aye, let's go posh at Terry's," the men are saying as they file out. "It's time we got up in the world!"

Up on the bridge Captain George is pacing as never before. It is supper time, the *Kelt* is ready for sea, and a lone straggler has held up sailing for more than half an hour. In between pacings George tugs repeatedly on the foghorn lanyard. The horn's loud blasts ricochet off the mountains surrounding Honningsvåg, shattering the snow-covered stillness of the little town.

"I'm getting blood pressure!" Captain George says, quite seriously. "I posted the time, I give strict notice, and then somebody goes off at the last minute to make a telephone call!"

Soon the last straggler returns. George swears and barks out a torrent of orders to the waiting deck crew. Two of them are a little slow in casting off one of the big stern lines. The *Kelt* already has some forward way. Suddenly, it is too late. The thick rope seizes on itself in the stern bollards; the two men dash for cover. There are brief straining noises and then a sound like a cannon shot as the line explodes in a burst of frayed manila fibers. And whiplashes, of course, just a little short of where the men were standing.

I sense that it is a deep humiliation for Captain George to have anyone witness so lubberly a spectacle. His anger, quite clearly, is too great for the amenities of further company.

Outside on deck there is another explosion — a quiet celestial explosion, that is — of ineffable brilliance. A large curtain of northern lights, the brightest I have ever seen, hangs over Honningsvåg. The curtain changes shape continuously as its shimmering folds drift and trail off at their lower ends. Nevertheless, for the moment, it seems positioned so low in the sky and so directly overhead as to be a fixed beacon, a departure point provided especially for the *Kelt* to set course for sea. The effect is friendly and calming. Standing alone on deck, I hope that it somehow reaches George.

Once out in Porsanger Fjord, the *Kelt* is gently pushed by a cold wind coming off the land. The northern lights remain with us, still very bright, flooding the rock-and-ice cliffs of the North Cape in a ghostly silver. Also bathed in the same light are some small Norwegian purse seiners, homeward bound. The little boats, overloaded as usual, are pushing hard to make Saturday night in port. The reds and greens of their running lights fade astern very quickly.

About five miles out, there is a low and unbroken roll of dark cloud. It is not likely to go away, since it marks the line where the cold land air reaches the warmer waters of the North Cape Current and condenses into low cloud or fog, depending on temperature differentials. The moment we cross this line, the last glow of the northern lights is abruptly extinguished. The south wind, having gained some sweep, blows stronger. The *Kelt* responds, rolling and yawing slightly to the following seas.

All is quiet below. The men know it is time to catch up on sleep, to make themselves fit for the endless rounds of twelve on and six off that will resume soon enough. In the deserted passage-ways there are only the steady sounds of air blowing from cabin ventilators, the throb of diesel engines, and loud snoring.

Late the next evening the *Kelt* reaches Tiddly Bank, there to compete with some thirty British, four Soviet, and two Norwe-gian trawlers. The fishing immediately improves. Some of the hauls average ninety baskets — the best of the trip so far. On each such occasion, Captain George is very pleased, proudly announcing that he has found yet another little fish shop, right under our keel. But almost as often he complains of the crowding (Tiddly Bank is but seven miles long and three wide) or becomes discouraged by a lower-than-usual catch. Veteran factory manager Arthur Myers, whose career began on the *Fairtry I,* watches George's moods very carefully. It is Arthur's duty to go up to the bridge and give him the tonnage totals after each catch is processed.

"Oh, yes, there'll be fire in the wigwam!" Arthur Myers says whenever he senses George is depressed or worrying about the generally slow pace of the trip. "I shan't stop off. I'll just stick my head in, give him my figures, and go."

A few days later or on the Monday after the fleet's expulsion from Tiddly Bank by the Soviets, a circular telegram from govern-ment and the company owners, sent through the United Kingdom Trawlers Mutual Insurance Company, reaches all ships. It reads:

AS OUR FISHING VESSELS HITHERTO FISHING IN DISPUTED ZONE
WERE DOING SO UNDER AGREED ARRANGEMENTS WITH NORWAY,
A NORWEGIAN PATROL VESSEL HAS CONFIRMED THAT U.K. VESSELS
ARE ENTITLED TO CONTINUE FISHING IN GREY ZONE AND SOME
ARE DOING SO WITHOUT MOLESTATION STOP YOU MAY THERE-
FORE PROCEED TO GREY ZONE WHILE CONTINUING TO EXERCISE
CAUTION AND RESPONDING TO INSTRUCTIONS FROM EITHER SIDE
STOP

The telegram is a matter for serious discussion, even though most of the captains do not find its contents very encouraging. The great fleetwide radio forum of the sea begins anew, with al-most as much vigor as on the original occasion of the expulsion:

"Well, that Norwegian, he's done his disappearing act again! I've not seen the famous patrol vessel in a fortnight!"

"Aye, and you could say we already got our instructions from the one side. Fookin' loud and clear they were, too, I'm thinking."

"I dun'no, Tom. It says you can fish with caution. 'Proceed to grey zone while continuing to exercise caution' is what it says."

"You know what that means, Barry? It means if you go in there and come out with some fish the gaffers will be fine with you, but if you get caught they don't know you. They don't want to hear about it."

Further discussion reveals that no one in the widely scattered fleet knows of any Norwegian patrol vessel in the area, much less of any British trawlers that have gone back to Tiddly to fish without molestation. The invitation to return to the gray zone, it appears, will be flatly declined.

In the afternoon, after tea, I see an elderly man dressed in a long underwear top and gray wool trousers sitting on the coaming of a fire door in one of the central passageways.

"I'm the fellow they told you about," he says. "My real name is Lionel Eade, but they call me Andy. I'm the one they took for dead." No, he wouldn't mind telling me all about it, he adds. I excuse myself, run to fetch pencil and notebook, and return to record his story.

"It was on the *Kingston Andalusite,* in nineteen forty-seven. It was a blackout I had from the war, a blackout from shell shock. They laid me out with the fish. Aye, they laid me right on the ice, with a canvas over me. I was that way for twenty-four hours, they say, before I woke up.

"No, at first I did not know where I was. I started to cry. Then I seen this stanchion and I knew I was in the fishroom. I pulled myself by the stanchion over to where the hatch was. I banged on the hatch. Soon the mate, he comes along and opens it. Then he slams it shut, thinking I'm a ghost. I was careful and had me head down. That was lucky. I might have been killed if I'd not had me head down!

"After a time, the mate he opens the hatch again. He just stares at me, scratching his chin, not believing what he sees, and then he walks away. I was hungry, so I went for the galley. When I gets there, the cook he climbs right out through the skylight. They all thought I was a zombie, you see.

"Then when we come home, there was my family on the dock all dressed in black.

"No, no, they didn't have no radio officers those times. The captain, he runs the wireless. He forgot to send the second wire saying I was alive. We were bound home, and he was playing that, that . . . what d'you call it? Aye, dominoes. He was playing dominoes all the way home. He forgot."

I thank Andy Eade for his patience and stammer something about how fit he looks now, or none the worse for the experience. He replies that he still feels a deep chill now and then, even in summer.

"Aye, and they still call me the zombie," he adds. There is a trace of pride, rather than hurt or self-pity, in the way he says this. His is a unique story, after all, one that everyone wants to hear and no one else can tell.

After supper the *Kelt* is off by herself. Earlier in the day Captain George had grown restive with too many close neighbors and decided the time was right for a little exploration, a little lone scouting, as he prefers to call it. The results so far have been excellent and he is in a correspondingly good humor. Now, however, one of the older stern trawlers steams up out of nowhere with her net on deck. One has to be suspicious under the circumstances, George thinks. His new neighbor will either shadow the *Kelt,* waiting to observe a haulback, or her captain will start making radio inquiries. The thing to do, therefore, is beat the intruder to the draw. George switches on his VHF transmitter and begins the difficult game of information exchange, British style. It is peculiarly polite and reserved, without any of the intricate sparring or sarcastic jokes practiced by other nations:

"Hello there, *St. Jerome.* I say, Tom, what are your intentions?"

"Well, George, it's all what you want to do. By the by, have you come into any fish over here? How was your last haul?"

"A fair haul, it was, but too many squatties. I'll be coming to port a bit now, following the hundred-fathom pitch, I expect."

"Righto, George. I'll be falling off to starboard then. It's all what you wanted to do. I didn't know what you wanted to do."

Captain George waits until the *St. Jerome* makes her move — until she commits herself by shooting her trawl — and then has a slight change of mind, as he chooses to call it, setting a different course from what he had announced. It is one designed to let his electronic track plotter take over and give him another good pass, he hopes, close to the last little fish shop he found. This done, he turns over the watch to Des Hendrickson and goes to his cabin, his good spirits restored.

The fishing continues, slowly. Six days have passed since the fleet left Tiddly. The *Kelt* has been working some small grounds known as the Groves and a long and shoal bank called the Finger. Both are "around the corner," or to the southeast of the North Cape and just on the safe side of the gray zone line. They are also only a scant twelve to fifteen miles from the Norwegian coast, which means this is one of the few occasions in distant water fishing when one may occasionally glimpse land. Today, however, the glimpses are rare. Showers of large snowflakes, heavy and wet, pelt down on us almost continuously, melting quickly on deck. When they lift briefly, there is a dim view of two low mountains covered with grayish snow and a strange assemblage of dome-shaped buildings, concrete silos, saucer antennae, and RDF towers. ("That's what the Russians worry about," Captain George says of it, claiming he has reason to believe the mountaintop installations constitute one of the most powerful early-warning stations in the Arctic.) At the foot of the mountains is a low island dotted with warehouses and small homes. This is the port town of Vardö, the largest in Norway's northernmost province of Finnmark. It has none of the snugness of Honningsvåg, nor are its approaches anywhere near as spectacular.

In the afternoon the weather suddenly clears. For some two hours after dark there appeared to be an exceptionally long sunset, or at least a small and low-lying band of brilliant light that lingered in one quadrant of the horizon. It was, however, in the wrong place, much more to the south than to the west. As it happened, a deckhand came along and set things straight for me. He explained the light was just the reflected rays of a sun that was stealing away from us, a sun that was still making the short days a little longer down to the south of us, under the horizon. "That's all you ever see of it when the long dark begins," he added. "You know it's down there, but it won't never come to you."

Early the next morning Vincent the galley boy falls headfirst down a ladder while taking down Captain George's breakfast tray. He thinks he has broken his arm. Des Hendrickson, the *Kelt*'s unofficial doctor, rigs him up with a thoroughly professional splint and a comfortable-looking sling. Nevertheless, Captain George thinks it would be better to have Vincent examined by the doctors in Vardö and gives orders to go there around midday, when there is some daylight. For his part, Vincent, who is all of sixteen and not at all sure about continuing his career in fishing, thinks this is a grand idea. "I'm packing it in this time, mates," he tells his friends, very jauntily. "You'll not catch me out on this bloody pitch again!"

But when the moment comes — when he is being lowered in a wire stretcher to the Norwegian pilot boat from Vardö by strange hands speaking a strange language — a look of sheer fright clouds Vincent's youthful features. Once in the boat he looks imploringly at his shipmates lining the rail. Captain George senses what the matter is. "You'll be all right, lad," he shouts down. "They'll take good care of you."

Going back to the bridge, George tells me the crew is already minus one deckie learner who complained of chest pains earlier in the trip and was put off at Honningsvåg. "Now I think that seeing it was only the lad's second time out, it was just that he discovered he didn't like fishing," he says.

But you can never be sure, George believes, and safety first and prompt medical attention should always be the rule. He has seen too many people hurt in his time. Like his nephew who was killed by a running winch, taken around five times, after some part of his body hit the full-speed lever. He doesn't even like to think about it.

In the evening we learn from the Norwegian doctors that Vincent has not broken any bones. His right arm is strained and badly bruised, however, and the company has decided to fly him home.

"He ought to get an Oscar for that performance," says Brian Pepper, the tattooed second cook, when he hears the news.

Three weeks have passed since I first joined the *Kelt*. Earlier, before we left Tiddly Bank, Terry Towle and others liked to tell me the crew would never allow a visitor who brought any kind of luck to leave the ship. ("No, they won't stand for it; you'll be with us the rest of the trip!") Now the subject is no longer mentioned. And the visitor for all practical purposes is not on the scene, being confined to his bunk with a back injury for all but mealtimes.

"I had to walk to school barefoot in all seasons, in short pants with a patch on the ass," Des Hendrickson is telling me, as he takes a powerful unguent labeled "Fiery Jack" from his medicine kit and goes to work on my back. "My father would lend me his boots for church and sometimes for school, but if I mucked them up the least bit he'd give me a good hammering."

Rubbing in the strong-smelling salve, Des says it reminds him of the goose fat his mother used to store in jars as a cure for colds. She firmly believed the older it got the better it penetrated and had the years marked on the jars. When she made a vintage selection, Des claims, he reeked so of the stuff he didn't dare go to school. Des says he likes to talk about his boyhood memories on quiet occasions — they are not, after all, the kind of thing you unburden on your shipmates around the wardroom table — and he wants to be sure I know they were not all bad. His father was an extremely stern man who had it in for him most of the time, but every now and then he would do a very nice thing. Des especially remembers one Sunday after church — he was still in his patched-up short pants — when his father took the family on an excursion to Swansea, a fishing port west of Cardiff, out where the Bristol Channel grows big and broad. It was Des's first real look at the open sea.

"I was in awe of it!" he exclaims, the deep fire returning to his eyes. "At first it was low tide, and all I seen was the flats. But then the tide comes rolling in and there were all these ships rising to it and riding at anchor. I felt the pull of it! I was in awe of the whole spectacle."

The pull remained and the sight of fishing vessels rising to the tide never left his mind, Des maintains. This was why he returned to Swansea at the age of sixteen, right after the war, and went to sea on a small steam-powered fresher called the *Tenby Castle*. From there on it was good to find a world where a man was accepted, by and large, solely on how he could do his job. That and his religious faith, which has given him the drive to get ahead, Des thinks, make up the rest of the story.

"I don't much care what other classes of people say about us," he adds, carefully packing up his medicine kit. "For as long as I live, whenever I hear the word *fisherman,* there will always be endearment in my heart."

My convalescence is also much enlivened by visits from Harold Norfolk, the *Kelt*'s most experienced winch operator. Harold is fifty-six and has been to sea almost continually since he took his first pleasuring trip at the age of twelve. He has an uncle who saw the last of the "boxing fleet," in the infamous days before World War I when the sailing smacks of the North Sea were forced to stay on the grounds for six to twelve weeks and deliver their catches to steam-powered carriers that shuttled back and forth to fishing ports. It was an efficient way to do things, Harold believes, one that in fact used the same principle as today's mother ships and catcher boats. But the business of heaving one-hundred-pound fish boxes from small rowing launches onto the carrier decks in all kinds of weather was extremely dangerous, so much so that Harold thinks he never would have gone into fishing in those times. Harold himself has had more than his share of danger, although he will never express it that way, when he was assigned to both minesweeper and Murmansk-convoy duty by the navy during the war. He saw "many a nasty crack-up" and was a principal contributor to the well-known book about the Murmansk run, *Convoy to Hell,* by Paul Lund, with whom he still corresponds. Like many of the older crew members, Harold thinks the comforts of the filleters more than compensate for the long trips. He always loads up with books borrowed from the London Seaman's Library before each sailing — he is reading one now about the Mayo Clinic — which are a great help in passing the time. He also does not swear, smoke, or drink and thinks that tattoos automatically brand you as "another breed of person." Summing it all up, Harold considers himself satisfied with the pay and working conditions of factory trawlers, but unsure about what he will do when his fishing days are over. Near the end of each visit he usually mentions the fact that he will probably be forced to retire next year and that it doesn't seem to him that fishing prepares you for anything else in life. If not, he will invariably close with a remark on the weather.

"It's getting to be that time," Harold will say. "You feel it in your bones and you know what's coming." That time, of course, is the day when the sun will no longer show itself, now only two weeks off. What is coming are the dread winter storms of the high Arctic. It is perfectly true, he and all the other older hands will agree, that you have more bad weather and the storms are more frequent down south. But when they do come up here, they can be the longest and worst of all.

The next day, shortly before supper, a factory worker rushes breathlessly to the bridge to tell Captain George that Arthur Myers "stook his finger up!" This is immediately understood as getting it caught in a filleting machine. Further questioning, in fact, reveals that Arthur's right index finger appears to be lopped off at the first joint and is of course bleeding badly.

"Ah, that's terrible!" George exclaims. "I'm shattered, that's what, absolutely shattered!" Nevertheless, he issues a string of orders with impressive despatch. The factory hand is sent to wake up Des Hendrickson, and Tony Scannell in the nearby radio shack is asked to start trying to raise Vardö immediately. George himself goes to his chart desk and quickly plots an estimated Vardö arrival for 0130 GMT. This done, he notifies the nearest British trawler that he is leaving the bridge on autopilot and rushes down below for a quick look at Arthur.

While Tony Scannell is talking, the Vardö operator excuses himself. Very politely, he explains that a West German freighter is in distress down around Tromsö, battling gale seas with a sixty-degree list. Not only that, a Norwegian salvage tug sent out to meet her has struck a reef. In such circumstances, the operator says, one must of course clear all channels and stand by. Ten minutes later he is back on the air. Yes, he says, the situation down south is improving and he has already arranged for a doctor to be on hand when the *Kelt* comes in.

Hobbling down to Arthur Myers's cabin, I find him sitting stoically in a chair staring at his well-bandaged finger, which he makes sure to hold upright. He seems more in a state of shocked bewilderment than anything else. The pain of it isn't so bad, he says, but he is worried about causing yet another interruption in fishing time and he still can't understand how he could have let such a thing occur. Nothing like it ever happened to him before, not in twenty years of working the machines. "It was the tip of my glove got caught, I think," he finally decides, speaking very slowly.

The night is clear and, fortunately, very calm. After the last haulback most of the crew gratefully turn in for a few hours of extra sleep. The *Kelt* then steams fast to the difficult harbor of Vardö, drops off Arthur, and quietly returns to sea.

A fresh gale, not strong enough to halt fishing, has blown for four days. The original plan for my departure was to take leave of the *Kelt* when she returned to Vardö to pick up Arthur Myers. But after two days of indecision the owners have finally decided to fly Arthur back home, since they are concerned that his finger might get infected and contaminate any fish he handled. Meanwhile, the gale has prevented any possibility of making port. The approaches to Vardö, the men tell me, have many off-lying shoals and skerries, ending in a cul-de-sac with man-made breakwaters just wide enough to admit a ship the size of the *Kelt*.

Today, however, there is another reason to go into Vardö again. Only last night, while hauling back in the gale, a fifty-five-year-old deckhand named Will Petty took a nasty spill, which Des Hendrickson thinks cracked one of his floating ribs. He is out of action in any case, whatever the final diagnosis. The consensus is that he should be dropped off while we are still near the coast, since there are rumors the owners will order a trip extension and send the *Kelt* far to the north, to Bear Island and Spitsbergen, in search of better fishing.

Today, also, the weather appears to be breaking. A stiff wind is still blowing from the east, but it seems to be moderating and the glass is steady. Captain George will give it a try, at least. He would be very grateful if I escorted Petty back to England — the ship's agent will take care of the tickets — since injured fishermen often feel confused and helpless when left to themselves in a foreign land. Then, too, there will always be a few who use up their travel allowance on a binge and get stranded somewhere along the way.

A light snow has started to fall. I watch from the bridge as the morning advances, bringing the now-precious daylight and another shrouded view of the headlands near Vardö Island. Captain George is apologizing about the trip. He hopes that I enjoyed it, but he wishes there had been better fishing for me to see and not so many interruptions. When I remind him that his unfailing search for those little undersea fish shops seems to have produced better results than others fishing near us, he is very pleased. Yes, he says, perhaps the trip won't turn out so badly, all things considered. Down in the fishhold there are now some 240 tons of frozen fillets; that's well over half the capacity, he has to keep reminding himself, and no one is coming home with a full hold these days anyhow. George also concedes that the lads have kept their good spirits and are working well, although of course the crews nowadays don't measure up to the kind of men you had in better times.

"The real problem is that we're too good for the resource," he says, after a moment of reflection. "With all the new gear the fish haven't got much of a chance."

"Yes, and the pelagic [mid-water] trawls have made a hash of it," says Des Hendrickson, who has joined us. "There's no rest for the fish. There's no fish safe on the bottom and there's no fish safe all the way up to the top! You think of the Germans with a net that the whole of Wembley or your Madison Square Garden would fit into the mouth of it. It's efficiency, yes, but —"

"Aye, it's that and the fact we got no place to go!" George breaks in. "Nobody loves us anymore. You'd think the Norwegians would be grateful to us after all we did for them in the War, right up here! Sometimes I think there's not enough understanding in this world."

Captain George is pacing the bridge. The mere mention of the future of British fishing, he claims, depresses him. He would rather talk about more cheerful things, like Christmas. What with the slow fishing and the possibility of a late return to Hull, he has been thinking, maybe the gaffers won't have the heart to send the *Kelt* out on the winter trip before the holidays.

"Of course, I can take a trip off and have Christmas any time I want, right at home with fine wine on the table and all that," he adds, smiling at the thought. Unmentioned is the fact, as he told me earlier in the trip, that he has not done so in three years. Or that the owners take a dim view of any officers or men who consistently skip the winter trip, and consequently assign them to older and less efficient ships.

We are closing rapidly on Vardö. Foaming seas surge and recede over rocky ledges to both port and starboard. Farther ahead small explosions of spray mark the line where waves rear against the harbor breakwaters. Presently a Norwegian pilot, an elderly man with ruddy complexion and the improbable name of Captain Øy, climbs nimbly up the accommodation ladder and guides us expertly through the narrow breakwater opening. He talks merrily to Captain George, all the way to dockside.

Des Hendrickson has rushed down to his cabin and returned

with a tape recording of "Amazing Grace" played by a Scottish bagpipe band. The bagpipes are a bit out of the ordinary, he says apologetically. But it's still his favorite hymn — the melody at least comes through clearly — and he wants me to have it.

Tony Scannell gives me letters of introduction to his district M.P. and a lecturer at the University of Hull, where his son is reading law. I will surely enjoy meeting the addressees, he says, since they are both gentlemen of distinction with much to say about the fishing industry or the economic problems of Yorkshire.

Harold Norfolk comes to the bridge with a note he has written containing all the facts and figures for the great Humber Bridge that will soon link Hull and Grimsby. It will be one of the longest single-span bridges in the world, he says, and I shouldn't miss the opportunity of seeing it under construction.

"Ooh, Bill, I wants to be going with you," sighs Brian Pepper, pumping my hand at the gangplank. "I wants to be slipping up the Humber right now. I tell you, that fookin' muddy river, it's the greatest sight in the world!"

"You're not after going to Bear Island with us?" Buster South and Terry Towle shout down from the rail, laughing and feigning surprise. "You sure you'll not be changing your mind?"

Captain Øy, who, it appears, is also the Vardö harbormaster and agent for the *Kelt*'s owners, deposits Petty and me in a stove-heated shack at the far end of the wharf. He apologizes for the fact that there is no other qualified pilot on duty today and he must therefore excuse himself to take the *Kelt* out again. But it will only be a matter of ten or fifteen minutes, he insists. After that there will be a hospital visit, a trip by taxi to the airfield at Kirkenes on the Soviet border, a night flight to Oslo, and then on to London in the morning. He has it all arranged.

The shack is overheated and stifling. After making sure that Will Petty is comfortably settled, I go out on the wharf again for a breath of air. The snow is now falling more heavily, stilling the east wind. In between its dying gusts it is possible to catch glimpses of the *Kelt* standing out to sea. Some of the crew are laying down the mooring lines in neat coils, while others move quickly to ready the trawl deck for a return to fishing. I picture Captain George as very pleased, snapping out his orders in proper Royal Navy fashion.

One final gust wraps the *Kelt* in a swirling curtain of snow. For a brief moment, after it lifts, I can see a lone figure walking out to the starboard wing of the bridge. It is Captain George, unmistakably. He turns toward the wharf, extends his right arm, and makes a vigorous thumbs-up signal. Then the swirling curtain descends again, silently closing down around him.

Three weeks later, on a windy morning in late November the day after the *Kelt*'s return home, I met with nearly all of her crew members again. They stood crowded in a narrow and drafty hall adjoining the owners' offices at St. Andrew's Dock in Hull, waiting for their first settling or trip pay. Later they would get additional pay for the fishmeal tonnage, quality bonuses, and any overages in the original catch estimates, several of the men informed me. But right now they would wait all day if necessary for the first settlement, which was much the larger of the two sums. The younger deckhands, dressed for the most part in tight-waisted jackets, flaring slacks, and their best high-heeled shoes, passed the time exchanging brief impressions of their first twenty-four hours ashore and debating about whether or not to make the winter trip.

Back in the rear of the hall, on an otherwise bare table, someone had left a pile of fishing journals which few if any of the crew had bothered to examine. One of the journals, the latest issue of London's *Fishing News* weekly, carried a banner headline proclaiming "NORWAY BLOWS THE WHISTLE!" The accompanying story told how the Norwegians had suddenly canceled all remaining foreign quotas in their two-hundred-mile zone for the rest of the year because of continued overfishing by European Community member states. A slightly older edition of Hull's *Trawling Times* ran a front-page item on the imminent departures of three high-earning filleters, the *Othello, Orsino,* and *Cassio,* for an extended joint venture in Australia, perhaps not to return. Both papers reported that large quantities of fish from Iceland were beginning to enter commercial or "nonfishing" ports all over the United Kingdom. Their editors agreed that this was making a mockery of the Hull bobbers and the Grimsby lumpers, who had steadfastly refused to unload any Icelandic vessel since the 1975 cod war.

In the front of the hall close to the entrance was a large blackboard, drawing much more attention. Many of the older crew members clustered around it, silently reading some typewritten notices pasted on its surface. It was called the orders board, Terry Towle told me, and it announced the last possible date and hour by which you had to sign on for a given trip, even though sailing time might be four days to a week later. Nobody was thinking about orders at that particular moment, Terry said, but the men were curious about the board because it was so bare. Usually it listed a wide variety of ships and dates. But today there were only two notices, both already outdated. One gave the orders for the factory trawler *Pict*, the deadline of which had passed two days before; the other, the sailing time for her sister ship, the *Norse*, two days later. No one, in fact, could ever remember so slack a board.

At about eleven o'clock a paymaster began issuing the settling checks. Shortly thereafter I saw Captain George in a small office one door down from the hall entrance. He was talking to the ship's runner, the company official most responsible for helping fill out crews. George immediately excused himself and took me outside to say that he had just heard the *Kelt* might be sent to fish for mackerel off the Cornwall coast on her next trip. This was certainly an odd role for a ship designed to cross oceans, George thought, but the mackerel had been fetching a good price ever since the North Sea herring ban and so maybe it would work out well. Then, too, he added, he would surely get home for Christmas.

Later in the day Des Hendrickson took me for a ride around the Hull waterfront in his Austin Healey sports car, which he had carefully put on blocks in a neighbor's garage while he was at sea. At the Albert Dock we saw five rusting side trawlers, rafted, or tied up abreast. Three of them, the *Boston Comanche, Boston Boeing,* and *William Wilberforce,* were familiar, or at least quickly recogniz-able. I had seen them on the Labrador grounds the previous win-ter, stretching the limits for ice-filled freshers in what the press had called a daring experiment. Des said he knew the experiment had failed, falling far short of meeting trip expenses, and that the three had not since been out to sea. The word was, in fact, that they might soon be towed away to the breakers for scrap. This was certainly a sad end, he thought, for able ships in basically good condition.

We finished our sightseeing at the locks that give entrance to the St. Andrew's Dock basin. All ships coming into Hull had to wait on high water and go through lock gates, Des explained, because the Humber had a tidal range of over twenty feet. But now the St. Andrew's locks were very rarely opened. They were too narrow for the big filleters, and even most of the sidewinders didn't have room enough to swing in the basin inside. So except for the various owners' offices, some chandleries and ropeworks, and the big U.K. Trawlers Mutual Insurance Company building, where you got your charts and the latest notices to mariners, St. Andrew's was for Des a kind of a dead place. He hoped that wasn't what was in store for the larger Albert Dock and the other fleet facilities in Hull. But he had a feeling it might be. As a result, he confided to me, he had been thinking about a berth on one of the trawlers recently converted for offshore oil-rig support work. He planned to go up to Aberdeen very soon to look into the matter.

"It's because I still have the drive to get on!" Des concluded, rather abruptly, with the fire coming back to his eyes. "And maybe now is the time to get ahead of the game."

I thought about this for a moment, while we watched the brown waves of the Humber race downstream on an outgoing tide. I had to agree. The end of the game — the high-stakes game of modern distant water trawling — seemed closest at hand in the land of its birth.

# SEVEN

# *To the* Seliger

A T 50°00′ W and 43°15′ N, on the morning of June 14, 1978, a new poster appeared in the mess room of the Soviet factory trawler *Seliger*. Freshly painted in sweeping red, green, and black letters, still glistening wet, the text read:

BALLS OF FIRE!

The Brigade of Second Fishmaster A.T. Abybikhanov,
with the joint effort of their comrade watchmates,
has processed

5 TONS, 570 KILOGRAMS

STEADY AS SHE GOES!

Although the new poster took its place with no fewer than seven others, all enjoining the *Seliger*'s crew to higher production quotas, it nevertheless stood out clearly from the rest both for its gaudy appearance and the exuberance of its message. In truth, however, the poster merely announced what the *Seliger*'s political officer, First Mate Oleg Sokolov, happened to consider a commendable twenty-four hours' work under difficult and unusual circumstances. Sokolov had waited some time, in fact, to insert just such an optimistic note in his daily exhortations on the need for greater collective efforts.

That morning, back on the *Seliger*'s stern bridge, Captain Oleg Amelichev directed the first haulback of yet another dismally foggy dawn. Below him helmeted deckhands manhandled heavy cables with drill-like precision. Presently a long and deep-throated extension piece, characteristic of Soviet ground trawls, snaked up the ramp. Dragging across the deck, it jingled with the sounds of thin-shelled clams, small pebbles, and clumps of mussels. Soon thereafter the giant *kutok* (cod end) rose up on deck. Streams of sea water gushed from its interstices, forced out by tightly packed fish. The big bag seemed at least two thirds full, with perhaps seven or eight tons of gray sole and yellowtail flounder.

"*Normalno, normalno,*" Amelichev said, very quietly, repeating the much-used Russian word for "average" or "just fair."

Captain Oleg Yakovlevich Amelichev, thirty-eight, might be excused his subdued reaction to what in fact was a good haul of flatfish in any waters. He saw no reason to celebrate, much less tack up congratulatory posters, if only because of long experience and intimate acquaintance with the grounds the *Seliger* now fished. His youth notwithstanding, Amelichev had been a fisherman for almost twenty years, beginning at nineteen as a cadet aboard one of the fine old square-riggers that the Soviets like to use as fishery training vessels. More to the point, he had first come to these waters in 1962 as fourth mate of a large factory trawler, back when the Soviet fleet was building up to a peak strength of 250 such vessels on the Newfoundland Grand Banks alone. He could remember, therefore, that in those days a factory shift producing five and a half tons of processed fish (out of fifteen to seventeen tons in the round) was commonplace or even below average. And flatfish at that! In his first years on the Banks no one ever bothered with the slippery and thin-bodied little "witches," or gray sole, nor even the yellowtails, except as incidental catches. Not when there were fat roe cod and redfish for the taking, twenty tons to the haul.

Also witnessing the early morning ritual was a group of eight or ten factory workers, temporarily idled. With what seemed like a decorous sense of place, they did not join the captain up on the stern bridge, but instead crawled out to a spare-net platform under the bridge and just above or almost on a level with their comrade watchmates of the deck. Here they observed the haulback in complete silence. Only when the big bag came into full view did they break into smiles and lively discussion.

"Oh, yet, it is always so," one of them explained. "We are happiest with the good catches. The time passes quicker."

"But the *moiva,* the *moiva,* the *moiva!*" said another, chanting the Russian word for the capelin. "When the little fish come, then you will see the results."

Unmentioned by either worker, but known to all of them, was a disturbing question. Where *were* the capelin? At this time of year the seas should have been alive with great schools of offshore spawners. Capelin, used in the Soviet Union for both fishmeal and human consumption, were what sent the daily tonnage figures spiraling, what the *Seliger*'s crew counted on to fulfill the ship's plan, or trip quota. The middle of June and still no sign of the little fish. No one had heard of such a thing. When would they come?

Now the deckhands busied themselves with emptying the cod end and hoisting the foreparts of the net high up on the stern gantry to shake the mesh clean of clogging weed and small fish. Captain Amelichev remained on the after bridge, watching and guiding the work. A huge man of medium height with blond hair, blue eyes, and a bushy, square-cut beard, he looked as though he could easily crush the strongest in his ship's company in an overly friendly bear hug. Everything about him bespoke authority. A stranger coming aboard without introductions would not have to be told; his bearing, his actions, his sheer physical size all spelled captain. But behind the rough beard and imposing stature were muted reserves of warmth and patience. As only his quiet smiles occasionally revealed, Oleg Yakovlevich Amelichev was, for all his commanding presence, a very kind and considerate captain. A captain, in short, who would never think of burdening his crew with his inner concerns.

Thus, if Captain Amelichev also worried about the nonappearance of the capelin, he spoke not a word of it. Faced at the moment with more immediate problems, he made a routine call to the forward bridge. The junior watch officer quickly answered his questions, one by one. No, there were no other ships lurking dangerously close in the fog. The ground ahead was about seventy meters deep, sandy-bottomed, and even. Yes, there were at least twenty miles of it, more than enough for a three-hour tow. No, it would not take them inside the big red arc prominently marked on the chart as the "Buffer Zone."

"*Tak derzhat, tak derzhat* (steady on, steady as she goes)," Captain Amelichev ordered. He left the stern bridge to go forward to his cabin for breakfast.

Unconsciously, to be sure, Captain Amelichev had borrowed a phrase from his first mate's garish poster. But to Amelichev it meant simply one more course heading, one more tow, to be entered duly in the logbook along with the weather, water temperature, ground consistency, and other essential observations for the proper conduct of fishing.

Normal. Steady as she goes. Business as usual.

Any one of these expressions might well describe the optimism or the general attitude of wishful thinking that buoyed up the Soviet fishing industry in the second year of two-hundred-mile limits. Clearly, there were problems. To keep the world's largest fishing fleet gainfully deployed under the severely reduced quotas and restricted areas imposed by nearly all coastal states would require some ingenuity and new approaches. But showing the way was no less a figure than a crusty Alexander Ishkov, the same fisheries minister, now seventy-four, who had first visited Canada to negotiate Soviet membership in ICNAF twenty-two years earlier. In 1975, despite the clearly foreseeable trend toward exclusive economic zones, Minister Ishkov had boldly projected a thirty to thirty-two percent increase in the 1975–1980 Five-Year Plan, a buildup of from 10,400,000 to 14,624,000 metric tons. Now, three years later, with two-hundred-mile fishery regimes an established fact in nearly all the world's best known fishing grounds, he gave specific guidelines on how this was to be accomplished. "To reach the targets set by the current Five-Year Plan," Ishkov declared in a *Novosti* press release, "the Soviet fishing industry will have to increase the efficiency of its fleet, start large-scale fishing beyond the two-hundred-mile zones and at greater depths, and expand fishing in our coastal waters." Given these new directions, he added, the people of the Soviet Union could look forward to eating up to forty-six pounds of fish per capita by 1980, double the average consumption during the 1960s.

In the Northwest Atlantic there was another alternative, not mentioned by Minister Ishkov, and not found in any official guidelines on the future of Soviet fishing. I had wondered about it before joining the Soviet fleet. So, too, had the Canadians, I later discovered. Wondered and worried, in fact.

The key to this unmentioned alternative lies with the geographical coordinates given at the beginning of the chapter. Map lovers may wish to make a rough plot on any suitable physical relief map of North America; 50° W and 43° N, they will find, lies near the tip of a great bulge in the North Atlantic coastal shelf, drooping southward like a falling teardrop, far out at sea. Using finger and thumb for easy measurement, the geographically curious will next discover that the tip of the bulge is more than two hundred nautical miles from Newfoundland's Cape Race, the nearest point of land. Such is the extent of the Grand Banks, in fact, that this tip is one of a few places in the world — the northeastern half of the Bering Sea, part of Norway's coast, and the Patagonian Shelf are among the others — where a clearly defined coastal shelf extends beyond any two-hundred-mile arc, however measured. Nearly everywhere else the rich shelf waters lie within newly drawn extended economic zones.

The tip is called the Tail of the Bank. It is the same ground where the *Fairtry* and the *Pushkin* first met and it is well known to all North Atlantic fishing nations as a shoal-water mixing ground where offshore branches of the cold Labrador Current swirl and clash with what are known as warmer slope-water currents. Not a bad place to fish, seasoned captains will tell you, except that you can't count on what's coming from one day to the next. Flatfish are often present in good numbers on the sandier shoals — gray sole, dab, yellowtail flounder, and, more rarely, Atlantic halibut — but they tend to be mixed and spotty or uneven in distribution.

Then, too, you may get short runs of cod, redfish, or even some stray pollock lured north and east from their normal haunts by the warm currents. But, mostly, you go for flatfish on the Tail. A place to scratch around, Captain Carl Spinney of the *Tremont* would call it, fishing by memory and the seat of your pants, hoping for the best, since even the most refined echo sounders are virtually useless in detecting flatfish, who spend much of their time buried in the bottom and for the most part lack the swim bladders that return, or "bounce back," electronic signals.

In the late spring of 1978 the *Seliger* was doing just that: hunting and scratching around on the Tail, digging out an occasionally good bag of sole or flounder. A 2,900-ton factory trawler built in 1968, she was one in a company of fourteen other ships of approximately the same vintage, nearly all from the *Seliger*'s home port of Kaliningrad, doing much the same thing. This small fleet may not have been what Minister Ishkov had in mind when he called for large-scale fishing beyond all two-hundred-mile regimes, but it was there for good reason. Hunting and waiting might better describe it. A number of the ships, the *Seliger* included, had licenses to mid-water trawl for capelin within Canada's two-hundred-mile zone. Canada, in fact, was still offering the Soviet Union one of its best opportunities to fish on traditional or familiar grounds, especially for fish neglected by Canadian processors. Included in the U.S.S.R.'s 1978 quota allocations in Canadian waters were 22,420 tons of redfish; 24,750 tons of the ugly grenadiers, or rattails, unwanted by anyone else except the East Germans; and, most significantly, an overwhelming 266,320 tons of the offshore-spawning capelin, five times more than Norway, the nearest competitor.

But with not a sign of the capelin runs, what was to be done? From the Soviet point of view there was everything to be gained by keeping the ships licensed for capelin busy on the grounds outside the zone while they waited. On the other side of the line, after all, it was gloriously free, unregulated fishing, given the collapse of ICNAF and Canada's failure to promote a successor organization with some international controls over every part of the Grand Banks. Then, too, a place like the Tail was ideal for Soviet fleet strategies, which require all trawlers to fish in systematic grid patterns and exchange full information with the *nachalnik* (manager), as the Russians call their fleet commanders, four times a day. With such constant searching and reporting, therefore, even a dozen ships could easily blanket the Tail and find the flatfish concentrations, no matter how scattered or how useless the sonars. And thus from time to time, as on the foggy dawn of June the fourteenth, do quite well.

The way to visiting a Soviet trawler at sea is a long one. Some patience is required, especially of those without official mission or support. In the writer's case, preparatory steps included long-unanswered correspondence with the Soviet Embassy in Washington, four days of anxious harborside waiting in St. John's during which first one and then another trawler he had been instructed to meet failed to appear, numerous phone calls to an unknown official in the Soviet Consulate in Halifax whose name had been provided "in case of any small problems," and, finally, the fortuitous appearance of a fleet-support tug, or what the Russians by appropriate coincidence call a *spasatel* ("rescue vessel").

The name of the tug was the first of many surprises. СМЕЛЫЙ, the large Cyrillic characters on her bow proclaimed. Native speakers will immediately recognize this as the Russian word for "bold." They will also know that unfortunately it cannot be transposed into the Roman alphabet in any form other than *smelly, smyelly,* or *smeli,* take your pick. That her masters were well aware of this unhappy circumstance, there was little doubt. Flying in the face of all accepted rules of Russian-English orthography, they had added a final consonant on the English-language signboard that hung, as required by Canadian law, high up on her pilothouse. *Smelij,* it said. Very boldly.

A fine ship of modest dimensions, the *Smelij* (I will go along with the alteration, wishing her no slight) provided much the same range of services as the West German *Fischereischutzboote,* although without the latters' engine-room computers, weather-map teleprinters, and other fancy extras. Ruggedly built in Finland in 1958, the *Smelij* had been well kept up and showed not a sign of old age. Her forty-foot beam and 210-foot length made for a profile typical of Soviet and other oceangoing tugs, which is to say a high and short superstructure perched forward on a blunt-bowed hull that carried a long trail aft to a round stern, very low to the water. Admirably suited to towing, with a 2,000-horsepower engine and a top cruising speed of seventeen to eighteen knots, the *Smelij* also managed to encompass several other functions within her cramped living and work spaces. The most notable of these included a five-bed hospital ward, a pump and hose room to fight fire on other ships, a well-equipped machine repair shop, a radio shack manned around the clock, and a therapeutic sauna bath, much appreciated in cold weather. True to the Soviet insistence on fleet self-sufficiency — which sometimes extends to replacing damaged propellers at sea — the *Smelij* also carried diving equipment and two master deep-sea divers ready at all times to don the traditional steel helmets and cumbersome lead-weighted suits still preferred by professionals. Thus provided, the *Smelij* and her crew of thirty-eight kept station on the North Atlantic for trips of exactly five months, just as the trawlers do. Five long months of service to the Soviet fleet and to any other vessels in distress, whatever their flag, in accord with the oldest and most honored of sea traditions. Five long months of waiting, towing, and repairing, relieved only occasionally by quick passages to foreign ports for fresh vegetables and other small things that give comfort to trawler skippers at sea.

I first found the *Smelij* tied up to a wharf near some large coal and sand dumps in an obscure part of St. John's harbor. Spatters of rain and rising winds, uncharacteristically strong for early June, swept her black hull and orange-colored superstructure. Alone on the long poop deck, a blond-haired young lady wearing a blue ski parka paced nervously back and forth, exhibiting all the signs of channel fever. As I prepared to address my first question to her, a short and stocky man with dark hair and jet-black eyes ran down the gangplank, introduced himself as the *starpom* (the Russian abbreviation for *starshi pomoshchnik*, chief mate), and cheerily led me to his cabin, which he insisted would be mine for the duration of our trip out to the fleet.

Minutes later, after my brief vodka and caviar reception in the captain's cabin, a scratchy public-address system barked out a stream of orders. Crew members, working quietly and without confusion, deftly slipped heavy mooring lines without the help of anyone on the wharf. The *Smelij* eased off smartly, her heavy engines chugging with the gentle and rhythmically pleasing pulsations of slow ahead, and made the harbor mouth in ten minutes, there to drop the pilot. Once outside the Narrows, she began to dance a wild saraband. The *Smelij*'s design, it was immediately apparent, made for the kind of quick-rolling response that knowledgeable seafarers call "lively" and consider highly desirable in terms of seaworthiness and safety. Comforting as this liveliness may be, it also produces the kind of wrenching motion to which one prefers a more gradual introduction.

Near to my tiny cabin was the officers' mess, a small room with dark red walls and a table accommodating ten persons at a sitting. Its monochrome decor was without ornamentation except for a ship's clock, a portrait of Lenin, a television set, and a book rack containing foreign-language editions of the standard Soviet propagandistic works with which most Russian vessels making calls abroad are usually supplied. Prominent among the book titles were *The Socialist World and the Liberation Movement, Soviet Citizens — Their Rights and Duties, At SALT Crossroads,* and *China and the Developing Countries: Political Gambling and Trade.*

At precisely half past three in the afternoon, a loud voice on the PA system said "fifteen-thirty o'clock, fifteen-thirty, crew to drink tea," twice repeated. Shortly thereafter four or five junior officers entered the mess, greeted me affably, and tuned into a local Canadian program on the television set, which was without sound. A girl named Nadezhda placed teakettles and plates of raw halibut, butter, and dark bread on the table. Outside, gale-force winds and rain lashed at the portholes and all but obscured a distant Cape Spear, the easternmost point of North America. Ever more lively, the *Smelij* continued to roll and pitch. She shuddered with each heavy head sea, but rose quickly to meet the next. *China and the Developing Countries* flew out of the book rack and skidded across the mess. The television set strained at its fastenings as the program changed to a professional wrestling match from Toronto, which appeared all the more grotesque for being acted out in silence. Two of the junior officers, losing their shyness, asked me what exactly they were watching with such bewildered fascination. Explaining the difference between professional and amateur wrestling, one quickly discovers, can be a severe test when putting a limited knowledge of Russian to its first practical application. But the men, evidently satisfied with my attempts, lost all remaining reserve. Soon they talked of many subjects and urged me to take more servings of raw halibut, in the most typical manifestation of Russian hospitality. This was, of course, another severe test, for a different part of the anatomy.

The days aboard the *Smelij* passed pleasantly enough, with gradually improving weather. I freely inspected all parts of the ship, practiced Russian, and watched a good many movies. Among the further surprises, and a very agreeable one at that, was Alexander Petrovich Korobetskom, the *Smelij*'s political officer. As such, he was the person who Washington experts on Soviet security had told me would be very difficult to identify. ("If the crew likes you, they may take you aside and tell you to watch out for him; that's how you'll know" was the exact advice I received from one State Department source.) Like much that I had been told before, this was hardly accurate. Whatever the cover or cryptic practices of former years, the Soviets are now quite open about their political officers. Aboard the *Smelij*, Korobetskom was immediately introduced to me as "our friend the commissar" amid good-natured laughter during the captain's reception. Aboard all Soviet merchant and fishing vessels, in fact, political officers now regularly occupy the position of first mate, which alone is free of watch duty. In return for this boon, Alexander Korobetskom worked especially hard at keeping up crew morale, which the best political officers instinctively perceive to be their principal function. He was also responsible, like all his counterparts, for personnel evaluations, ship inspections, the conduct of meetings, and many other more routine administrative chores, each carrying considerable paperwork. An extremely courteous man in his early thirties, Korobetskom was unique among his shipmates in keeping his cabin open at all times. (Russian seamen value their privacy; nothing is more characteristic of Soviet vessel living space than long rows of closed cabin doors.) Here he brewed good coffee or tea, received crew members coming and going between watches, and held court on such diverse topics as Antarctic whaling, factory ship duty, or the virtues of *spasatel* service, all drawn from his personal experience.

"I began as a cadet on a whale catcher boat and then had four years on the floating factories, but the *spasatels* are much the best," Korobetskom liked to tell me. "I like the sense of mission, ready at all times to assist others."

On other occasions Korobetskom clearly enjoyed talking about Murmansk, home port of the *Smelij* and the residence of most of her crew. He was, to be sure, the city's most ardent booster, followed closely by the second engineer, his next-door neighbor (a nautical academy classmate) and the ship's doctor, a plumpish woman in her late thirties whose soft speech and soothing tone of voice belied an earthy sense of humor and an admirable tolerance for the male world of ocean-going tugs. In this company the first mention of Murmansk was usually the signal for all three to ply me with astounding facts and figures about "the world's largest city north of the Arctic Circle." Murmansk and its population of 375,000, they wished me to understand, was one of the fastest-growing cities in the Soviet Union. True, the midwinter months were entirely dark, but the climate was milder and more salubrious than generally supposed. In reality, Murmansk was the ideal home for the outdoorsman or athlete, witness the fact that it played host every March (when sufficient daylight returned) to an Arctic Olympiad with ski races, skating, and cultural events for all. It was also a city of the young, with an increasingly youthful median age. This last, the lady doctor never failed to explain, was because the older residents did not properly appreciate the brisk climate and tended to move out, to be replaced by industrious younger workers, for whom there were nearly always good jobs and opportunities.

"The entire city has been awarded the Order of Lenin," Korobetskom would always conclude. "It is a great honor."

Equally friendly, though of a different stripe, was Anatoliy Anatolevich Mikholazhin, the popular chief mate of the *Smelij*.

"Look, I am a gypsy!" Anatoliy Anatolevich liked to exclaim at social gatherings, laughing uproariously and pointing to his black eyes and dark complexion. "It is true! A gypsy at sea!"

Happily, the crew always laughed with him. Anatoliy Anatolevich had learned that to make ethnic jokes at one's own expense is in many situations the only route to minority acceptance. He had chosen the route, the reader should understand, because like so many Northern Hemisphere countries, the Soviet Union is not without prejudices about its southerners (they are "lazy" and "clannish" or "distrustful") and, more generally, about any of its darker-complexioned peoples. This is especially true, incidentally, of the Soviet fishing fleet, where a strong majority of officers and crew are Great Russian.

At more serious moments Anatoliy Anatolevich would return to the cabin he had so kindly vacated for me, hug me around the shoulders, insist that I call him comrade or use his first name and patronymic, and unburden himself of his life history in a mixture of Russian and badly fractured English. True, his father had been a gypsy — he had died honorably in the defense of Moscow — but his mother was pure Russian. His son and daughter, he took pains to point out, "they grow orange hair [meaning blond, I always assumed], not black like me." His daughter was already a university instructor, and his son, he would make sure, was soon to enter one of the college-equivalent nautical academies that are a prerequisite for all Soviet deck officers. These facts established, Anatoliy Anatolevich would invariably go on to give me a rapid exposition of his *Weltanschauung,* most typically as follows:

"All peoples is O.K. War is terrible. The United States and the Soviet Union will come together. Our people now travels; your peoples now comes to our country. We are friends. But the United States government treats us badly in port! I have been to New York; we could not leave the ship! And why does your government not permit us more fish? Two hundred miles! Is it not true that the ocean is of no man?

"We have a good life at sea. I am satisfied. I am happy to be *Starpom*. But I will never be captain because I did not join the Party. For others it is fine to be a party member, but I cannot do it. You understand it is because I don't want to change myself. I am what I am.

"But you must know — you with your experience, you can see it — that the Soviet fleet is the best in the world! I have traveled to many countries and have also seen others. There is too much rank. They have too much formality; it sticks in the throat. With us you are what you work, and we all work together."

For Anatoliy Anatolevich the exercise was cathartic. If I but nodded in agreement with any of his views, he would return to the bridge a happier man. "We are friends," he always said on leaving.

In the evening of the second day out, Captain Mikhail Semyonovich Otvodenko, a tall and quiet man with aquiline features, informed me of a change of plans. The *Smelij*, already well on its way to the Tail of the Bank, would now have to alter course and proceed north and west full speed to Flemish Cap to take a distressed trawler in tow. The trawler was adrift with a badly damaged propeller and would most probably be ordered to Saint-Pierre and Miquelon. Considering the slower towing speed, the captain explained, it might be a week before the *Smelij* could fulfill this mission and then return to the main body of the fleet on the Tail. He hoped this would not be too inconvenient.

Two days later, shortly after a breakfast featuring raw sand eels, we closed with the disabled trawler, a thirteen-year-old ship of the Mayakovsky class named the *Gubertas Borisa*, from the Lithuanian port of Klaipeda (Memel). Eschewing any coil guns, one of the *Smelij*'s more rugged crew members effortlessly threw a heaving line high above the helpless ship's bow. Very handily and without problems, the *Borisa* was taken in tow. Her crew, standing atop the bridge and lining the boat decks, watched the maneuvers with great interest and cheered lustily, glad as crews always are to be relieved of the uncomfortable feeling of being a cripple at sea.

That night Captain Otvodenko again called me to his cabin for a conference. I would not have to stay with the *Smelij* for the trip to Saint-Pierre, after all, he said. We would be meeting a trawler, to which I would transfer at eight o'clock the next morning. He gave no explanation for this second change of plan, nor did I ask him any, not wishing to press my luck. Anatoliy Anatolevich, who was also present, smiled broadly; his obvious pleasure on my be-half seemed guarantee enough that a convenient and happy devel-opment had somehow occurred. I merely asked the name of the ship.

"Oh, I don't know the name," Captain Otvodenko said ca-sually. "It's trawler number two hundred and something. Anatoliy Anatolevich, do you remember the name?"

Anatoliy Anatolevich, his face now frowning, could not remem-ber. To him also it was just a number.

Not at eight, but sometime before six in the morning, the helmsman of the watch burst into my cabin and shook me awake. In excited Russian and sign language he made it abundantly clear that the assigned and still anonymous trawler was within close ra-dar range. Fifteen minutes later, after frantic packing, I gained the after deck just in time to see a large conventional lifeboat with a rachitic engine stroke come rolling through the fog. The legend on its bow read *"Seliger,* Kaliningrad, Capacity 56 Persons." The lifeboat circled around to a convenient gate in the port rail and kept running alongside, without making fast any lines, while the *Smelij* retained steerageway, slow ahead. Anatoliy Anatolevich handed down my gear. A large swell raised the boat almost to the level of the gateway.

"Jump now!" yelled its coxswain, a tall man with a long mous-tache, who was wearing a handsome full-length sheepskin coat. Strong arms caught and steadied me in the lifeboat. The coxswain instantly veered off. I could not see the *Gubertas Borisa;* only a taut cable running off the *Smelij*'s stern indicated that she was still safely in tow somewhere back in the fog. Without seconds, the *Smelij* itself was similarly lost.

If the reception aboard the *Smelij* was cordial, the *Seliger*'s was warmly hospitable, festive, and, evidently, well prepared in advance. Climbing out of the lifeboat onto the boat deck, I went instinctively to the person I thought was the captain and addressed him as such. Captain Amelichev, pleased by the recognition, shook my hand hard and said welcome many times both in English and in Russian. He would await me in his cabin for breakfast, he said, as soon as I settled in. A younger man with close-cropped hair — the chief mate, I later learned — shouldered my luggage and led me to an antiseptically clean cabin on the same deck, just aft of the *Seliger*'s large funnel. The cabin had a private bath with numerous handholds and a bunk with white-enameled guardrails, two amenities which immediately suggested infirmary or sick-bay use. It was just that, the chief mate said in answer to my question, or what the Russians in an uncharacteristic bow to ancient usage call the lazaret. (The word now generally means any between-decks storage space, but its original connotation was an isolation ward or quarantine station, said to derive from a corruption of *nazaret* from the fifteenth-century Santa Maria di Nazaret church-hospital in Venice.) Additional luxuries of the lazaret included a long working table with a strong light, fresh towels in all sizes, clean bed linen, an easy chair, and a small metal night table. Neatly placed on the latter was a bar of soap, a pack of mild Lithuanian filter-tip cigarettes, and a bag of candy and sugary Nabisco-like wafers, the label of which announced them to be "Waffles, Price 10 Kopeks."

In Captain Amelichev's dayroom — large, with wall-to-wall carpeting, and luxurious by any standards — a voluptuous woman with red hair and a suggestion of Eurasian features stood by to serve us fresh oranges, boiled eggs, cheese, dark bread, assorted pickles, and tea. These delicacies barely consumed, she placed on the table a second course of veal cutlets and french-fried potatoes, accompanied by fresh pots of tea and a bottle of export-quality vodka. At this point we were joined by First Mate Oleg Sokolov. Both he and Captain Amelichev seemed in remarkably good humor, considering the early hour. The vodka, of course, helped. We drank repeated *zdorovye*'s and exchanged many toasts.

The breakfast reception was highly informative. Captain Amelichev explained that the *Seliger* was a BMRT of the Leskov class built in Gdynia, Poland, in 1968 and named after a large lake near Kaliningrad that forms part of the Volga River headwaters. At 275 feet length overall and 2,900 gross tons, she retained the approximate dimensions and many of the basic design features of the pioneer Pushkin and Mayakovsky classes. The *Seliger* was of the same family tree, no doubt of that, Captain Amelichev said, but with later refinements and improvements. Although now quite old in terms of Soviet fleet development, the class was one that he liked very much and considered just as good as the newer and larger Altais, Atlantiks, and Super-Atlantiks. The factory arrangements of the Leskovs were in fact much more sensible. This was important, he thought, since good fishing can bog down with the overly automated or newer and fancier factory systems that break down all too often. First Mate Sokolov agreed. Then, too, Captain Amelichev added, the maintenance crews in Havana had done an excellent job in conditioning the *Seliger* for this trip and he certainly hoped he would get as good a ship on his next.

This last led to an interesting revelation: namely, that Soviet captains, as well as their crews, have no regular assignments. Seldom, in fact, do they know what ship they will be boarding from one trip to the next. The present voyage, Captain Amelichev explained, was his first on the *Seliger*. It had begun on April the twenty-third at Moscow's Sheremetievo Airport, where he and his crew of ninety-three first assembled and flew nonstop to Havana. From there the *Seliger* put to sea two days later. The trip, moreover, would end on September the twenty-fifth, after exactly five months at sea and in exactly the same way. On that much-awaited day the crew would fly home from Havana, leaving the *Seliger* behind to be readied by maintenance and repair crews, half Russian and half Cuban, for another trip with an entirely different complement. So much was this the accepted practice that as far as either Captain Amelichev or First Mate Sokolov knew the *Seliger* had not been in the Soviet Union for two years. Given its good condition, they doubted it would go home following this trip. "It is difficult to say how often a ship will return to the Soviet Union," Captain Amelichev volunteered. "Sometimes it is after one trip, sometimes after four or five. It all depends on where the ship is and what has to be done."

As I listened, I could not help but wonder about the system. The question foremost in my mind, as it would be to anyone familiar with Western fleets, concerned the remarkable bond that can build up between a ship and those who man it. Not to have this — to miss the strong sense of ship identity that comes with continued assignments — is unthinkable to most capitalist fishing countries. Owners recognize its value, witness the British challenge cups and the blue ribbons awarded top-earning trawlers of other fleets, and fishermen tell their life histories in terms of protracted association with this or that vessel. For this reason, as Captain Amelichev went on to explain that he had to contend with an almost entirely different crew on each trip, I could not resist the opportunity to get his views on the subject. Supposing, I asked, he had an outstanding crew that knew each other and got along and worked well together. Would it not be advantageous to continue their association? Would he not want to keep them?

"Oh, I'm used to it," Captain Amelichev replied. "And perhaps the opposite is just as true. Have you considered that crews may work better when they don't know each other too well?"

It was, as the Soviets might say, a lesson in dialectics. The contrary view had not, of course, occurred to me. But given further thought, it was certainly valid. Not to be forgotten are the tensions and lax discipline that occasionally build up among those who go to sea together trip after trip — the Spanish, for example — on voyages as long as the Soviets'.

As the breakfast reception ended Captain Amelichev told me we were returning to the Tail of the Bank, from which the *Seliger* had come halfway to meet me, to fish for yellowtail flounder and other flatfish outside the two-hundred-mile limit. The trip so far had been *normalno* — not good, not bad — beginning with licensed fishing for hake on Sable Island Bank off Nova Scotia. The crew had already had one recreational shore visit to Halifax, he added, and might get one more in St. John's before the trip ended. (Soviet trawlers make at least one port call in each five-month trip, but often minor supply needs may dictate a second.) He hoped the flounder fishing would be productive, but was eager to begin mid-water trawling for capelin, in which he knew I was interested.

That afternoon, I busied myself by studying a poster in the crew's mess. It bore a primitive hand-painted picture of a large trawler breasting a pea-green sea and was entitled "Ship's Organ — BMRT *Seliger*." Pasted on the poster board were neatly typed articles contributed by various crew members, which I thought might be interesting. One of the first to catch my eye read:

> Now the end of the first month of fishing has revealed initial results of socialistcompetition. During the time we worked on hake, our brigade showed that collective brigades can approach solidarity and work with full-efficiency strength for the fulfillment of trip quotas. Every member of our brigade tried to work quickly and correctly. The result — first place in the socialistcompetition!! It is hoped that the good work of Comrade Seaman Cernov V., Malkov V., Kuznetsov A., and others will be noted. Now the brigade awaits the start of capelin fishing. I congratulate my comrades for victory and wish them success in their future efforts.
>
> Seaman Akatov U.

Equally sparkling contributions filled much of the poster.

Early the next morning two figures rushed by the lazaret portholes. They appeared to be the third mate and a helmsman, running aft as fast as the fog-drenched and slippery surface of the promenade deck would permit. Seconds later Captain Amelichev followed, at an only slightly more dignified pace.

There was, however, no emergency. The grinding of winches

soon announced the beginning of a haul. Captain Amelichev, the third mate, and the watch helmsman were all merely making a routine transit from the forward to the stern bridge, from which latter point they would steer the *Seliger* throughout the haulback. The need for them to do this, should the reader remain confused, can be restated very simply. If in the design of the trawler you choose to have what has previously been called a passenger-liner appearance — that is, a lengthy upper deck with cabins, the funnel housing, and other structures immediately aft of the bridge — you cannot of course also have rearview bridge windows with direct visibility of the trawl deck astern. Rather than rely on relays or shouted orders or hand signals (as the *Fairtry I* eventually came to do), the Russians continue to use the small second, or stern, bridges that are standard design on all their older factory trawlers. (Not until 1969 and the *Altai,* the maiden vessel of the ninth major class in the evolution of the Soviet fleet, did Soviet designers switch to the high and isolated forward bridge with rearview windows.) The stern bridge is known in Russian by the ungainly phrase *rubachka rulevaya po korme,* which would seem difficult to sing out in a snappy order, and it may be found on over 650 ships of the older classes. On the *Seliger* it consisted of a cozy little shack perched on a narrow, rail-guarded platform that extended the full width of the ship. Inside the shack was a complete replication of all the instruments most necessary to the control of a large vessel, from a speed log and foghorn button to automatic steering and propeller pitch settings.

Normal procedure at the beginning of each haul, therefore, was for the watch officer and helmsman to scan the horizon (or radar) to satisfy themselves no nearby vessels might be on potential collision courses, check the steering and other automatic controls, and then sprint for the *rubachka rulevaya po korme.* Later in the trip I was often to find myself completely alone on the forward bridge under these circumstances. The automatic pilot would click away with its customary rhythm, adjusting to every swell. Lorans continued to track course. A black-box transponder in the chartroom unfailingly blinked out latitude and longitude in digital readers and stood ready at the press of a button to broadcast the ship's position in event of an emergency. And the *Seliger* would surge quietly and confidently ahead, so much so that it seemed totally unnecessary to worry about leaving her unattended. Still, one understands why the men ran. There is something ghostly, something inherently wrong, about a deserted bridge and a great ship left to purely mechanical devices, no matter how brief the interval. Thus, to see the watch running by the lazaret portholes at any hour of the day or night may have been an undignified spectacle, but it was reassuring.

First observation of the Soviet deck work reveals a striking difference from the practice of other nations. Most noticeably it is a matter of attitude and pace. There is no frenzy. One thinks of the British deckhands in their self-styled image of combat troops as they rush about the deck, often goaded by their captains. Or the Spanish bosuns crossing themselves as they descend into the pit, knowing full well they must react quickly at all times or be injured or killed. By contrast the Russians seldom run. Nor do they shout, except under the most trying circumstances. Although they might lose out by a few seconds in a stopwatch contest with, say, the West Germans or the English, their work is not really slower. Rather, it is ordered and methodical. In the language of the Spanish bullring, Soviet deck crews have good *temple,* the ability to keep a controlled pace during fast-moving or unexpected events.

Reasons exist for this. On Soviet trawlers there are, first of all, more hands to help. Each deck watch consists of six men; four or five is the more usual number on comparable-sized trawlers of other flags. In addition there is a chief bosun of the deck, known either as the *tralmaster* or *starshi master dobychi* (literally, "senior catch master"), who, although free of assigned watches, is most often on deck to help. Consequently, there is not quite so much for each man to do and less reason to hurry about. There is also the running gear, especially on the older factory trawlers, which is comparatively safe. The main winches are well forward, tunneled underneath the boat deck, in a location where the lethal whiplash of a parted cable is to some degree contained. The heavy blocks on which doors are hung are equipped with ingenious safety devices. Some Soviet trawlers even have a grillwork of steel bars, which is lowered over the stern ramp to protect men from falling down it. Trawlers of other flags ignore this danger, doing no more than stringing a rope across the ramp edge in heavy weather.

These provisions undoubtedly contribute to what appears to be enviable safety records. In a month aboard the *Seliger*, I saw not a single serious accident, nor even a cut finger or bone bruise. (Indeed, had there been a serious accident, I would have been moved from the lazaret and thus the first to know about it.) During the same period, moreover, the ship's doctor, a pleasant woman in her forties whose family name was Skorokhodova ("fast walker" in Russian), held no more than three sick calls and then only for a total of six or seven patients who had either skin infections or headaches. Dr. Skorokhodova had kept some records, she told me later in the trip, during her five years of seagoing practice. Serious accidents, which she defined as those requiring evacuation, since she herself was not qualified for surgery, occurred at the rate of one every eight months. More interestingly, Dr. Skorokhodova had not been able to discern any time-of-day patterns to the accidents. Studies among Western fishing fleets show a marked concentration of injuries near the end of long watches, just as clearly as ski-patrol records reveal that a majority of accidents will occur among tired skiers who insist on "just one more run" at the end of the long day. Asked about this, Dr. Skorokhodova found correlation not with hours of the watch, but rather seasons of the year. She and her colleagues in the fleet, she said, had found only that serious mishaps occur more often with rough winter seas.

If the above is at all representative, then much of the credit must go to the Soviet watch system. None is kinder. As against the crushing fatigue induced by the twelve hours on and six hours off of most European fleets, Soviet deck crews and factory workers go around the clock with equal time, or eight hours each, for rest and work. The same holds true for the remainder of the crew: the galley helpers, in which capacity, incidentally, five of the *Seliger*'s seven women were employed; the so-called special groups, who do engine and electronic repair; and even the lowly engine room wipers, whom the Soviets prefer to call "motorists." All enjoy their eight and eight. The only exception comes at periods of heavy catches, when off-duty personnel may be sent down to help clear the factory of fish.

Ironically, as members of the classless society, officers have a still easier schedule. It is one that even yachtsmen on pleasure passages might envy: four on and eight off. Nor do the deck officers suffer any of the enforced solitude common among other fleets, where captains and chief mates succeed each other in lonely twelve-hour vigils. On Soviet trawlers the fourth mate, ranking just above a cadet or apprentice, is usually paired with the *starpom* (chief mate). The second and third each has a *matros rulevoi* (seaman-helmsman) to help him; in addition, the third is also usually under the guidance and observation of the captain. In their defense, however, it must be noted that the Soviet deck officers have additional off-duty responsibilities — one may be in charge of ballasting or cargo and fish storage, another serves in effect as the purser or supplies officer, and so on — and that they, too, may be called to the factory to deal with extraordinary catches.

To their credit also, at least as a gesture to classlessness, officers never refer to themselves as such. The term *officer* is proscribed in civilian vocabulary. (Its use is considered proper only to the military.) Accordingly, Soviet fishermen go to great lengths to avoid it. When it is necessary to speak of the officers collectively — to make some differentiation from the crew, that is — one must call them the captain's company, or simply the company. The crew, paradoxically, is known as the command. Even signs on the doors of the *Seliger*'s two messes made this distinction very clearly, although to the uninitiated their meaning was exactly the opposite of what one might assume. *Kayut-kompaniya* (company's cabin) said one; *stolovaya komandy* (crew's dining room), the other. At the first regular meal, searching for my assigned place at the captain's table and thinking the first sign indicated a boardroom for high-level meetings, I of course entered the wrong one.

To provide such properly restful working conditions, Soviet

trawlers have large crews — extraordinarily large, in fact, relative to others. The Germans, for example, made do with crews of sixty on trawlers like the *Wesermünde*. But ships of the Seliger's class, smaller in every dimension than the *Wesermünde* and her sisters, are invariably manned by ninety-three to ninety-five persons. This is not atypical, and much the same holds true for the big nonfishing mother ships, which the Soviets call *plavzavody:* literally "floating factories." On these ships crews of three hundred to six hundred are not uncommon. Unlike those of the trawlers, over half of their crews will be women. The *plavzavody* also have excellent theaters, libraries, and occasional visits at sea by top concert artists from Moscow. "The social opportunities are more interesting," the *Seliger's* second mate, who had served on one, said to me of all this.

Soviet fleet operations, then, may run the full gamut from generous crew staffing and maximum self-sufficiency at sea to the provision of different movies every night or seagoing concert troupes. None of these practices can be defended on balance sheets or purely economic grounds, nor in the Soviet view are they necessarily supposed to be. The West Germans, more meticulous than most in cost accounting, estimate the operating costs of a factory trawler of the *Seliger's* size at $12,000 a day. The Atlantic hake and other less desirable species that the Soviets fish under license in Canadian and American waters rarely command much more than seven or eight cents a pound, undressed, on international markets. By these standards fifty tons of hake, which is a very good day's catch, would theoretically produce a daily operating loss of about $4,000. Project this figure to a five-month cruise and the sum is not inconsiderable. But, again, it becomes a question of what values are most important on the balance sheet. "The supreme goal of social production under socialism is the fullest possible satisfaction of the people's growing material and cultural and intellectual requirements," intones Chapter II, Article 14 of the Soviet Constitution. Accordingly, full employment is a sacred principle of the Soviet Union.

Nevertheless, Western economists take great relish in poking fun at the inefficiencies of Soviet factories clogged with too many managers and workers, as the Soviets themselves often do, or the official nonexistence of unemployment. But the fact remains that the goal is largely reached; unemployment, if not underemployment, *is* negligible in the U.S.S.R. Few workers have better job security. Or are harder to fire, depending on how one wishes to view the matter.

The early-morning haul of the first day aboard the *Seliger* strained the net, but not with fish. By some ill luck the trawl had managed to drag through one of those inexplicably dense concentrations of invertebrate bottom life. In this case the offending organisms were the familiar "potato" holothurians — more than five tons of them, in fact — which the Russians, as we do, call sea cucumbers. Also in the net were huge and slowly oozing accretions of light gray mud. Rarely will a ground trawl pick up large samples of the bottom it travels, but when one does, it is almost a sure sign that you have gone a little too far "over the edge," where the fine silts of outer continental-shelf slopes may ball up with claylike consistency. In any event, crushed between the globs of mud and the cucumbers was less than one ton of flounder and witch. The deckhands immediately noticed this, of course, and looked up accusingly at Captain Amelichev, as all fishermen do to their skippers or watch officers after a lost or nearly wasted tow. To him, however, the tow had been but a necessary probe, part of the methodical patterns of total search and experimentation. He immediately ordered a 180° course change for the next set and told me the fishing was bound to get better.

By supper Captain Amelichev was in good spirits. He was pleased to report the catches had improved, as predicted, throughout the day and he claimed they would be even better by night. "It is very curious," he said. "Even the flatfish rise up from the bottom and swim more after dark."

As the *Seliger* continued to work the Tail of the Bank, the first week aboard rolled by smoothly and without great event. True to Captain Amelichev's observation, the best catches came by night. Sometimes there were eight to fifteen tons of yellowtail flounder, which pleased the factory workers because of this species' relatively high yield. On other occasions the thinner witches and the Canadian plaice, or dab, predominated. But with us at all times was the curse of the Grand Banks in June of thick and unrelenting fog. To all outward appearances, the *Seliger* was a solitary ship quietly parting a permanent veil of gray on an ocean all of its own.

It was probably for this reason or the loneliness that comes in the private world of fog that Captain Amelichev seemed to enjoy his four-daily *soviety,* as the Russians call their radio meetings with other ships in the near vicinity. (The word *soviet* in Russian can mean a council or meeting of any kind.) Punctually, twice in the morning and once each after lunch and supper, he would enter the radio shack with pencil and paper and would himself take over from the chief operator the turning of the myriad dials and crank handles necessary to good reception. One by one the ships reported, terse and to the point:

"BMRT KB278, fishing grid M-62, thirteen tons cod, six redfish."

"Good evening, comrades. This is the *Polotsk,* grid 3N-78. We have twelve tons, all flatfish. Seas are calm, wind southwest."

Captain Amelichev would dutifully copy down all the catch totals, simply for his own understanding of overall patterns, and patiently wait his turn to report.

"We have about forty ships in all the Northwest Atlantic this year," he explained on one of these occasions. "It is nothing compared to earlier times, of course. We divide into three *raioni,* or general areas: Labrador and Newfoundland, the Nova Scotia banks, and the American zone, from Georges Bank to Norfolk. Each area has a *nachalnik,* a manager, or what you would call a fleet commander. Here in the Labrador-Newfoundland *raion* we now have about twenty-five ships, five out on Flemish Cap fishing cod and redfish and fifteen on the Grand Banks proper. Many of the ships on the Banks are outside the two-hundred-mile line, as we are, but two or three are inside. This is because there are still no capelin. When they come, we will have more ships licensed like ourselves for capelin, going inside the Canadian zone."

He was not quite sure, Captain Amelichev added, about the total numbers in the Northwest Atlantic. This was because all Soviet trawlers in the American zone had left there a week or so earlier, frustrated by very small "windows," the prescribed areas of latitude and longitude in which they were allowed to fish, and the presence of a great many large offshore lobster pots, strung together with cables or rope by American lobstermen, which constantly fouled the trawlers' nets. As of the moment there was not a single Russian trawler in American waters; that much he knew. He supposed, therefore, that some of the ships that had been there might be coming north to join us, while others would head for Africa or more distant shores.

In this and similar conversations on fleet operations, Captain Amelichev and a number of officers, or rather members of his "company," showed a keen interest in the practice of other nations. My accounts of the latters' various subterfuges and deceptions — of the West Germans continually trying to break each other's company codes, for example, or the Spanish *patrones* giving true information only to close relatives — seemed totally incomprehensible to them. Their reaction was hardly surprising. It could scarcely be otherwise among the citizen fishermen of the world's most systematized fleet, long accustomed to four-a-day councils and entire oceans neatly divided up in twenty-by-twenty-mile quadrates, or grid squares.

The systematization is not to be ridiculed. To see it in action was to be completely convinced of the value of cooperative fishing. From the beginning, one supposes, Soviet fleet managers understood that they were starting from scratch without any tradition or knowledge of distant water fishing and that they would thus have to rely on a full exchange of information to gain maximum information about unfamiliar grounds in the shortest possible time. Individualistic captains jealously guarding hard-gained knowledge — and passing it on generationally, if at all — may do well enough for others. But something more was necessary for the Soviet skippers. "It's all that talk, you know," Captain George Renardson used to say of them on the *Kelt*. "That's how they know where to dig up a good bag of fish."

Nevertheless, a paradox remains. Competition also plays an important role in Soviet fishing. Or "socialistcompetition," to be more precise. Here again we must be careful of terms. *Competition* in the usual sense is not a favored word in Soviet vocabulary, fraught as it is with capitalist connotations. One must rather say *sotssorevnovanie* or the tongue-twisting two-words-in-one for the socialist variety of the phenomenon, officially defined as competition that does not exploit but instead educates workers through emulation and mutual instruction. Definitions notwithstanding, some classical competitive stratagems — American personnel-management experts would call them employee motivation and recognition systems — are everywhere present both on individual trawlers and in the fleets at large. A majority of the crew on every factory trawler is divided into two "Complex Brigades," teams of deckhands and factory workers sharing the same watch, who compete in tonnage for a monthly award, usually a red and gold pennant hung prominently in the crew's mess hall. The same award also goes to the best engine-room watch or special technical group. Similarly, front-rank production prizes, usually a lapel pin and the posting of one's name and photograph on the *doska pochyota* (honors board), are given to individuals at the end of each trip. More significantly, the fleet manager keeps a close watch on the relative catches of ships fishing for the same species in the same general area. These are in turn converted into rankings which are posted in each trawler's mess along with all the other performance indices. During my visit, I was always happy to note, the *Seliger* regularly occupied first or second place.

"I don't like this 'who catches the most' business; I don't like the thought of a *konkurentsiya*," Captain Amelichev said to me of this. "Look, you have seen that today we moved to the northwest, scouting all by ourselves. You have seen how the catches are better here. So I told the others to come and join us right away."

Other captains in the same situation, I imagined, might not be quite so cooperative. They could conceivably delay or spread out their increased catches, reporting them in later soviets, and thus enjoy the considerable advantages of undisturbed fishing before the mob joined in. But not for very long. Captains in most Western fleets can and do underreport their catches for an entire trip; the discrepancies do not appear until their catches are spread out in all their surprising glory on the auction piers. But Soviet factory trawlers unload to refrigerated fish carriers at sea, at least two or three times per trip.

Going into the second week, the *Seliger* and four or five other ships that had heeded Captain Amelichev's call continued to make fair hauls in the fog-draped seas of the Tail. On the eighth morning a variable northerly breeze picked up strength and eventually settled down before noon in the northwest quadrant at about fifteen knots. Very soon the fog began rolling away to the east. The sole herald of this happy event was a brief moment of "foggy bright," with the warming feeling of a close-overhead yet still hidden sun. Five minutes later the *Seliger* broke through the wall of the vast fog mass that had enveloped us for over a week. In a dazzling sun and bright blue ocean she rose and fell gently to long swells crowned with small whitecaps. Unexpected numbers of shearwaters quickly joined us, soaring beautifully in the fresh wind except when disturbed by the feint of a predatory skua. For the first time, other ships were visible.

"Here on the port bow is the *Yuri Kostikov*," volunteered the third mate, normally a very taciturn individual, as we looked over our neighbors from the bridge. "It is the same as us, a sister ship. The other ship to starboard is the *Gulf Strim,* of the Altai type. It is much larger and more modern than us, built in the Soviet Union, with a one-thousand-ton fishhold. Ours is seven hundred. But I don't like the Altais. *Kak kachayet, kachayet* [how they roll and roll]! And how they list on every turn."

Obviously cheered by the good visibility, the third mate continued to talk. Soon our conversation entered the rarefied world of naval architecture. Cautiously, I asked if perhaps the basic Altai design was at fault, with too high a metacenter.

"It is just so," he promptly replied.

As the day wore on, more than our neighboring ships came into view for the first time. Following lunch and changing of the watches, many crew members I had not noticed before came out to enjoy that splendid feature of the older Soviet ships, not found on any other factory trawlers, which I have often chosen to call the promenade deck. Officially it is known as the *shlupochnaya paluba* — the *shlup* deriving from the ancient root word for a sloop, shallop, or small launch of any kind — and is thus more correctly designated the boat deck. But a promenade it certainly offered, with thirty yards on each side and a complete circuit of over seventy if one elected to use a break or a narrow transverse passageway through the forward superstructure. Around this route lady crew members now walked hand in hand, faces turned up to the sun. The men gathered in small groups, talking animatedly and smoking either the classical *papirosa,* which is in effect a cardboard tube with a short butt of black tobacco, or more modern filter cigarettes. One of the *ofitsiantki* (galley waitresses), who also doubled as a chambermaid charged with the daily cleaning of the lazaret and other cabins, sat on a fireplug reading what she described as a very romantic novel. An eager young factory worker named Valery Deinega, whom I helped with English lessons, greeted me in high spirits. He had thought of a joke, he said. The weather was so beautiful, he struggled to convey in both his best English and sign language, that surely I had influenced the captain and the *Seliger* was now off the coast of Florida, U.S.A. Unlike other fishermen, so indifferent to fair weather or foul, the Russians worship the fine days at sea.

Later in the afternoon another galley waitress, whom I knew only by her first name of Svetlana, told me she had seen me jogging on prior occasions. In addition to her regular duties, she carefully explained, she was the *sportsmenka* (physical instructress) on board and also the secretary of the *Seliger*'s Komsomol, or Young Communist League. Would I care to join her, she asked, in running and other exercises shortly before supper?

By evening the fog had returned. Little beads of moisture collected on the *Seliger*'s railings, and the decks were as slippery as usual. Nevertheless, Svetlana appeared at the appointed hour, equipped with good jogging sneakers and a trim blue and white warm-up suit. We started to run at a dizzying clip — faster than my customary and cautious pace, at any rate — using the full seventy-yard circuit. Very soon she began to add some of the rhythmic calisthenics to which Russians seem so addicted.

"Reach for the skies!" Svetlana commanded, alternatively scissoring her arms or lifting them high overhead as she pranced down the straightways in a series of balletlike *grands jetés*.

"Make like an airplane!" she next instructed, as with arms extended we banked around the slippery corners.

The reader will understand. It was one of those moments in life when questions about what we are doing in a totally improbable situation suddenly strike with embarrassing force. Stronger still was my embarrassment about what several husky crew members standing around on deck might think of the spectacle. But in truth, not one of them jeered. Or even raised an eyebrow.

If nothing else, the incident at least illustrates that physical culture is a thoroughly accepted (and sometimes mandatory) leisure activity on Soviet ships. On the big *plavzavody* the men and women working in the factory take required breaks from their fixed positions on the assembly lines to do loosening calisthenics to loudspeaker commands every two or three hours. On factory trawlers, where the work is apt to be harder and more varied, there are no such prescribed exercise periods. Even so, given their reasonable watch schedules, many Russian fishermen apparently enjoy keeping fit on their own. Two barbells were available on the *Seliger*'s boat deck; the stronger crew members used them often. Others, including the women, jogged, skipped rope, did knee bends, or, most commonly, paced endlessly around the promenade.

Whenever possible, Soviet fishermen also like to practice competitive sports. In addition to the ubiquitous chess tourneys and Ping-Pong, some crews attempt volleyball on the trawl deck, with the ball prevented from sailing overboard by a shock-cord tether.

On the return trip aboard the *Smelij*, First Mate Alexander Korob-etskom ingeniously organized a "Ship's Olympiad" on the occasion of Fishermen's Day, one of the thirty-four professional group holidays on the Soviet calendar. Almost the entire crew turned out to engage in boisterous tug-of-war, chinning, weight lifting, and standing broad jump contests; that night the victors received little prizes in a splendid mock ceremony at a banquet enlivened first by vodka and later by balalaikas, singing, and the ear-shattering whistles that spur on Cossack dancing. "It [the state] encourages the development of mass physical culture and sport," proclaims Article 24, Chapter III of the Soviet Constitution. Aboard the fishing fleet, it would seem, official encouragement is hardly necessary. Like anything else that breaks routine, exercise and organized sport are welcomed.

Other mainstays of morale and well-being for the Soviet fishermen are reasonably good food and, as already suggested, frequent motion-picture showings. All Russian ships at sea have four meals a day. On the *Seliger* lunch and supper were standardized and quite predictable. Each began with a large bowl of very tasty soup, most often potato, cabbage, or vegetable borscht. (The only questionable variety was a watery mix of fish bones and boiled potatoes called *ukha* which no one seemed to like.) Next came a small plate of fried meat with kasha, noodles, or other such starchy accompaniments. Two kinds of dark bread (but not butter) and a communal dish of chopped raw onions rounded out the main offerings. Rather than a true dessert, every lunch and every supper finished without exception with what the menu extolled as "compote." It was in fact a weakly flavored beverage made from dried fruits and served cold in teakettles.

The surprises came at breakfast. Like many other peoples of the world the Russians believe that the digestive system can best handle rich and hearty foods after a good night's rest — a proposition with which nutritionists do not necessarily disagree — and thus make no concessions in the direction of cereals or other blandities. Instead one receives the dark bread (with butter), tea, and one fairly stout main dish. The latter might be thick slices of raw bacon, Polish sausage, a wedge of cheese, cold fish, frankfurters, or, mercifully, twice a week, fried or scrambled eggs.

Some of the best food came at tea, which Captain Amelichev called *poldnik* (literally a midday snack) and insisted on translating as "lunch," although it was served from 3:30 to 4:30 in the afternoon. Bread and butter and freshly fried fish were always available at this time, plus delicacies such as *pirozhki,* the classical Russian buns with spicy meat fillings; *oladyi* (potato pancakes); *vinegret* (a coleslawlike salad); and *eekra,* which is the word for caviar, but in this case meant a cold puree of eggplant and other vegetables. The most popular of these — the *pirozhki* and the *eekra,* for example — were always starred or capitalized on the official menus posted ten days in advance on the messroom bulletin boards and countersigned by the chief mate, the second mate, Dr. Skorokhodova, and the chief cook. Teatime was also the occasion when the officers might indulge themselves with little extras. (The basic menu for all meals was, however, the same for officers and crew.) These might be Bulgarian plums or slices of lemon in a sugary syrup — the lemons were eaten rind and all — purchased from the ship's store. Alternatively, there was always the possibility of raw herring, Captain Amelichev's favorite, or cod roe, brought fresh from the trawl deck. The roe, served ice cold and spread with bread and butter, was excellent, being somewhat akin to a true and not-too-salty caviar and quite different from the rather tasteless canned variety. One may have many opinions of Russian diet — and new tastes to acquire it — but it is never uninteresting.

Movies were shown promptly after every lunch and supper, to accommodate both watches, from a projection booth at the forward end of the crew's mess. In order to provide a new program each day, the *Seliger* usually had about forty feature films aboard at any given time and regularly replenished this collection by exchange with other ships. The same was true of the "journals," newsreellike short subjects — "Ten Minutes Around the U.S.S.R.," "Soviet Sport," and "World Hockey: The Duel of Bobby Hull and Vyachislav Fetisov" were typical titles — that preceded every feature. First Mate Oleg Sokolov chose the films and usually presided over every showing. If not enough of an audience appeared, he seemed to think it a personal affront. Nervously pacing the mess as he counted heads, he would often delay the projection for five minutes and send an emissary or himself go to familiar gathering places throughout the ship to drum up more trade. Sometimes, knowing of my interest in the journals, he might even burst into my cabin to announce an exceptional offering.

"Oh, what a really excellent journal tonight!" Sokolov would shout. "It is about the BAM [the Baikal-Amur Magistral, the new trans-Siberian superhighway and railroad, now under construction]. You will see Siberia! And a great enterprise of the state! Come!"

So it is that, willingly or not, a visitor to the fishing fleet becomes an expert on contemporary Soviet cinema. As befits a nation that continually relives World War II, films about the Great Patriotic War, as it is more properly termed by the Soviets, far outnumber any others. The most eagerly received of these feature courageous *partizanki,* women guerrilla fighters in action-packed epics set behind enemy lines. (Notably absent from all of them is any reference to Stalin or, for that matter, to the possibility that other allied nations might have helped in the general cause.) The next most popular genre has surprising affinities to the American western. Instead of peaceable homesteaders against the open-range cattle barons and their hired guns, it pits soldiers of the Revolution returning to their homelands to form agricultural kolkhozes versus wealthy kulaks or remnants of General Denikin's White Army. Sooner or later in all of these films there comes the archetypal scene. Sun-bronzed young women, their hair tied up in kerchiefs, are pitchforking hay and singing happily against a blue sky with racing clouds; their menfolk are off purchasing or repairing a prized tractor. Then, over the brow of a distant hill, not Indians or a corrupt sheriff's posse, but a band of mounted kulaks and their hirelings suddenly appears. The men, of course, return just in time, and virtue in the form of a happy and productive commune eventually prevails. So popular is the genre, in fact, that Soviet directors have succeeded in transposing it to modern times.

One such film was shown aboard the *Seliger,* at least. True to form, the men had to go off to deal with reactionary forces, leaving their women to run the kolkhoz. But in this case the enemy was the Chinese, never actually shown in the film, but continually mentioned as lurking across a broad river and ever ready to make damaging border raids if constant vigilance was not kept. But the fact that the film was not shot on location blunted much of its impact for the *Seliger*'s crew. Realists all, they were quick to notice and criticize this detail.

"That's not Siberia!" yelled one. "It's not the Amur! It's the Upper Volga."

"No, it's the Dnieper, or somewhere in Byelorussia," said another.

"Comrades, such things are not important," a party stalwart finally interposed. "Let us be quiet and let the film speak for itself."

Among other recreational resources of Soviet fishermen alcohol plays no part, at least officially. Drinking was *"Nelzya, sovsem nelzya* [forbidden, absolutely forbidden]!" in the words of Dr. Fastwalker, as I sometimes could not help thinking of Dr. Skorokhodova, who was a strict party disciplinarian.

But in practice drinking at sea is widely tolerated. Like the British, the Soviets prohibit the possession of any liquor or spirituous beverages aboard ship, but captains are expected — indeed, almost required — to overlook the regulations on appropriate occasions. As mentioned in the official recommendations for inspection at sea, Soviet skippers are instructed to offer vodka or brandy to foreign inspectors or other visitors of note. For the rest, much depends on what individual captains consider appropriate. Some will be very generous, passing out vodka from their personal supply to the crew for holiday banquets, or, alternatively, not inspecting very closely the packages the crew members bring aboard after shopping sprees in foreign ports. Other captains are quite rigid; parties and drinking are largely confined to the captain's company and then only on very rare special occasions. On such ships the crew will resort to home brew. They whisper and pull you aside into the most unlikely places to uncover gauze-capped jars of a potent, milky-white fluid — called *vrak* (rubbish) in Russian — made from fermented raisins or other dried fruits. The effects of this little ceremony are not always pleasant, but the intent is admirable and typical of the extreme generosity of Russian seamen, who run some risk in doing this kind of thing with foreigners.

The first appropriate occasion on the *Seliger* came the second week out, on Doctor's Day, one of the thirty-four Soviet professional holidays. ("For us they are holidays of the soul," an electrician's mate explained, meaning that at sea work continues throughout all of them.) Promptly at 8:45 P.M. nine of us squeezed into the tiny single cabin of the straight-lining Dr. Skorokhodova for a late supper. Captain Amelichev came in resplendent uniform, navy blue with brass buttons and the customary four gold-braid stripes; the chief mate and commissar Sokolov were in mufti. On the distaff side, in addition to Dr. Skorokhodova, were the waitress who doubled as my chambermaid; the voluptuous redhead named Annalise who presided over the reception breakfast in Captain Amelichev's cabin and regularly served as the *bufetchitsa,* or "stewardess," of the officers' mess; a kindly older woman with handsome peasant features, who ran the *Seliger*'s experimental canning unit; and Svetlana the *sportsmenka,* who outshone all the others, all very well attired, in a trim green dress with high-heeled shoes and a string of imitation pearls. Crowding Dr. Skorokhodova's small dressing table were bottles of vodka, various salads, raw herring, Atlantic halibut from the experimental cannery, black lumpfish and red salmon caviar, salami, cheese, breads, and many other similar delights, with not an inch of space to spare.

Amidst much joking about the inadequacies of our banquet space and frantic lunges for dishes or bottles sliding with the ship's roll, there came that first prerequisite of all Russian parties: a round of formal toasts. Captain Amelichev led off with a splendid tribute to the medical profession in general and, more particularly, to the gentle sisters who served at sea. Dr. Skorokhodova responded with equal grace, nothing loath in the process to take decorous but full-measure sips of the forbidden spirits. Captain Amelichev, ever considerate, made a special effort to put everyone at ease. An admirer of the cannery and one of its best customers, he toasted the canning-unit lady and gently coaxed her into a reply. Carefully choosing her words, she made a brief declamation about her gratitude to be aboard the *Seliger* and her joy in her work. All hands roared approval, especially First Mate Sokolov.

Next, of course, came song. Captain Amelichev led off in a husky voice alternating between baritone and bass, which made up for any deficiencies in timbre with sheer enthusiasm and decibels. The ladies giggled, but he did not mind. His efforts produced just what he wanted. All joined in; the women, especially, had beautiful voices. Surprisingly, for a nation without a long fishing tradition, many of the songs concerned fishermen or life at sea. Most were very much in the heroic mode, as in the popular and rollicking *"Zvezda Rybaka"* ("Fisherman's Star"):

> *The fisherman has his fortune;*
> *Each from childhood with the sea betrothed.*
> *Here where storm and wind,*
> *Where all life's struggle,*
> *Makes courage our law of the sea.*

> Chorus: *At distant moorings alien lights*
> *And glare of beacons for someone search*
> *O salty waves! O salty days!*
> *But in the sky there shines,*
> *There shines*
> *the fisherman's star.*

Still others, such as the hauntingly melodic "Nadezhda" ("Hope"), which as in English is a girl's name, approached poetry:

> *Again we are separated.*
> *Between us once more are cities*
> *And the runway lights of airfields.*
> *Out here ours are the fog and the rains;*
> *Ours, too, the frozen dawns.*
> *Here, along unknown lanes*
> *Wait difficult, intricate things.*

> Chorus: *Hope, you are my earthly compass;*
> *Fortune is but the reward of the bold. . . .*

A small wave of homesickness and other private sorrows swept through the group whenever this song was sung. Sometimes the ladies' eyes grew moist, although none ever allowed a tear to form. But Captain Amelichev and Mate Sokolov were quick to notice and act accordingly.

"*Khod polny* [full ahead]!" Sokolov would bellow, thrusting forward an imaginary telegraph signal with his fist.

"That's right, all clear ahead and good health to you all," Captain Amelichev would reply, hoisting his glass.

And thus, tempo restored, the party would continue. It continued, in fact, for three full hours in its initial phase in the doctor's cabin. Then came a slight intermission — "The ladies must refresh themselves," First Mate Sokolov explained — after which we moved up to Captain Amelichev's spacious dayroom. Here Annalise and her charges had laid another excellent table. There were some repeat items — the cheeses and meat salad, for example — but also new delicacies such as true sturgeon caviar, fresh oranges, cookies, candy, and Canadian coffee. When the latter was served, nearly everyone laced it with Latvian *balzam,* a medicinal-tasting liqueur which Russian dictionaries define as "a grass infusion." Captain Amelichev explained that it was "to cure oneself," against ailments not specified, and that it was something a person like myself, unaccustomed to stronger spirits, might drink with impunity. As I did so, my toasts seemed immediately to improve.

Soon the singing and toasting gave way to dance music on reels of tape from First Mate Sokolov's collection. As Soviet protocol requires, each man danced in turn with each of the ladies. We swayed slowly to the romantic ballads, with the ladies giggling when the ship's motion caused us to bump or stumble. Sokolov next put on some Soviet jazz selections. Jitterbugging, at which Svetlana was particularly adept, was then in order. Captain Amelichev laughed uproariously when I called for more such decadent and hooligan music. Only the chief mate held back. Fortunately for all of us, it later proved, since he had the bridge watch starting at 4 A.M.

When I excused myself at 2:30, Captain Amelichev was giving yet another splendid rendition of the "Fisherman's Star," so loudly that his voice was already cracking and raspy.

"*Khod polny!*" First Mate Sokolov continued to shout, as he shuttled back and forth to his nearby cabin, trailing long ribbons of spilled tape.

The ladies continued to giggle.

The next day all participants seemed friendlier, exchanging knowing glances, and in excellent humor. Our select little party was exactly what such events should be at sea — a catharsis or total restorative from the monotony of routine. Only some grim news about the fishing spoiled an otherwise relaxed and pleasant day.

# EIGHT

# Steady On

"THE Japanese, the Norwegians, and some of our ships are still looking for the capelin," Captain Amelichev said in the radio shack the next day, after the noonday soviet. "The *Norglobal,* the big Norwegian factory ship, is at anchor on Southeast Shoals. But no one has reported any good catches."

"Our trawlers on Flemish Cap are doing all right, taking some cod and redfish," he went on. "But even with them it is nothing like last year."

Captain Amelichev frowned. His thoughts kept turning to the capelin. For the first time he began to express doubts that they would come at all. It was now so late that one had to consider this possibility, he said, although in all his years on the Banks he had never known it to happen.

"The capelin stocks in the Barents Sea are now more normal," he added in afterthought. "Our government has imposed closed seasons and quotas, and we are making an agreement with the Norwegians to do the same. Our position is that if we fish the capelin too heavily, we won't have enough cod."

It was Captain Amelichev's only mention, in the course of many talks, of the need for conservation. Although he might often complain of the decreasing opportunities and the difficulties of fishing within extended economic zones, he nevertheless viewed the future with great promise and a hope that recovering fish stocks might soon bring about a return to free fishing. His optimism was understandable. Fishing had been good to Oleg Amelichev. He had dreamed since childhood of going to sea. Now, after seventeen years with the fishing fleet, the dreams had been realized; he could look back with satisfaction on a rewarding professional career.

"Oh, yes, I read many novels and many historical works about the sea as a boy," he continued. "I am from Bryansk, a small town near Smolensk, far from any coast. My father was a *dorozhnik,* a road worker. It is true that I have an older brother who was in the merchant marine, but I'm sure it was all those books I read. In any case, at twelve or thirteen I was seriously thinking of going to sea.

"When I was nineteen I was accepted as a cadet on a training ship. It was the *Tropik,* a Finnish-built brigantine, a fine ship. Really, there is no better training than sail. You learn everything you need to know of the sea, and it makes a man out of a boy."

Captain Amelichev paused. He smiled and made a little pantomime of climbing the rigging as he continued to reminisce about his training cruise. "But what a pity!" he added. "Now the *Tropik* is like the *Queen Mary*. They say it is tied up in some Baltic port as a floating restaurant and nightclub."

From the training cruise onward, he admitted to my questions, his career had advanced quite rapidly. He had finished nautical college and on-the-job training in three and a half years, to be assigned at the age of twenty-one as third mate and navigator of a small side trawler fishing the Baltic and North Sea. Two years later he held the same position on a large BMRT in the transatlantic fleet. Then came an assignment that most Soviet officers dislike but accept uncomplainingly to further the cause of international socialism. In the years 1965–1966, Amelichev was sent to Ghana as part of a fishing aid mission, teaching the Ghanians the rudiments of ground trawling. Like others on the *Seliger* who had participated in similar missions, he did not harbor any deeply felt racial prejudices toward his black pupils. Instead, he had been shocked to discover that not all the citizens of the world share the Soviet work ethic.

"The Africans don't work the way we do," he simply said of the experience.

"But can you guess what happened?" he added. Captain Amelichev smiled as he posed the question, as though he was sure I knew. "One day all the statues of Nkrumah came tumbling down. And so we were out!"

Soon after the aid mission, however, Amelichev was rewarded with the critical promotion to *starpom*. He was then twenty-eight. Four years later, in 1972, he got his four stripes.

"That was the best trip!" he laughed. "You keep asking me about my best and my worst experiences, but I don't think of such matters. Look, it doesn't matter if it's Labrador in the winter! The first trip as captain is always your best."

In sum, Captain Amelichev thought, it was a good enough life at sea. To be sure, one missed one's family — indeed, upon retirement he would look forward most "to getting acquainted with my son" — but then there was a genuine satisfaction in knowing how necessary fishing was to the Soviet Union. Often he spoke with true missionary zeal about the need for more fish, about how his family, his friends, and all the people of the Soviet Union required more animal protein. It was true, he admitted, that in such places as Leningrad or the Baltic ports there was often a surplus of fish in the shops, whereas in some interior cities fish from the sea were not even known. But Secretary General Brezhnev had recently spoken of the plans for improved processing and distribution. There would soon be new marketing centers, he felt sure, all over the Soviet Union.

Captain Amelichev also firmly believed that if two-hundred-mile regimes were someday to come to an end with improved fishing, the prospects for world fish trade would be almost limitless. Increased foreign trade, he maintained, was the key to good relations among all countries and especially between the U.S. and the U.S.S.R. Well informed on the subject, he had on earlier occasions told me how important the big U.S. grain sales were to the Soviet Union and how much they had been appreciated by the people. Conversely, he had been chagrined by the breakdown of the 1974 U.S.-U.S.S.R. trade agreement and once asked me if Senator Jackson remained a presidential hopeful or a figure of importance in America. More specifically, returning to fishing, he knew that a major New England processor (Gorton's of Gloucester) had long had a contract with the Polish fleet to fill out such supplies as did not come from Canada. "Why do you buy from the Poles?" he asked me on that occasion. "We catch twenty times more fish than they."

Yes, there was still a great future to world fishing, Captain Amelichev now insisted, and I should not consider the small fleet of which we were part as in any way representative of present Soviet operations.

"You must not think that my company, that the KBTF [the Kaliningrad Base Trawling Fleet, a state-owned company that administers the older BMRT's of the Kaliningrad fleet] is all that we have," he said. "There is also another company in Kaliningrad, the KBEL, or Kaliningrad Base for Expeditionary Fishing, which manages all the newer classes, like the Super-Atlantiks. It is they who fish the new grounds in the South Atlantic, the Antarctic, and the Indian Ocean. The same is true of the Murmansk Company. Look, I have been in some of those waters. Did you know that there is an excellent new fish in the southern oceans? There is not even a name for it yet; we call it *nototeniya,* from its scientific designation [*Notothenia rossi,* now coming to be called the 'Antarctic cod']. It's about three or four feet long and has the same coloration as cod. But it has more fat and is a much better eating fish. Eight or ten years ago we caught many of these fish, from South Georgia in the Antarctic to the Kerguelen Islands in the Southern Indian Ocean."

I listened to this last with special interest. Even as we spoke, European fishing journals were hailing *Notothenia* as an important new discovery. The West Germans, in fact, were conducting extensive consumer tests, promoting the fish as excellent tasting and "having affinities with both redfish and cod." But Captain Amelichev seemed to be talking of it in the past tense or as a resource that had been already overexploited.

"You know about the krill in the Antarctic," he continued. "And then there are all the fish of the deep oceans! Who knows how many new fish are in deeper waters?"

In each example — new grounds to explore, the promise of the open oceans, and fishing at greater depths — Amelichev echoed the guidelines of Minister Ishkov. When I told him that the prevailing scientific opinion now viewed abyssal and deep-slope waters as relatively impoverished, he politely disagreed.

"Look, I have fished at depths of fifteen hundred meters [4,950 feet or 825 fathoms] and more in the South Atlantic," he answered. "We caught good fish, many of them not yet well known to the scientists. We have had much experience in this. And if you stay with us a little longer, you will see some deep fishing! The *Seliger* has a license to fish grenadier within the Canadian zone, beginning the seventh of July. Sometimes we fish the grenadier down to a thousand meters. Stay with us and you will see!"

Captain Amelichev's optimism was infectious. Ingenuous though it might be, the more one knew of his life the easier it was to understand. He had grown up with the Soviet fleet during the years of its maximum expansion, when constantly rising catches had made the fishing industry an outstanding success story in the Soviet Union. Now it was simply a matter of finding new grounds, and the success story would continue. Any thoughts that all this could be undone — that scientists might be right in assigning 80 to 90 percent of world fish stocks to the continental-shelf zones, for example, or that diplomats sitting at conference tables drawing odd lines on charts might be establishing permanent sovereignties in these same zones — were as yet too alien for him to grasp.

At the end of our long conversation, Captain Amelichev asked me how the cod and haddock fishing were going in New England. He knew, of course, that these two species had been prohibited to foreign fleets for almost a year and a half. I told him the stocks had improved dramatically and much sooner than biologists had expected, although full-grown fish were still relatively scarce.

Captain Amelichev was pleased to hear this. He remained in the radio shack adjusting dials and searching various frequencies for reports from other fleets. Perhaps, at last, there might be some word on where the capelin were.

A week later Alexander Zakharov, the *Seliger*'s youthful chief radio operator, heard that the *Norglobal* had weighed anchor. As far as he could determine, the world's largest factory ship had given up on the capelin and was heading home. Her satellite catcher fleet of the world's most efficient purse seiners had been unable to supply more than a pathetic fraction of what her factories could process at full capacity.

For some time before this, the *Seliger*'s deck crews had been readying new lines and checking out the Japanese-made headrope sonars, so essential to mid-water trawling. But the nets themselves — the huge mid-water trawls with a very small mesh newly made of clean white synthetic twine — stayed neatly piled on the platform below the stern bridge.

Unknown to us, a major alteration was taking place in the ecology of the Northwest Atlantic. A decade of what some management experts had so ardently espoused as harvesting at the secondary trophic level — taking smaller bait fish, that is, rather than their immediate predators — was suddenly showing a sad result. The little capelin that drew cod inshore and provided the lifeblood for Newfoundland's small-boat fishermen could nowhere be found, inshore or offshore.

Back in St. John's a long-standing debate was bursting out in the press with renewed vigor. The *St. John's Daily News* called for an immediate ban on all foreign capelin fishing in both headlines and editorials. "No!" answered an official of Fisheries Products Limited (Newfoundland's largest integrated fishing and processing company), which had pioneered in shore-based capelin-reduction plants supplied through a joint venture by Icelandic vessels. "Not until we increase research activity . . . until we know all the facts involving the capelin fishery." One government scientist held out hope. He reminded readers that considerable fluctuation was normal in capelin stocks, reported a good scull of beach spawners in one particular locality, and surmised that everywhere else "a lot of capelin are late spawning this season because of cold water." Not many agreed with him. Compounding the concern was the suspicion that many foreign trawlers licensed for capelin might be fishing for other species while they waited just outside the two-hundred-mile line. "We want to find out what they are doing out there!" cried Arthur May, director of resource management for Fisheries Canada, in an interview widely quoted in the Canadian press and international fishing journals. Although the almost constant June fogs had seriously impeded the aerial surveillance so essential for total fleet counts, Mr. May nevertheless suspected (far more correctly than he knew at the time) that on occasion more foreign vessels might be fishing outside the line than inside. This was not illegal, of course, but it flouted the spirit of Canada's fisheries legislation and was thus all the more reason to press for wider international controls through an ICNAF successor organization.

Later in the summer the president of Fisheries Products Limited gave me a more candid and succinct assessment of the capelin problem. "What we have seen is a total wipe-out, a biological disaster," he said, speaking of the offshore capelin fishery as a whole. "I cannot remember any worse season." A compensating late spawn had never occurred, he further explained, and the Norwegian fleet had gone home with a total catch of about 3,000 tons, no more than one day of full production aboard the *Norglobal*. His Icelanders had fared little better. He was thinking of dropping the venture, in fact, or converting to squid.

None of these events — unknown in their totality, but partially sensed by everyone aboard — seemed to discourage the *Seliger*'s crew. Although the absence of capelin could mean fewer rubles in their pockets, they went about their business with unfailing good cheer. The morale of all hands — officers, deckhands, factory workers, and the engine-room gang — remained uniformly high. The more the trip progressed, in truth, the more I came to a surprising realization. The *Seliger* was a happy ship, with the most highly motivated crew I had seen on any distant water factory trawler.

How much of this could be attributed to the unflagging efforts of First Mate Sokolov was a question that never ceased to engage me. Like all in his profession, he was, of course, much disliked by some of the crew. On one quiet evening, after Sokolov and I had finished a brief chat on a lonely deck, a crew member rushed out from nowhere and asked in whispered tones if I understood who he was and what he did.

"Watch out for him!" my informant cautioned, true to the State Department scenario given me before the trip.

"I despise that man!" he added, hissing through his teeth, as he quickly moved away.

But to the majority of the crew Sokolov was a genial and friendly presence. A tall man with dark hair and a strong build that was beginning to go soft from too much desk work, he had an India-rubber face that contorted in automatic reflex to his every mood, from dark scowls caused by disappointing production to ecstatic smiles of socialistcompetition satisfaction. The smiles, however, predominated. Most of the time, the crew well knew, First Mate Sokolov could be counted on for a good joke or a kind word of encouragement.

"Ah, so you say the fish are too small, not more than half a kilo?" I once heard him ask the crew, spreading his arms, raising his eyebrows, and letting his jaw go slack in mock astonishment. "But truly it is said that two small fish make one good fish. And, comrades, remember that grams make kilos and kilos make tons. And tons mean rubles! Work with goodwill, think of that, and then tonight how peacefully you will s-l-e-e-p!" He drew out the last word exquisitely, eyes closed, with a long sigh of relief. As always, the men laughed with him. Yes, they said, it would be nice to dream of those extra rubles. Perhaps, after all, they could fulfill or exceed the trip plan, even with the flatfish.

In these and all other counsels, First Mate Sokolov spoke from experience. He had himself been a fisherman, and this the crew respected. Born in the Far East port of Magadan on the Sea of Okhotsk, Sokolov had moved with his family to Astrakhan as a small boy. There, at the age of sixteen, he entered one of the numerous fishery trade schools where nearly all Soviet fishermen begin their training. He graduated three years later, alternating classroom instruction with job training aboard a small drift netter fishing the Caspian Sea. Then came what for all fishermen is the school of hard knocks, the long way up from a simple seamandeckhand. For ten years Sokolov had worked on heaving trawl decks, first on side trawlers in the Baltic and then on factory trawlers crossing the Atlantic or journeying north to the Spitsbergen and Bear Island grounds. During this time he advanced to the *starshi master dobychi* position that is roughly equivalent in other fleets to chief bosun of the deck. Finally, in 1969, at the age of twenty-nine, he was selected for the Higher Party Leadership School in Leningrad. After six years there, also interspersed with supervised training at sea, he had earned his rank as first mate.

Much of Sokolov's time was spent in paperwork, about which he always jokingly complained. The most onerous of his bureaucratic tasks centered around a little pamphlet known as the *Klasifikator,* which was in effect a demerit system with percentage-point coefficients, which he applied against other or more positive standards to give a trip mark for every member of the crew, from captain to seaman. Most of the *Klasifikator*'s rule violations or examples of bad work came under separate headings for different components of the crew, as, for example, "poor quality and improperly timed preparation of food, substandard baking of bread," to be docked at .2 for the galley crew, or "incorrect sorting of fish by grade, size, or species," rated at .08 for the factory workers. Others were general, or shipwide, ranging from violation of the rules of conduct for Soviet seamen abroad to inattention on watch, both worth one full decimal point. "If they add up to .9 or more," Sokolov would explain, "that is very bad, that means 'out'!" He hammered a nail through an imaginary board as he spoke the last word.

Significantly, a copy of the *Klasifikator* was always on prominent display, hanging by a string from a bulletin board in the crew's mess. Here, too, in what was the *Seliger*'s one and only social center, were many other examples of Sokolov's handiwork. In addition to the already-mentioned honor lists, ship standings, and the painful compositions of crew members (which always seemed to me to bear strong traces of Sokolov's forcing hand), a patient inspection of the mess decor also revealed such items as a "Cabin Cleanliness List" carrying the names of senior cabin leaders and a marking scale of one (very poor) to five (excellent) and a weekly health bulletin called the "Health Corner," done in collaboration with Dr. Skorokhodova, which covered such topics as alcoholism, personal hygiene, skin infections, and Vitamin C insufficiencies. Dominating all else, however, was a large poster near the aft entrance to the mess, which, unlike all others, drew almost constant scrutiny from the crew. "ECONOMIC INDICES OF WORK: TRIP TO-TALS," it proclaimed in the boldest letters of all. This was, of course, the *Seliger*'s quota or trip plan. Here the captain's production assistant filled in daily tonnages in neatly divided columns, for every kind of fish and for every method of processing.

Such was the mess hall's inventory of exhortations and instructions. From time to time First Mate Sokolov also added flash bulletins, most often announcements of meetings or international Communist festivals ("Let There Be Strength: Long Life to Soviet-Cuban Friendship!") or more rarely his colorful "fireball" posters praising high factory production. Then, too, there were periodic calls for voluntary action, or so at least it seemed when large signs cheerfully urged, "Everyone Out for the Subotnik!" On land in the Soviet Union a *subotnik,* which derives from *subota,* the Russian word for Saturday, is a true example of civic spirit in which citizens voluntarily give over their Saturdays off to simple repair projects or neighborhood cleanups. More officially defined, a *subotnik* is "a day's labor freely given to the government." At sea, unfortunately, it is the day's wage that is given and there is no choice in the matter.

Many of these devices, but by no means all of them, are to be found in the workers' clubs or in the "Red corner" reading rooms of every Soviet factory, the use of which is voluntary except for meetings. But on a factory trawler, the place where workers eat, socialize, and presumably relax is also inescapably their schoolroom. A schoolroom, that is, where messages from the principal's office and both individual and collective grades are ever on display.

Another of Sokolov's duties, apparently, was the care of foreign visitors. With me he was a model of patience and politeness, never missing an opportunity to point out events he thought worthy of attention. The latter might vary from a detailed description of a passing ship of another class to a shouted reminder that it was *banya* day — complete with a vigorous pantomime of scrubbing and toweling — the one day in ten when the *Seliger*'s shower room and steam bath was open to all. More important, neither he nor anyone else ever placed any restrictions in my way. I enjoyed full run of the ship, free at any time to make unannounced visits to the bridge or to work in the factory sorting fish and learning how to pack freezer trays. Another example of his courtesy and consideration, I thought, was the nearly total absence of anti-American statements in the daily news announcements he made over the ship's public-address system during the lunch hour. This was the more remarkable since first mates on other ships regularly use these and similar occasions for intense political commentary. (I have met Soviet captains in port who, after a few drinks, complained bitterly that their first mates devoted more time to lecture-tirades on international affairs than to anything else.) To my knowledge Sokolov made but a single public reference to the United States and then only when he quoted from a *Christian Science Monitor* editorial cautioning our policy makers not to forget the common interests of the U.S. and the U.S.S.R. in the new flush of excitement over improving relations with mainland China. Instead, Sokolov habitually rushed through his noonday broadcast with what passes for news in the Soviet Union — construction projects, meetings of the Supreme Soviet, or endless bulletins from cosmonauts Vladimir Kovalenok and Alexander Ivanchenkov, at the time well along in their record-breaking sojourn in space — with such enthusiasm that he sometimes had to stop to catch his breath or find his place in the wireless bulletin from which he read. Then came the reading of telegrams ("Congratulations and a happy holiday to Seaman Nikolai Markov, father of a boy, Yuri Nikolayevich, born June

2r"), changes of watch schedules or other ship's business, and, finally, a short homily on the virtues of sufficient rest, good health,
and proper collective spirit in the daily battle to conquer the ocean's
riches. In the officers's mess the more sophisticated among his audience might laugh when he tripped over his own words or wink
at me to show their boredom with either his sermonettes or the
news announcements. Next door in the mess hall, the crew listened with more attention.

But rather than the impersonality of microphones and public
address systems, Oleg Sokolov clearly preferred the dynamics of
the numerous meetings it was his duty to conduct. These proved
his shining hours, especially if they were festive in nature. On such
occasions he seemed much more the friendly tour director of a
cruise ship than the commissar of a factory trawler. The first of
them during my visit came on the eve of the Day of Soviet Youth,
under the sponsorship of the *Seliger*'s Komsomol. Svetlana the
*sportsmenka,* in her capacity as secretary of that organization, opened
by reading the minutes of the preceding meeting to a full audience
crowding the mess hall. The minutes approved with a thunderous
*da,* she then introduced Sokolov. He gave a rousing speech,
thanking one and all for the *subotnik* they were contributing the
next day, including, even, the distinguished visitor from the United
States, whom he understood to be no stranger to the factory.
(Cheers, laughter) Then, very soon, it was time for the testimoni-
als from the audience that are considered essential to meetings of
this kind. Now Sokolov was at his best. He kept up the momentum in a manner not unlike an American coach in a locker-room
pep talk.

"Would not the audience like to hear the mature opinions of
the distinguished trade-union delegate and hydroacoustic me-
chanic?" Sokolov asked. The sonar technician, as he would be called
on other ships, was a respected person in his early forties, popular
among all. Shouts of approval greeted this suggestion.

"Yes, comrades, it is true that I have more years than most of
you," the sonar technician began, seriously and modestly. "This
itself is not important, except that perhaps it has given me more

opportunity to see how far our beloved country has progressed, how far we have come in what is now the sixty-first year since the glorious October Revolution."

But, like university commencement speakers, the sonar technician knew that the future must lie with youth. "It is important to remember the young people who hold in their hands all our hopes," he concluded. "That is why I am so pleased that we celebrate the Day of Soviet Youth and that is why I thank our Komsomol for this festival."

"That's clear, that's clear enough," Oleg Sokolov responded, even before the applause had stopped. "What more? Who is next? Can it be that we will not hear from the factory sections? Who will speak for the brigades?"

All along the rows of *obrabotchiki* (factory hands), who always stuck closely together, there were nervous downward glances. Sokolov's inquiring eye soon came to rest on my friend Valery Deinega. Yes, he was the one! He, with his international experience, was the logical choice!

Valery Deinega blushed, bit his lip, and looked at the floor. His friends watched eagerly, happy they had not been chosen. But for Deinega there was no escape. Why had not the assembled group spoken more of the international youth movement, Sokolov asked rhetorically. By this and similar persuasions he virtually lifted Deinega to his feet.

"Comrades, as many of you know, I have had the opportunity to travel to distant lands and seas," Valery Deinega began. "On the *Anton Lopatin,* on the *Malakhit,* and on the *Akvamarin,* I have been to Montevideo and the southern oceans, to South Georgia, the Coronation Gulf, and the very continent of Antarctica." He spoke slowly and paused after every phrase, feeling his way and making sure he spoke in complete sentences.

"You know, too, that I have fished shrimp with our Cuban comrades in the Gulf of Mexico and worked with the shore crews in Havana," Deinega continued. Now he felt more confident. His eyes sparkled and his voice took on a more sincere tone as he moved to his conclusion. "Comrades, it is true that in some foreign lands they look at us strangely and know little of our progress in the Soviet Union. But there is understanding among the young people of the world! I know this from Cuba. I know this from the strong bonds of friendship forged through the Komsomols with our Cuban comrades! That is why I, too, am glad we celebrate the Day of Soviet Youth."

A wave of relief swept over Deinega's factory-shift friends. They laughed and exchanged approving comments throughout the general applause. Most of them, of course, had heard his story before. But Valery had done it. That was important. He had given a good testimonial and spoken well. And was that not an admirable thing?

"Oh, excellent, excellent!" boomed Oleg Sokolov. Sensing that the meeting had reached a zenith, he wisely moved toward rapid adjournment. "If there are none against it, I declare that this festival for the young, this our celebration of the Day of Soviet Youth, is now closed.

"And on with the show!" he added, yelling over the crowd and almost pushing the motion-picture operator into the projection booth.

The crew rose to their feet, clapping loudly. Some moved off to the work from which they had been briefly excused, talking and smiling more than when they had assembled. The rest stretched themselves, rearranged their chairs, or otherwise made ready for the nightly movie.

The outsider watches and reflects. Somehow, there comes to mind the elegant rhetoric of Arthur Koestler, who once described Soviet society as condemned to "living in a climate of perpetuate adolescence." He might have written differently aboard a Soviet trawler. At sea, at least, this adolescence has an undeniable charm and energy. And breaks the routine, wherein its value.

Later that night the *Seliger* crossed to the western side of the Tail on a solitary scouting expedition. The next morning it was as though we had entered another ocean. As the fog rolled away, bits of sargassum weed could be seen floating in the troughs of azure-colored seas. Incredibly, Portuguese men-of-war drifted close by. They held their course easily, cresting up and over gentle white-caps, with iridescent air sacs that acted as staysails. Clearly visible under the surface were their long trails of tentacles, each studded with deadly stinging cells. Fulmars, who have a notable preference for boreal waters, were suddenly nowhere to be seen in our avian escort. The shearwaters, in fact, had the ship's wake to themselves.

The day grew very warm with the rising sun; off-duty strollers crowded the promenade deck. Nearly everyone now repeated Valery Deinega's joke. Yes, they said, the captain had listened to me and the *Seliger* was bound full ahead for Florida. Well they might have thought so. On the bridge the water-temperature thermometer registered an unbelievable 16° centigrade (61° Fahrenheit), up from 8° (46° Fahrenheit) the day before. In truth, not Florida itself, but one of its physiographic by-products was the cause. A deviant eddy of Gulf Stream water, known to scientists as a "warm-core ring," was paying us a visit. (Such rings may be likened to the whirling eddies left in the wake of a canoe by a strong paddle stroke; for reasons not yet fully understood, the Gulf Stream generates similar eddies, which have both the size and strength to travel long distances.) Even under normal circumstances the western edge of the Tail of the Bank, affected by the previously noted slope-water currents, will be warmer than the eastern, which is more subject to the Labrador current. But when a wandering warm-core ring reaches the area, water temperatures are doubled. Thus the southernmost extension of the Newfoundland Grand Banks becomes, however briefly, a small outpost of the Caribbean Sea.

Up in the net came extraordinary quantities of mollusks — mussels, clams, moon snails, and small whelks — similar to what one might typically find on a New England beach. But, incredibly, at our exact position on the southwestern tip of the Tail, the coast of New England lay over 1,200 miles away. The abundance of such coastal organisms so far from land can have but one explanation. Water depth, more than currents or eddies, was in this instance the critical factor. The larvae of many mollusks drift far and wide —

clear across the Atlantic in some cases — during their brief free-floating existence on the sea's surface. When at the magic moment of metamorphosis they must sink down to permanent and sedentary existence on the bottom, they cannot survive if the water is too deep. Over much of the Grand Banks the microscopic larvae will perish as they filter down to a hostile sea floor with excessively high water pressures, low temperatures, or a combination of both. But here and on other shoaler portions of the Tail they drop down to no more than fifty or sixty meters to congenial sand and weed bottoms that provide them little islands of safety — Elysian gardens ideal for molluscan growth — far out at sea. So it was that all through the day shells scraped, jingled, and tumbled as they dragged across or fell onto the trawl deck. Many were so familar that they made me homesick for summer beaches. Among them were razor clams, cockles, both smooth and ribbed mussels, multicolored scallops, and numerous whelks, some of which harbored live hermit crabs, not to mention brittle stars, sand dollars, red and purple starfish, and tons of short-finned squid. But not many fish.

Captain Amelichev took the poor results stoically. "It is always so with such warm water," he explained. "I cannot say why. All I know is that it makes the flatfish rise and scatter widely." I could see he was disappointed, nevertheless, not to be able to report a good discovery — not to have the satisfaction of summoning the other ships — as he had done before.

The next day we moved north and east to dead center of the Tail at its widest point, very close to the two-hundred-mile line, fishing depths of eighty to ninety meters. Right away, the variety of molluscan fauna dropped off and the fishing improved. Now the haulbacks regularly produced ten or more tons of flatfish, mostly the preferred yellowtail flounders.

The *Seliger* remained in the area, working it hard day and night, for over a week. The good fishing held, or enough so, at least, to keep both the deckhands and the factory workers busy around the clock. Not only the work, but also many small incidents and schedule alterations forestalled all possibility of monotony.

One day we entertained a visiting delegation from the *Polotsk,* a sister ship that Captain Amelichev told me had not been doing very well because the deckhands in general and the *tralmaster* in particular were not familiar with the Leskov-class deck equipment or the proper rigging of nets for flatfishing. For over three hours, therefore, Captain Amelichev and company cordially entertained and seriously instructed the visitors, in an extreme example of the cooperation that is unknown to Western fleets.

Schedule alterations, or, more precisely, extra duty, occurred during the heaviest night catches, when off-watch officers and even women crew members were called down to the factory to help speed up processing. It was difficult not to sympathize with the women, whose galley work and general cleaning chores gave them more than enough to do without additional burdens. My chambermaid, especially, always looked out of place and disconsolate in the factory. In order to ward off its damp chill, she habitually wore a handsome gray wool turtleneck sweater of good quality. The men had loaned her one of the traditional oilskin aprons used for factory work, but it covered only a small part of her upper torso. Fish scales flew into her face, stuck in her hair, and spattered all over what was surely her best sweater.

In the middle of the week we made rendezvous with the *Ostrov Russki,* a huge Swedish-built tanker and refrigerated fish carrier, to take on diesel fuel. Captain Amelichev paced back and forth on the port bridge wing, nervous as captains always are when faced with this most difficult of high-seas maneuvers. The *Ostrov Russki* held a fixed course at about two knots, just enough to maintain firm steerageway. The *Seliger* approached from astern at a very shallow, or near-parallel, angle. Coming closer, we could see that the *Yuri Kostikov* was already lashed to the *Ostrov Russki*'s port side, unloading fish, and a third trawler lay in her wake waiting for a fuel hose from astern. On her near, or starboard, side, ready to receive us, the *Ostrov Russki* was festooned with loops of old truck tires and a chain of five sausage-shaped "Yokohama bumpers," inflated rubber fenders, each weighing half a ton, that floated at her waterline. As we inched up ever closer, Captain Amelichev snapped out quick and decisive orders. Although some ground swell was running, he brought the *Seliger* alongside in perfect eggshell conjunction. Only the Yokohama bumpers absorbed the gentle impact; the loops of truck tires hanging above them never touched. Then, very quickly, a veritable cat's cradle of light heaving lines whistled through the air, crisscrossing between the two ships. The lines gave way to ropes and the ropes to heavy cables. In this manner, in less than five minutes, the *Seliger* and the *Ostrov Russki* were firmly united. They remained so for six hours, as empty fuel tanks slowly filled. As the time went by, a few crew members from both ships lined the rails to chat, conversing in normal tones when the rolling was synchronized. They were forced to yell, however, whenever the rail of one or the other ship dropped down fifteen or twenty feet in an unharmonious roll, while the Yokohama bumpers squeaked in protest and great geysers of sea water sloshed up in the narrow chasm between the two ships' walls. Presently some of the crew started sending messages for transfer to friends on the *Yuri Kostikov,* stuffing them in fishing gloves, which they tied to heaving lines with a clove hitch. First Mate Sokolov paced the deck throughout, watching them closely, to be sure that just messages and not contraband articles passed over the side.

It was during these days, moreover, that a short list of trawlers fishing in the immediate vicinity, posted near the radio telephones in the forward bridge, grew somewhat longer. Almost every other day, it seemed, a new ship would join our select little company on the Tail. I thought perhaps some had come from the recently abandoned New England hake fishery. The second mate told me, however, that most had been waiting for the capelin inside Canadian waters. Now, thoroughly discouraged, they had moved out to join us on the other side of the line.

Among the new arrivals was the first foreign, or non-Soviet, vessel. She was, in fact, Cuban, one of the giant Río-class factory trawlers that the Castro government had kept purchasing even as two-hundred-mile regimes were being everywhere enacted, much to the surprise of the world fishing industry and the delight of the

Spanish shipyards that got the contract to build them. *Río Jicopoa,* Havana, it said on her fantail.

"Yes, the large Cuban trawlers have Soviet captains," Captain Amelichev said, in answer to my question. Ever the diplomat, he said no more. But the weary tone of his reply was commentary enough. Soviet training of Cuban fishermen, the gift of training vessels, and heavy investments in the Havana fishing port had begun in 1962. Now, sixteen years later, the Cuban fleet was still not making it entirely on its own.

The remarks of the crew were much more forthright. "They don't know how to work, those Cubans," one after another would say. "Listen, when you are with the port crews in Havana, you have to watch them all the time. They disappear like magic if you don't! Oh, yes, they are good enough for music and dancing, but don't look to the Cubans for work!"

As we crossed astern of the *Río Jicopoa,* dead fish littered her wake, among them numerous skates and small cod and flounder. All could have been kept for fishmeal, and some of the cod and flounder seemed large enough for normal processing. But, apparently, the Cubans did not wish to bother with them.

"What a waste!" exclaimed one of the junior officers watching the spectacle from the bridge. "Aren't they the lazy ones!"

By the end of the week a small group of activists, led by Svetlana the *sportsmenka,* began preparing for the most important of all Soviet professional holidays for the fishing fleet, the *Dyen Rybaka* (Day of the Fisherman), falling on July 9. Forgoing the nightly movie, Svetlana, who was the lead vocalist; the assistant cook, a proficient accordionist; and two deckhands, who struggled with varying degrees of success on guitars, met in the officer's mess to rehearse their routines. Alexander Zakharov, the energetic young radio operator, ingeniously rigged up amplifiers for all of the instruments using odd bits of equipment borrowed from the radio shack. On the tables were mimeographed copies of a pamphlet entitled *Recommendations and Suggestions for Recitations, Dialogues and Song* (*Holidays and Evenings of Rest Aboard Ship*), put out by the Cultural Support Staff of the Kaliningrad Base Trawling Fleet Company. Among other things, leaving nothing to chance, the recommendations urged celebrants not to forget the ladies. A suggested recitation began:

> Women! In this one word what a world of joy and hope! What friendship is theirs, what warmth. . . . But all who have worked as fishermen know of women's wondrous capacity for work (here name the leaders in socialistcompetition, energetic members of the Komsomol, etc.) as well as for the happiness they bring to all.

But, it was pleasing to note, Svetlana and her devoted band of accompanists mainly worked out their own material. A handsome machine-shop specialist with sideburns prepared a dialogue to precede the singing of "The Fisherman's Star." Alexander Zakharov practiced a monologue in which a drunken father from the provinces attempts to call his city-dwelling daughter from a public telephone booth, eventually overcoming irascible operators and the complaints of other customers who waited their turn in line. It might not have met the standards of the company's Cultural Support Staff, but it was riotously funny.

Next door in the crew's mess, both before and after the movies, crew members looked over the daily tonnages on the big ECONOMIC INDICES: TRIP TOTALS poster with increasing attention and concern. Talk of revision of the trip plan, taking into consideration the absence of capelin, was everywhere in the air.

"Oh, yes, it is possible that the plan will be changed," Alexander Prokofievich Yurchenko, a deckhand who was always both friendly and frank, explained to me at the time.

"You know, really, we nearly always fulfill our plan," he added with a sly wink.

Plan alteration, in which managers and government planners join in a benevolent conspiracy to rationalize downward revisions, is relatively common in Soviet factories on land. Much more rarely has it been necessary at sea against the background of historical success of the Soviet fishing fleet. For over twenty years, from the birth of distant water trawling to the advent of two-hundred-mile coastal jurisdictions, individual ship quotas and the successive Five-Year Plans of Minister Alexander Ishkov have nearly always been met and far exceeded.

But what is important to the Soviet fisherman, whether plan revision occurs or not, is the degree of fulfillment or, more accurately, overfulfillment. Contrary to the popular belief of Western fishing captains, who insist that Soviet crews receive only token bonuses or medals and trinkets for going over quotas, the base pay of Soviet fishermen actually depends on a combination of both catch-shares and plan-fulfillment bonuses. The latter are not inconsiderable. They may range from twenty percent for simply meeting the plan to forty percent for "one hundred and twenty percent plan fulfillment": i.e., exceeding the trip quota by twenty percent. In practical terms, to a second-class seaman of the deck this means the difference between 300 and 450 rubles a month (U.S. $420 and $630 in 1978) for poor or excellent trips, respectively. This is very good pay, with high purchasing power, in the Soviet Union.

"Oh, yes, we get at least two or three times more than the merchant fleet," one constantly hears from the deckhands, who are well aware of their privileged position in the Soviet wage hierarchy.

"It is clear enough," the factory workers echo. "We are paid three times what you get for doing the same work on shore." Unlike the differentiation found aboard other distant water trawlers, the Soviet factory shifts receive exactly the same pay as the "combat troops" out on deck. It could scarcely be otherwise, in fact, since on Soviet trawlers the deckhands and the factory workers are invariably organized as fellow members of the previously noted complex brigades.

In this and other ways the Soviet pay system embraces all the incentives of capitalist fishing fleets. In reality the system is a mixture of the American or Canadian "lay" — that is, individual crew shares based on total catch value — and a variant of the German or English tonnage premiums, expressed in terms of overfulfillment rather than straight tons. At the beginning is a fixed price (about fifty-four rubles per ton of flounder, for example, at the time of my visit), which the government pays to the fishing company for the catches of its trawlers. The amount so received for each trip is divided into equal shares, the captain receiving no more than an engine-room wiper. The plan-fulfillment bonuses are then added to the basic share. Next comes a *koeffitsient raiona* — literally, a regional coefficient — that is something akin to the post differentials or hardship pay of the American foreign service. The Newfoundland Grand Banks, for example, rate an additional seventy percent; South Georgia or the Antarctic seas merit a full one hundred percent. Then, finally, after the individual shares with fulfillment bonuses are multiplied by regional coefficients, there comes another important differential. The final sum is multiplied by "position coefficients," beginning at .98 for second-class seamen and similar ratings and going up to 2.2 for the captains. In this way, in the Soviet fishing fleet, is due recognition given to rank and responsibility.

What these figures signify in simpler terms, averaged out to fair or good fishing, is 360 rubles a month to the lowest ratings, or approximately double the earnings of a shop manager or foreman on land, and 700 rubles a month for captains, which in the Soviet Union equals the salary of a cabinet minister. To these must be added overtime increases, nearly full pay for vacations of twenty-fours days per year (plus Saturdays and Sundays falling within the vacation period), and compensatory leave during the turn-around time between trips, averaging about twenty-six days a year, based on the number of Sundays and holidays spent at sea on each five-month trip.

Added all up, the bonuses, coefficients, and other benefits provide distant water fishermen with some of the highest earnings in the Soviet Union, paralleled only by Siberian BAM workers, Spitsbergen coal miners, and a few others who enjoy the dispensations for "heavy or hazardous work in isolated areas." Not incidentally, they also give the fishing industry a competitive edge in the chronically short Soviet labor market. Indeed, the industry has seldom, if ever, suffered for want of recruits. From all over the Soviet Union they come, although a large majority in the Kaliningrad and Murmansk fleets will inevitably be Great Russian. To many, distant water fishing is an end or career in itself; willingly they suffer the long absences from home for the opportunity of real savings. Others view employment with the fleet as temporary, or a well-paid stepping-stone to other professions. Some simply cannot make up their minds. Time enough to think about it, the latter say, during the long months at sea.

"Oh, certainly, I will continue until retirement," Captain Amelichev liked to say. "That is at fifty-five for the crew and the captain's company. Unfortunately, for the captains themselves it is five more years, at sixty. But when it comes I will build a dacha in the country and enjoy life. Best of all, as I have said before, I will get to know my son!" Amelichev, of course, was thoroughly the careerist.

Equally career-oriented was the second mate, Vladimir Alexandrovich Petrov, a young man of twenty-seven with long hair and a drooping moustache, who continually wore bell-bottom slacks and a flashy plaid sports jacket. Petrov's ambitions were quite evident, even in such small details as the decorations of his neatly kept single-berth cabin. Pasted up at the foot of his bunk were the good things of life: a discreet pinup calendar obtained in Halifax, for example, to which he had affixed labels from bottles of high-priced vodka and cognac. But above his writing desk, staring him always in the face, were a large hand-drawn map of the Newfoundland fishing zones and typed copies of lengthy bridge-watch instructions and emergency procedures. Near to these was a color reproduction of a romantic portrait of Lenin addressing students at the University of Kazan.

A witty and soft-spoken person who had almost completely overcome what must have been a serious stuttering problem in his boyhood, Petrov was unique among the *Seliger*'s officers — and possibly the entire crew — in having a father serving aboard a factory trawler. As he himself explained, however, this was not very surprising, considering that the Soviet fishing fleet was much too recent a phenomenon to have the kind of generational succession found in Great Britain or other older fishing nations.

"But my father did not encourage me," Petrov always maintained. "I myself chose the career. I finished middle school at seventeen and enrolled directly in a higher institute." By this he meant he had skipped one step in what is probably the world's most complete fisheries-training curriculum. In the Soviet Union most candidates for deck officer or engineer positions finish their training at one of the twenty-five nautical colleges spread throughout the nation, which provide excellent vocational instruction, approximately of the caliber found in the German *technische Hochschule,* plus general education that is the equal of a good American junior college. Fewer numbers will go on, however, to the university-level higher institutes, which are obligatory only for captains, chief mates, and chief engineers. Petrov had done this at an earlier age and more quickly than most, graduating after five years of the usual alternation of classroom and on-the-job training at sea. Not only that, he had taken a double course load and received two diplomas, one for deck officer and the other for high-school teaching. The latter may have been incongruous and a little unusual, he granted, but as an additional and certified qualification it gained him some extra pay.

Petrov found job security one of the most comforting aspects of his profession and liked to cite a dramatic example to prove it. "I was second mate on the *Taras Shevchenko* when it was seized and taken into Boston Harbor," he once told me. "Your Coast Guard kept saying they were sorry for me and the others of the captain's company; they knew we would be dismissed when the *Shevchenko* returned to the Soviet Union. Silly things like that. Look, I was second mate then, and you can see with your own eyes I remain so today. The same is true of the man who commanded the *Shevchenko* on that trip. He is still captain."

Never did Petrov express any bitterness over the experience, however, unlike a crew member who had shared it and said that it felt "like being an animal in a zoo" when the curious crowds came down to look over the *Shevchenko,* week after long week. To Petrov it was merely boring and a great waste of time, except for the opportunity to practice his English and to acquire from a member of the armed guard with whom he had struck up a friendship a Zippo lighter engraved with a Coast Guard shield. The lighter was one of his proudest possessions, at least, on a par with the plaid sports jacket.

"Yes, I'm still second mate," he repeated with a broad smile, unable to conceal his pride in what he wanted to tell me. "But now I have my high-seas navigation diploma — a captain's license, you would say — and will soon make *starpom*. In fact, something tells me it will be the next trip!"

To many of the crew, however, especially the women, high earnings rather than long-term career prospects were the most immediate and important consideration. My chambermaid, for example, was quick to say she had gone to sea for the money alone. It was only her second trip, moreover, and she was not at all sure about continuing. At the opposite extreme — in length of service, at least — was the woman who ran the *Seliger*'s laundry. She was forty-one years old, she never hesitated to say, and had served continuously with the fleet since she was twenty-five. On one occasion when I dropped by the laundry to thank her for her excellent and prompt work, she seemed overcome with emotion. (Such praise, apparently, was unique in her experience.) In a flush of gratitude, she invited me to her lower-deck cabin near the bow, where she shared with the older woman who managed the experimental cannery unit the heavy pitching and closed portholes common to that location. From her bureau she extracted a small packet of old and much-thumbed photographs, carefully wrapped in brown paper and string. The first sequence of pictures showed her enjoying shore leave at Las Palmas in the Canary Islands — either at the beach or strolling the island's mountainous roads in the company of handsome young men — wearing a belted bathing suit or the long skirt, sandals, and white ankle socks once so popular with Russian women.

"As you can see, I was a more attractive woman in those times," she said, not immodestly. "Now here we have the celebrations of crossing the Equator! Oh, how we made merry, how foolish we were! Look, here is King Neptune — really he was the first mate — ready to initiate his new subjects."

She paused. "This is my sister and brother-in-law. And here their children! Are they not truly lovely? You say you have six children? How wonderful, how very fortunate! I, you must understand, have never been married."

As we continued her voice reflected many moods, changing abruptly from deep melancholy to extreme elation. Imagine, she suddenly exclaimed, these snapshots are from Saint Helena, the very island of Emperor Napoleon's exile! Yes, that was a most interesting visit, since the island had many lovely and strange flowers, many exotic things you could not see anywhere else in the world. Then next in the little packet came more photographs of relatives. She paused again. Here was a brother. And another sister. Both with fine children, as one could see.

Although never stated, there was a conclusion. The years at sea had meant too much denial, too many missed opportunities. Except for the money, she seemed to be saying, it was a wasted life.

Just the opposite, new and challenging horizons, beckoned factory manager Yosef Sheek. A dark-eyed native of Azerbaijan, Sheek was the prime example of those who prepare themselves for other professions by arduous study both at sea and while on home leave. Like Vladimir Petrov, he was a graduate of a higher institute with a coveted *tekhnolog* degree, which, while not necessary to his position, earned him extra pay.

"In all I have been with the KBTF for thirteen years," he preferred to say of his career. Because he had done some service at a large company *kombinat* (shore processing plant), Sheek knew the Kaliningrad Base Trawling Fleet Company better than most and tended to think of it rather than this ship or that as his immediate employer.

"Of course, the KBTF is not a company in the sense of your General Motors," he told me one evening, laughing, over a glass of tea. "But it employs over six thousand workers, is the largest in the Baltic, and is second only to the Murmansk Company in the western Soviet Union. After the *kombinat,* I went to sea for two trips as fishmaster. Then it was factory manager, for twelve years, on many different BMRT's."

Like many of the *Seliger*'s officers and not a few of the crew, Sheek was a voracious reader. He knew the Russian classics well, admired Shakespeare, and was especially interested in American novels. In the latter category he had gone well beyond Jack London and Hemingway, the all-time favorites of the Soviet fleet, to Dreiser, Sinclair Lewis, and Faulkner. More recently he had read Arthur Hailey's *Airport.* He seemed puzzled why this and other disaster novels, evidently much pushed in the Soviet Union, constituted the new American literature.

Most remarkably, Sheek also found time to read weighty volumes on government and comparative law. It was not until I asked First Mate Sokolov, who was proud to have a person of Sheek's qualifications among his charges, that I found out that throughout his twelve years at sea he had studied hard as an "extern" for a law degree. On his next shore leave, in fact, Sheek would take the final examination for his doctorate in jurisprudence. All who knew him were sure he would pass.

Among the undecided or those with ambivalent career views were many of the factory workers. Valery Deinega, for example, was cheered by the fact that his fiancée had sent him a telegram during the trip saying she had acquired a new apartment less than one kilometer from the University of Kaliningrad. She was studying there to be an economist, he was proud to say, and he had in turn wired her telling her to save her vacation until his leave period. Perhaps, with her help, he, too, might be accepted at the university.

Without ever saying so, however, Deinega appeared to have some slight misgivings about his next move. As often as he spoke of his ambitions, he also mentioned his high earnings.

"You understand, I have long hoped to go to the university or a higher institute," he might typically tell me. "But it has been necessary for me to postpone such thoughts. My father, who worked in the Dombas, died when I was very young. My mother soon became very sick. I had to go to work in a factory at seventeen, for two years. Then it was two years in the army. When I was twenty-one, I joined the fishing fleet. I do not like living at sea, but the pay is very good and I have a good career. But now I am twenty-nine. It may be that it is time for a change. Imagine, a new apartment so near to the university!"

The deckhands also tended to be undecided about their work and their career prospects, if indeed they thought they had any. Unlike the others, however, they talked of such matters with a refreshing insouciance and a strong belief in the virtues of carpe diem. During idle moments on deck I liked nothing better than to listen to their halfhearted complaints or their endless arguments on the ultimate rewards of their profession. Although quite unlike the discussions of the rest of the crew, the deckhands' open forums had a thoroughly familiar ring:

"The devil take it! This is my last trip, for sure. There is more to life than money in the pocket."

"Pyotr Alexandrovich, you said that the last trip."

"Hey, here is an idea! You can help us. You speak to the captain and tell him you have a family emergency; you must go immediately to New York. Then we all go to Broadway and get a little *fooky-fook!* Is that not an excellent idea?"

"Horny bastard, you."

"I save it all for when I get home. You know what I do? First, permit me to explain that I never smoke at sea, as you may have seen. Nor do I drink. There is, shall we say, a private manufacture of spirits on this ship and opportunity enough. But I save it all for home leave! I smoke and drink good vodka around the clock. Oh, how glorious! It is better that way."

"Ha! And then the *militsioneri* catch you drunk driving!"

"Yes, they are so strict! One offense and your permit is gone! Is it not true that the same happens in the United States? We see many films of drunk drivers in the United States."

"On my last leave, I walk into the house and my daughter asks, 'Who is this man?' "

"The trips are so long. We are happy to have you visit with us, but how would you like five months of this? It is so boring, that is the problem, so very boring!"

"I am not bored when we catch good fish."

"Let the fish go fuck themselves! This is my last trip. This time I am sure of it."

Alone among the crew, the *Seliger*'s deckhands were the universal fishermen.

On the evening of July 6, almost midway through the *Seliger*'s five-month cruise, Captain Amelichev announced what everyone already knew. There would be no capelin fishing, at all. Shortly before supper, the deck crew quickly finished the last haulback and put away the lightly rigged trawl used for flatfishing. Presently a new and more powerful throb from the engine room raced in small shock waves through every part of the ship. The *Seliger* began steaming to the opposite end of the Grand Banks, some 360 nautical miles to the north.

"We are going here, inside the Canadian zone, to fish for grenadier," Captain Amelichev explained to me in the chartroom. He pointed to an area on the seaward side of the banks the Portuguese and Spanish call the *Gran Norte*. Examining the chart, I found a unique steplike pattern. Almost everywhere else along the circumference of the Grand Banks, the continental shelf terminated rather abruptly in what fishermen call steep edges or foul pitches. But in the area of our destination, it was easy to see, the shelf descended in fairly even steps — small plateaus, one might better call them — that went down from 800 to 2,000 meters. Here we would fish.

"We have a forty-day license for the grenadiers," Captain Amelichev continued. "Some of our ships are already up there, on the grounds. So, too, is the *Smelij*, which can take you to St. John's whenever you wish." He hoped, however, that I would remain aboard much longer. There was the deep fishing to observe, he added, and soon would come Fisherman's Day, time for another splendid party.

All the next day we steamed due north. A strong northwest

wind brought clear and bracing weather. Occasionally, without any regular rhythm, the *Seliger*'s bow slammed into a cresting wave, causing the hull quivers and the hollow, gonglike noises so reminiscent of winter seas. Down in the officers' mess Annalise the stewardess cursed in a rich vocabulary worthy of the Boston Fish Pier. A full teakettle had spilled, and rivulets of water poured down onto the settees from each of six forward portholes, which, although closed, had not been well tightened. Out on deck, not the least affected by the pitching, men worked all day rigging up a new groundrope that was chocked solid with the heavy bobbins necessary to deep fishing. Long-absent fulmars returned to trace effortless arcs above our wake. Soon they outnumbered the ubiquitous shearwaters, who cackled in protest at the intrusion.

That night the entire crew, minus only minimal or standby engine-room and bridge watches, jammed the mess hall for a long-announced general meeting to review the past month's production and set goals for the next. Neither Captain Amelichev nor First Mate Sokolov presided; both sat down at the mess tables like any-one else. Instead, the soft-spoken sonar technician, now acting in his role as official representative of the All Union Central Soviet of Professional Trade Unions, opened the meeting.

"He is our George Meany, our Mister Meany-Meany," Captain Amelichev whispered to me, in what was one of his favorite jokes. The comparison, in point of fact, was not entirely farfetched. Soviet labor philosophy maintains that all workers are inherently good and productive; managers who fail to provide proper leadership or working conditions are most often held to blame when things go wrong. Thus all Soviet bosses, including captains of ships at sea, are aware of the potential power of their union delegates and listen seriously to what they have to say.

But, for the moment of this occasion, the union representative merely exercised his titular role of convening the meeting. He moved quickly to the election of a three-man presidium — it was customary to vote a different one for every major meeting, Captain Amelichev explained — and from within the three a *predseda-tel* (presiding chairman). The man so chosen was the fishmaster, or factory foreman, of the first complex brigade. Earlier in the day, I had seen him bent over a table, intently studying the *Klasifikator,* copies of the ship's regulations, and other official-looking documents.

There was, it appeared, no fixed agendum. Instead, the presiding chairman called for motions from the floor to suggest the order of business, each being voted for or against. In this manner, duly suggested and approved, we heard reports from Captain Amelichev, First Mate Sokolov, Production Assistant Sheek, and the chief bosun. The latter was pleased to say that the decks were clear and that all gear was rerigged and ready for grenadier fishing. Captain Amelichev gave a detailed report on the catches and general progress of other ships in the fleet. Production Assistant Sheek reviewed catch tonnages and factory production to date in still greater detail and announced the revised plan, taking into account the absence of capelin, the figures of which caused some crew members to whistle through their teeth with surprise.

Only First Mate Sokolov provided a true note of drama, in a report that was quite different in tone and substance from his youth festival address. He began by reminding one and all of the goals of the current Five-Year Plan, quoting in the process from Secretary General Brezhnev on the importance of increased protein production and the plans for new and improved fish distribution throughout the Soviet Union. Sokolov sincerely hoped, therefore, his voice now rising, that everyone realized this meant doubly high standards of work and proper attention to the ship's routine. It meant, moreover, that *kachestvenny trud* (quality work) and not just quantity must everywhere prevail! Not only that, he also expected that all were fully aware that the brigades had to work as units, with the collectivist spirit flowing harmoniously from the fishing deck through the factory and freezing chambers down to the very depths of the fishhold.

Sokolov paused briefly. He had taken a recent inspection tour of living quarters, he wanted all to know. And what had he found? Why, cabin portholes carelessly left open! Teapots spilled and unnecessary lights left burning! The engine room, moreover, was if anything worse. He had found certain valves left continually open in obvious contravention of safety regulations. Why, he could not possibly understand how such carelessness might have occurred!

"All of this is bad, very bad!" he said, pounding his fist in his palm. "Comrades, there is a great need for *systematic recommendations!*"

Commissar Sokolov sat down, his face frozen in a dark scowl.

The pace of the meeting now quickened. In view of the first mate's report, the union representative suggested a technical safety committee to further his investigations and present recommendations at the next meeting. The motion carried unanimously. The chairman next announced that the captain of the *Turmalin* had been chosen to represent the Northwest Atlantic fleet at a fisheries conference in Kaliningrad the next month. Several crew members immediately proposed Captain Amelichev instead, but he gracefully declined by saying that he was a fisherman first and foremost, and not one for the conference tables. The red and gold pennants for the best group performances of the month were then awarded, to perfunctory applause.

Now it was time to throw the floor open for any complaints or individual grievances. In all such meetings this is the occasion when, theoretically, at least, the hallowed Leninist principle of democratic centralism — briefly defined as free discussions of any questions followed by binding adherence to such decision as the party leadership may make from them — should have its fullest expression.

Only Annalise the stewardess spoke up. She asked why it had been necessary to assign women to off-duty factory work during the preceding week. Predictably, the union delegate and other party stalwarts patiently explained the necessity of clearing the factory at times of peak catches, of the importance of sharing heavy burdens. Still others spoke of proper collectivist attitudes. But Annalise held her ground.

"We had better catches earlier in the trip, and no women were called to the factory," she answered back, her sloe eyes fairly smoldering. "How does one explain that?"

"Because it is so!" snapped Oleg Sokolov. There was no more discussion. Democratic centralism had run its course.

The meeting was not quite over. Surprisingly, considering the length and the intensity of his first peroration, First Mate Sokolov was again called to speak. The reason was clear as soon as he stood up. Gone was the commissar's dark scowl. In its place was the cruise director's friendly smile. The crew, in short, was ready for more homespun humor, and Sokolov could barely wait to oblige them. He began with a variation of his parable on how two small fish made one good fish, transposing it to how ugly fish might magically be made to seem beautiful. Few creatures of the sea were more hideous looking than the grenadier, he had to admit, shuddering with revulsion. But cut off the ratlike tail, remove all those raspy scales, throw away the bony head! And what did you have? Beautiful round fillets, white and glistening fillets, in tray after tray and row upon row in the freezing chambers. Truly a sight of great beauty! That was the way to think of the grenadiers.

His audience was mildly amused. Sokolov, sufficiently encouraged, moved on swiftly to his punch lines. A great new thought had occurred to him, he said. The crew listened eagerly.

"Yes, comrades, I have been thinking how our Hero Cosmonauts Ivanchenkov and Kovalenok are breaking all records in their long journey in space, as you well know," he said. "But soon the cosmonauts will have to return to earth. Splendid, you say, but what has that to do with us? Comrades, have you thought that we, too, must soon leave the empty spaces of the sea and get back to earth? [Laughter] It is possible, of course, that the Hero Cosmonauts will receive more acclaim and more glory than we! [More laughter] But for us, too, there will be some cheers, some praise, and surely the warm welcome of our loved ones. Yes, comrades, let us fulfill the plan! Let us return home as *Hero Fishermen* to all our families and all our friends! Think of that as we work with collectivist solidarity through the second half of our long journey in space. Think of that and tonight, oh, how peacefully you will S-L-E-E-P!"

Again Sokolov shut his eyes, smiled beatifically, and drew out the last word. Again the crew laughed and agreed it was a good thought. On this note the monthly production meeting came to a close. The *Seliger* steamed serenely through the night.

The next night, approximately twenty-four hours later, I was aboard the *Smelij* on the first link of a long homeward journey. That morning the *Seliger* had barely finished laying out three miles of cable on the grenadier grounds when Captain Amelichev was ordered by the fleet *nachalnik* to start for Flemish Cap, 220 miles distant, before the end of the day. Captain Amelichev was visibly upset. It meant still more time lost in steaming, and the nets would have to be rerigged again for cod and redfish. He could see no reason for the costly move. I thought to myself that perhaps the small detachment of trawlers out on the Cap was not doing well and that Amelichev was being sent there to lead them or even provide tutorial assistance, as we had done with the *Polotsk*. Whatever the reason, the move presented a difficult decision. The *Smelij* was in the vicinity, as promised, waiting to take me to St. John's. Captain Amelichev, however, urged me with great warmth and sincerity to remain. The very next day was Fishermen's Day, he reminded me, and he was sure that arrangements could be made with one of the trawlers on Flemish Cap to take me back, with perhaps a loss of only a few days. It was hard to resist. But one month at sea had already passed, and any visitor learns from experience that nothing is more unpredictable or subject to constant change than the movements of a trawler fleet. One always takes the bird-in-hand in the problematic business of getting home. With extreme reluctance, therefore, I opted for departure that night.

The last day was beautifully clear and crowded with event. Some twelve ships, all Soviet except for one big Cuban dead in the water with engine trouble, worked close together, slowly crisscrossing one of the small plateaus in a tight concentration that brought to mind the cities-at-sea of an earlier day, before two-hundred mile limits. The northwest wind held steady, fresh and cool, at a pleasant twelve knots. Pods of small pilot whales broached and spouted, all in unison, throughout the day. A big West Greenland berg was said to be nearby.

There was time during that day, although just barely, to observe one complete tow for the rattailed grenadiers. Shortly before noon, finding a clear track in the congested waters, Captain Amelichev ordered the heavily weighted trawl down the ramp in what the chart indicated was a depth of 1,400 meters, slightly less than a mile. The main winches slowly ground out cable for a full hour before Amelichev judged the requisite three-to-one ratio of cable length to water depth had been reached and ordered them stopped. During this time the *Seliger* hardly seemed to be moving ahead. Indeed, Second Mate Petrov periodically threw wood chips overboard and paced down the promenade deck with a stopwatch timing their float, to ascertain if the *Seliger* was making true forward progress over the bottom or merely maintaining way in wind and current. It was necessary to creep at such a snail's pace, Captain Amelichev explained, to allow time for the net to sink. Any faster advance would trail it astern too much and thus prolong the set. This action completed, the net was then left to drag the stygian depths for four and a half hours at a speed of little more than two knots. This was all the *Seliger* could manage with engines full ahead because of the trawl's great weight, not to mention six miles, three on each side, of the heavy steel towing cables which themselves weighed hundreds of tons. It was not until after teatime, therefore, and an additional forty minutes of labored grinding of the winches — the stern sections of the *Seliger* shook under the strain — before the first bag of fish was on deck. In it were about three tons of *Macrourus berglax,* "rough heads," one of an estimated 300 species of grenadier. Both Captain Amelichev and I agreed that they were a sorry sight. Prolonged tumbling and dragging in the net had caused the fish to rub against each other and file away their sharp scales. Their flanks, in fact, were scraped entirely raw, down to the tips of their long whiplike tails. Only the finer scales of their blunt and bony heads — not sharp, but mildly abrasive like a safety-match striking surface — had withstood the long friction. Many of the fish had gaping sockets where their eyes should have been; the extreme changes of water pressure had completely popped out their large and curiously ringed eyeballs. Mixed in with the mangled grenadiers was a sprinkling of hardy Greenland halibut, which along with its Atlantic cousin is one of the few market fish to live comfortably at depths of over 2,000 meters; some thorny-backed tapir fish, also deep dwellers; and a lone specimen of a small and pale eellike fish with an upturned mouth and tiny vestigial eyes, which could not be identified by anyone and looked as if it belonged in a cave.

The tow had provided a clear demonstration of some of the difficulties inherent in fishing for underutilized species. For a decade I had listened to oceanographers use the Macrouridae as a prime example of the almost inexhaustible bounty of deeper seas. The "rattails" were not much to look at, they always said, but they were reasonably good to eat and of course they abounded — they fairly teemed — in the slope waters of many latitudes. Now I wished that my oceanographer friends might be standing on the deck of the *Seliger*. It had taken us six hours, double the time of a conventional tow, to catch three tons of the rough heads that are said to be one of the few grenadier species large enough to produce a respectable fillet. As factory managers on land would never argue, a 50 percent production slowdown is not an inconsequential matter. We must think in the same terms of large trawlers, with their operating costs of $10,000 to $20,000 a day. The Soviets and other Communist-bloc nations, desperate for animal protein and equally desperate to avoid sudden layoffs of ships and fishermen, may fish the grenadiers for some years to come. But who else? Not the hard-pressed inshore fishermen, who most need new species and new markets. Their boats are too small to reach the grounds. Even if they could, it takes a ship at least the size of the *Seliger* — larger and higher-horsepowered vessels would do even better — to support the heavy equipment necessary to get down to where grenadiers swim in any numbers. Such are the considerations that the apostles of oceanic plenty, the projectionists of total marine biomass, have long overlooked.

There was time also during the last day, Captain Amelichev made sure, for a proper farewell party. At six in the evening he invited me to his dayroom, where once again Annalise had laid out a sumptuous spread. Also on hand were First Mate Sokolov and Production Assistant Sheek. Much vodka and the supposedly curative Latvian *balzam* flowed in swelling accompaniment to our toasts and little jokes, told and retold, about various incidents that had marked my visit. So, too, did souvenirs and gifts. Earlier in the trip I had received a folk-art bird carving, lacquered spoons, Lenin pins, a bottle of "International Solidarity" cologne, and tins of halibut, hake, and cod livers from the experimental cannery unit. To these were now added more substantial items. Captain Amelichev insisted that I keep his short-length watch coat, olive drab and lined with imitation fleece, that he had loaned me for cold nights. It was just what the BAM workers in Siberia wore during the milder seasons, he explained, and the thought of a BAM coat in Washington, D.C., amused him greatly. This in turn inspired First Mate Sokolov. The "journals," the newsreels! That was what I had liked, he exclaimed, that was the thing to take back! In a matter of seconds he returned from his cabin balancing a stack of film cans like pie plates. Yes, and it was also necessary for me to sample more fish, Captain Amelichev then decided. He had forgotten the raw herring in my cannery selection and promptly sent a seaman to fetch some. And magazines, of course, Sokolov added. Here were several copies of *Krokodil*, the famous Soviet satirical magazine, the very one I had been asking about! Any protestations that my duffle bag could contain no more were quickly brushed aside. String shopping bags appeared from nowhere and rapidly filled. Periodically, we lumbered down the promenade deck to add them to my luggage pile. These brief interruptions proved salutary, or so I thought, breathing deeply of the cold wet air in vain attempts to clear my head. On one such occasion I saw a small light to starboard, refracted by the fog into what looked like a faint and tiny star. The *Smelij* was running alongside, waiting.

Hours passed. At one point the duty officer called on the telephone to ask what was going on and to report that the bridge watch on the *Smelij* was getting impatient. We all laughed as Captain Amelichev swore, told him and the *Smelij* to mind their own damn business, and slammed down the receiver. He would allow nothing, it was clear, to interfere with the proper course of the farewell. At more serious moments he told me how no one had known what to expect when I first came aboard, but now all would miss their good colleague and friend very much. Oleg Sokolov and Yosef Sheek nodded in agreement, proposed more toasts, and issued repeated invitations to come to Kaliningrad.

Sometime around ten o'clock, to the best of my memory, we at last made our way to the lifeboat. Captain Amelichev hugged me three times. Sokolov and Sheek followed suit. Crew members came up and pressed into my hand ballpoint pens they had carefully purchased in Halifax. Someone noticed that my hands were bare and said the night was cold. Instantly a bag of two dozen cotton gloves, of the kind fishermen use as inside liners, was added to the parabola of luggage now flying into the lifeboat. The woman who operated the laundry darted out from a hidden corner of the deck to give me a small vial of perfume. "For your lovely wife," she said.

Many have written of it. All who experience it forget their politics and agree. To work and to live closely with the Russian people is to know generosity, warmth, and a sense of community matched by none.

A few days before my departure, Captain Amelichev had inquired once again about the fishing in New England. Again I had reassured him, citing the rapid improvement of stocks.

"I am so glad to hear that," Amelichev replied. "It means that the same may happen in coastal zones all over the world.

"So tell me," he continued. "Do you not think that in five or ten years the fishing will be so much better — the stocks will so rise — there will be no more need for all these two-hundred-mile limits? Do you not see the return of free fishing?" His voice was uncharacteristically earnest. Unlike other occasions, he did not preface his question with a joke or any attempt at humor. He wanted to know.

The question took me aback. It was surprising, on reflection, coming as it did from someone so relatively well informed as Captain Amelichev. I wondered if perhaps it were not based on some new directive from Moscow designed to maintain morale, to hold out continued promise for the Soviet fleet. Whatever the inspiration, I could not find it in my heart to say that it was unlikely, that nation states, once having extended their sovereignties, are seldom disposed to withdraw them. Or that, granted some quota relaxation, the nation that had a world reputation for overfishing and stock depredation might not be among the first to gain favored status.

"Oh, yes, it is certainly a possibility," I said. In the meantime, however, I supposed it would be a matter of *tak derzhat,* steady on course, steady as it goes. Of business as usual, within the restrictions.

"Yes, *tak derzhat, tak derzhat,*" Captain Amelichev answered.

# NINE

# Epilogue

$V$ERY few factory trawlers now traverse the great arch of the North Atlantic. Floating cities — the massive concentrations of one hundred or more distant water vessels once so common on prime grounds — are no longer found anywhere along its way. In the North Atlantic and elsewhere, factory trawlers themselves, not the fish they catch, appear doomed to extinction. The leviathan ships once hailed as fishing technology's greatest leap forward are proving too costly to operate under the low quotas assigned them by coastal states around the world. The big ships are also particularly ill suited to chasing down new species in the broad expanses of the tropical and subtropical seas where for the most part they are forced to fish. Rather than the most effective of all fishing machines, factory trawlers now seem like lumbering dinosaurs, unable to adapt to the changing environment of world fishing they themselves did so much to create. An era of fishing history is in fact fast coming to a close.

In the first summer of the United States' two-hundred-mile enforcement, the West German factory trawler *Wesermünde* did not return to Georges Bank for what her fishermen used to call "the herring trip that makes the year." Only two ships from the Hanseatische Hochseefischerei company fleet did. This may have been just as well, the company director later informed me, considering the very low quota and severely restricted fishing area allowed them by the U.S. The two that he did send, the *Karlsburg* and the *Geeste*, in his words, "found not 1 (one) herring in the so-called 'window' where we had the licence to fish from 15 August to 30 September." Since the two ships each had daily operating expenses in excess of U.S. $13,000, he had in fact ordered them home after about ten days of searching for not one herring.

Instead of Georges or other North Atlantic grounds, the *Wesermünde* eventually found her way to New Zealand, where she fished in an experimental joint venture for almost two years. Like the British factory trawlers *Othello, Orsino,* and *Cassio,* which preceded her to Australia, the *Wesermünde* at first caught too many different kinds of fish and not enough of any one for efficient factory processing. Then, just when she was beginning to discover some marketable species in good quantity, the New Zealand government imposed catch limits and seasonal closures of the best grounds. This was done at the insistence of the local fishermen, who were becoming increasingly concerned over the growing number of joint ventures New Zealand was entering with other nations. These restrictions and an almost astronomical rise in the cost of diesel fuel made further fishing by the Germans a losing proposition. The venture was therefore terminated; the *Wesermünde* went home to Bremerhaven. By the time she got there, at the close of 1980, it was no longer a very active fishing port. Many West German factory trawlers had already been sold to developing nations or refitted for offshore oil surveying, and nearly all the large fresh-fish stern trawlers that once made a specialty of fast trips to Iceland had been laid up or sold for scrap. Today the situation is even more disheartening for German fishermen. From a peak of slightly over one hundred ships, the West German distant water fleet now counts only twenty-eight. Among the survivors, however, are the *Wesermünde* and her three "third-generation" sister ships, which remain the Federal Republic's largest and best equipped. Thanks to generous government subsidies, they make occasional trips to the notorious East Greenland grounds, where they have been offered relatively good quotas mainly because no one else wants to do battle with the area's omnipresent ice, bad weather, and foul "rock garden" bottoms. Sometimes, too, they go hunting for blue whiting, a small and extremely abundant pelagic fish, near the Faroe Islands or west of Great Britain's fishery zone. The sisters also make a few trips to Canada, which allows West Germany to fish for approximately 5,000 tons of cod a year, or to Norway, which permits even less. Mostly, though, they wait for better days in what might be called a government-sustained holding pattern. "We all hope for better quotas in the future," the Hanseatische company director has recently written, but with something less than complete conviction.

The men of the *Wesermünde* have been more fortunate than most. Captain Ernst Hörhold, First *Steuermann* "Jupp" Merkler, *Fischmeister* Jürgen Blum, Radio Officer Ernst Schmiedeberg, and a large part of the crew have stayed with her throughout her wanderings. Nevertheless, they are not entirely sanguine about their future. They understand very clearly that only their government's help has kept them afloat. And that it may be a long time, if ever, before adequate quotas again permit them to display the kind of fishfinding wizardry that once was the envy of others. Sobering as these facts may be, the fate of many of their colleagues is even more so. An estimated 2,600 West German distant water fishermen are now retired or working ashore.

After her autumn trip of 1977 to Tiddly Bank and the North Cape, the *Kelt* made two more trips to the Norwegian Arctic. Since both were losers, she was subsequently ordered to join the growing flotilla of British trawlers of every size and description fishing for mackerel off the Cornish coast out of Falmouth or Milford Haven. Then, in January of 1980, the *Kelt* made an experimental trip to the Bay of Biscay to fish for scad, or "horse mackerel," for the Ministry of Agriculture, Fisheries, and Food. The thought at the ministry, which was then also subsidizing test fishing for blue whiting, was that these and other species previously taken only for fishmeal or oil might be converted through imaginative processing into good table fish.

But neither the scad nor the blue whiting found much market

acceptance — both fish had too much dark meat — and subsidized fishing for underutilized species soon came to an abrupt end. In May of 1982, after a long lay-up, the *Kelt*'s owners sold her to a Norwegian firm for conversion to offshore oil support work in the North Sea. She thus joined a growing fleet of some fifteen British trawlers previously put to similar use. The principal duty of the *Kelt*, now rechristened the *M/S Sub Surveyor*, is to launch and re-cover unmanned mini-submarines used to inspect seabed pipelines and rig foundations for possible faults. She thus has more inter-esting work than the others, at least, most of which remain contin-uously on station close to an oil rig on "rig standby duty," ready to serve in effect as king-size lifeboats and hospital ships in the event of distress. Former fishermen find the standby work very easy, of course, but also extremely boring. The boredom is most oppressive when dodging or riding out gales with no place to go, a crew-member friend has told me. There is then not even the prospect of a change or something to wait for, like a return to fishing. Just more of the same, endlessly keeping the sea, my friend says.

For as long as the *Kelt* kept fishing, Captain George Renardson remained with her. Before one of her last trips, at the beginning of the unsuccessful experiment with scad, he even began to feel cau-tiously optimistic about the future. ("We will be taking four bot-tom trawls and two mid-water, so I hope it is a success for the sake of the fishing industry," he wrote with some enthusiasm at the time.) But today Captain George has no more such hopes. Since the *Kelt*'s sale he makes only short and irregular trips with one or another of the dozen-odd factory trawlers and whole-fish freezers still fishing seasonally for mackerel off Cornwall. This is because "England has no place else to go," as he so often predicted on Tiddly Bank. And the dozen ships are all that is left, operation-ally speaking, of the British distant water fleet.

Mate Desmond Hendrickson has found a berth as second in command of an American supply ship serving an oil exploration task force off Nigeria. Radio Officer Tony Scannell has told me that a number of the *Kelt*'s younger deckhands have also gone abroad, answering the advertisements of foreign governments for experienced fishermen-teachers. Scannell himself has been out of work for over a year, however. So, too, have many of the *Kelt*'s older deckhands and factory workers. It is useless for them to look for any kind of employment along the waterfront, Scannell tells me. In February of 1980, the Hull Fishing Vessel Owners Association, the port authority that operated all of the city's fishing docks and associated services, declared itself in liquidation. Since then Hull, once Europe's busiest fishing port and the principal base for Britain's distant water fleet, has been notable mainly as a graveyard for long-idled and rusting trawlers. Except for the occasional unloading of a foreign trawler, the Albert and St. Andrew's dock areas are a dead and ghostly place. Exactly as Des Hendrickson had feared, in fact, when we toured them on a blustery November afternoon in 1977.

The Spanish pair trawler *Terra* is an exception. She and the *Nova* — always together, of course, the two working as one — are the only vessels among those I visited that are fishing today, just as they did six years ago, on virtually the same grounds. They do so more out of desperation, however, than by any preconceived plan or design. The desperation traces back to 1979, when Canada and other countries began to come down very hard on Spain for the wasteful practices of her pairs. At the beginning of that year, in fact, Canada announced she would allow only two Spanish pairs inside all her two-hundred-mile zone. But the pair captains and owners, true to their *individualismo,* could not agree among themselves which two should go. The following spring, therefore, nearly all the remaining Spanish pairs, the *Terra* and *Nova* among them, crossed the Atlantic anyway, without licenses, ostensibly to fish Flemish Cap or some of the small outer segments of the Grand Banks coastal shelf that jut beyond the two-hundred-mile line. Soon after they got there, however, the Canadian government ordered them off the Cap and the borderline grounds, citing as authority Spain's refusal to join the Northwest Atlantic Fisheries Organization (NAFO) [1] and threatening to force all the pairs into St. John's for stem-to-stern inspections. The outlaw fleet therefore went home after only a few days of fishing. Subsequently, the Spanish government relented, joining NAFO and thereby committing all her fishing vessels to a system of voluntary quotas and other conservation measures. Canada, mollified, has since allowed the Spanish pairs to fish outside her zone without molestation, although she now gives them no quota at all inside it.

At this writing, therefore, a dozen or so Spanish pairs annually make their way across the North Atlantic to fish Flemish Cap or the borderline grounds. In this elite group are the *Terra* and *Nova,* still going strong after fourteen years of hard campaigning. But the fishing is nothing like the grand days of "fifty tons salted" I saw on Southeast Shoals or the Platier in 1977. Other nations are fishing the Cap very heavily, and it is getting more and more difficult to bring home a paying catch. The *Terra* and *Nova,* for example, fished all through the hard winter of 1981-82, one crew member has written me, only to get 340 tons of salted cod, about one third of their joint capacity. Moreover, one campaign a year rather than the customary two is now the rule. One has to think how long that kind of fishing can continue, my correspondent concluded.

By the close of 1979 José Antonio Larruskain, the successful *patrón de primero* of the *Terra,* was seriously thinking of leaving fishing for all time. After the aborted trip of that summer, following the expulsion from Flemish Cap, all the Spanish pair crews went on strike. When the strike might be settled nobody knew, José Antonio wrote at the time, but it was not a matter of great importance to him. He had already decided that pair fishing was a thing of the past. Nevertheless, he made a few more trips. Then, while on vacation abroad, José Antonio broke his hip and one leg in a glider crash. He can no longer fish.

Manuel ("Manolo") López Muñiz, the poetry-quoting nautical

---

1. The international agency, established in 1980, that succeeded ICNAF and uses its previously established system of fishery conservation zones, some of which extend beyond two hundred miles.

captain of the *Terra,* has switched to another pair in the small fleet that continues to fish "beyond the line" on the Grand Banks. In a recent long-distance telephone conversation, just before setting off on another campaign, he was his cheerful and optimistic self, eager for what he liked to call the soul-cleansing satisfaction of returning to sea. He admitted, however, that he often has quite different feelings at the end of a campaign. It is then that he thinks hard about his future and broods over the present state of the Spanish fleet. Although Spain has become an expert in setting up multinational fishing consortia and transferring her fishing vessels to flags of convenience, it is usually only the officers and a few crew members of the big factory trawlers that benefit from such arrangements. "We in the pairs are forgotten," Captain Manolo says of this. "It is always so."

The recent history or whereabouts of the *Seliger* are not easy to pinpoint. Two months after starting inquiries through official channels, I received a telephone call from a Soviet Embassy staff member in Washington, who said he was pleased to report the *Seliger* was still in service. This was not surprising, he volunteered, given her sturdy Polish construction. But as for her most recent activities, he could only say that "the *Seliger* fishes the whole wide world, from the Barents Sea to the Falkland Islands, and enters to many joint ventures." The mention of the latter, however vague, is of particular interest, since many older Soviet factory trawlers have been used in joint ventures merely to process and not to catch fish. They keep station off the coasts of widely separated host countries — Guinea-Bissau, Senegal, South Yemen, Japan, and the United States — creaking and groaning as they roll ceaselessly to ground swells, waiting around the clock for what are erratic and frequently disappointing catches by the local fishermen. Or, what is perhaps less boring, in the case of developing nations, giving instructions to the locals on demonstrational cruises.

To anyone who knew her in her more active days, it is difficult to imagine the *Seliger* in this role. Without the stimulus of fishing she must be a tired and dull ship, with no more rollicking parties or exuberant songfests. Without the spur of between-ships "socialistcompetition," political officers must be hard put to hold the kinds of rousing pep rally I witnessed in her crew's mess. Perhaps even the monthly production meetings have gone by the board. Or at least become more perfunctory and routine, if that is possible.

Efforts to find out how some of my Soviet shipmates are faring have not been much more successful. Shortly after my trip I wrote to many of the *Seliger*'s former crew members, enclosing photographs taken aboard, postcards, recent stamp issues, and other things they had said they would look forward to receiving. With the sole exception of Captain Amelichev, who sent a brief well-wishing telegram while at sea in command of another ship, I received no answers for a long time. Then in the spring of 1979, almost a year after my writing, there came a sudden flurry of replies. All of them offered effusive best wishes, news of their families or questions about mine, accounts of their vacations, and other well-meaning generalities. But any answers to my various questions about where they were fishing, what ships they were on, or how they were coping with new restrictions were either not forthcoming or very brief and in a different tone. "The brigades continue to work well with proper collectivist spirit," one correspondent wrote. "We have fulfilled all trip plans," another said. "The fishing has certainly changed, all over the world," a third volunteered. "But goals can be met with new kinds of fishes." It was almost as if First Mate Oleg Sokolov, more in his role of strict commissar than friendly cruise director, was leaning over their shoulders. Two correspondents said they would write again, with more details. But they never did. Neither, under the circumstances, did I.

Today, six years after the rush to two-hundred-mile zones, fishing has indeed changed all over the world — not just for the Soviets, but for all nations who relied heavily on distant water trawling for much of their catch. The most noticeable change is in fishing-vessel construction. No new factory trawlers have been built since the first years of extended fishery regimes. Even the Soviets, who were the last to do so in 1979 with a class especially designed for very deep trawling, have now announced that future construction will focus mainly on medium-range or small stern trawlers. Similar-sized ships, equipped with small freezing units, refrigeration, or ice (but not costly and space-consuming factory sections), are becoming universally popular, especially with developing nations seeking a quick buildup of their coastal fleets. Western European nations are also scaling down the average size of their fleet vessels. Much in favor are combination, or "all-purpose," vessels that can both seine and trawl and ingenious "autoliners," or automated longliners, which bait, set, haul back, and unhook fish from their 15,000-hook lines entirely by machine. The only big ships now being built comparable in size to factory trawlers — in length, if not tonnage — are giant seiners modeled after the highly successful California tuna clippers. Too many of them, one is already tempted to say, under a bewildering array of flags.

Not only ships, but the fish they catch and the principal world areas where they pursue them have also changed very radically. King cod, as the British used to call *Gadus morhua,* no longer reigns supreme. Since the early 1970s the Alaska pollock, a species that in spite of its name was long spurned by Alaskan fishermen, is now the world's most often caught and heavily consumed fish, presently at about 5 million tons a year. The herring that was formerly the standard or almost exclusive species of the fishmeal industry was long ago replaced by the Peruvian anchoveta. Then, after wanton overfishing caused this incredibly rich fishery to collapse in the early 1970s (from 13 million tons to less than 2 million in three years), the fishmeal plants of northern Europe regained their leadership through a systematic search for suitable alternatives. Next in line was the capelin, which held brief sway as the world's highest-volume fishmeal species from 1975 to 1978. Since its near-collapse (a drop from 4 million to about 2.5 million tons in three years) the search has again become more global. The current leaders are *Sardinops sagax* and *Sardinops melanostica,* better known as the Chilean and Japanese pilchards, two sardinelike fish that are already showing signs of overexploitation. Coming up fast in the North Atlantic is the blue whiting, the fish that so recently failed all its human-consumption tests. It is now pursued very eagerly for meal by the Norwegians and the Faroese, who have discovered dense schools four or five miles long and sixty or seventy meters thick. They fish these schools with enormous new mid-water trawls capable of bringing in five hundred tons in a single haul. Such hauls are an absolute record in the history of trawling, most experts agree. How long the blue whiting can withstand them is a more difficult question.

The table fish that will probably rise most dramatically — in value, not volume of catch — are the scombrids, the large family that includes most of the mackerels and tunas. The latter are now heavily fished not only by the United States, but also by Japan, France, Spain, Italy, Mexico, and Panama. All of these nations, plus a few more on the waiting list, are in the process of acquiring respectable fleets of "superseiners," as the big tuna clippers two or three hundred feet in length overall are now called. The Soviets, too, have recently entered the race, trailing American clippers in the Pacific for days on end to learn the high art of modern tuna seining. Nor are the classic grounds off the west coast of Central and South America any longer sufficient to supply a growing worldwide demand for tuna. Led by the Americans, the superseiners now range the breadth of the Pacific, fishing waters unclaimed or loosely guarded by the new island nations, from Samoa to the western Carolines. But problems already loom on these far horizons. All three of the most favored tuna species — the yellowfin, skipjack, and big-eye — seem already to be fished at their maximum sustainable yield; their combined catch has remained remarkably static at approximately 1.45 million tons over the last five years, in spite of a greatly increased fishing effort. As might be expected, the search for acceptable substitutes is already under way. American housewives may soon therefore have to settle for Spanish and king mackerel, jacks, or other scombrids as "tuna." And the day is not far off when chunky tidbits of prime yellowfin will no longer go into Nine Lives and Puss 'n Boots cat food.

In other parts of the world minuscule fleets of remaining factory trawlers fish far and wide, in what seem improbable places. The Soviets drag their trawls across isolated seamounts, the small flat-topped rises that dot the deepwater expanses of both tropical and temperate seas. They, the Japanese, and other distant water nations also patiently scour the vastnesses of the Indian Ocean and both coasts of Africa. Generally speaking, they stick to the rules and fish according to quota or joint-venture agreements when inside established fishery zones. But none can resist the occasional temptation to poach, wherever enforcement is weak. Or search out more continental-shelf grounds that lie beyond two hundred miles, as on the Grand Banks. A good example, until the recent hostilities, was the long spur of the Patagonian Shelf that reaches out to the Falkland Islands.

Some new groundfish species show promise. In Australia and New Zealand, a deep water fish known as the "orange roughie" is finally being caught in quantity and finding a good market. The same is true of *Notothenia rossi,* the codlike fish of the southern oceans that Captain Amelichev claimed the Soviets have fished since the late 1960s. The French, too, are now said to be doing well with it, fishing south of the Kerguelen Islands, down where cold polar seas and the warmer waters of the southern Indian Ocean meet in what oceanographers know as the Antarctic convergence. But the biology of these fishes has not yet been studied. Not enough, at least, to predict if they may someday be the southern analogues of, say, the Atlantic cod or the redfish.

Other species have not lived up to the high regard oceanographers once accorded them. The prime example is the krill, the small shrimplike crustacean that is the principal food of the Antarctic's fish, penguins, seals, and whales. So abundant are Antarctic krill stocks that some scientists estimate a safe annual harvest of 50 million tons, which is close to the world catch of all marine fish and invertebrates. Understandably, therefore, conservationists have been alarmed at this prospect. It now appears they may rest easy. Factory trawlers have fished and continue to fish the krill at catch rates that occasionally make newspaper headlines. But the little crustaceans, which are difficult to process and which spoil quickly, are finding poor acceptance on world markets other than in Japan, where they may occasionally be a constituent of *surimi,* fish-paste sausages, and the Soviet Union, where they are used mainly for low-grade fishmeal. What is more important, this situation is not apt to change unless there is an unprecedented world shortage of both fish and soybean meals and oils. Accordingly, the present krill catch is not in the millions, but approximately 400,000 tons. Much the same is true of the grotesque rattails, or grenadiers, still spurned by all but the Soviets and the East Germans. At less than 100,000 tons a year, none of the various grenadier species rate mention in the FAO's annual rankings of principal commercial species. There are other examples. They are all fish that are either too unappealing or too difficult to catch. Or, as in the case of most deepwater species, a combination of both.

Among all these and other shifting patterns of world fishing, there seems to be but one that is unlikely ever to change. The one constant, the one certainty, is that the richest meadows of the sea — the continental shelf and slope waters that are home to eighty-five percent of the world's harvestable fish — are now a staked plain. Almost everywhere, moreover, the stake lines that nations draw out to 200 miles fully encompass this plain. The fishing commons of the oceans have been enclosed.

What this restructuring will mean to commercial fishing over the long run is difficult to predict. How well the new enclosures will be managed, what further potential resides in pelagic or open-oceans fishing, or how many underutilized species will ultimately make the grade are all questions that cannot yet be answered.

Meanwhile, however, a few major phenomena — problems, some call them — are already discernible. First and foremost, the total world catch of marine fishes and invertebrates has not significantly altered, in spite of continuing increases in the worldwide fishing effort. Rather, it remains at the 60-million-ton plateau first reached in 1974. More specifically, according to the FAO's most recent estimates, the world sea catch has totaled 59.6 million tons in 1974, 59.2 in 1975, 63.5 in 1976, 61.5 in 1977, 63.3 in 1978, 63.9 in 1979, and 64.6 in 1980. This leveling-off (after many years of annual increases of approximately eight percent, we must not forget) raises the disturbing question of whether or not the world oceans are already yielding a maximum of economically usable fish. Almost equally disturbing is the fact that the two giants of world fishing, the Soviet Union and Japan, claim to be catching just as much as always. Although the Soviets have by conservative estimate lost 2 million tons through prohibited fishing or reduced quotas in the traditional areas they formerly fished, they continue to register an annual catch of approximately 9 million tons, just as they did in the peak years before widespread application of extended fishery zones.[2] So, too, with the efficient Japanese, who in spite of some of the same difficulties still edge out their Soviet rivals by about 1 million tons a year.

This, in turn, leads to another question. Those who see problems ahead ask why the world catch has not decreased or what, if anything, has been achieved in fishery conservation by curbing the great factory trawler fleets of the past. This question is especially puzzling because fishing within the now-universal two-hundred-mile zones has been severely restricted by some coastal states, appreciably reduced by many others, and regulated to some extent by all. Yet instead of decreasing the world catch as we have seen is slowly inching up towards the 70 million-ton mark.

To this second question, at least — what has been done for conservation — there appear to be some positive answers. One is that instead of intense Northern Hemisphere concentration there is now a diffusion of fishing effort: a great global diaspora. This in itself is salutary. The greater the diffusion, the less is the probability of dangerous overfishing, or the kind of "targeting" on a few key species that characterized the factory trawler era from its begin-

2. There is no compelling reason to doubt their figures; what has probably changed most in Soviet fishing is that it is now more widespread but probably less profitable than ever as a result of explorations, experimentation, and marginal joint ventures.

ning. Stated another way, a larger number of smaller vessels are now competing for smaller amounts of a greater variety of fishes over a wider expanse of the world oceans.

Another answer concerns the threat of critical reduction of fish stocks. To understand it the reader must bear in mind that before two-hundred-mile zones the most massive harvesting power in the history of fishing was narrowly directed at some of the world's densest concentrations of fish. What the great distant water fleets were doing — the pulse-fishing rows of two hundred or more factory trawlers plowing the best North Atlantic grounds like disk harrows in a field — was reducing fish stocks to a borderline point. The borderline may be defined not as species extinction (although that was always a possibility) but rather reduction to levels that can no longer sustain viable fisheries. Commercial extinction, if the reader prefers. A prime historical example is the Atlantic halibut, once so plentiful that it was the fresh-fish prize of nineteenth-century New England schooners, but now so rare throughout the North Atlantic that today's trawlers take no more than five or six of the fish in a week of continuous fishing. In modern times the same fate appeared to await the Georges Bank haddock, as its catch plunged from 155,000 to 5,000 tons in what scientists thought was an irreversible decline. And, quite probably, nearly all of the targeted species of the factory trawlers — the yellowtail flounder, the cod, the slow-growing redfish, the Atlantic herring. Given free or unregulated fishing, the list might have been very long.

Today the most massive harvesting power in world fishing is no more. Not since 1974 have the annual armadas of one thousand or more distant water fishing vessels crossed and recrossed the Atlantic. It has been more than twelve years since American fishery agents have counted as many as two hundred Soviet trawlers off Cape Hatteras or on Georges Bank. Even the forty or fifty I saw off the Labrador in the winter of 1977 were the last of that number, as Captain Hörhold of the *Wesermünde* had suspected.

What the decline of factory trawling has meant, therefore, is that the threat of commercial extinctions no longer exists. Nor will it ever, if all coastal states show themselves to be good stewards of their new oceanic preserves. The proof, theoretically speaking, is already at hand. The great arch of the North Atlantic — the world's most severely tested fishing laboratory — is providing it. Almost everywhere along its way, fish stocks are rejuvenating. The good market fish, the key species, are coming back.

Iceland, the first and most vigorous of the good stewards, has benefited most. In the eight years since establishment of a two-hundred-mile zone, the island republic has seen an overall catch increase of 58 percent. The United States has had almost equal success. The endangered haddock has risen fivefold from its 1974 low, and the cod catch has almost doubled. Even the Atlantic herring once so coveted by foreign trawlers are coming back strongly from what Maine fishermen, who catch them as juveniles for packing as sardines, thought was the end of their inshore fishery. Now, five years after the cancellation of all foreign herring quotas, the Maine sardine canneries are glutted with more than they can handle. Canada, for her part, has been witnessing what fishery officials like to describe as bonanza years. Both the cod and the yellowtail flounder catches have doubled since 1976, and haddock have risen over 100 percent.

Capelin are still down, but the offshore stocks (now all but denied to foreign trawlers) are at least sufficient to support a growing Canadian fishery. Perhaps, someday, the same will be true inshore. Perhaps, that is, Newfoundland outports will once again celebrate the "sculls," the annual arrival of the beach-spawning capelin, with scoffs and soirees. And the cod, of course, that follow them in.

The one major exception is Norway, especially the tired waters of the Norwegian Arctic. From Spitsbergen and Bear Island to the North Cape and Skolpen Bank, the grounds where generations of foreign trawlers came "to dip and fill" for most of this century are still yielding far less than in the days of their prime. Nevertheless, there are some hopeful signs. The precipitous decline of various capelin stocks has been halted, and the catches of cod and herring seem to be stabilizing. Thus, given further restrictions on European Community and Soviet fishing and on her own large fleet,

Norway hopes that a turning point or an overall catch increase is not far off. The same may be said of Europe's most overworked fishing ground. In November of 1981 British scientists for the first time noted some exceptionally good year classes of the long-banned herring of the North Sea. With almost indecent haste the ban was lifted.

In summary, therefore, the fishing laboratory put to the hardest of all tests is giving a positive answer. Throughout the North Atlantic arch, at varying paces, there is rejuvenation or the promise thereof. The cycle begins with the smaller fish — the younger year classes that are always more abundant than the old. Then, with patience, as records already show, there come the fully mature fish, the optimum-size classes that were almost never seen when factory trawlers dominated the grounds.

The cycle begins with the smaller fish. Sometimes, as it happens, with a sudden or explosive increase that neither scientists nor fishermen expect.

In August of 1977, barely five months after implementation of the United States fishery conservation zone, I witnessed just such an explosive increase while taking a second trip with Captain Carl Spinney on the *Tremont*. As we steamed out of Boston Harbor, Captain Carl summoned me to the bridge to tell me about what he called an incredible discovery on his previous trip. He had gone way up to the northern tip of Georges — nearer to Yarmouth than Boston — between what the chart calls the Northern Edge and the Northeast Peak. Dropping his voice and looking instinctively over his shoulder, he then told me he had found a small thirty-four-fathom knoll that yielded some fantastic hauls. Many of the fish were small cod and haddock, not illegal, mind you, but rather the scrod sizes that often bring the top price at the Fish Pier. It was all so incredible, he said, because the whole area had long been the Spanish pairs' favorite winter ground, one that they continually "dried out." Now we were heading right back there, of course, especially since Carl thought he knew where he might find some larger fish, too.

As we steamed through the night, we saw not another fishing vessel, either American or foreign. The absence of the latter was to be expected. A handful of Russian trawlers were being allowed to fish for some hake, but way out over the slope waters at the other end of Georges. There might also be some Germans and Poles, but they were confined to a herring window down by Jim Dwyer's Ridge, plus a few Spaniards, widely scattered, who could now fish only for squid. The important thing, Captain Carl said over coffee in the messroom, was that practically speaking the foreigners were kicked out. He had been thinking it over and come to the conclusion that the removal of the continual bottom disturbance and scarring of the grounds by the foreigners, was the only way you could explain the fishes' coming back in four months. The National Marine Fisheries Service had been telling him and all New England fishermen that it would be years before they might expect any good results; they would have to wait for the maturing fish. But it certainly looked like some were coming back a lot sooner.

"You've seen the big trawls the foreigners use," Captain Carl added, as he left for his cabin. "You have to think how they kept chewing up the bottom. You have to think how they never let the fish bunch up and rest."

Norman Blake, the *Tremont*'s twine man and fish hailer, agreed. "The skipper's right," he said. "You'll see tomorrow."

At eight-thirty the next morning the first haul produced a bagful of dogfish, the curse of Georges Bank. Captain Carl moved to less sandy grounds. Then it came. Two hours later, winches straining to full power, the *Tremont* shuddered as a cod end filled to the bursting point rose up on deck. It held its maximum capacity of ten tons, by Carl's estimate, and there were plenty of ten- and twenty-pound cod as well as the scrod.

The fishing held throughout the afternoon, with more scrod cod and only slightly less big ones. After early supper another great bag, ten tons or more, squeezed up the ramp and came to rest covering all the working deck space between the coamings. As all good captains will, Carl then went down to help out in the *Tre-*

*mont*'s fish cleaning room, which was now badly backed up. He asked me to take the bridge watch. The sea was flat calm, but the tidal current was strong and we were now joined by a half dozen Canadian scallop boats from Lunenberg. I should nudge the *Tremont* out of the way if any of them drifted down "too handy to us," as Carl put it.

The *Tremont* rolled slightly on a glassy sea, to the steady plop of trash fish tumbling out of her discharge port. Large rafts of resting shearwaters floated by, unwilling to make the effort of feeding in the windless calm. Sensing their opportunity, little Mother Carey's chickens — Wilson's petrels, they were — flew in from everywhere and began their delicate aerial plucking dance to feed on plankton or choice morsels in the gurry of the *Tremont*'s wake. Soon what seemed like thousands of them fluttered up and down close above the surface, their legs dangling like those of toy men on strings, backlighted by a pale setting sun. At about the same time some small needle-billed fish known as sauries, or skippers, raced up in small groups to the fish-cleaning waste water spurting from the *Tremont*'s side. Individuals darted in to snatch some tiny prize and then instantly bounded away, jumping three or four times in a row. Down below I could hear the men shouting and joking, though some had been on their feet all day, as they attacked the overflow of ungutted fish. Just before dark, about two hundred yards off the port bow, a large black object repeatedly broke water. It kept appearing and disappearing, in slow lunging motions. With binoculars I immediately saw it was the blunt head of a sperm whale.

After dark a light breeze stirred the water. With it came patches of fog that briefly obscured the Canadian scallopers. A dense school of small sand eels, or lance — a beautiful pencil-shaped fish with a back of burnished blue and gold — swarmed around the ship, clearly visible in the *Tremont*'s strong working lights. Out beyond in the dark I sensed the petrels were still feeding, by the sound of whirring wings and excited peepings. Then suddenly two, three, or more of the little birds began to crash-land on deck with every passing fog patch. Apparently unable to take off without a pattering run on the water, they hopped disconsolately all over the main deck, some even finding their way to shelter under the messroom table. In the clear spells I ran down from the bridge, caught them easily, and launched them one by one over the side. As they flew back into the night, they uttered what sounded like calmer peeps, as if in gratitude.

With the darkness the current seemed to increase, until the *Tremont* was drifting so fast that small eddies and whirlpools trailed from her bow and stern. About an hour after nightfall, first one and then four or five triangular dorsal fins knifed into the circle of the *Tremont*'s lights. They were great blue sharks, five and six feet long, and they quickly took up positions at the bow and stern eddies. I watched in fascination — their very color, the deep cobalt blue of their topsides, commands nothing less — while they effortlessly swallowed small fish or cod bellies. The sand eels suddenly disappeared, probably sounding far down to the bottom. Burrowing is their best defense mechanism, and I imagined them doing so now, forswearing further night rises to the surface. The skippers remained, but by now there were the torpedo shapes of mackerel flashing about underneath them. Thus, to the steady splashes of the skates, pouts, and other large waste fish, there were added other sounds — the swirl of mackerel chasing the skippers, or the boil and snap of the more energetic blue sharks that swam up to the discharge port to take on a big skate. Long into the night the laughter from belowdecks continued. And, out in the black, the whirring and peeps of the petrels.

As the watch wore on, I came to realize I was witnessing an extraordinary spectacle. Certainly, it was not one that had occurred on my trip of the previous October. Then, there were only the great floating cities — the massed lights of the foreign trawler fleets — to command our nocturnal attention. Now they were gone.

The sea, as a result, seemed newly alive.

# Appendix I

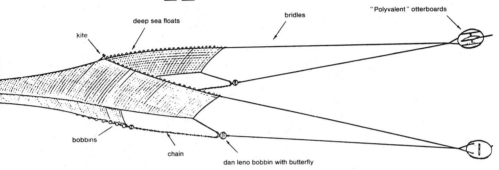

A modern high-opening ground trawl. The "kite" is a planing board with its own floats, positioned in an upward angle at the center of the headline, which helps to open the trawl to a height of over thirty feet.

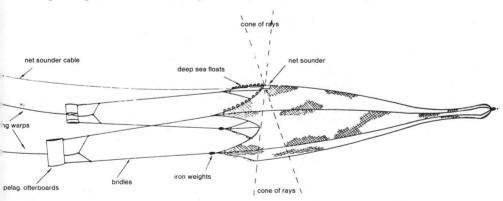

A pelagic (mid-water) trawl. Nets of this kind, each requiring 120 miles of twine, now have mouth openings that average 130 feet in height and 200 feet in width. Fishing depths and net spread are controlled by an intricate combination of factors: bridle length, ship speed (slower is lower, generally speaking, with wider openings), towing weights, and, above all, "a great deal of experience and constant attention by the skipper." Courtesy Hermann Engel & Co., Manufacturers

# *Appendix II*

Schematic drawings of the netsounders, underwater sonars used in mid-water trawling. Some fishing captains prefer to use single downward-ranging netsounders, relying on the ship's sonar for forward and lateral scanning. But most modern netsounders are now multidimensional, as pictured. The most common practice, therefore, is to use them in conjunction with the ship's sonars. The ship's sonars customarily have greater forward range and may be augmented by acoustic lateral sounders, which give louder "pings" as they sweep toward the densest part of a school. Recently, color sensors have been added to sonar equipment and are said to be very useful in "targeting," or distinguishing between different fish schools. Courtesy Honeywell ELAC

# Appendix III

## BEAUFORT WIND SCALE

| Beaufort Force | Knots* | M.P.H. | Weather Service Descriptive Terms | Sea Effects |
|---|---|---|---|---|
| 0 | 0 | 0 | Calm | Sea like a mirror. |
| 1 | 1–3 | 1–3 | Light air | Ripples with appearance of scales are formed, but without foam crests. |
| 2 | 4–6 | 4–7 | Light breeze | Small wavelets, still short, but more pronounced. Crests have a glassy appearance, but do not break. |
| 3 | 7–10 | 8–12 | Gentle breeze | Large wavelets; crests begin to break; foam of glassy appearance. Perhaps scattered whitecaps. |
| 4 | 11–16 | 13–18 | Moderate breeze | Small waves becoming longer. Fairly frequent whitecaps. |
| 5 | 17–21 | 19–24 | Fresh breeze | Moderate waves taking a more pronounced long form; many whitecaps are formed. Chance of some spray. |
| 6 | 22–27 | 25–31 | Strong breeze | Large waves begin to form; the white foam crests are more extensive everywhere. Probably some spray. |

*A knot is a measure of both distance and time, signifying one nautical mile (1.15 land miles) per hour.

Source: *Marine Surface Weather Observations,* National Oceanic and Atmospheric Administration, U.S. Department of Commerce; January, 1982.

| | | | | |
|---|---|---|---|---|
| 7 | 28–33 | 32–38 | Near gale | Sea heaps up, and white foam from breaking waves begins to be blown in streaks along the direction of the wind. |
| 8 | 34–40 | 39–46 | Gale | Moderately high waves of greater length; edges of crests begin to break into spindrift. The foam is blown in well-marked streaks along the direction of the wind. |
| 9 | 41–47 | 47–54 | Strong gale | High waves, dense streaks of foam along the direction of the wind. Crests of waves begin to topple, tumble, and roll over. Spray may affect visibility. |
| 10 | 48–55 | 55–63 | Storm | Very high waves with long overhanging crests. The resulting foam, in great patches, is blown in dense white streaks along the direction of the wind. On the whole, the surface of the sea takes a white appearance. The tumbling of the sea becomes heavy and shocklike. Visibility affected. |
| 11 | 56–63 | 64–72 | Violent storm | Exceptionally high waves. Small and medium-size ships might be for a time lost to view behind waves. The sea is completely covered with long white patches of foam along the direction of the wind. Everywhere the edges of wave crests are blown into froth. Visibility affected. |

| 12 | 64 and over | 73 and over | Hurricane | The air is filled with foam; sea completely white with driving spray. Visibility seriously affected. |

# *Acknowledgments*

A NY reader who has come this far will know that this book
could not have been written without the good offices and
help of a great many people. Ironically, among those I wish to
thank most are two persons whose names I never learned.

The first of my anonymous benefactors was a Russian seaman
of the watch who, midway through my trip on the *Seliger*, loaned
me his shortwave radio set (surely his or any other Russian fisherman's most precious possession), which gave me the great con-
solation of a window to the outside world. The second was an elderly fishmeal-plant worker on the *Wesermünde* who periodically
lumbered up to my cabin with a fresh supply of girlie magazines
from his private collection. These, too, I must confess, gave con-
solation and distraction, especially in the dark night of winter
storms.

The actions of my two unknown friends were not atypical. "As
generous as a fisherman" is a saying in many languages. I believe
it is true — true of fishermen of all nations and without the connotation of profligacy and wild shore-leave extravagance many of
the sayings imply. As a group the fishermen I sailed with were the
most open, friendly, solicitous, and sincerely generous people I
have met. First and foremost, then, I want to thank them all.

For their good offices — specifically, for granting permission to
visit ships of their fleets — I would like to thank Jack Fulham of
John Fulham and Sons of Boston, Günter Ohlrogge of Hansea-

tische Hochseefischerei of Bremerhaven, José Ignacio Serrat of Expes of San Sebastián, and Graham Hellyer of British United Trawlers of Hull. In addition, although I had no meetings or exchange of correspondence with Ambassador Anatoliy Dobrynin of the Soviet Embassy in Washington, I have reason to believe he had much to do with my being able to visit the *Seliger*. If so, I wish to thank him most sincerely. Intermediaries who helped with the requisite permissions include Dr. Hinrich Wachhorst, formerly with the Embassy of the Federal Republic of Germany in Washington, and José Arambarri, a former Spanish trawler captain now with the Harvey shipping agency in St. John's, Newfoundland, whose first-hand knowledge of foreign fishing fleets was of great practical use. And I must again thank all the captains, those of the text, who took me aboard. In each case the final decision was theirs alone — "at the captain's discretion," as fleet owners like to say.

Getting off distant water fishing vessels is sometimes as problematical as getting on. I would therefore like to give special thanks to Captain Karl Egner of the West German factory trawler *Geeste* and Serafín Martínez Graña and Enrique Pujales Rivas, *patrón de pesca* and nautical captain, respectively, of the Spanish pair trawlers *Lasaola* and *Lasaberri*, who went out of their way to start me on my homeward journeys.

Waiting in port for ships of irregular call can at times be a very frustrating experience. It was never so in St. John's, a city for which I have great affection, thanks mainly to congenial faculty members of the Memorial University of Newfoundland. Elliott Leyton and Judy Adler of the university's department of anthropology gave me constant hospitality, help, and, at discouraging moments, the will to persevere. Joseba Zulaika, formerly of the same department and now at Princeton University, prepared me as no one else could for my trip with Spanish Grand Banks pair trawlers; I thoroughly recommend his book, *Terranova,* to all who would learn more of the sociology of this unique fishery. Talks with Raoul Andersen, maritime historian, George Story, author of the *Newfoundland English Dictionary,* and the staff of the university's marine research laboratory at Logy Bay also helped put the waiting times to very good advantage.

In Washington Milan Kravanja, Chief of the National Marine Fisheries Service's International Fisheries Analysis Division, has been a steadfast source of expert help on world fishing, as have his able assistants Matteo Milazzo and Dennis Weidner. A dedicated public servant and one of the world's few authorities on Eastern-bloc fishing, Kravanja has created what I like to think of as a little State Department of the sea, where current and accurate information on the complexities of international fishing is always available.

In Newfoundland and Nova Scotia, Dennis Monroe, president of Fishery Products Ltd., and Lou R. Day, formerly Executive Secretary of ICNAF, contributed much to my early education in offshore fishing. So, too, with answers to specific and sometimes difficult questions, did Wilfred Templeman, Alister M. Fleming, Thomas K. Pitt, Richard Wells, and D. A. MacLean, biologists all, with the Canadian government's Department of Fisheries and Oceans. And William Warshick, a veteran enforcement agent for the same department, whose experiences in keeping foreign fleets in line have been of great interest.

In London Peter Hjul kindly allowed me to rummage in his busy offices for back issues of the monthly *Fishing News International,* which he edits, and the weekly *Fishing News,* now in its seventieth year. Together these two journals are a priceless resource for fishing historians. Much the same, in a more contemporary sense, can be said of Hjul's anthology *The Stern Trawler,* a unique technical source book on the development of factory and other stern trawlers.

If the fieldwork for this book was long and at times arduous, so also, as it proved, was the writing. Here again, I benefited from the help of many friends. My brother, Charles K. Warner, has as always been a wellspring of encouragement and sound advice. My wife, Kathleen, and my sons and daughters, six in number, have at times played a similar role, at least when I could catch their busy ears. Phyllis Theroux and Cristy West have cast their discerning eyes on certain chapters which I once thought might be diffi-cult for the lay reader. If they are no longer so, much credit goes to them. Kate Winthrop Jackson patiently typed much of the first draft and offered helpful suggestions throughout. Connie Gray did much the same with the second.

Finally, with all the gratitude I can muster, I wish to thank my good friend and editor, Peter Davison, for his patience and under-standing support. Fishing is as broad and engaging a subject as the oceans it encompasses; the dangers of wandering off course are many and tempting. I did so, often. But, always, there was the polestar, the master compass of my editor to bring me back. If, then, the reader has found this work within tolerable bounds of general interest, join me in thanking him.